VEILED THREATS

VEILED THREATS

The Logic of Popular Catholicism in Italy

MICHAEL P. CARROLL

THE JOHNS HOPKINS UNIVERSITY PRESS

Baltimore and London

© 1996 The Johns Hopkins University Press
All rights reserved. Published 1996
Printed in the United States of America on acid-free paper

05 04 03 02 01 00 99 98 97 96   5 4 3 2 1

The Johns Hopkins University Press
2715 North Charles Street
Baltimore, Maryland 21218-4319
The Johns Hopkins Press Ltd., London

Library of Congress Cataloging-in-Publication Data will be found
at the end of this book.

A catalog record for this book is available from the British Library.

ISBN 0-8018-5290-0

He criticized devotion to sacred images, saying that it was idolatry. Moreover he would sometimes kneel in front of the sacred images found in the prison and mock them using coarse and irreverent gestures.

Testimony given to the Inquisition in the proceedings against Giordano Bruno by one of his fellow prisoners (cited in Mercati 1961, 92)

To GIORDANO BRUNO, born at Nola in the shadow of bleeding madonnas and liquefying blood relics; who spent his fifty-two years challenging smug interpretation and accepted wisdom wherever he happened to be; who offended in turn the Catholic Church in Italy, Calvinist authorities in Geneva, and Oxford professors in England (and that's the short list); who could not stop speaking his mind plainly even when he should have kept his mouth shut; condemned by the Roman Inquisition and burned alive in the Campo dei fiori at Rome in 1600.

Contents

List of Illustrations and Tables   ix

Preface and Acknowledgments   xi

Prologue   1

Introduction: Adrift in the Italian Indies   3

Chapter 1. Powerful Images   16

Chapter 2. The Church Adapts to Image Cults   49

Chapter 3. "Preaching to Their Eyes"   77

Chapter 4. The Cult of the Dead, I   116

Chapter 5. The Cult of the Dead, II   139

Chapter 6. Relics   163

Chapter 7. Reformation and Ricettizie   186

Chapter 8. "Preserved Whole and Entire"   208

Conclusion: Back to Beginnings   226

Epilogue   247

References   251

Index   267

Illustrations and Tables

Figure

2.1. Number of supernatural favors attributed to the Madonna di Pompei, 1876–87 73

Plates

Facade of the sanctuary of the Madonna dell'Impruneta (near Florence) as it appears today 104

The veiled image of the Madonna dell'Impruneta being carried in procession (detail) 105

Edicola at Naples 106

Rural *edicola* just outside Gimigliano 107

Pilgrims seeking favors from the Madonna di Loreto outside her sanctuary near Ancona 108

Edicola in honor of the Madonna di Pompei at Catanzaro 108

A votive offering being carried to the sanctuary of the Madonna dell'Arco near Naples 109

Holy Saturday procession at Nocera Terinese 110

Flagellation during Holy Saturday celebration at Nocera Terinese 111

Facade, Church of Purgatory at Bitonto, depicting the souls-in-a-sea-of-flames motif 112

Sanctuary of the *morti della fossetta* at Ghedi 113

The sanctuary of the Madonna di Pompei at Pompei 114

Edicola honoring the beheaded souls at Palermo 115

Perimeter entrance to the area containing the Catacombs of S. Callisto 115

Tables

1.1. Miraculous madonnine images found in churches in Lombardy,
Bologna, and Sicily   26

1.2. Static and dynamic miraculous madonnine images   29

1.3. The images found in *edicole,* three communities in Apulia   34

3.1. Italian sanctuaries dedicated to the Addolorata and to delle Grazie
or dei Miracoli madonnas   95

6.1. Relic collections, selected Neapolitan churches   174

8.1. Saintly bodies preserved incorrupt in Italy   213

Preface and Acknowledgments

This book is meant as a companion volume to my 1992 book, *Madonnas That Maim*. While some familiarity with that earlier work would be useful to the reader, it is not necessary. Most of the material presented here is new, and where my arguments do depend upon the 1992 volume, I provide a summary of the relevant material.

Some of the data reported here I have gathered; for the most part, however, I rely on materials assembled by Italian scholars. I make no apologies for this. During the 1970s and 1980s, Italian scholars published a number of truly first-rate studies dealing with popular Catholicism and the Catholic experience in Italy. Unfortunately, these studies have generally not been translated into English, and with each passing year the likelihood that they will ever be translated diminishes. Making these studies more familiar to English-speaking audiences, if only in summary form, is a major goal of this book. Needless to say, the original investigators are not responsible for the uses to which I have put their data.

Chapter 1 is concerned with image cults, that is, cults organized around images (usually paintings or statues) that dispense miraculous favors. Such cults have been (and still are) central to the Catholic experience in Italy, and the underlying logic of these cults is one of the most important constraints to which the institutional Church in Italy has had to adapt over the centuries. The precise nature of this adaptation is explored in the following two chapters. Chapter 2 is concerned with the ways in which the Church hierarchy has shaped its variant of Catholicism in the face of a public unshakably committed to image cults. Chapter 3 is concerned with those religious orders that have had a special commitment to popular preaching and with the new religious devotions that emerged when these orders sought to merge their Christocentricism with the logic of popular Catholicism.

Chapter 4 is concerned with popular devotion to the souls in Purgatory. Although the modern *idea* of Purgatory may have emerged in the twelfth century, as scholars like Jacques Le Goff claim, the evidence from Italy suggests that a truly popular cult organized around the souls in Purgatory did not emerge until the late sixteenth and early seventeenth centuries. This chapter explores the reasons for this delay between intellectual invention and cultic popularity. Chapter 5 is concerned with a second cult of the dead in Italy, which is organized around the skeletal remains of executed criminals and plague victims and is a cult not much discussed in the English-language literature. Although Italian commentators tend to see this second cult as being tied to an archaic and agricultural past, I argue that it was a creative response "from below" to the more official cult organized around the souls in Purgatory and that it emerged only after this first cult had established itself. These two chapters are likely the most important in this book because they provide a particularly clear illustration of how new devotions emerge from the interaction between the logic of popular Catholicism and the logic of official Catholicism.

What images are to madonna cults in Italy, relics are to cults organized around saints. Relic cults were mentioned only in passing in *Madonnas That Maim,* and so they are considered in detail in chapter 6. Contrary to the impression conveyed by many English-language accounts, the golden age of relic cults was the early modern period, not the Middle Ages, and one of the goals of chapter 6 is to explain this historic pattern.

Chapter 7 considers the differing responses of northern Italy and southern Italy to Reformation ideas imported from northern Europe. These differing responses are related, first, to a reform tradition in Italy that to some extent developed independent of the Reformation and, then, to a specific type of local church, the *chiesa ricettizia,* that flourished in the south. (This chapter is a much revised and expanded version of my 1992 article, "Religion, *Ricettizie,* and the immunity of southern Italy to the Reformation," *Journal for the Scientific Study of Religion,* and is published here with the permission of the Society for the Scientific Study of Religion.)

Chapter 8 considers a special sort of relic cult, one organized around the incorrupt body of a saint. Although a belief in saintly incorruption existed in the Middle Ages, cults organized around incorrupt saintly bodies experienced a dramatic surge in popularity during the Counter-Reformation, and this was mainly due to the efforts of Church elites, not of the general public. This chapter considers why this particular type of relic cult was especially appealing to Counter-Reformation prelates.

In the conclusion, I present a frankly speculative explanation for many of the distinctive features of popular Catholicism identified in earlier chapters. Finally, I offer some suggestions for systematically comparing popular Catholicism in Italy with the variants of popular Catholicism associated with other national traditions.

Unless otherwise noted, all translations from Italian to English are my own.

Without the constant encouragement of my parents, Olga Ciarlanti and William Carroll, and their willingness to promote the education of their three sons even when it meant serious financial hardship for themselves, I would never have enjoyed the luxury of an academic career and the chance to pursue this investigation. More than anyone else, they must be thanked.

I must also thank the Social Sciences and Humanities Research Council (SSHRC) of Canada for two grants, which financed the research reported in this book. In an era of shrinking resources, SSHRC's continued commitment to scholarly investigation is something for which everyone in the Canadian academic community must be thankful.

The publication of this book was also aided by a grant from the J. B. Smallman Publication Fund, Faculty of Social Science, University of Western Ontario. This, too, is gratefully acknowledged.

VEILED THREATS

Prologue

Lòrsica is a village that clings to the upper slopes of the Val Fontanabuona in Liguria, and it was in Lòrsica that my great-grandfather Felice Demartini was born, in 1868. Sometime during the 1880s he emigrated to the United States and ended up in San Francisco, where he earned his living as a bartender in that seedy but colorful area of the city called the Barbary Coast. After a few years Felice started returning to Lòrsica on a regular basis. He wasn't wealthy, but he was talented enough to defray the cost of his passage by playing the accordion on the ships that moved between San Francisco and Genoa. In 1895, on one of his trips home (there was never any doubt that Lòrsica, not San Francisco, was "home"), he met and married Antonietta Demartini (no relation, despite the same last name), my great-grandmother. A year later Felice and Antonietta were back in San Francisco, and it was there that their first child was born. They named her Aurelia, and she was my maternal grandmother. When she was weaned at age two, my grandmother was sent back to Lòrsica to be raised by relatives.

An old photo of Felice shows a handsome man with a dapper look, and family tradition suggests that "he could charm the birds down out of the trees." But my great-grandfather had a dark side. In 1902 he insisted that Antonietta accompany him back to Italy even though she had pneumonia; she died when they reached Genoa. Sometime circa 1907, while living in Lòrsica, he had some minor dispute with his younger daughter, my great-aunt, and chased her out of the house. He refused to let her return. Relatives were forced to apprentice her to a family in the nearby city of Chiavari as a domestic servant. She was five years old.

My grandmother lasted longer in her father's household than her sister, but only by a few years. As a young girl my grandmother worked at a loom on the third-floor patio of the family home in Lòrsica. Most of the time she made the sort of colorful sashes favored by male dandies of the period. Every so often, her sashes were taken to a market in the valley floor and sold to supplement the family income. In 1911, Felice—now back in Italy for good and needing money for some purpose or other—demanded that Aurelia increase the number of sashes she made. She did, but the more she made the more he wanted her to make. Eventually, driven to tears, she told her father that she could not do more than she was doing. Given his temper, it was a brave thing for a fifteen-year-old girl to do—and would turn out to be a decisive event in the history of my family.

Felice flew into a rage. He chased my grandmother around the house with a club, intent on beating her senseless. She escaped only by running outside and into the house of Felice's own father. As Aurelia would later tell the story, her grandfather shook his head sadly and wondered aloud how he could have produced such a monster of a son. Meanwhile, Felice placed his hunting rifle in his front window, with the barrel pointing at the path leading to his house. To anyone who would listen he said he would shoot his daughter if she dared return. Family members took the threat seriously, and my grandmother was shipped off to San Francisco.

As Italian family stories go, this one is not as dramatic as the opening incident in a Francis Ford Coppola movie. In the end, after all, nobody gets killed. Still, my grandmother's story does run counter to many of the stereotypes that so often guide the thinking of Anglo-Saxons when they confront Italy and the Italians. A strong emphasis on family solidarity? A special regard for children? Not in my great-grandfather's household. And what about the Italian countryside? Populated by peasants tied to a traditional and changeless rural culture? Lòrsica was, and still is, a relatively out-of-the-way community, and most of its inhabitants were indeed engaged in agricultural pursuits. Yet my great-grandfather regularly traveled between Lòrsica and San Francisco, and my grandmother worked at a loom making a product destined for an urban market.

I doubt that my grandmother's story is typical of Italian family life of the time (although I suspect that readers would be surprised to learn how many Italian Americans can tell similar stories), and the story makes no reference to Italian Catholicism, which is the subject of this book. Still, this particular story has always been important to me as a cautionary tale, a reminder to develop an image of Italy and Italians using the perspective and experiences of ordinary people, even if the result differs considerably from what those of us living in Anglo-Saxon countries have come to expect. It is a tale I have kept in mind while writing this book.

Introduction

Adrift in the Italian Indies

I n the two centuries following the Council of Trent (1545–63) thousands of Catholic missionaries were sent out from Europe to convert local popula-tions throughout the world to the new tridentine orthodoxy. But at the same time, Catholic missionaries were sent into the European countryside, and there they encountered nominal Catholics who seemed as ignorant of core Cath-olic beliefs as any of the heathens in far-off lands. The situation seemed especially bad in southern Italy, and it became commonplace for Counter-Reformation mis-sionaries to call this area of Europe "our Italian Indies."[1]

To convey to European audiences just how abysmal the state of the Church was in these Italian Indies, missionaries were fond of reporting the "silly" answers that southern Italians gave to simple and obvious questions. They especially liked reporting the answers given to the question, How many gods are there? presum-ably because these answers seemed especially ridiculous. For example, in his 1651 account of Jesuit missionary activity in the Kingdom of Naples (southern Italy), Scipione Paolucci, himself a missionary, describes a community in Basilicata in this manner:

> They were men, but really they had only the appearance of men. In terms of their
> abilities and knowledge they were little better than the beasts they herded. Not only
> were they entirely ignorant of the prayers and the various mysteries of the Holy
> Faith, but they were even devoid of any knowledge of God Himself. . . . Asked how
> many gods there were, some of these people said "a hundred," some said "a thou-
> sand" and some gave an even larger number. The larger the number they gave, the
> more they considered themselves to be knowledgeable. To them, increasing the

1. On the use of the "Italian Indies" metaphor in missionary reports, see Di Palo (1992, 37–38); Caponetto (1987, 20–25; 1992, 403–8); Prosperi (1980).

number of gods was like increasing the number of animals in their herds. (Cited in
Di Palo 1992, 15)

To the dedicated but smug purveyors of tridentine Catholicism (both the missionaries and the educated elites who formed their intended audience) a response
that suggested there were hundreds if not thousands of gods was obviously wrong.
But was it?

Suppose we approach the matter from the perspective of the people being
questioned. Complete strangers come into their community claiming to be Catholics. Although obviously well-meaning and self-sacrificing, these strangers speak
a different type of Italian and in their sermons seem obsessed with issues that are
either irrelevant or peripheral to the local Catholic experience. Then there is the
matter of their questions. They ask, How many gods are there? The very structure
of question presumes that the term *god* can exist in the plural; indeed, the question seems to imply that there *are* several gods. But what does the term *gods* (*dei*)
mean? Saints and madonnas—these are the supernatural beings familiar to real
Catholics. Saintly relics and images of various madonnas, after all, can be found
in local churches, and everyone knows that these are the objects most infused with
supernatural power. That power, after all, is why these objects are carried in processions to secure a good harvest or to end a drought and why good Catholics
turn to these objects when they need a favor. But what do gods have to do with
any of this?

But let us suppose that our local Catholics wanted to please their well-meaning visitors by providing a reasonable answer to this puzzling question about gods.
How might they proceed? One way would be to listen carefully to the sermons
preached by the missionaries and to search for contextual clues that provided
some insight into what a god was. Since missionary preachers often paired the
term *god* with statements evoking connotations of great power, listeners might
reasonably conclude that a god was anyone whom these missionary preachers saw
as having power. Since there are lots of people with power in the world, there are
quite obviously lots of gods—which is just what local populations said when
asked, How many gods are there?

My reconstruction here is speculative but not particularly fanciful. Paolucci's
account (cited in Di Palo 1992, 15) goes on to say that when people were asked to
name various gods, they named the pope, the local padrone, and the Jesuit missionaries who were instructing them. In short, they did seem to understand *god*
as connoting people whom the missionaries associated with power.

Now let us turn the situation around. Imagine that in the encounter between Counter-Reformation missionaries and southern Italian Catholics it had

been the latter who had asked the questions. Suppose, for instance, they had asked the missionaries, How many madonnas are there? Good tridentine Catholics that they were, these missionaries would have said, One. After all, the position of the Church has always been that every madonna is a representation of the Virgin Mary, that simple maid of Galilee whom New Testament mythology describes as having given birth to Jesus Christ. But this answer would have seemed absolutely ridiculous to ordinary Catholics living in the Italian countryside (and, as we shall see, ridiculous as well to ordinary Catholics living in urban areas). To ordinary Catholics it would have been obvious that there were several madonnas, all differing in the amount of supernatural power they possessed, all capable of acting independent of one another, and each associated with a particular image located at a particular sanctuary. One madonna? I don't think so.

The general lesson to be learned from all this is that popular Catholicism in Italy (or anywhere else) must be studied on its own terms, which means that we must seek to understand what this variant of Catholicism meant to the people who practiced it. Not what it might have meant to smug Jesuit missionaries or anyone else committed to the Catholicism of the tridentine Church, but what it meant to the great mass of people living in the hamlets, villages, and towns of Italy.

The Unpopularity of Popular Religion

It has become fashionable among scholars studying popular religion in Western Europe to begin their analyses by criticizing the term itself. For Christian (1981) *popular religion* too often connotes peasant religion and so precludes the study of popular religion in urban areas; his preferred alternative is *local religion*. Badone (1990) finds the term *popular religion* problematic because it suggests a "mistaken" perception of official religion, and this, she argues, prevents us from seeing popular religion as forming a consistent system of symbolic meanings in its own right. Harline (1990) argues that the line separating official religion from popular religion, which seems so clear in the abstract, often becomes fuzzy when specific groups are considered; he holds up the examples of traveling monks (presumably, he means friars) and parish priests as especially problematic groups in this regard. Duffy (1992) does not like the term because it implies that popular religion and official religion are necessarily different (a view that he rejects in the case of late medieval England); he substitutes the term *traditional religion*.

Whatever merit these criticisms might otherwise have, they all rest upon a methodological conceit: that there exists some single definition of popular religion (or traditional religion, or local religion, or whatever) that will be useful across all cultural and historical contexts—and this cannot be taken for granted. Definitions of popular religion must be tailored to particular contexts. In the present case, this means developing a definition that proves useful in the case of Italy. Such a definition may prove useful in other cultural contexts as well, but that can only be decided on a case-by-case basis.

The Study of Popular Religion in Italy

De Rosa (1983, vii) suggests that up until the 1960s the study of popular religion in Italy was dominated by a "two monads" model, in which Italy, southern Italy in particular, was divided into two camps. On the one side stood the Catholic Church, which used its power to impose its beliefs and practices on as large a proportion of the population as possible. On the other side were "economically dependent" groups, mainly peasants, who were attached to a range of magical beliefs and practices inherited from a distant and pagan past. These two monads did not exist in isolation. On the contrary, the economically dependent groups (or so the model suggests) accepted some Catholic elements and rejected others, with the result that popular religion in Italy was a syncretic mix of pagan and Catholic elements.

De Rosa does not address the question of why the view of popular religion in Italy as a mixture of pagan and Catholic elements proved to be so popular for so long, but I can think of at least two reasons. First, many of the scholars who studied popular religion in Europe had a personal commitment to religion as a meaning system. They were, in short, religious. Quite often (especially in Italy) they were clerics. In portraying popular religion as consisting largely of survivals from a distant and pagan past, they set up an implicit contrast that suggests that official religion—the religion to which they themselves were committed—was both modern and progressive. Second, to say that popular religion in Italy consists of a mix of pagan and Catholic elements is to portray the great mass of Italians as essentially passive, as clinging to what they inherited from the distant past and as accepting what was transmitted from on high but as being incapable of religious innovation. Such a view denies to ordinary Italian Catholics the creativity routinely accorded the intellectual elites who have dominated the history of the official Church. It is thus a view that flatters those intellectual elites and so, by extension, flatters modern scholarly investigators, who usually identify with these elites.

The two monads model still has its adherents. Some commentators remain so committed to this model that, when an analysis of Italian Catholicism fails to make use of it (the pagan-survivals hypothesis), this failure is taken as a deficiency (see Greeley 1993). Nevertheless, at least since the 1970s the two-monads model has generally been displaced within the Italian scholarly community by what De Rosa (1983, ix) calls "dialectical" models. *Dialectical* in this case means that these models see religion as having been shaped by the interaction between distinct social groups, each pursuing different political, religious, or economic goals. The proponents of these new dialectical models do not deny that magical beliefs and rituals have been widespread in Italy or that these beliefs and rituals have often been mixed with elements borrowed from the official Catholic tradition. What they do suggest, De Rosa (1983, 10–13) argues, is that the study of Catholic-pagan syncretism is of secondary importance in coming to understand the history of popular piety in Italy.

Seeing religious belief and ritual as shaped by the interaction between different social groups is not uniquely associated with the Italian scholarly tradition. During the 1970s this same emphasis could be found in the work of a number of non-Italian scholars, notably Jean Delumeau, Jacques Le Goff, and Natalie Zemon Davis. Still, the theoretical tradition that emerged in Italy was somewhat different from the analogous traditions that emerged elsewhere, and much of that difference can be attributed to the influence of Antonio Gramsci (d. 1937).

Gramsci was a political philosopher whose comments ranged widely over a number of subjects. His views on religion, however, are summarized in the following passage, which has become a mantra for historians of religion in Italy:

> Every religion, even Catholicism (in fact *especially* Catholicism, precisely because of its efforts to maintain a superficial unity and not allow itself to be fragmented into national churches or along class lines) is really a multiplicity of religions that are distinct and often contradictory: there is a Catholicism of the peasant, a Catholicism of the petty bourgeoisie and urban workers, a Catholicism of women, and a Catholicism of the intellectuals. (Gramsci 1966, 120)

Gramsci's contribution, in other words, was to suggest that in a society like Italy there were several variants of Catholicism, each different from the others. The scholar's task is to study the nature of these different variants and the ways in which they interact, not to decide which variant is "more authentic" or "more Catholic." Gramsci's formulation has always been especially popular with Marxist scholars in Italy, presumably because Gramsci (himself a founder of the Italian Communist Party) related his different Catholicisms to the groups (the petty bourgeoisie, urban workers, women, intellectuals, etc.) that have always been central to Marxist thought.

Within the Gramscian perspective, we can associate official Catholicism, like all Catholicisms, with a specific social group. Official Catholicism consists mainly of the bishops of the institutional Church. In other words, these bishops and the intellectuals and administrators who surround them are simply one social group among many, and their Catholicism only one variant among many. But there is no scholarly reason for calling this Catholicism more legitimate than the other variants.

Gramsci's formulation raises an obvious question: Does "being Catholic" mean the same thing within the various Catholicisms that exist and have existed in Italy? For most of the past few centuries, the answer to this question is almost certainly no. The Mass, confession, Holy Communion, papal authority, the Real Presence—these elements, so central to official Catholicism, were either absent from or peripheral to the experience of most other Catholicisms. As for the bishops themselves, who were so fond of reiterating their claim to spiritual authority, they were seen by most Italian Catholics as distant figures of no particular religious importance except on those infrequent occasions when they or their designates deigned to make a pastoral visit. Even then, these visits were significant mainly because the associated costs had to be borne by the local community, something that became a continuing source of complaint as pastoral visits became increasingly frequent in the centuries following the Council of Trent.

What, then, did "being Catholic" mean for most Italian Catholics? Within the Italian scholarly community, the most influential answer to this question is the one given by De Rosa.[2] Since the late 1960s, De Rosa consistently argues that popular Catholicism in Italy is best viewed as official Catholicism adapted to local conditions. The history of Catholic piety in Italy since the Council of Trent is, in his view, the story of how individual bishops, all committed to the same variant of Catholicism, have adapted that variant to the distinct conditions they encountered in their dioceses. Since these conditions varied from region to region, the Catholicisms experienced at the local level also varied from region to region.

De Rosa is not a sociologist or an anthropologist. He does not distribute surveys or conduct ethnographic research. He is most of all a historian who has sought to recapture the history of Catholic piety at the local level by scrutinizing archival records. The most important of these records, in his view, are reports of pastoral visits that bishops made to the communities in their dioceses. In the mid-1960s De Rosa and his associates began the task of cataloguing these reports for dioceses in the Veneto. Shortly thereafter he turned his attention to the study

2. I am not aware of any English-language source that provides an overview of De Rosa's life and work; for Italian-language materials by and about De Rosa, see the various essays in De Rosa (1971; 1983; 1987); Cestaro (1980).

of pastoral visits in the Mezzogiorno, the Italian South, a task that was substantially more difficult given that archival materials in the Mezzogiorno were far more fragmented and disordered than in the Veneto. In addition to the reports of pastoral visits, De Rosa and his students made use of parish registries, the records of diocesan synods, and the reports *ad limina*,[3] which bishops made to Roman authorities.

What De Rosa found is that the experience of Catholicism at the diocesan level had little to do with the grand events of Church history (like councils, the publication of encyclicals, the election of a new pope, etc.) or even with the grand events of Italian history (like the Risorgimento, Unification, etc.) but had a great deal to do with local conditions (like disputes between bishops and the central government, rates of emigration, the penetration of capitalism into the countryside). He is particularly proud of the "discovery" that popular Catholicism in the Mezzogiorno was shaped more by the *chiesa ricettizia* (a type of local church prevalent in the Mezzogiorno prior to 1800 and that is discussed at length in chap. 7) than by anything else.

De Rosa's emphasis upon adaptation to local conditions led him to pay special attention to bishops in peripheral dioceses, that is, in dioceses outside the immediate influence of large urban centers like Naples and Palermo. In the second (and substantially revised) edition of his *Vescovi, popolo e magia nel Sud*, De Rosa (1983, xv) tells us that his favorite essay in the book is the one describing the career of Angelo Anzani (1703–70), bishop of Campagna (Campania). For De Rosa, Anzani's struggle with the ricettizie clergy, with a population equally at home with madonnas and magic, and with a royal government unsympathetic to Rome epitomizes the "struggle to adapt" that faced all southern Italian bishops after Trent—and he is proud that his archival research rescued Anzani from historical oblivion.

De Rosa's work has provoked an intellectual revolution in the study of popular Catholicism in Italy. The fact that his most important books have still not been translated into English is a measure of the isolation that prevails between the English-speaking and the Italian-speaking scholarly worlds. Nevertheless, as important as it is, De Rosa's approach to popular Catholicism can be faulted in at least one regard. Notwithstanding his programmatic statements about the need to look carefully at the interaction between the various groups in a diocese, the

---

3. Very early in the history of the Church, bishops were in the habit of making a visit to the tomb of the Apostles (ad limina Apostolorum) at Rome and reporting to the reigning pope on the state of their dioceses. Sixtus V made these visits and the accompanying ad limina reports mandatory in 1585. Italian bishops were supposed to make these visits every three years; bishops outside Italy made visits less frequently.

only individuals granted any significant agency in De Rosa's analyses are reform-minded bishops, whom De Rosa obviously admires. In other words, just like the two-monads model that he criticizes, De Rosa's analyses allow creativity to Church elites while denying it to ordinary Catholics.

For example, in his discussion of Angelo Anzani (his "favorite" bishop), De Rosa (ibid., 68–69) tells us that Anzani worked hard to stamp out the widespread practice of having women "cry" over corpses at funerals. The reference here is to the ritual lamentations that were part of the traditional Mediterranean funeral (this type of funeral, and the Church's campaign against it, is discussed in chap. 3). The severity of Anzani's campaign against these lamentations is most evident, we are told, in the events that unfolded in the community of Pietrafesa in 1755. On November 30 of that year Anzani decreed that he would not allow the Church of S. Rocco at Pietrafesa to be blessed by the local clergy (something that the community greatly desired) unless and until the practice of these lamentations was stopped. On at least three different occasions over the next few days, he repeated this threat from the pulpit of the main church in Pietrafesa, and on each occasion he was assured by the women in the audience that they would stop participating in the lamentations. On December 8, he repeated his threat from the pulpit and this time indicated that promises "from the women" were not enough. He demanded that the men of the community also promise not to engage in the lamentations and that they forbid their female relatives from engaging in the practice. The men in the audience made the promises demanded of them, and Anzani finally allowed the local archpriest to bless the Church of S. Rocco.

Anzani is the only person who emerges as a truly active protagonist in De Rosa's account. Just as in the older pagan-Catholic-syncretism literature, the ordinary Italian Catholics of Pietrafesa clung to old practices and only accepted or rejected what came to them from on high; they did not innovate. The contrast that emerges between "active" bishops and "passive" laity, recurs throughout De Rosa's work.

A Modified Model: Interacting Logics

In an earlier work (Carroll 1992), I propose a modification of De Rosa's conceptualization of popular Catholicism, suggesting that the implicit logic of official Catholicism establishes two very broad constraints within which a religious belief or practice must fall in order to be deemed legitimately Catholic. The first of these constraints is that, to be Catholic, a belief or practice must be at least loosely associated with the supernatural beings considered important in the pantheon of the official Church, which usually means Christ, Mary, and the saints. The second constraint is that public rituals must be legitimated by the clergy, at least the local clergy. Popular catholicism is the Catholicism that develops within these broad constraints at the local level. Precisely because these constraints are broad, the popular Catholicism that develops at the local level can be quite different from official Catholicism.

Just as important, and the Gramscian emphasis on class differences not-withstanding, I found certain elements are common to virtually all forms of popular Catholicism that have emerged in Italy. Saints and madonnas, for instance, are always more powerful than Christ, and these saints and madonnas have a fearsome dark side, which has no counterpart in the idyllic world of the triden-tine pantheon (see ibid., 14–29, 67–87). Still, although the formulation just summarized provided a useful framework for describing the logic of popular Catholicism in Italy, I have come to realize that it is incomplete.

Generally, De Rosa and his school take official Catholicism to be unproblematic. For them, it is a variant of Catholicism that can be accessed by consulting the pronouncements of popes, bishops, councils, and synods. By contrast, a number of other investigators, mainly non-Italian, suggest that official Catholicism is problematic. In the usual case, the point being made by these investigators (see for example Harline 1990) is that there was a divergence of opinion within the Church hierarchy, and within the hierarchy of the Italian Church in particular, on important doctrinal and devotional issues even after the Council of Trent.

But the presence of diverging opinions among Church elites is not the only thing that makes official Catholicism problematic. What I argue throughout this book is that the Catholicism favored by Italian bishops was shaped by a process that is the mirror image of the process that shaped popular Catholicism. In other words, the logic of *popular* Catholicism in Italy established some very broad constraints to which the official Church had to adapt. This means that even before official Catholicism comes to be adapted to unique local circumstances (in the manner described by De Rosa) it is already a cultural product, shaped by its interaction with the logic of popular Catholicism.

In the end, this book argues that the Catholic experience in Italy was shaped by the dynamic interaction between the two logics, one associated with official Catholicism and one associated with popular Catholicism, with new devotions and beliefs constantly emerging, sometimes from above but very often from below, as each variant adapted to the constraints imposed by the logic of the other.

Other Approaches

Several recent studies of popular religion in Western European societies suggest that the content of popular religion is affected most of all by the power wielded—or not—by political elites committed to some particular religious ideology. This emphasis upon power and upon imposing religion from the top down seems to be especially popular with Anglo-Saxon scholars. Duffy's (1992) account of traditional religion in England just before and just after the Reformation and Wuthnow's (1987, 311–30; 1989, 25–156) account of the Reformation in England and France are examples of this approach.

Duffy challenges the view, held by many historians of the Reformation, that the English public was becoming disenchanted with traditional Catholic practice in the late 1400s and early 1500s. On the contrary, he argues, traditional Catholicism was widely popular during this period, and there was, if anything, a devotional renaissance among English Catholics. So why did England become Protestant under Henry VIII and Edward VI? Duffy's answer: They didn't. The repressive measures enacted by Henry and Edward may have had the effect of extinguishing the outward signs of Catholic practice, Duffy argues, but they did not extinguish the commitment of ordinary people to Catholicism. In support of this view, Duffy mounts an impressive array of evidence from a variety of sources that suggests that, when the repressive measures enacted under Henry and Edward were repealed under Queen Mary, Catholic devotion at the parish level emerged as strongly as ever. It was only with the accession of Elizabeth I and the enactment of measures far more repressive than anything done previously that the English public began to abandon Catholicism—and then only because embracing Protestantism was the path of least resistance.

Wuthnow (1987, 311–30; 1989, 25–156) advances a similar argument in addressing a somewhat different question. Wuthnow starts his analysis by pointing out that there was significant support for Catholicism in England and significant support for Protestantism in France. Yet England become a Protestant nation and France remained (largely) Catholic. Why? For Wuthnow, the key lay in the degree to which the central government, notably the king himself, could act independent of the landed aristocracy. In Wuthnow's reconstruction, the landed aristocracy was strongly committed to the old religion in all areas of Christian Europe during the early years of the Reformation. Given this, Protestantism was most likely to be successful in those areas where a central government could act independent of the landed aristocracy, as in England. Conversely, Protestantism was least likely to be successful in those areas where the central government was heavily dependent on the landed aristocracy, as in France.

The arguments advanced by Duffy and Wuthnow are important because they show that the outcome of the Reformation in England and France was far more problematic than is generally recognized. Furthermore, there can be no denying that the ability and willingness of political elites to enact repressive measures in support of one religion over another has always had an effect on religious practice at the local level. Nevertheless, implicit in both analyses is, a model in which ordinary people are essentially passive beings, who change only as a result of force applied from above. The issue is not whether such a model is true or false but whether it is useful or not. In the case of Italy, as I hope to show, a model (any model) that denies a creative role to ordinary Catholics causes us to misperceive much of what has happened over the past few centuries.

A second approach that must be mentioned here, if only because it is so strongly associated with Italian scholarship, is the microhistorical approach pioneered by Ginzburg (1980; 1983).[4] Microhistorians like Ginzburg have sought to uncover popular traditions that have remained hidden from scholarly view because they were part of an oral culture that left no written records. This is best done, they argue, by focusing upon those infrequent and highly circumscribed situations in which popular and elite traditions have unexpectedly collided. In *The Cheese and the Worms,* the microhistorical analysis that is likely most familiar to English-speaking readers, Ginzburg (1980) uses the records of the Inquisition in Udine to reconstruct the worldview of a miller named Menocchio who was brought before the Inquisition in the 1580s on a charge of heresy. In Menocchio's testimony, Ginzburg argues, we catch sight of long-standing popular traditions that existed alongside the more familiar traditions associated with Italian elites. Menocchio, for instance, believed that life on Earth had originated by means of a "rotting" process, which gave rise to angelic beings in the way that rotting cheese (it was believed) gave rise to worms.

In an even earlier book (but translated into English only after the success of *The Cheese and the Worms*) Ginzburg (1983) used the records of the Inquisition to reconstruct an agrarian cult whose members called themselves *benandanti.* The term is not easy to translate, but "righteous travelers" is a close approximation. The benandanti believed that at certain points in the year they were called out to the fields surrounding their local community to do battle with witches. The fertility of the fields depended upon the benandanti winning these "night battles." Ginzburg demonstrates that the Inquisitors were totally baffled when they first began to hear about the benandanti. As members of the Church hierarchy, they simply had no knowledge of this popular tradition. Slowly, over the

---

4. For an overview of the microhistorical tradition, see Muir (1991).

course of the next century or so, the men who ran the Inquisition in Udine learned to "make sense" of the benandanti by assimilating them to the familiar category "witch." Over time, the benandanti themselves came to accept this view of themselves.

At first sight, the emphasis by microhistorians upon the interaction between popular and elite traditions would seem to make their work relevant to the concerns of this book. Unfortunately, the popular traditions that have been of most concern to the microhistorical school rarely have anything to do with Catholic beliefs regarding saints or madonnas or with the rituals associated with these beings. In other words, although the microhistorical school has much to say about popular tradition, it has little to say about popular Catholicism. Menocchio, for instance, was just what the Inquisition said he was, a heretic who denied the existence of Purgatory, who denigrated the clergy (from the pope down to the local priest), and who criticized the excessive emphasis placed on Mary. He was certainly not part of the Catholic tradition, popular or otherwise. The benandanti appear to have considered themselves good Catholics, but they also seemed to have kept their Catholic beliefs separate from the beliefs that defined their benandanti role. At any rate, Ginzburg has nothing to say about how popular Catholic traditions might have influenced the benandanti cult.[5]

The general disinclination of microhistorians to confront popular Catholicism constitutes an interesting puzzle in the sociology of Italian social science. Whatever the solution to that puzzle might be, the practical effect of this disinclination is that there is little in the microhistorical literature of value to the understanding of popular Catholicism in Italy.

Historical Periods

All periodizations of history are arbitrary. No cultural ethos, institutional innovation, or social process ever emerges ex nihilo, and it is always possible to argue that something that appears to be new is to some extent a continuation of something preexisting. Even so, the fifteenth century has always struck students of Italian history as the obvious divide between the medieval period and the early modern period, especially in matters relating to religion. This, after all, was the century that witnessed that explosion of artistic and literary creativity that would come to be called the Italian Renaissance. This was also the century that saw an end to the Great Schism and its three competing papacies, that saw the reestab-

5. Ginzburg aside, the tendency to ignore popular Catholicism or consider it only in passing is also evident in other microhistorical analyses; see the essays in Muir and Ruggiero (1991).

lishment of the papacy at Rome, and that saw the emergence of a strong Papal State in central Italy. Finally, this century witnessed a dramatic intensification of those reform movements that had began to develop within the mendicant orders, the Franciscans and the Dominicans in particular, during the closing decades of the fourteenth century. For all these reasons and, more pragmatically, because so much has been written about the fifteenth century, this century seems a convenient place to begin consideration of the topics discussed in this book.

The terminus ad quem of my analysis is less clear. In northern Italy, many of the processes described in this book were clearly on their way out by the early nineteenth century. For reasons discussed later, these same processes continued to operate for a longer period in southern Italy. It is also the case that there has been a decline in religiosity in all regions of Italy since the end of World War II. On the other hand, neither the differences between northern and southern Italy nor the general decline in religiosity over the past few decades should be exaggerated. As is shown in chapter 1, cults organized around wonder-working images have for centuries been a central element in popular Catholicism, and such cults still exist in both the South and the North. Further, as the discussion of the sanctuary at Ghedi (see chap. 4) makes clear, cults of a decidedly non-orthodox nature can still be found in northern Italy.

Popular Catholicism in Italy may not be as popular as it once was, but it is still sufficiently popular to justify the designation.

Chapter One

Powerful Images

O n July 21, 1864, a fifteen-year-old boy named Giovanni Belloni was working in a field near Fara d'Adda in Lombardy, when he suddenly fell to the ground unconscious. All attempts by his father and the other men working nearby to revive him failed, and Giovanni was carried home and put to bed, still unconscious. His parents called in a local doctor, but nothing he did could rouse the boy. When Giovanni's condition seemed to worsen, they sent for a priest to administer Extreme Unction.

At this point, while awaiting what they thought was their son's impending death, Giovanni's parents heard about a new miraculous image, a fresco of a madonna painted on the exterior wall of a farmhouse in the nearby community of Arcene. Although the image had been painted centuries before, it was new in the sense that it had only recently begun to dispense miraculous favors. Giovanni's parents left for Arcene immediately. There they prayed in front of this newly empowered image and held up one of Giovanni's shirts so that it might be blessed. Returning home, they wrapped the shirt about their son, and at that moment he regained consciousness for the first time since his fall. Within two weeks, Giovanni was well enough to travel to Arcene with his parents to thank the madonna for his health. During this visit, he and his parents provided the local parish priest with an account of these miraculous events.[1]

As miraculous image stories go, this one is fairly tame. There is nothing particularly mysterious about a teenager fainting while hard at work in a field. Nor is regaining consciousness after several days as impressive as being able to see after having been blind since birth or having a mangled limb restored to perfect

---

1. This priest's account is reproduced in Cornaro (1868, 253–54) and is the source for the story reported here.

health, favors that have often been dispensed by miraculous images in Italy. What makes this story valuable is that it throws into relief an important element in Italian Catholicism: the need for direct contact with a particular image when asking for a favor. In the story, for example, it does not occur to Giovanni's parents to pray to the generic Mary of the tridentine Church. On the contrary, they feel compelled to go to Arcene and pray in front of a particular image. Just as important, they feel the need to establish a physical link between Giovanni and the image by means of the shirt. When Giovanni is finally healed, nobody thanks Mary. The family goes to Arcene to thank the image that was seen to be the source of the miracle.

Over the past six centuries, Italy has been home to hundreds, possibly thousands, of miraculous images like the one at Arcene. Occasionally, these images depict a saint or Christ, but the vast majority are images of a madonna. Although these madonnine images are associated with a wide variety of titles,[2] the most common is Madonna delle Grazie. Quite often, even when a madonna's official title is something else, ordinary Catholics will call her Madonna delle Grazie.[3] This title, more than any other, conveys the core meaning of these images to Italian Catholics: they dispense favors (*grazie*).

The official Church, of course, has always viewed miraculous images differently. In line with its Christocentric biases, the Church argues that prayers to a madonnine image are really prayers to Mary, and that any favors obtained are the result of Mary having interceded on our behalf with her Divine Son. For Church officials, the popular belief that some madonnine images have an intrinsic power is an "abuse" that needed to be eradicated. Fortunately (for us), official accounts of this particular abuse are often fairly detailed, with the result that these accounts often provide us with glimpses into popular Catholic practice that are not available from other sources. The critiques of one reform-minded segment of the Italian clergy, in particular, are especially valuable in reconstructing the logic of popular Catholicism in Italy.

2. Most discussions would likely call these Marian images. Such a label, however, presupposes the view promulgated by Catholic theologians, namely, that these are representations of Mary. In fact, although all madonnas are vaguely associated with the Mary of the official Church, it is fairly easy to establish that different madonnas are seen as having distinctive personalities (see Carroll 1992, 52–66). For this reason, the term *madonnine* seems more appropriate.

3. Servetti Donati (1970), for instance, reproduces nearly a hundred testimonies describing the receipt of a divine favor from the Madonna dell'Olmo in the sanctuary at Budrio, near Bologna. These testimonies were collected by the staff of the sanctuary over a two-hundred-year period, starting in the mid-sixteenth century. While the title Madonna dell'Olmo does appear in these testimonials, the madonna is just as likely to be called questa Madre di grazie, Santa Madre di grazie dell'Olmo, Santissima Vergine di grazie, Nostra Donna delle grazie, etc.

Italian Jansenism and the Elimination of "Pernicious Custom"

Jansenism, a Catholic reform movement, emerged during the seventeenth and eighteenth centuries, mainly in France and northern Italy. Older Catholic commentaries tend to depict Jansenism as a movement dominated by cheerless intellectuals with a pessimistic view of human nature and an overly rigorous attitude toward the sacraments (see, e.g., Forget 1913). More recent scholars, however, both Catholic and non-Catholic, approach Jansenism in less judgmental terms.[4]

At least in Italy, Jansenists saw themselves as being driven by two interrelated concerns: to restore the Church to the primitive purity of the earliest Christian centuries and to eliminate those Catholic practices that diminish the centrality of Christ. Unlike Protestants, who wanted much the same things, Jansenists were thoroughly committed to maintaining the organizational integrity of the Church. True, their focus on the "early Church" led them to argue for a reduction in papal power, but this never translated into an outright denial of papal primacy. Moreover, Jansenists accepted all the important doctrinal pronouncements associated with the Council of Trent. The important point is that their unyielding Christocentrism and their emphasis upon the early Church led Jansenists to take a sharply critical look at popular practices associated with madonnas and saints. They were especially concerned with image cults, and the most influential of the Jansenist critiques leveled at image cults emerged at the Synod of Pistoia.

The Synod of Pistoia was held in 1786 in response to an initiative by Peter Leopold, Grand Duke of Tuscany, who wanted to promote in Tuscany the same sort of reforms regulating the relation between Church and state as had been enacted in the Hapsburg dominions by his brother Joseph II. The Grand Duke wanted a Tuscan synod that would eliminate the various abuses that had been introduced into Ecclesiastical practice. As a preliminary to this synod, Tuscan bishops were asked to convene synods in their dioceses. The bishop who responded most favorably to this initiative was Scipione de'Ricci (1741–1810), the Jansenist bishop of Pistoia and Prato.

Ricci convened his diocesan synod in Pistoia on September 18, 1786, and it met for ten days. Although the pope was recognized as head of the Church, the synod made it clear that he should operate within certain constraints. In partic-

---

4. For a brief overview of the Jansenist movement in Tuscany during the late eighteenth century, see Miller (1994). For more detailed discussions of Italian Jansenism, see Molinari and Fappani (1982); Signorotto (1983a); Bontempi (1983); Verzella (1993). Verzella is particularly useful in demonstrating the varied nature of Jansenism in Italy, something that has allowed Italian scholars to focus on selected aspects of Jansenism in order to develop critiques that reflected their particular political or religious concerns.

ular, the synod decreed that a pope should not introduce new doctrines, that is, doctrines not already evident in Holy Scripture or the writings of the Church Fathers. Pistoia encouraged bishops to reclaim their rights over a variety of matters that had been given to them by Christ but that had been usurped by the Roman Court. The synod also proposed a variety of reforms designed to rationalize Catholic practice. All the regular orders, for instance, were to be reduced to a single order with a single habit, and all churches were to contain only a single altar.

The synod made a number of recommendations in regard to image cults. One of these dealt with the matter of using various titles to denote madonnine images: "This holy Synod also recommends an end to the pernicious custom of distinguishing between images, in particular those of the Virgin, with special titles. Such titles are for the most part useless and childish" (Stella 1986, 202).[5] Why the use of different madonnine titles was so offensive was spelled out in more detail in the decree that Peter Leopold later issued in order to put the Pistoian reforms into operation: "No church is to have more than one image of any given saint, and in particular, more than one image of the Most Holy Virgin. These different images have led to thousands of strange ideas among the people, such as the idea that there are several different Virgin Marys because there are several different titles given to Mary" (cited in Ricci 1980, 2:337–38).

These passages of course are evidence of the fact that ordinary Catholics did see the various madonnas as separate and distinct supernatural beings. But another "error" identified at Pistoia suggests that Italian Catholics did more than just differentiate among their madonnas: "Authorities should remove those images in which the public seems to place a special trust or to recognize some special power. . . . Such an image can be recognized by the fact that a special cult attaches to it and that people turn to it more than other images, as if God and the saints might pay special attention to prayers that are said in front of this particular image" (Stella 1986, 202). In other words, the variant of Catholicism that the reformers at Pistoia wanted to eliminate was a Catholicism in which madonnine images were often infused with supernatural power and in which some of these images were so powerful as to be deserving of a special cult.

The fact that madonnine images represented separate and distinct madonnas, with some images being especially powerful, explains something else mentioned at Pistoia: the practice of keeping madonnine images veiled, an abuse that the Pistoian decrees condemn over and over again:

5. Stella (1986) provides a photographic reproduction of this document, which was originally published in Florence in 1788.

Bishops should be required . . . to inspect all the pictures and images in their churches, removing those that might be indecent or duplicates [of others already in the church]. There are many images that until now have been kept covered on the pretext that this increases devotion; these must be uncovered. (Ibid., 60)

All country churches should be required to have only a single altar. This altar should have a Crucifix, and possibly a painting of the local patron saint and a painting of the Holy Virgin. But the practice of routinely covering images, whether it involves a crucifix or an image of the Holy Virgin or some other saint, constitutes an abuse and should be stopped, since this practice has no purpose except to inspire superstition. (Ibid., 63)

The abuse of keeping certain images covered should also be stamped out. Not only does this practice lead the people to suppose that a special power resides in the image but it destroys the usefulness of the image. (Ibid., 202)

To the rationalist clerics at Pistoia, covering an image seemed to negate the whole purpose of making an image. After all, what is the value of an image that cannot be seen? Moreover it seemed silly to cover some images but not others, since they all depicted the same Mary. One anonymous defender of the Pistoian reforms, for instance, would later ridicule the practice of "keeping one image of the Virgin in a church covered while ten, fifteen, even twenty or more other images of the Virgin in the same church were uncovered" when "the original behind each image was in all cases the same" (Riflessioni in difesa 1796, 383). But the fact remains that madonnine images were veiled in Italy, and this practice met with the approval of both ordinary Catholics and the local clergy (who, after all, had physical custody of these images). The delegates at Pistoia needed to go no further than Tuscany to find well-known examples of veiling.

One of the most important and powerful madonnine images at Florence, for example, was the Nunziata (Annunciation) in the church of the same name. The Nunziata was veiled and was uncovered only on special occasions and only under tightly circumscribed circumstances. In 1588 when the clergy of the church allowed a procession in front of an uncovered Nunziata, they were rebuked by the Grand Duke himself, Cosimo I. Cosimo commented upon the "confusion" and "disorder" that this act provoked in the assembled crowd and ordered that in the future it not be uncovered without his express permission (the relevant passage from Cosimo's letter is cited in Andreuci 1857, 95). An inventory published in 1783 (see ibid., 92) indicates that the Nunziata had three separate veils, one of which was a silver veil inlaid with precious stones.

The Madonna dell'Impruneta was another powerful image in Tuscany. Although usually kept at a sanctuary in the community of Impruneta (just south of Florence), this image was often brought into Florence and carried in procession during times of crisis, especially those provoked by rain or drought. There were seventy-one different processions of this sort between 1354 and 1540 (del Grosso 1983, 54). Yet whether carried in procession or held in its sanctuary, the Madonna dell'Impruneta was kept veiled. Even today, pilgrims to the Impruneta sanctuary will normally find the image veiled.

A third veiled image could be found in the Cathedral at Pisa. The madonna in this case was called S. Maria sotto gli organi, and the records of the cathedral make it clear that her image had been kept continually veiled, even when carried in procession, from (at least) 1494 until 1789. Her veil was removed only on December 13, 1789, upon the orders of Peter Leopold, acting under the influence of the Pistoian decrees.[6]

It is possible that the delegates at Pistoia were thinking specifically of these three veiled Tuscan images when they framed their decrees. But the veiling of powerful madonnine images has occurred throughout Italy. Mondello (1882, 48–58) tells us that at Trapani (Sicily) it was customary for people who believed themselves to be possessed by diabolical spirits to gather in front of the veiled image of the Madonna di Trapani on August 14. The image would be uncovered, and at that moment the possessing spirits would be forced out of the bodies they had invaded, a process that was accompanied by shouting and speaking in foreign tongues. Bystanders would at the same moment place rosaries and other holy objects to their mouths to ensure that the departing spirits would not enter them. According to devotional accounts, the force of the spirits rushing out of the possessed was sufficiently strong to extinguish the flames on a lamp in the ceiling.

Why were especially powerful madonnine images kept veiled? The reformers at Pistoia almost got it right when they suggested that covering an image "leads the people to suppose that a special power resides in the image." But it is not veiling that leads to perception of power; rather it is the perception of power that leads to veiling. The underlying logic here was spelled out some time ago by scholars like Robertson Smith (1972, 148–64) and Durkheim (1915, 317–21). Both theorists suggest that supernatural power, even if it is generally beneficent, was nevertheless perceived as potentially disruptive and dangerous to human beings. The way to guard against such danger is to surround objects infused with supernatural power with prohibitions that limit and regularize the contacts between that object and human beings. These two theorists are talking about non-Western religions (the religion of the ancient Semitic-speaking cultures of the Middle East, in the case of Robertson Smith, and the religion of the Arunta in Australia, in the case of Durkheim). Nevertheless, the Italian practice of veil-

6. The story of this image is recounted in Carmichael (1901, 165–66).

ing madonnine images is to be explained in the same way: veiling ensures that contact, even visual contact, with an especially powerful image occurs within precisely defined limits, to minimize the danger associated with that image.

That Italian publics did see miraculous images as potentially dangerous shows up in the folk traditions that coalesce around these images. A story preserved in the archives of the Cathedral at Pisa (reported in Carmichael 1901, 166), for example, tells us that in 1607 the archbishop of Pisa, who was from Piemonte (and thus a foreigner), decided he wanted to see the image of S. Maria sotto gli organi. In the presence of two of the cathedral's canons and a workman, he started to remove the veil. But before he could finish, he was seized with a shivering fit and yelled out "Cover it! Cover it!" The archbishop died soon after; one of the canons committed suicide by cutting his throat with a razor; the other canon died a little later in poverty. And the poor workman, who was after all just following orders? He simply went blind. Such are the penalties, this story would suggest, for those who seek contact with powerful images outside the bounds prescribed by tradition.

Most madonnine images in Italy were not veiled. Even so, veiling is the logical outcome of the popular belief that concrete images could be infused with supernatural power. Given this, the reformers at Pistoia were quite correct (in light of their goals) to single out the veiling of images for special condemnation. The reforms promulgated at Pistoia were meant to be applied to the Church as a whole. For that reason there was great interest in the synod in all areas of Catholic Europe. When the *Atti e decreti* was published in 1788, it was quickly translated into Latin, French, German, and Spanish and became the object of wide discussion.

In the end, however, the Pistoian reforms failed for a number of reasons. As might be expected, Pistoia's attempt to constrict the powers of the pope ensured the opposition of the papacy. As well, the outbreak of the French Revolution in 1789 predisposed much of the hierarchy of the Church against the sort of radical organizational changes proposed at Pistoia. The Tuscan National Council envisioned by Peter Leopold and Ricci failed to materialize. In 1790, Peter Leopold became emperor of the Austrian dominions, and his son and successor as grand duke, Ferdinand III, was less supportive of Ricci and his reforms.

Within Tuscany, however, one of the most serious obstacles to the Pistoian reforms was the strong resistance of the general public and the local clergy, especially their resistance to the reforms relating to image cults. Ricci's memoirs suggest that, even before the synod, his attempts to restrict or eliminate image cults always provoked strong outcries from the public and the clergy (see Ricci 1980, 1:236–40). This pattern was exacerbated after the synod. The most serious disturbances occurred at the end of April 1790.[7] Rumors that Ricci was about to move against a madonnine image that was the focus of an especially popular cult led to public disorders at Prato and Pistoia. Very soon, the disorders spread to the rest of the diocese and into other areas of Tuscany, including Florence. Ricci was forced to flee. Later that year he resigned as bishop, and the government revoked many of the Pistoian reforms.

Rome began a formal investigation of the Synod of Pistoia, and in 1794 Pope Pius VI issued the bull *Auctorem Fidei,* which condemned eighty-five of the propositions passed by that synod and labeled seven of these propositions as heretical.

Two years after *Auctorem Fidei,* an outdoor image near the Trevi fountain at Rome, called the Madonna dell'Archetto, began to move her eyes. This behavior was repeated many times over the next two months and was witnessed by a large number of people. A French cleric who was an eyewitness to the phenomenon reported: "There I saw first with my naked eye, and afterward with the help of my spectacles, the eyes of the blessed virgin painted on the canvas, 1. move horizontally, as if they had been animated; 2. open wider than usual, of which I was able to judge from having often said mass at that altar; 3. shut quite close so that the hair of the upper eyelid hung down over the under one" (Anon. 1796, 8).

Over the course of the next six months other madonnine images in Rome would also move their eyes. The official commission set up to investigate the phenomena authenticated twenty-four of these images as being associated with truly miraculous events (see Marchetti 1797). It also listed another seventy-two images in which "movement of eyes" or something similar had been reported and which the commission had not investigated. Finally, during this same period eighteen madonnine images in other areas of the Papal states also moved their eyes or did something similar (ibid., 279–93). Never before or since in Italian history have so many madonnine images displayed such visual wonders in so short a period of time.[8]

A cynic might suggest that the pope's condemnation of Pistoia in 1794 and the madonnine miracles of 1796 both derived, ultimately and in different ways,

7. This incident is described in Maselli (1980, 44).

8. In addition to the 114 madonnine images that moved their eyes, Marchetti reports that there were (in all areas of the Papal States, including Rome) five images of Christ and two images of a saint that displayed similar behaviors. Such data constitute a particularly clear illustration of the general assertion made at the beginning of this chapter: miraculous images in Italy are overwhelmingly madonnine images. The Madonna del'Archetto, the very first of the madonnine images at Rome to move its eyes in 1796, still exists. It is maintained in a private oratory located in an alleyway a few blocks from the Trevi fountain; the oratory is open to the public in the evening.

from the same thing: the threat of a French invasion. But another explanation was offered in a report on these madonnine miracles published in 1797 (cited in Stella 1986, 166); this report suggests that the miracles were an admonition sent from Heaven on account of the outrages promoted by the Jansenists. It is only a short step from this to another possible explanation, and one that must have occurred to many Italian Catholics: the miraculous images of central Italy were going out of their way to demonstrate the absurdity of the Jansenist view that they lacked an inherent power. These images were, in short, gloating.

What Miraculous Images Look Like

When Italians look at a miraculous image, just what are they looking at? In their survey of Catholic sanctuaries in Western Europe, the Nolans (1989, 183–87) found that nearly half of the sacred images enshrined in sanctuaries in Italy were two-dimensional (paintings or frescoes), the rest being statues or reliefs. Significantly, this is not the pattern typical of Catholic Europe as a whole. On the contrary, the Nolans found that the images most associated with sanctuaries in France, Spain, and Portugal were usually three-dimensional (statues or reliefs).[9] Only in German-speaking regions like Austria did the proportion of sanctuaries organized around two-dimensional images come close to what is found in Italy.

The Italian Catholic predilection for two-dimensional images is long-standing. In 1608, the painter Francesco Cavazzoni identified fifty miraculous images that were the object of devotion in the city of Bologna, and he presented a sketch of each image and a brief account of each image's history. Varese (1969) reproduces these sketches and summarizes Cavazzoni's text.[10] While fifty might seem a small number to anyone familiar with the output of Bolognese artists in the centuries prior to 1600, it must be remembered that Cavazzoni was concerned only with miraculous images, that is, images that had become objects of special devotion because they were believed to dispense favors. His sample thus did not include the hundreds of nonmiraculous images that would also have been found in Bologna. In any event, of the fifty miraculous images identified by Cavazzoni, sixteen were paintings, sixteen were frescoes, thirteen were statues, and five were reliefs. Two-dimensional images, in other words, outnumbered three-dimen-

9. The results of the Nolan survey, and in particular the fact that two-dimensional images are rare in sanctuaries in France and Spain, clearly undermine Dupront's suggestion (cited in Russo 1984, 436) that a preference for two-dimensional images is part of a Mediterranean cultural heritage.

10. Cavazzoni's in situ sketch of the Madonna di San Luca, the single most important image in Bologna, shows a retractable veil on each side of the image. Almost certainly this means that the image was usually kept veiled.

sional images by a ratio of almost 2:1. Russo (1984, 436) finds a similar preference for two-dimensional images in her consideration of the sacred images mentioned in the pastoral visits made to outlying communities in Campania between
1598 and 1754.

As to content, madonnine images in Italy are relatively standardized. The
madonna is always fully clothed. She usually wears a cloak over a tunic, with her
head covered by the cloak's cowl. Although a few images are of the madonna as a
young girl, the vast majority depict her as an adult. But the one iconographic element that most distinguishes these images from images of, say, female saints is
that the madonna is usually holding a child. In other words, most miraculous
images of a madonna in Italy are images of a Madonna con Bambino, a madonna
with child.

Table 1.1 presents the frequency of three madonnine patterns (Madonna con
Bambino, madonna with the adult Christ, madonna without any depiction of
Christ) in churches in three regions. The images that were the objects of cults in
Lombardy are derived from Arrigoni and Bertarelli's (1936) description of the
sacred images depicted in popular prints dating from the seventeenth through the
early twentieth centuries. The miraculous images at Bologna in the early 1600s
were described by Cavazzoni (see earlier remarks). The madonnine images that
were the objects of cults in Sicily are derived from Cocchiara's (1982) account of
the madonnine images depicted in popular prints on file at the Museo Pitrè in
Palermo. Cocchiara does not associate particular prints with particular dates, but
his discussion suggests that the prints date from the eighteenth through the early
twentieth centuries.

The images considered in table 1.1 were objects of popular cults and thus
constitute only a very small proportion of the paintings, statues, and reliefs found
in Italian churches and museums. They are generally not the images studied and
commented upon by art historians. Nevertheless, these images—objects of popular cults—provide insight into the preferences of ordinary Italian Catholics.
What the data in table 1.1 demonstrate is that ordinary Italian Catholics clearly
prefer their madonnas to be con Bambino.

This Italian Catholic predilection to take their important madonnas con
Bambino is worth emphasizing, if only because this is not the pattern among
modern Catholics generally. For example, the three Marian shrines outside Italy
that today draw more Catholics than any others are dedicated to Our Lady of
Fatima (in Portugal), Our Lady of Lourdes (in France), and Our Lady of Guadalupe (in Mexico). None of the Marys associated with these shrines holds a
child. Similarly, the Mary who appears on the Miraculous Medal, which is the
single most popular Marian medal of the nineteenth and twentieth centuries,

Table 1.1. Miraculous Madonnine Images Found in Churches in Lombardy, Bologna, and Sicily

Image	Lomabardy, 17th to Early 20th Centuries		Bologna, Early 17th Century	Sicily, 19th to Early 20th Centuries
	Milan	Outside Milan		
Madonna con Bambino	71　(53%)	93　(68%)	40　(80%)	34　(81%)
Madonna with adult Christ	22　(17%)	12　(9%)	6　(12%)	1　(2%)
Madonna only	40　(30%)	31　(23%)	4　(8%)	7　(17%)
Totals	133 (100%)	136 (100%)	50 (100%)	42 (100%)

Sources: Lombardy: Arrigoni and Bertarelli (1936); Bologna: Varese (1969); Sicily: Cocchiara (1982).

carries an image of Mary as the Immaculate Conception and also lacks the Christ child. Finally, the Mary who has been appearing at Medjugorje (Bosnia-Herce-govina) for more than a decade and who has attracted the attention of millions of Catholics worldwide is a lone Mary, without the Christ child.

The temptation to attribute the popularity of the Madonna con Bambino pattern to an Italianate love of children should be resisted. Although there is anecdotal evidence that children are today highly valued in Italian society, it would be hazardous to project this cultural value onto the past; there are simply too many indicators that Italy was not always a child-loving society. Some of the most dramatic evidence in this regard comes from studies of child abandonment, the rates of which have been high, at least in certain regions of Italy, for most of the modern era.

Between 1500 and 1700, for instance, the proportion of newborns aban-doned at Florence never went below 12 percent (Kertzer 1993, 72). In Italy as a whole, rates of child abandonment increased dramatically following the sharp increase in Italy's population that began in the eighteenth century (see Cappel-letto 1983; Corsini 1988, 12; De Rosa 1983, 263); and by the nineteenth century child abandonment had reached horrendous levels. During the decade 1841–1850, 14,613 abandoned children were taken in by the Ospedale di S. Maria degli Innocenti at Florence, equivalent to 39 percent of the children baptized in Flo-rence during the same period (Corsini 1976, 1039). At Cosenza (Calabria) dur-ing the 1820s, 39 percent of all newborns were abandoned (Kertzer and Bretell 1987, 101). Similarly, about a third the children born in Milan during the 1840s were also abandoned (Hunecke 1989, 181–82). Although in Italy as a whole most abandoned children were illegitimate, there were important exceptions to this pattern. At least during the nineteenth century, a majority of the children aban-doned in cities like Milan, Brescia, and Florence were legitimate (ibid., 28).

It is easy to see parental poverty as a driving force behind child abandonment, and almost certainly poverty figured prominently in the conscious calcu-
lations that parents made in deciding whether or not to abandon their offspring.
Nevertheless, as Kertzer (1993, 170–72) points out, efforts to find a correlation
between the extent of poverty in an area and rates of abandonment have generally failed. Clearly factors other than poverty were at work as well. For instance, a
common method of abandoning a child was to place the child in the *ruota* set
into the exterior wall of a convent or foundling home. A ruota was a revolving
drum or cylinder, open at one side, into which an infant could be placed and
which could then be rotated so the infant would be inside the building. The most
obvious consequence of using the ruota was that it permitted parents to abandon
their children anonymously. In her survey of child abandonment in communities near Siena in the mid-nineteenth century, Bruttini (1983, 229) finds that, in
communities that used a ruota, the average number of children abandoned each
year was 195; in communities that did not use a ruota that figure was 3 per year.
In other words, it appears that the easier child abandonment was made for parents, the more readily they abandoned their children.

The ways in which children were abandoned in Italy also reveal cultural attitudes toward children. In many areas it was common practice to abandon children in hazardous places even when less hazardous places were available. A man-
ual published at Rome in 1584, for instance, instructs parish priests to work
against the abandonment of children but (if abandonment was necessary) to at
least instruct people "to abandon their children at hospitals or other places prepared to receive them and not at crossroads, or along public streets, or in those
places where the children might easily expire" (cited in De Rosa 1983, 263). Two
hundred years later, children were still being abandoned on public roads in
Calabria and still faced the danger of being attacked and eaten by dogs or pigs
(ibid., 270).

Italian attitudes toward children can also be assessed by looking at societal
reactions to infanticide. Officially, infanticide was defined as a serious crime in
most Italian legal codes, and in most Italian dioceses it was one of the few sins
that only a bishop could absolve. Even so, Casarini's (1982) analysis of mothers
charged with infanticide at Bologna during the early 1800s, shows that in practice, judges were relatively tolerant of the crime and searched for circumstances
that might justify clemency.

Finally, Del Panta (1980, 79–80) suggests that smallpox was the least feared
of all the epidemic diseases in Italy precisely because it was a disease that was
most likely to strike children rather than adults. When members of the middle or
upper classes did express fears about smallpox they were more likely to be con-

cerned with their own facial disfigurement than with the threat posed to their children.

All of the above make it difficult to argue that in centuries past Italy was a society characterized by that strong love of children that is now so much a part of the Italian stereotype. But if the Italian Catholic predilection for the Madonna con Bambino pattern did not derive from an especially positive valuation of children, where did it come from? Many modern Catholics might see in this preference nothing more than a simple affirmation of Church doctrine. The Church, after all, has always argued that Mary was the mother of Jesus Christ and that it is this maternal link that makes her such an effective intercessor with her divine son. Given this doctrine, stressing that maternal link by pairing Mary with the infant Christ would seem to make perfect sense.

The problem with this interpretation is that it ignores the realities of Italian Catholicism. Virtually every investigator who has studied popular Catholicism in Italy has concluded that the saints and madonnas of Italy are seen as more powerful than Christ.[11] Italian madonnas, in other words, do not derive their power from anyone, and certainly not from Christ; they themselves have power. But if madonnas have independent power, they have no need to be paired with Christ. So, the question remains: why do Italian Catholics prefer their madonnas to be con Bambino?

Since the most obvious consequence of associating a madonna with a young child is to make the madonna a mother (not necessarily the mother of Christ, just a mother), I suggest that this is why it is done. Italian Catholics, in other words, find that a powerful female supernatural being is more appealing if she is also a mother of a young child. This is a point to which we will return in the concluding chapter of this book.

One final characteristic of miraculous images in Italy is easily overlooked: these images are generally static, that is, they do not depict a scene from a recognizable narrative. True, the madonna and child who appear in a miraculous image are often engaged in some recognizable activity (e.g., the madonna is gazing at the child, the madonna is nursing the child, the child is touching the madonna's cheek, etc.), but these activities are not associated with a commonly known story.

The fact that miraculous images tend to be static is the more noteworthy given that dynamic images of a madonna (i.e., depicting a scene from a recognizable narrative) are abundant in Italy, which is awash with paintings and frescoes depicting scenes from Catholic mythology. Many images, for instance, de-

11. For an overview of the relevant literature, see Carroll 1992, 14–29).

Table 1.2. Static and Dynamic Miraculous Madonnine Images, in Churches in Lombardy, Bologna, and Sicily

Image	Lomabardy, 17th to Early 20th Centuries		Bologna, Early 17th Century	Sicily, 19th to Early 20th Centuries
	Milan	Outside Milan		
Static madonna	84 (63%)	98 (72%)	42 (84%)	32 (76%)
Dynamic madonna				
Addolorata	25 (19%)	17 (12%)	6 (12%)	2 (5%)
Madonna in New Testament scene (apart from Addolorata)	9 (7%)	4 (3%)	2 (4%)	2 (5%)
Immacolata	13 (10%)	4 (3%)		4 (9%)
Madonna in apparition scene	2 (1%)	12 (9%)		
other		1 (1%)		2 (5%)
Totals	133 (100%)	136 (100%)	50 (100%)	42 (100%)

Sources: Lombardy: Arrigoni and Bertarelli (1936); Bologna: Varese (1969); Sicily: Cocchiara (1982).

pict New Testament scenes, such as the Annunciation, the Visitation of Mary and Elizabeth, Mary in the stable at Bethlehem, and the Holy Family traveling to Egypt. Others depict events that do not appear in the New Testament but that nevertheless have been a part of Catholic tradition for centuries, like Mary's Assumption or her being crowned Queen of Heaven. But such dynamic images rarely become miraculous images and rarely become the object of a popular cult.

Just as surprising, perhaps, given the number and importance of madonnine apparitions in Italy, images depicting an apparition are also unlikely to miraculous images. Table 1.2 presents the frequency of static and dynamic madonnine images for the three regions in table 1.1. Static madonnas predominate in all cases.

The only dynamic madonna who shows up with any regularity in the popular tradition in Italy is the Addolorata, the Sorrowing Madonna. The Addolorata is the Mary of the New Testament, who is grieving over the suffering and death of her son, Jesus Christ. Being tied so explicitly to the Passion narrative, she is very much a dynamic madonna. The Addolorata cult constitutes an interesting episode in the history of Italian Catholicism, but for reasons that will become clear it is better discussed in the next chapter.

Origin Stories

For many miraculous images, the circumstances under which they first began to dispense favor are unknown. Others have an origin story, which spells out those circumstances in great detail, often giving even the precise date and time of day associated with an image's first miracle. Summaries of the origin stories associated with the most important miraculous images still extant in Italy can be found in Medica's (1965) guide to madonnine sanctuaries; more detailed versions of all these stories can be found in various specialized publications.

The devotional view is that these origin stories describe what actually happened. An alternative view, and the one adopted here, is that these stories are folk narratives that were shaped during oral transmission by the beliefs held about the images. Given this, these stories tell us the expectations regarding the miraculous images.

One expectation is that images do not become miraculous as soon as they are made. Every origin story, without exception (as far as I know), starts with an image that has been in existence for some time, often for centuries. Many images that became miraculous after 1400, for instance, are believed (by ordinary Catholics, not art historians) to have been brought to Italy during the eighth century as a result of the Iconoclast controversy that was then raging in the Eastern Church (see chap. 2). In other cases, an origin story will say that the image was hidden many years earlier and has only just been discovered. In still other cases, the story might give no specific details concerning the time or place of the image's manufacture, but the implication is that the image antedates, considerably, the events to be described.

A second expectation reflected in these origin stories has to do with location. Although the aisles and side chapels of Italian churches have long been well stocked with images, and although these have sometimes become miraculous images, most miraculous images were originally located somewhere outside of a functioning church. Some miraculous images, for instance, first started dispensing favors while located in a private residence. Still others were found on the walls of abandoned churches or small oratories. But an even larger number were located outdoors when they first began dispensing favors.

Consider for instance the origin story surrounding the sanctuary dedicated to a delle Grazie Madonna at Budrio (Emilia-Romagna). The earliest version of this story is in a report published in 1596 by Pompeo Vizani, who together with his brother had founded the sanctuary in 1589:

> [The inhabitants of Budrio and the surrounding area] went humbly to pray before an image of the Glorious Virgin that was found within a small and roughly made niche [un picciolo, et assai rozzo tabernacolo] set into an oak that grew in a field within the Commune of Budrio. As the size of the crowds coming to the site increased, so too did their devotion. They brought alms, they lit candles, and they

attached items of clothing, wax images, and painted ex-voto[12] to the oak in testimony to the graces received. (Cited in Servetti Donati 1970, 16–17)

Miraculous images have been encountered in other outdoor locations, as well. The following two stories are taken from Donato Calvi's almanac of important religious and secular events in the diocese and province of Bergamo:

> 1602: In the middle of the day, a bright light appeared near an image of a madonna that was painted on a wall in Borgo di Saint Caterina. The faded colors of the image were miraculously renewed. People ran to the image, and innumerable prodigies and miracles were dispensed. (Calvi 1676b, 594–95)

> 1604: Frightened by thunder and lightening, the horses drawing a carriage bolted. The reins snapped, and the horses continued to pull the carriage at high speed toward certain disaster. Suddenly, the gentleman in the carriage caught sight of a Madonna con Bambino painted on the wall of a house and appealed to her for aid. The favor was granted immediately, and the horses came to a stop. (ibid., 475–76)

In the Papal States (mainly in the city of Rome) in 1796, accounts of the twenty-six madonnine images that "moved their eyes" also indicate that the vast majority of these images were located outside, in a street or a piazza (see Anon. 1796).

These examples, along with innumerable others, make it clear that miraculous images in Italy are most often located outdoors near to where people congregate or go about their daily business. Since the nature of these outdoor images might be unfamiliar to anyone who has not actually visited Italy, a digression seems in order.

The Edicole of Italy

Italians use various terms—*tabernacolo, romitoria, santella, pilastrino, celletina, sacella, cappelletta, capitello, maestà*—to designate the structures that contain outdoor images. Terms may vary from region to region, so that *capitello* is the preferred term in the Veneto, *santella* and *madunin* (madonnina) in Lombardy, *maestà* in Tuscany, and so forth. The most common term, however, and the one used most often by Italian scholars, is *edicola*.

Most edicole found in urban areas are niches set into the exterior wall of a

---

12. The wax images were almost certainly body part ex-voto, that is, wax representations of that part of a person's body (the head, the eyes, an arm, a leg, etc.) that had been cured as a the result of a favor from the madonna. Painted ex-voto are painted tablets showing some danger from which the person had been delivered. Thus, a painted ex-voto might show someone being run over by a cart, falling from a building, tumbling into a well, etc. These tablets are still found in many Italian sanctuaries. For a discussion of ex-voto, see Carroll (1992, 82–87).

building. These niches are usually framed with a border (which can be plaster, marble, wood, or metal) and are surmounted by a small "roof." Today, most niche edicole have a pane of glass that protects the image inside from the elements. Many are backlit with a small electric light. Though the illumination thrown off is minimal by modern standards, these lights were in many cases the only source of nocturnal illumination along some streets during the late nineteenth and early twentieth centuries. Another type of edicola found in urban areas consists of a "box" attached to an exterior wall or to the corner where two exterior walls meet. A third type, less commonly encountered, resembles a small altar that has been set up against an exterior wall. In this case, the image is placed in an enclosure set above the altar.

In the countryside, especially in the past, an edicola might be nothing more than a image painted on a board and stuck onto a tree. The image that began dispensing favors at Budrio in the late 1500s was a tree edicola. Sometimes a countryside edicola is a large niche set into one of the stone walls that run along country roads. More typically, especially today, countryside edicole are free-standing structures, often a low wall or pillar in which a niche has been carved to contain an image, with some sort of framing added to protect the image from the elements. Some countryside edicole resemble sentry boxes and contain a small altar; others are like small chapels, with room enough inside for two or three people (although the entrance is usually blocked by an iron grate).

Edicole in the countryside were particularly likely to be found at crossroads. Some commentators (e.g., Lanari 1986, 23) suggest that this was a protective measure, designed to ward off the demons and evil spirits that were believed to frequent these locations. A simpler and more prosaic explanation is that edicole are the object of cultic activity (see below) and were placed at crossroads because this is where people gathered when returning from the fields in order to talk, play games, and generally socialize.

The historic origins of edicole are obscure. Moroni (1986, 32) argues that niche edicole derive from similar structures used in ancient Rome to hold images of household gods. Certainly there is a structural similarity between the two types of niche, which is why surviving Roman niches were often adapted to Catholic use. Breda (1979, 218), for instance, reports finding a niche of apparent Roman origin housing an image of S. Rocco in the community of S. Giorgio (in the Veneto). Nevertheless, no one has yet demonstrated that Italian Christians in the first centuries of the Christian era used edicole, and certainly no one has documented a continuous tradition of edicole stretching back to this early period.

Documentary references do establish that edicole were being used in Italy during the thirteenth and fourteenth centuries (Moroni 1986, 33). In the thirteenth century, Pietro Martire (1206–52) suggested that Florentines put lit candles in the edicole found in Florence and the surrounding area to provide a measure of safety for people traveling at night. Not only was the suggestion accepted, but the Signoria of Florence often released condemned men from prison or remitted their exile on the condition that they maintain the lit candles at some particular edicola for a period of five years (Andreucci 1857, 27). Some of these early edicole still exist. In their survey of 279 edicole in Bologna, for example, Ferrari and Lanzi (1985) find that four can be dated with certainty to the fourteenth century. Given that edicole use seems to have been well established by the thirteenth century, I suspect that most investigators would not dispute Oltranto's (1982, 13) claim that edicole first began to be used widely in Italy during the eleventh and twelfth centuries.

Prior to the nineteenth century, most explicit references to edicole by local bishops were hostile. In 1652, for example, the bishop of Brescia ordered the destruction of an edicola dedicated to S. Rocco at Pontasio, while in 1740 the archbishop of Milan issued an edict discouraging the inclusion of profane elements "in the sacred images that are painted or hung on the walls of the *contrade* or found within workshops and houses" (both incidents are reported in Niero 1986, 314). In the early 1600s, Church authorities at Naples discouraged the practice of painting sacred images on exterior walls on the grounds that people often piled manure near these walls and that men urinated against them (De Maio 1983, 178). But the more general pattern was for bishops to ignore edicole, and they are only rarely mentioned in reports of pastoral visits.

A decided shift in official opinion occurred during the closing decade of the eighteenth century and the early decades of the nineteenth century, when Italian bishops began co-opting the popular devotion centered on edicole by associating it with indulgences. In the usual case, a bishop would place a marble plaque on an edicole indicating the value of the indulgence (often forty days or some multiple of forty days),[13] the specific prayers that had to be said to earn that indulgence, the name of the bishop involved, and the year the indulgence was first authorized. One such plaque on an edicole along the road leading to the sanctuary of S. Maria dei Miracoli near Andria in Puglia reads: "Monsignore Giuseppe Cosenza, Bishop of Andria, concedes 40 days indulgence to anyone who recites a Credo and three Gloria Patri's—AD 1845." The inscription beneath an edicole in Monreale (near Palermo) reads: "Monsignor Lancia di Brolo Archbishop of Monreale with a decree dated 3 August 1897 concedes a 40 day indulgence to the faithful who with piety recite a Hail Mary in front of this image of Maria Santis-

---

13. An indulgence of forty days was usually called a *quarantina* (quarantine).

Table 1.3. The Images Found in *Edicole*, Three Communities in Apulia

Community and Image	Number of Edicole
Lucera (55 edicole)	
Madonnas	52
Madonna della Vittoria[a]	46
Immacolata	2
Madonna del Rosario	1
Addolorata	1
Madonna delle Stelle	1
Unknown Madonna con Bambino	1
Saints	1
Unknown male saint	1
Christ	2
Christ carrying cross	1
Pietà	1
Bari (99 edicole)	
Madonnas	61
Addolorata	27
Madonna di Constantinople	7
Madonna del Carmine	6
Madonna di Pompei	4
Madonna del Rosario	3
Immacolata	3
Madonna di Fatima	2
Unknown Madonna con Bambino	8
Other unknown madonna	1
Saints	24
S. Nicola[a]	12
SS. Medici (holy doctors)	3
S. Michele	2
S. Rocco	2
S. Giuseppe	1
S. Antonio di Padua	1
Unknown male saint	2
Unknown female saint	1
Christ	14
Christ crucified	11
Sacred Heart	2
Christ meeting Veronica	1
Lecce (35 edicole)	
Madonnas	15
Madonna del Carmine	5
Madonna di Pompei	2
Madonna del Rosario	1
Madonna del Latte	1
Annunciata	1
Unknown Madonna con Bambino	4
Other unknown madonna	1

Table 1.3. (continued)

Community and Image	Number of Edicole
Saints	12
S. Antonio di Padua	4
S. Oronzo[a]	3
Unknown male saint	5
Christ	8
Sacred Heart	3
Pietà	3
Christ crucified	1
Other Christ	1

[a]A supernatural patron of that community.

sima delle Grazie." Similar inscriptions can be found attached to edicole in all regions of Italy.

Sometimes the image in an edicola depicts a saint or Christ, but the one finding that emerges over and over again in the studies of edicole by Italian scholars is that these structures most often contain madonnine images. Cisotto (1979, 250) summarizes the results of a number of studies of edicole in the Veneto; the percentage of edicole in each community containing madonnine images are as follows: Valdagno (62%), Nove (81%), Thiene (78%), Marostica (68%), Asiago (66%), Vicenza (66%), Zanè (61%), Cittadella and Camposampiero (58%), Sandrigo (52%), Colli Berici (51%), Lonigo, (50%), and Padova (33%). Also in the Veneto, Breda (1979, 224) finds that 20 (71%) of the 28 edicole in the community of Marano and 45 (80%) of the 56 edicole in the community of San Pietro were dedicated to a madonna. Similarly, Ferrari and Lanzi (1985) find that 173 (68%) of the 256 edicole in the old city of Bologna contained madonnine images. Table 1.3 gives the results of surveys I conducted in the historic centers of Lucera, Bari, and Lecce, all communities in Apulia.[14] The finding that emerges from all these studies is that edicole containing madonnine images account for 60–80 percent of the edicole in any particular community.

Edicole are not merely decorative; they are the focus of cultic activity. For most of the year, the image in an edicola is honored (at least in the present day) by the placing of fresh flowers or lit votive candles in front of that image. Some-

14. Oltranto (1982, 16) suggests there are "about 120" edicole in the old city of Bari, without giving a breakdown by type of image contained. This number is higher than the number of edicole (99) that I found at Bari. In part, this is likely due to the fact that I missed some. But it also appears, from the photos included with in Oltranto's book, that some of the edicole he surveyed were found in private courtyards. I limited myself to edicole that could be viewed from public streets.

times these flowers or candles are ex-voto (that is, given in thanks for a favor), but often they are simply tokens of veneration. In their study of edicole at Bologna, Ferrari and Lanzi (1985) found fresh flowers at 61 (22%) of the 279 edicole in their sample. In my own studies, I found fresh flowers at 22 (22%) of 99 edicole at Bari and at 15 (43%) of 35 edicole at Lecce (Apulia).[15] Remember that the edicole were observed only once; if they had been checked regularly throughout the year, it seems certain that the evidence of cultic activity would have increased.

In addition to these daily acts of veneration, it is common to decorate edicole with special draping and floral arrangements just before some especially important festa. At Naples, in the days preceding the festa of the Madonna dell'Arco, each of the groups that will travel in procession to this madonna's sanctuary stages a series of rituals at specially decorated edicole in their local neighborhoods. These rituals include music (provided by a band or a "boom box" or both), a special sort of shuffling dance, and the dipping of banners before the image in the edicola.

Several investigators note that edicole are found along the routes known to have been associated with important processions (Lazzaretto 1978, 306–7; Ferrari and Lanzi 1985, 155). This link between processions and edicole can often be detected in documentary accounts of particular processions if we pay careful attention to the incidental details. Thus in 1671 an eyewitness to a particularly important and elaborate procession in honor of S. Gaetano at Naples wrote:

> This procession then reached the Church of S. Paolo . . . where it was greeted by His Eminence, Archbishop Caracciolo. After the archbishop received the banner and dispensed the incense, he intoned the *Te Deum.* . . . A wide variety of beautiful altars could be seen in all the streets where the procession passed, each altar being decorated with sumptuous silverwork and other charming ornamentation. (cited in de Blasis 1889, 58)

The altars mentioned here were almost certainly edicole that had been elaborated and enlarged for the occasion.

Who maintains the edicole? Occasionally a plaque beneath an edicola will indicate that the structure was established by a confraternity or simply by the people living in a certain street. However they were erected, most edicole, at least most niche edicole in urban areas, are today maintained by individual households. This is why edicole are usually very near the main entrance of a household and why they are most frequent along streets bordered by residences. The link with particular households is most obvious in those cases where edicole are set

---

15. At Lucera, however, a substantial number of edicole were located on second-story balconies, and I could not clearly see if the flowers they contained were fresh or plastic.

into a second-story wall reachable only from the porch of a particular household.

There is a reason why most scholarly studies of urban edicole in Italy (including my own) focus on the historic centers of particular cities: modern neighborhoods in most Italian cities contain few if any edicole. In some cases, this can be explained in purely practical terms. People living in a modern high-rise apartment building often do not have access to their outside walls. In other cases, the reason is less clear. Apartment buildings in Italy often have balconies, yet even here edicole (though they occasionally appear) are rare. It would be easy to attribute all this to secularization, and no doubt secularization is a factor, but there is another process at work as well.

While a given edicola might be maintained by a particular household, Italian Catholics have never considered edicole to be the locus of a purely domestic cult. The images set into edicole are meant to be seen by members of the community in general. Furthermore, it is important that the images themselves see the people passing in the street. This last point might seem strange to Anglo-Saxons, but it is an attitude encountered often in connection with edicole. One recent commentator, writing from a devotional perspective, suggests:

> An edicola is . . . not just something that adds a dash of folkloristic or devotional color to its surroundings. The madonna or saint represented is a "presence" that is unobtrusive and friendly. From its niche the image listens and sees [ascolta e vede] literally everything that happens around it. It is aware of prayers as well as the stench of everyday life. It hears exclamations of joy as well as the blasphemies uttered in moments of rage. It hears the characteristic sounds of the people when they are moving, talking, and working, as well as the odd silences of the night. (da Langasco 1992, 8)

In the winding and cramped streets of an old city, where few buildings are more than two or three stories high and where people still spill out into the streets to cook on low firepits or simply to socialize, both expectations can be fulfilled: an image in an edicola can see and be seen. But this is precisely what cannot happen if an edicola were to be built into the wall of a balcony of a modern high-rise apartment. It is thus the architecture of modern neighborhoods, at least as much as a loss of religiosity, that works against edicole.

Supernatural Signs and Miraculous Images

Sometimes an image comes to be considered miraculous simply because appeals to that image bring forth miraculous favors (someone blind or mute or lame is cured, a devastating plague stops, rain comes after a prolonged drought, etc.). But in many cases, an image attracts attention to itself by means of a supernatural sign that is observable by anyone who happens to be on the scene. Most commonly, an image

—exudes blood or sweat,
—sheds tears,
—moves like a human being,
—changes color, or
—becomes surrounded by a mysterious light.

The origin legends summarized in Medica's (1965) guide to madonnine sanctuaries credit any number of miraculous images with having displayed these signs. These same origin legends make it clear that these signs are not mutually exclusive, so that in some origin stories images both cry and move, shed tears and bleed, and so forth.

In all cases, the immediate effect of the miraculous sign (within the context of the origin story) is to alert people to the fact that the image is infused with supernatural power. The physical sign, in other words, is a signal to the public that supernatural power is present in the image and is willing to be used. Phrased differently, these origin stories indicate that Italian Catholics expect images infused with power to announce themselves to the public by a visible sign. This cultural expectation is sufficiently strong that a supernatural sign element will often be added to an origin legend if it was not there in the earliest versions of that legend.

Consider the origin stories surrounding the miraculous image found at the Church of S. Maria della Sanità at Naples.

This church had been the resting place of S. Gaudioso, an early bishop of Naples who died circa 450 A.D. But in the ninth century, S. Gaudioso's body was removed to a more centrally located Neapolitan church, and over time the original church fell into disrepair. D'Engenio (1623, 611–12) says that by the late 1500s a sword maker named Cesare had planted a garden on the land containing the ruined church and was using the crypt as a cellar. On November 9, 1569, a severe rainstorm hit Naples, and a torrent coming off the nearby mountain smashed into Cesare's house, killing him and his wife. Ownership of the property fell to Cesare's nephew, but since "he continued to use the church in a profane manner like his uncle, God sent him an infirmity," namely, his toes fell off, and a short time later he died (ibid., 611).

The nephew's heirs, being more sensitive to the proper uses of a sacred place, opened a path into the old church and collected alms to subsidize the saying of masses there. When diocesan authorities learned that there were crosses painted on the wall of the building, they understood that this was a consecrated structure and, in 1577, turned it over the Dominicans. Not knowing the original dedication of the church, it came to be called S. Maria della Sanità, partly because the valley in which the church was located was called "la valle di Sanità" and partly because an image of a madonna found in the abandoned church had begun to dispense favors. Nothing in D'Engenio's account associates this miraculous image with a visible supernatural sign.

Some seventy years after the publication of *Napoli Sacra*, Celano (1860, 350–54) published (in 1692) another version of the origin legend associated S. Maria della Sanità. This version was virtually identical to the version published by D'Engenio but did add one detail: "The colors of Holy Image," says Celano, "had remained bright even though the image had been buried for such a long time." He stops short of saying explicitly that the image's failure to fade even though it had been buried was a miracle, but it is implied. This version of the origin legend, then, has moved closer to the cultural expectation that miraculous images announce their power with a visible sign.

In 1716, almost a full century after D'Engenio's original account, a third version of the origin legend appeared in a manuscript written by the Dominican Francesco Maria Luciani. Luciani's account, summarized in Miele (1963, 308–9), says that in 1576 the owner of the property—whom Luciani calls Giulio Cesare Mascolo—died and in his will instructed his heirs to reopen the abandoned crypt and subsidize the saying of masses there. The heirs—three sisters—entrusted these tasks to a friend of the deceased, one Anello di Stefano, who in turn obtained a chaplain for the crypt. So far, the story seems to be a shortened version of the accounts by D'Engenio and Celano, with a few changes being made to names and genders. But then Luciani mentions an incident that has no counterpart in either of the two earlier accounts.

The chaplain appointed to say masses in the crypt, Luciani says, was lax in his duties and so Heaven intervened directly in the matter. On the night of November 2, 1576, Anello di Stefano was looking from a window of his house and "saw a strange procession of friars leaving and reentering the crypt." The vision frightened him so much that he fell ill. Some days later, the madonna herself appeared and promised him that he would get better. She also said that the crypt was precious to her and asked that it be renovated and turned over to a religious order. After various negotiations with the archdiocesan authorities, Mascolo's heirs turned the church over the to Dominicans. It was while the crypt was being cleared out by the Dominicans that the miraculous image of the Madonna della Sanità came to light. In this third account, then, the miraculous image is very clearly associated with a supernatural sign (the mysterious procession of friars who enter and exit the crypt) and, just as important, this sign appears before the image is discovered. In effect the sign announces the presence of a powerful image, just as the cultural formula requires.

Devotional historians, seeking to reconcile the different versions of the S. Maria della Sanità origin legend, have sought to decide which is the more trustworthy. Miele (1963, 308) believes that Luciani's account is closer to the historic truth. But if we view these stories as folk traditions, as I suggest, we need make no such choice. All three stories are versions of the same folktale. The earliest versions did not contain an element required by the cultural expectations surrounding powerful images, and so this element came to be added in a later version.

Appealing to a Miraculous Image

In 1594 a madonnine image located in a roadside edicola near the town of Mondovì (Piemonte) began dispensing favors and quickly became the object of pilgrimage. The cult that formed around this image in the years 1595–1600 was described by Giuseppe Alamanni (d. 1630), a Jesuit missionary who came to Mondovì in 1595 and who witnessed the events he describes.[16] Alamanni's report is valuable for two reasons. First, although Alamanni believed the image was miraculous, he is not an uncritical observer. On the contrary, Alamanni admits that some cures were only partial and that others were clearly faked. Second, he is attentive to the behaviors of those who came to Mondovì. His report is thus a rarity: a detailed first-hand account of popular Catholic practice as it was (rather than as Church officials wanted it to be) in the late 1500s.

In discussing the confraternities that came to venerate the image in 1595, Alamanni notes that, as their members approached the image,

> some threw themselves to the ground, some shouted "Misericordia," some were sobbing so much they were unable to speak, some used their finger to make the sign of the cross in the dirt and then kissed it, some conveyed their prayers to the Holy Virgin with loud shouts, some disciplined themselves with iron chains or rosettes, shedding so much blood that it was sometimes necessary to take away these tools. (cited in Mellano 1986, 137)

As unusual as these behaviors might seem to modern readers, they were not the behaviors that struck Alamanni as being most interesting. The really interesting behaviors (and those to which Alamanni devotes an entire chapter) started toward the end of August 1595, when a substantial number of pilgrims began to experience bodily tremors and falls (ibid., 141–42). Sometimes these tremors would

16. Mellano (1986) reprints Alamanni's report in its entirety and provides, as well, information on Alamanni's career before, during, and after his stay at Mondavì.

affect only a part of the body (an arm or a hand, for instance), sometimes a person's entire body would shake. The tremors would usually be followed by a fainting spell that caused the person—even if on horseback—to fall to the ground, where they might remain for several hours. While on the ground, some people would lay immobile, others could move only a foot or a hand. Often they would grind their teeth, sweat copiously, and experience heart palpitations. When these people awoke, they often experienced pain or intense itching in the part of their body that had been seized by tremors. Several women (Alamanni does specifically say women) ran and jumped about furiously, threatening divine castigation, and then fell to the ground. It was common for some individuals to experience three or four separate falls.

At one level, the events at Mondovì are worth noting simply because they occurred in northern Italy. The modern expectation is that religious events permeated with emotionalism are to be found in southern Italy, and to a large extent this expectation conforms to the reality.[17] But as I argue elsewhere (Carroll 1992, 88–111), the differences that existed by the late nineteenth century between northern and southern Italy were less evident at the beginning of the modern era. Alamanni himself (see Mellano 1986, 141) specifically mentions that the same phenomena—people being affected by tremors and falls—had been observed at Lucca (Tuscany) in 1588. Further research would undoubtedly uncover other examples of such behavior in northern Italy during the sixteenth and early seventeenth centuries.

In trying to explain what happened at Mondovì, much depends upon what we count as "explanation." If we focus solely on proximate causes, that is, on the factors immediately preceding these behaviors and that might have precipitated them, then we need go no further than Alamanni's own report. Good Jesuit that he was, Alamanni sets about explaining the events at Mondovì by systematically examining a number of logical possibilities. He eventually settles upon four possible causes. Two of these were supernatural in origin, namely, that they (1) were produced by the devil and (2) were caused by God.

---

17. When modern investigators do occasionally come across outbursts of emotion at religious events in northern Italy, they feel compelled to note that it goes against the prevailing pattern. Tocchini (1972), for instance, reports that people who were "possessed" would be brought to the sanctuary of the Madonna di Caravaggio at Caravaggio (Lombardy) on the occasion of her festa (May 26) in order to be exorcised. The struggles of these possessed individuals as they resisted being brought into the sanctuary contributed to the emotional tension, which would peak when the possessed were liberated from their affliction. After describing these events, Tocchini (1972, 284) notes that readers unfamiliar with this festa will likely be surprised "to find that rituals and beliefs of this sort, more easily attributable to the technologically backward areas of southern Italy, are still to be found in northern Italy, an area more usually associated with connotations of progress . . . and rationality."

But Almanni also identifies two natural processes that were likely at work as well. First, the tremors and falls could be the result of physiological processes. Many pilgrims had come a long distance to the sanctuary and under conditions of great physical stress. Some had come barefoot, for instance, and some had made the journey while fasting on bread and water. In these cases, they may have fainted simply because of their weakened state. Other pilgrims probably had pre-existing physical disorders (Alamanni names epilepsy, heart problems and fee-blemindedness) that made them susceptible to fainting. A second cause of the falls and tremors, Alamanni argues, and one that has been identified for certain in some cases, is simple faking: some people mimic the experience of tremors and then voluntarily fall to the ground. Fakers are easy to spot, he says, because they do things (move their eyes, swat flies, etc.) that someone who had truly fainted would not do.

Stress, preexisting disabilities, and faking almost certainly did account for some of the tremors and falls at Mondovì. But Alamanni's account implies that there was something else at work. In the section where he discusses the possibility that the falls and tremors were sent by God, Alamanni notes that most of those who received some favor from the madonna had been afflicted with tremors and falls just prior to their receipt of that favor. Since the favor itself is assumed to come from God (through Mary's mediation), Alamanni concludes that in these cases the tremors and falls must also have come from God. But the data could also be read as suggesting that pilgrims at Mondovì saw the experience of tremors and falls as a necessary (though not sufficient) precondition for receiving a favor. In other words, people expected tremors and falls to precede the receipt of a favor from the madonna, and this cultural expectation guided their behavior. Actually, Alamanni himself comes close to saying just this. In explaining why some people fake their tremors and falls, Alamanni says they do so because they think that such behavior will provoke favors from the image.

Why would Italian Catholics see tremors and falls in front of a madonnine image as something that made it more likely that that image would grant favors? A good question, and one whose answer, I think, sheds light on some of the core psychological processes that have shaped popular Catholicism in Italy. But here again, this is a question best considered in the conclusion.

By the nineteenth century, extreme behaviors of the sort observed at Mondovì in the late 1500s were no longer to be found at most northern sanctuaries, but they could still be observed at sanctuaries in the South. In May 1877, the Tuscan writer Renato Fucini paid a visit to the madonnine sanctuary at Montevergine. This was and still is one of the most important sanctuaries in Italy. Fucini describes the behavior of the people who crowded before the miraculous image:

It was necessary to believe that these people . . . imagine their celestial advocates to be deaf, such were the screams and shouts with which they commended themselves to [the madonna]. A great many times a raucous voice exploded next to my poor ears and I was tempted to tell my pious neighbor to calm down and to make him understand that . . . this sort of behavior was not appropriate in God's house . . . but I stayed silent. (Fucini 1977, 105)

Fucini (105–6) also reports that as pilgrims crossed the threshold of the sanctuary many of them threw themselves onto the ground and crawled forward to the image on their hands and knees. These behaviors appalled Fucini, good Tuscan intellectual that he was. He tells us that he was reminded of the "profanation of the temple" mentioned in the New Testament, and he laments that there was no one who would drive out these modern profaners the way Jesus drove out the money changers. After a short while, he left, disgusted.

Fucini's difficulty was that he was viewing the events at Montevergine through a lens shaped by intellectualized Christocentric biases. He assumed that the content of the exclamations uttered by devotees was what was important, and he saw the madonna as a simple intercessor. In fact, it was the shouting itself (not what was shouted) that was important, and its importance lay in the cultural expectation that shouting (like the tremors and falls at Mondovì) made it more likely that powerful images will dispense supernatural favors.

The extreme behaviors described by Fucini are still relatively common in southern Italy. For example, one of the most important festas in the South is the one in honor of the Madonna dell'Arco; it has been described by a number of Italian investigators.[18] On the Monday following Easter, dozens and dozens of different processions, each originating in some particular neighborhood in Naples or the surrounding area, converge on the small sanctuary dedicated to this madonna in the community of S. Anastasia. Thousands of onlookers also attend the festa. Some of the onlookers crowd inside the small church (where barriers keep them to the sides), and some line the street outside the church to watch the processions as they enter. Others simply mill about the streets around the sanctuary, which are lined with small booths and tables selling sausages, pizza, nuts, candy, and inexpensive plastic toys for the children who come with their parents. In 1993, when I last observed this festa, a small amusement park with kiddie rides had been set up in a field near the sanctuary.

The processions begin arriving around 9 o'clock in the morning and continue to arrive until late in the afternoon. A substantial minority of people in each procession are barefoot (quite a discomfort given the distances that some of them

18. See D'Antonio (1979); for an English-language account, see Tentori (1982).

have walked) or wear only socks. Many carry votive offerings. The most common offerings are flowers, but some people carry large candles that weigh as much as a person. Carabinieri and festa organizers, using barricades, allow only one procession into the sanctuary at a time. Once in the sanctuary, each procession moves up the center aisle toward the main altar, where the madonna's image is kept. Most people walk forward slowly, but a substantial number move forward on their knees, and a few (almost all male) lie face down on the stone floor and pull themselves forward using only their arms. When the procession reaches the altar rail the person carrying the group's banner dips the banner in front of the image. The members of the procession then break formation and move forward to kiss the gold rondels set into the altar rail at various points. After kissing a rondel, they move quickly out through the back of the church, and the next procession is allowed to enter. The Dominican priests who stand behind the altar rail seem concerned mainly with hustling people along and wiping clean the gold rondels. Quite often, these priests turn over these tasks to assistants.

Every so often, activities within the church deviate from the pattern just described. Sometimes a few members of each procession—and they include both women and men—collapse and drop to the floor somewhere between the threshold of the church and the altar rail. When that happens, two or three soldiers (from the contingent of soldiers specially sent to the sanctuary for this day) rush to the prostrate persons, pick them up, and carry them quickly to the first aid station outside. Often a person yells and screams and then collapses to the floor. When I viewed the festa in 1993, there seemed to be a gender difference in these cases. Women who yelled and screamed and then collapsed would usually lie motionless and offer no resistance as they were carried out. But the men who yelled and screamed and dropped to the floor usually flailed about in a serious attempt to be free of the soldiers (or other procession members) who were trying to carry them outside. These extreme behaviors, I should add, occurred only after the processions entered the church and came within sight of the image; they did not occur in the streets outside the sanctuary, nor did they occur in the neighborhood celebrations that I observed in Naples on Easter Sunday, the day before the festa.

The behaviors exhibited in front of the image of the Madonna dell'Arco in the 1990s are similar (though enacted on a smaller scale) to the behaviors exhibited in front of the image at Montevergine in the 1870s and in front of the image at Mondovì in the 1590s. Obviously, many Italian Catholics still consider yelling, screaming, and falling down to be the behaviors most likely to attract the beneficent attention of Italian madonnas.

Madonnas and Madonnine Images

Italian Catholics traditionally are confronted with a variety of madonnas and madonnine images during the course of their everyday life. Why do some of these, but not others, become miraculous? At least part of the answer can be traced to the Italian Catholic belief that madonnas crave veneration, with the result that an image that is neglected will start dispensing miracles in order to promote its own cult. As strange as such an interpretation might seem to outsiders, this association between neglect and dispensation of favors has often been noted by devotional commentators.

In discussing the madonnine miracles at Rome in 1796, for example, Marchetti (1797, xxii–xxiii) is careful to note that the single most honored image in the city (which he identifies as the Madonna della Pietà in the Church of S. Bartolomeo de' Bergamaschi) did *not* move her eyes. Another observer was even more explicit about the status of those images that move their eyes:

> The prodigy [movement of the eyes] has not been seen in any of those pictures that are most respected, exclusive of that of the Madonna dell'Archetto, in which it was seen for the first time on Saturday at 10 o'clock. It was seen in the neglected pictures that are about the streets; then it went on multiplying itself in churches, but only in those churches that have nothing particular to recommend them. (Anon. 1796, 21)

In other cases, commentators go beyond simply taking note of a correlation between neglect and likelihood of becoming a miraculous image and suggest exactly what I suggest here, namely, that the former *causes* the latter. Writing about the church of the Pietà near Naples, D'Engenio (1623, 262) gives this account of that image's early history: "Thirty-four years ago there was an image of the Madonna della Pietà that had been painted on a wall in the garden of Francesco di Sangro, Duke of Torremaggiore [a city near Naples]. *Not wanting to be held in such low regard* the image began to dispense a great number of miracles and favors." (Emphasis added.) In short, Italian Catholics see image cults as involving an exchange, with devotees giving veneration and images granting favors. The images themselves are assumed to have the same attitude, with the result that when they are neglected they seek to obtain the veneration they crave by dispensing favors.

It has been convenient to talk of madonnine images and madonnas as if these were separate things, but this is really only the official view. In the popular imagination, they are not separate and distinct categories. On the contrary, the popular conceptualization of any particular madonna is inextricably bound up with the concrete image of that madonna that resides in some particular sanctuary. At one level, this is why a madonna's power is seen to reside in her image and why physical proximity to her image is seen to make it more likely that she will grant requests. This tendency to conflate and merge the concepts madonna and madonnine image also explains, in the first instance, why the image itself is seen as animate, that is, as something that can bleed, cry, and move.

Conclusion

Folklorists call a specific set of motifs (incidents) that appear in more or less the same order across different stories a tale-type. In the example I want to consider here, a tale-type is defined by the following motifs:

1. Two or more men are playing a game somewhere near an edicola that contains a nondescript madonnine image.

2. Something about the game leads one of the men to explode in anger, and he strikes or throws something against the image.

3. The image bleeds where it has been struck.

4. Shortly thereafter the offending man dies.

6. The image becomes the object of cultic attention and begins to dispense divine favors.

Grigioni (1975) calls this the story of the impious gamesplayer. It is one of the most popular of all religious folktales in Italy and has been found in virtually all regions of the peninsula. Grigioni herself presents over a dozen versions, all drawn from the *Atlas marianus*, a devotional work originally published in the late seventeenth century. I have come across at least as many other versions in a variety of other sources.

As with folktales generally, not every version of the impious gamesplayer contains every motif that defines the tale-type. On the contrary, the tale-type becomes evident only by considering a range of stories. The following stories, for instance, though different in many of their details, are all recognizable as versions of the impious gamesplayer:

> [Bergamo, Lombardy]: On this date (24 August 1500) there occurred a miracle involving a perfidious gamesplayer. This man was playing cards with others just outside the Church of S. Bartolomeo di Trescorio. Upon losing at the game, he began to blaspheme against God and the Most Holy Virgin. He then took a *ronca* [a type of scythe] and struck an image of the Mother of God that was painted there . . . opening a wide wound in her breast. Although the man left to go to Gorlago, he got no further than the Torrone River, which is where he was later found cut to pieces. (Calvi 1676b, 19)

[Naples, Campania]: On the wall of this chapel [in the church of S. Eligio] there is a painted image of the most Holy Virgin. The gash in the Virgin's face was given to her by a gamesplayer in the year 1524. On that occasion fresh blood emerged from the gash. The gamesplayer fled to Florence, his place of origin. There he was seized by the Bargello when he was found (as a result of divine providence) near a dead body. Under torture, he confessed to the crime he had committed in Naples and was decapitated. (D'Engenio 1623, 442)

[Soleto, Apulia]: One evening in 1568 Giacomo Lisandro was on his way home after having been paid for his work in the fields. He stopped near an edicola to join a group of men who were gambling. Poor Giacomo lost all his earnings. In a fit of anger he struck the madonna's image with his hand axe, saying "I'll only believe in you if you can cause my death this very evening." His blow caused a gash in her cheek, which began to bleed.[19] Later, as Giacomo entered Soleto, he was accosted by Luigi Rullo, a man to whom he owed money. They fought, and during the fight Giacomo was stabbed to death. When the news of what had happened spread, people came to the image and it began to grant favors. Later, a sanctuary was built on this spot and the image installed above the main altar. (Summarized from Febbraro and De Benedictus 1988)

[S. Anastasia, Campania]: On the 6th of April 1450, some men were playing *pallo e maglia* [a rudimentary form of croquet] in the space in front of an edicola containing an image of a madonna. One of the player botched his shot and his ball hit a tree near the edicola. Angry, he retrieved the ball and threw it against the image. The madonna's left cheek, which is where the ball had struck, began to bleed. The young man wanted to flee, but found himself wandering aimlessly around the edicola. Very shortly, the impious gamesplayer was arrested and executed by the Count of Sarno. Subsequently, the image began to dispense miraculous favors. A few decades later, a sanctuary was built here to house the image.[20] (Summary based on the account in D'Antonio 1979)

Why has this particular tale proven so appealing to Italian Catholics? The answer, I think, is that the story of the impious gamesplayer epitomizes all the important beliefs that Italian Catholics have about miraculous madonnine images. Such images, for example, are animate, and in this story that is made clear in a particularly dramatic manner: the image bleeds when struck. Similarly, the images in

19. This image, a fresco, still exists in the sanctuary at Soleto, where I saw it in 1992. A blotch on the madonna's left check is still very much in evidence, and the reddish color of that blotch is more or less the same as the color of the madonna's cloak. Possibly this is the result of retouching over the centuries, or perhaps this is a replacement for the original image, and the blotch was added purposely.

On the other hand, if this is the original image, then possibly the "blood" mentioned in the original story was simply an undercoat that was uncovered by a actual axe blow. In this case, then, the "bleeding" may have been the misperception of a real effect.

20. This is the origin legend associated with the Madonna dell'Arco, whose festa is described earlier.

most versions of this story are outdoor images, located near where people routinely congregate and play games, and so are relatively neglected compared to those images given a place of honor in a church. But perhaps the most important element in the impious gamesplayer is implicit: the gamesplayer dies *because* he has been impious. What is being reflected here, I suggest, is the obverse of the Italian Catholic belief that images crave veneration. Thus, if an image receives veneration, it dispenses favors. But if an image is treated in manner opposite to what it desires, if it is abused, then it dispenses death.

Quite obviously the madonna who appears in the impious gamesplayer tale-type is quite unlike the Mary of the tridentine Church. This official Mary is, after all, a warm, reassuring mother figure, surrounded by esoteric doctrines relating to her conception and her motherhood, whose physical body reposes in some far-away Heaven, and who very much wants people to avoid "sin" and get to Heaven. The madonnas in these stories, like Italian madonnas generally, are powerful supernatural beings whose identity is inextricably bound up with a physical image located in one particular geographical location and who use their power mainly to promote their own cults. Each of these madonnas may be a mother by virtue of the child she holds in her hands, but unlike the official Mary her main concern is with herself, and she is quite willing to punish anyone who forgets that.[21]

21. The Impious Gamesplayer tale-type is not the only narrative in which madonnas punish. A great many apparition accounts portray a madonna as being willing to harm individuals who do not move fast enough to establish the church that she wants built in her honor; see Carroll (1992, 67–87).

Chapter Two

The Church Adapts
to Image Cults

B y the second half of the sixteenth century, image cults had become a central issue in the debates engendered by the Reformation. But Reformation-era arguments for and against image cults did not emerge ex nihilo. On the contrary, both Catholic and Protestant propagandists recycled arguments that had first been articulated in the distant past. An understanding of those ancient arguments, and of the societal contexts in which they emerged, is necessary for understanding the ways in which the Church has confronted the image cults that lie at the core of popular Catholicism in Italy.

Iconoclasm

Sometime toward the end of the sixth century, Serenus (d. 601), bishop of Marseilles, concluded that the people in his diocese were worshipping, not merely venerating, their sacred images. His solution to the problem was simple and direct: he ordered that all sacred images be removed from the churches under his jurisdiction. This action provoked the disapproval of Pope Gregory the Great (d. 604), and in one of several letters he wrote chastising Serenus, Gregory advanced the following argument:

> Not without reason has antiquity allowed the stories of the saints to be painted in holy places. And we indeed entirely praise you for not allowing them to be adored, but we blame you for breaking them. For it is one thing to adore an image, it is quite another to learn from the appearance of a picture what we must adore. What books are to those who can read, so is a picture to the ignorant who look at it; in a picture even the unlearned may see what example they should follow; in a picture they who know no letters may yet read. (cited in Fortescue 1913b, 668)

Gregory's images-are-books-for-the-illiterate argument would be quoted over and over again during the next thousand years and would be reaffirmed at the Council of Trent. And Serenus? He seems to have relented and restored the images to his churches. His temporary lapse into iconoclastic bad taste notwithstanding, he would become a saint, whose feast is still celebrated on August 9.

The dispute between Gregory and Serenus was not a dispute over doctrine. Both men agreed that concrete images should not be invested with supernatural power and should not be worshiped. Likely, as well, there was no disagreement over sociological realities; that is, Gregory would likely have conceded that many Christians, at Marseilles and elsewhere, did invest images with power and did worship those images. After all, several centuries earlier S. Augustine (d. 430) had leveled this same charge. Gregory and Serenus differed only in how to respond to this popular tendency. Serenus felt that the best response was to remove the occasion of sin by removing the sacred images from Christian churches. Gregory felt that the matter could be solved in a purely intellectual way: define the proper doctrine and ensure that Christians come to understand and accept this doctrine.

By focusing exclusively upon belief, Gregory's policy (unlike Serenus's) had the effect of leaving intact all the behaviors associated with image cults. There is nothing in Gregory's response to Serenus, for instance, that suggests that there is anything wrong with the popular tendency to differentiate among images, to pray in front of particular images, to append ex-voto to images in return for favors granted, and so forth. The practical effect of Gregory's policy, then, was that ordinary Christians were free to continue as usual in connection with image cults. Gregory simply insisted upon an interpretation of their actions that was almost certainly different from the interpretation held by the people involved.

Image cults became increasingly popular during the sixth and seventh centuries. Early in the eighth century, however, a reaction against such cults emerged in the Eastern Church. This was the beginning of what is usually called the Iconoclast controversy.[1] There are a number of different theories as to the general social and political conditions in the Byzantine Empire that gave rise to the Iconoclast movement (see Barnard 1974 for a review). What everyone agrees on is that the first active proponents of iconoclasm (the removal and destruction of sacred images) were several bishops in Asia Minor. Sometime around 725, these bishops gained the support of the Byzantine emperor Leo III. Shortly thereafter (the exact date is a matter of debate) Leo ordered that the holy images in his

---

1. The scholarly literature on the Iconoclast controversy is vast. Martin (1930) still provides a good introduction to the sequence of concrete events involved. More recent interpretations of Iconoclasm can be found in Barnard (1974); Fazzo (1977); Bryer and Herrin (1977).

empire be destroyed. Although this order was not fully effective, it did result in the destruction of many images.

In 730, Leo forced the resignation of Germanus I, patriarch of Constantinople and a supporter of image cults. Although segments of the lower clergy continued to oppose iconoclasm, both the new patriarch and most other members of the upper clergy in the Eastern Church accepted—or at least tolerated— Leo's policy. The hierarchy of the Western Church proved more resilient. Both Gregory II (715–31) and Gregory III (731–41) wrote against iconoclasm, even though they were technically subjects of the Byzantine Empire, and Gregory III convened a synod at Rome in 731 at which iconoclasm was condemned. Generally, Italy provided a relatively safe haven for anti-Iconoclast clergy who fled from the East (Ahrweiler 1975).

In 753, Constantine V, Leo's son and successor, convened the Council of Hieria, and this council approved the emperor's iconoclastic policies. As Martin (1930, 43–44) points out, the number of bishops who attended Hieria (338) contrasts with the number (150) who had attended the Ecumenical Council of Constantinople in 381 and the number of bishops and representatives of episcopal sees (260 or so) who would attend the Second Council of Nicea in 787, which would condemn iconoclasm (see below). It also contrasts with the 93 Western bishops who attended the synod held at Rome in 731 (Fazzo 1977, 345). In other words, the number of bishops attending the Council of Hieria and endorsing iconoclasm was relatively large when compared to the number attending these other assemblies and condemning iconoclasm. Following the Council of Hieria, Constantine escalated his attack on images, and his iconoclastic policies were maintained by his successor, Leo IV.

When Leo IV died in 780, his widow, Irene, assumed the throne as regent for her son Constantine VI and began to restore the veneration of images. Irene's greatest achievement (as far as the history of image cults in the Western Church is concerned) was to convoke the Second Council of Nicea in 787. This council was attended not only by monks and bishops of the Eastern Church but also by two papal representatives, who were given a place of honor in all proceedings.

Nicea II ordered the restoration of images and laid down a number of doctrines that legitimated image cults. The council distinguished between the worship that is due God alone and the reverence that is appropriately rendered to Mary and the saints. It specified that the veneration offered in front of images is directed not to the image itself but rather to the prototype that the image represents. Finally, it explained the usefulness of images: "For the more frequently they [Christ, Mary, angels, and saints] are seen by means of pictorial representation, the more those who behold them are aroused to give them greeting and worship of honor" (cited in Barnard 1974, 8). In other words, a concrete image helps to focus the mind upon the abstract and distant figure that the image represents. Nicea II's images-help-to-focus-the-mind argument would become as important as Gregory's images-are-books-for-the-illiterate argument, and it too would be reaffirmed at the Council of Trent. Significantly, the policies laid down at Nicea II, like those promoted by Gregory centuries earlier, left all the popular behaviors associated with image cults intact.

Iconoclasm did not end with the Council of Nicea. In 813, Leo V ascended the throne and initiated a new wave of official iconoclasm that lasted until 843. In that year, Theodora, another female regent (like Irene), called a council at Constantinople, which restored the veneration of images once and for all. This event is still celebrated each year in the Eastern Church on the first Sunday of Lent.

Although different in substance, the justifications for image cults offered by Gregory and the Council of Nicea had this in common: they both legitimated image cults and they were both formulated in response to acts of iconoclasm. In fact, this has always been the typical pattern. The popular behaviors surrounding image cults are generally ignored by Church authorities until these behaviors are attacked by reformers; Church authorities then provide a rationale for image cults, and it is always a rationale that permits the popular behaviors associated with these cults to proceed undisturbed. This is what happened in the dispute between Gregory and Serenus, this is what happened during the Iconoclast controversy, and this is what happened during the Reformation.[2]

Image Cults and the Reformation

Luther's position on image cults was relatively tolerant. Early in 1522, for instance, crowds destroyed the sacred images found in various churches at Wittenberg. In 1522, in response, Luther (1959, 81–83) preached that, although he himself was "not partial" to images, Christians generally were free to choose whether to use them or not. Somewhat later, in 1525, he would approve of iconoclasm when the images destroyed were clearly being worshipped (and here he singles out the destruction of images found at popular pilgrimage sites; see Luther 1958, 91–92). Even so, he still conceded that Christians could in good conscience reject iconoclasm.

Other Protestant leaders were less tolerant. During the 1520s Zwingli at-

---

2. Jedin's (1972) early article remains the best account of sixteenth-century doctrinal disputes regarding the veneration of images, and I have relied on it heavily in this section.

tacked image cults and called for the removal of images from churches. Zwingli had no in-principle objection to images that were purely decorative or informative; his concern was only with those images that became the object of cultic devotion. Zwingli's point was that, if images were allowed in churches, people naturally would tend to make them the focus of devotion. In short, like Serenus a thousand years before, he argued that the only way to eliminate image cults was to eliminate the occasion of sin.

Calvin discusses images in the first edition of his *Institutes of the Christian Religion* (published in 1536) in the course of his commentary on the Second Commandment (see Calvin 1986, 19–21). This commandment, he suggests, seeks to ensure that God's greatness is not diminished by trying to represent him in material form. Calvin goes on to consider two arguments commonly advanced in support of image cults. The first is that sacred images are not to be taken as supernatural beings but only to represent such beings. Calvin's main objection here is scriptural: although both the Jews and the gentiles of the Old Testament distinguish between idol and God, the use of idols is forbidden by God. But Calvin also advances a more sociological argument: theology aside, if we look at the behavior of Christians who use images it seems clear that they see the image itself as possessing some intrinsic virtue. How else to explain, Calvin asks, the fact that Christians so often prostrate themselves before particular images and so often "take up the sword" to defend these images?

Calvin then addresses Gregory the Great's contention that images are the books of the uneducated, and here he raises two objections. First, many images are far more an occasion of sin than a means of avoiding it. "Indeed," says Calvin (1986, 21), "brothels show harlots clad more virtuously and modestly than the churches show those objects which they wish to be seen as images of virgins." Second, Christ nowhere endorsed the use of images for instruction; the only method of instruction legitimated by Christ, Calvin argues, was the preaching of his word.

In the 1559 edition of his *Institutes*, Calvin (1960) repeats these earlier arguments and adds some more. He notes the absence of images in the first five centuries of the Church and cites the criticisms leveled against image cults by authorities like Eusebius (d. circa 340), the Spanish Council of Elvira (held sometime in the early fourth century), and St. Augustine (d. 430). He also discusses at length the distinction made by Catholic commentators between *latria* (the worship due to God alone) and *dulia* (the honor due the saints). Calvin, like Zwingli, suggests that, however much human beings might try to keep the worship of God separate from the veneration of saints, the use of saintly images inevitably leads to idolatry. To show the truth of this assertion, he goes back to the same event that was so important to Catholic apologists: the Second Council of Nicea, held in 787.

Unlike Catholic commentators, Calvin was less concerned with the anti-Iconoclast doctrines proclaimed at Nicea II than with the effusive comments about images made by the clerics who took part in that council. Thus, notes Calvin, one bishop at Nicea blamed the calamities that befell Greece and the East on their refusal to worship images; another said that the same honor is due images as is due the Trinity; still another said that it is better to admit all the brothels in the world into one city than to reject the worship of images, etcetera. For Calvin, such testimony was clear evidence of the patently silly extremes that inevitably follow upon the use of images.

Calvin's discussion of images in the 1559 edition of the *Institutes* was greatly expanded. His original arguments are developed in greater detail, and the discussion of image cults stands on its own, rather than being simply a part of his commentary on the Second Commandment. Between the 1536 edition and the 1559 edition, the removal of images from churches moved to the center of Calvinist doctrine.

Calvin's original (1986) attack on image cults did not evoke an immediate response from the prelates of the Italian Church or from Italian theologians. Jedin's (1972, 344) review of the literature suggests that nothing of importance was published in Italy in response to Calvin's attack on image cults until the late 1550s. Moreover, Jedin notes, the first work written by a Catholic apologist in Italy who seems to have actually read Calvin's *Institutes* did not appear until 1561, just as the Council of Trent was about to close.

Image Cults and the Council of Trent

Although the Council of Trent opened in December 1545, images and image cults were not considered until its twenty-fifth, and last, session, which began in December 1563. The most likely reason for this delay is that in its early sessions the council was dominated by Italians. Although Calvinism had made some headway in northern Italy (see chap. 7), it had not generated any significant and sustained outbreaks of iconoclasm. For the Italian prelates at Trent, then, iconoclasm was not a pressing concern. But as Jedin (1972, 368) points out, iconoclasm did become a pressing concern at Trent in late 1562 with the arrival of an important delegation from France. In France, not only was Calvinism gaining support, Calvinists were launching direct and violent attacks upon images. In 1561, French Calvinists had sacked churches at Orléans, in the Loire, at Rouen, at Lyon, in the Dauphiné, and in Paris. Writing in 1562, one French commentator (cited in ibid., 369) describes how Protestants had entered the Church of St. Médard in Paris in December 1561 and "had not left a single statue undisturbed, cutting off the head of each statue as if it had been a living saint." For French delegates, then, the issue of image cults was much more than a matter for abstract theological discussion; it was an issue they were forced to consider as the result of pressing and immediate events. At their insistence, the council addressed this issue.

Trent's position on image cults appears in a decree entitled On the Invocation, Veneration, and Relics of Saints, and on Sacred Images. The passages dealing specifically with image cults are based upon a similar document that French theologians had approved at Paris in 1562 (see ibid.). The tridentine decree starts by firmly and unambiguously endorsing the practice of placing images in churches and so clearly condemns the iconoclasm promoted by Calvinists. The decree goes on to give two basic arguments that legitimate image cults. First, it says, images are venerated not because some special virtue resides in them but because the veneration offered to an image is really being offered to the prototype the image represents—and here the decree notes explicitly that this was the view laid down at the Second Council of Nicea. Second, the decree notes that the stories depicted in paintings can be a method by which "the people are instructed and confirmed in the articles of faith" and that in depicting events from the lives of the saints images also provide the faithful with "salutary" models of piety that they can imitate (Schroeder 1950, 216). All this is of course a variant of Gregory's images-are-books-for-the-illiterate argument, although Gregory himself is not named.

The tridentine decree goes on to recognize that abuses have sometimes arisen in connection with image cults and calls for these abuses to be eliminated. Although scholarly commentators often cite this section of the decree as evidence that the prelates at Trent were truly concerned with the reform of image cults, the decree in fact singles out and discusses only two abuses in any detail, both involving fairly elitist issues. The first abuse consists of attempts to make images that portray "false doctrines." The reference is almost certainly to those attempts to portray complicated issues, like the meaning of the Trinity or the relationship between God the Father and God the Son, in some simple and concrete way. The second abuse consists of images that are "painted and adorned with a seductive charm" (ibid.). There is an echo here of Calvin's claim that some images were an occasion for sin. In any event, the reference is clearly to those artistic works that incorporate the Renaissance emphasis upon the human form (often entailing nudity) even when depicting religious subjects.

Completely missing from the tridentine decree is any suggestion that there is anything inappropriate about the behaviors that ordinary Catholics in Italy (and elsewhere) displayed in connection with image cults. As with statements issued centuries earlier by Gregory the Great and Nicea II, there is nothing in Trent's decree that forbids praying or lying prostrate in front of an image, nothing that forbids appending ex-voto to images, nothing that forbids making a pilgrimage to offer thanks to some particular image, and so on.

In the end, the decree that was passed so hurriedly at Trent did give the French Catholic Church a boost in its struggle with the Calvinists, and it did define inappropriate images (i.e., those that try to portray complicated doctrines or those involving nudity), but it says nothing that interfered with existing image cults.

The Driving Force Behind the Debates

The traditional scholarly view, and the one that still dominates Reformation studies, is that Protestant iconoclasm in the sixteenth century was driven mainly by intellectual or ideological concerns. Why, for instance, does Calvin devote more attention to image cults in the later (1559) edition of his *Institutes?* Battles (see Calvin 1986, 245) suggests that Calvin became increasingly aware of the literature relating to the Iconoclast controversy in the eighth and ninth centuries. Payton (1993, 230) suggests simply that he became a more "seasoned theologian" over time. Scavizzi (1992, 21) argues that two decades of debate among Protestant theologians on the matter of image cults provided Calvin with material that he could now use to buttress his original argument. And why did the practice of iconoclasm become more widespread in those areas of Europe where Calvinism became popular? For Eire (1986), whose work is the most extensive study of Reformation-era iconoclasm yet written, the answer is clear and obvious: the increasing popularity of Calvinist doctrine led to iconoclastic behavior.

There is no particular reason (apart from the intellectualist bias of most scholars studying the Reformation) for not suggesting that the causality underlying this traditional view is backward. In other words, the historical record could just as easily be read as indicating that Calvin gives more weight to the matter of images and image cults because this relatively minor element in his original doctrine proved to be enormously popular. It was, in other words, the popularity of iconoclasm with the people, at least the people in certain areas of Europe, that influenced Calvinist doctrine, not vice versa. The possibility I am suggesting (phrased in the language used at the beginning of this book) is that Calvin and his ministers adapted their doctrine to popular preferences, preferences which presumably derived from preexisting social and cultural arrangements that still need to be identified. Some support for such an interpretation is found in the fact that in many areas of northern Europe iconoclasm proved to be popular at the local level long before there was any clear understanding of the theological arguments being advanced by the Reformers (see Maarbjerg 1993; Kirk 1992).

Calvinism aside, what about the Italian Church and image cults? In this case, what is the causal relationship between official doctrine and popular practice? We have already seen (in the previous chapter) that in the popular imagination sacred images are invested with supernatural power and that ordinary Catholics can appeal to this power for miracles. We have also seen (in earlier sections of this chapter) that the Church usually ignores image cults until they are attacked by reformers and that, in responding to these attacks, the Church is always careful to promote doctrines that leave intact all the popular behaviors associated with image cults.

A parsimonious way to make sense out of all this is to suggest that Italian Catholics are predisposed (for some reason) to invest sacred images with supernatural power and that the Church has always taken this as a given. In the language introduced in the introduction, the popular predisposition to invest images with supernatural power is a constraint to which the Italian Church has had to adapt if it wanted (as it has) to maintain the nominal allegiance of Italian Catholics. Historically, that adaptation has always taken the same form: denying at the level of formal doctrine that images are invested with supernatural power while simultaneously legitimating all the popular practices that flow from this belief.

To best appreciate just how far the leaders of the Italian Church have been willing to go to accommodate the popular view of miraculous images, even after Trent, we must set aside those works written in response to Protestant critiques and look instead at what Church leaders have said to Catholic audiences who were fully convinced that holy images are the locus of supernatural power. Doing this, we will almost always find Church leaders implicitly confirming the popular view of miraculous images, however much that view is inconsistent with formal doctrine and despite Trent's apparent concern with rooting out "abuses" that had arisen in connection with image cults.

Two Official Views of Image Cults after Trent

Shortly after the close of the Council of Trent, Athanasio Nelli, a Dominican, wrote a Latin treatise (Nelli 1571) on the history of the sanctuary dedicated to the Madonna della Quercia (Madonna of the Oak) at Viterbo (Lazio). His text was revised and translated into Tuscan by Aurelio Cosimi Senese, a fellow Dominican, and was published in 1571 as *Origine della Madonna della Quercia a Viterbo*. The style and tone of this book reads like a sermon, and very likely that is what it was intended to be. At the very least it was meant to serve as a model to be used by other Dominicans in constructing their own sermons.

Although most of Nelli's book is devoted to the Viterbo sanctuary, the second chapter discusses image cults in general. Nelli starts by saying that the "Enemy of humankind" (the Devil) is always trying to take away those things that aid us in our search for happiness. This is why, he says, this "Enemy from the Abyss" has sent out from Hell a number of impious and wicked teachers (Nelli names Pelagius, Manichaeus, Arius, and Luther) to strip Christian churches of their holy images. Nelli (ibid., 6) then tells us why sacred images are useful:

> Either on account of sickness, wounding, or any of the other horrors experienced daily in this tearful life, people from all walks of life—popes, kings, cardinals, bishops, lords, soldiers, men, women, even the haughtiest sinner—are led to appeal to God, who is the source and giver of all benefits. But we can also appeal to the saints, who can act as intercessors with God; and often what reminds us of this is some small and simple image [of a saint] that we have seen while passing through the streets.

In suggesting that images are beneficial because they direct our attention to the supernatural beings they portray, Nelli of course is simply repeating the argument laid down at Nicea II and reaffirmed at Trent. But after repeating this standard argument, he (ibid., 7) directs our attention to what he regards as the clear and visible proof that his argument is valid:

> And if you would like to see visible proof of all this . . . go into any city or region or castle or church in which there are saintly images, in particular images of the glorious Virgin Mary. Hanging from the wall you will see all manner of ex-voto— some made of gold or silver, some painted or sculpted, and some made in other ways. These ex-voto demonstrate in the clearest possible way that when the saints are called upon during times of need they are ready to plead with God in order to secure our well-being.

Nelli then goes on to name a variety of sanctuaries, including the sanctuary at Viterbo, in which the votive offerings displayed are especially numerous.

   In evaluating the "proof" that Nelli offers, keep in mind that both he and the Italian Catholics to whom he is (ultimately) addressing his remarks knew full well that ex-voto were brought to a sanctuary because appeals directed to the particular image at that sanctuary had resulted in some supernatural favor being granted. Thus the ex-voto displayed at the Viterbo sanctuary were for favors obtained from the Madonna della Quercia, while the ex-voto displayed at the Nunziata (in Florence), at Loreto, and at all the other sanctuaries listed by Nelli were for favors received from the particular madonnas associated with these sanctuaries. Indeed, later in his book Nelli is at pains to provide examples of people who were saved from danger after appealing specifically to the Madonna della Quercia. This means that in pointing to ex-voto as proof that image cults are favored by God, Nelli is legitimating the practice that was being criticized by Protestants (and would come to be criticized by Jansenists; see chap. 1), namely, the practice of forming cults around particular madonnas at particular sanctuaries, rather than around the generic Mary of the official Church.

But the most significant part of Nelli's argument, given our concerns here, is that he is allowing the public belief in the miracles associated with madonnine images—a belief manifested in the ex-voto appended near or to these images—to serve as the final test of the legitimacy of image cults. In other words, for Nelli the miracles that flow from madonnine images are not pious delusions or vaguely embarrassing expressions of well-intentioned belief and they are certainly nothing that need to be questioned or scrutinized by Church officials. He accepts uncritically the popular view that miracles really do flow from these images; not from Mary, in general, but from specific images located in specific sanctuaries. What Nelli is telling his audience is that the fact of these miracles, more than anything else, shows that the Protestant rejection of image cults is wrong.

As preachers, Nelli and his fellow Dominicans (like the regular clergy generally) stood at the interface between the Church hierarchy and the people. That they should implicitly endorse the popular view of miraculous images may not be all that surprising. Perhaps more surprising is that Church leaders further up the hierarchy were willing to do the same.

After the close of the Council of Trent, Pope Gregory XIII appointed a four-person commission to carry out and administer the council's reforms. One member of that commission was Cardinal Gabriele Paleotti (d. 1597), bishop of Bologna. In 1594 Paleotti published *Discorso intorno alle imagini sacre e profane*. A section of that book deals with image cults, and as part of this discussion Paleotti (1961, 197–201) lists eight reasons for considering an image to be sacred and thus worthy of veneration, among them that God himself commanded that the image be made; that the image was formed by touching the body of Christ or a saint (Paleotti mentions as an example the Shroud of Turin); that the image was made by a holy person (like St. Luke); that the image was made miraculously, without human intervention; that the image was anointed with holy oil according to the older traditions; that the image was blessed according to the rites of the Church; and that the image depicts a religious subject or was made for a religious purpose. But I want to call special attention to the reason that appears fifth in Paleotti's original list:

> An image deserves to be called sacred when God clearly and unambiguously associates the image with signs and miracles. This happened, for instance, in connection with the Holy House of Loreto, which God transported from a distant country and through which he has operated so many miracles. . . . But it has happened as well with other images in other places. Thus God sometimes allows images to be seen

with their faces shining with a resplendent light, or shedding tears from their eyes
or exuding drops of blood, or moving in the way that a living person moves. Similarly, an image deserves to be called sacred if we see that God in his divine goodness
has by means of this image cured the sick, given light to the blind, and liberated
others from a variety of dangers. (ibid., 198)

The supernatural signs that Paleotti mentions in this passage should seem familiar. As we saw in the last chapter, ordinary Italian Catholics have always taken
these same visual wonders (the fact that images move, bleed, cry, etc.) as evidence
that an image has become infused with supernatural power, a view that Paleotti
comes very close to endorsing by suggesting that such signs are evidence of
sacredness. Notice too that in the last sentence Paleotti associates sacred images
with miracles. Despite the tridentine veneer (which identifies God as the source
of the miracles in question), his argument—like Nelli's—clearly legitimates the
popular view, which is that the supernatural power latent in images can be a
source of miracles.

Paleotti was only one of several members of the hierarchy who legitimated
and encouraged cults organized around miraculous images after Trent. As Scavizzi (1992) points out, influential prelates like Carlo Borromeo, archbishop of
Milan, and Casare Cardinal Boronio did likewise. One result of all this was that
there was a sharp increase in the number of miraculous images in the decades
immediately following Trent, especially in areas most subject to the authority of
the Church. Thus, for example, while there are only six recorded cases of miraculous activity associated with madonnine images in the city of Rome in the
period 1521–46, there were at least twenty-one such cases in the period 1550–
1600 (ibid., 237).

Thus the Italian Catholic tendency to infuse images with supernatural power
is a constraint to which official Catholicism in Italy has always had to adapt. Intellectualized approaches to religious change aside, no variant of official Catholicism that failed to adapt to this constraint can ever be successful in Italy. The result:
though the belief that supernatural power can infuse concrete images might be
denied at the level of official doctrine, the Italian Church has never taken steps to
stamp out the behaviors associated with the cults that form around favor-dispensing images. Moreover, when the Church has wanted to solidify its hold on
Italian publics (as it did during the Counter-Reformation) Church officials like
Nelli and Paleotti have always been willing to go even further, by legitimating—
at least implicitly—those beliefs (e.g., the view that particular images might be
associated with visual wonders or a source of miracles) that were central to the
popular understanding of image cults.

Episcopal Investigations after Trent

The Council of Trent passed a number of reforms designed to ensure that bishops take a more active role in regulating religious activities in their dioceses. Bishops were now required to be resident in their diocese and to make regular pastoral visits to the communities under their jurisdiction. They were required to regularly convene synods, at which the secular clergy were required to attend. Bishops were given also more control over the regular clergy, who now had to obtain permission from the bishop before erecting any new monasteries and convents.

Given this concern with strengthening the control of local bishops, it is hardly surprising that Trent also gave bishops more control over sacred images:

> [This] holy council decrees that no one is permitted to erect or cause to be erected in any place or church, howsoever exempt, any unusual image unless it has been approved by the bishop; also that no new miracles be accepted and no relics recognized unless they have been investigated and approved by the same bishop, who, as soon as he has obtained knowledge of such matters, shall, after consulting theologians and other pious men, act thereupon as he shall judge consonant with truth and piety. (Schroeder 1950, 217)

This passage gave bishops a procedure that could have been used to suppress cults—especially new cults—organized around images seen by the public to be infused with supernatural power. Moreover, commentators (see for instance Viscardi 1993, 26–28) often see in this procedure evidence of a desire on the part of the hierarchy to control "spontaneous" forms of religiosity that undermines the position of the official Church.

Nevertheless, if we examine one way Italian bishops after Trent actually chose to exercise their newly strengthened control over image cults, it becomes apparent that they were driven by a concern that had little or nothing to do with stamping out the popular belief that images were infused with power.

The Case of the Madonna del Pozzo

The sanctuary dedicated to the Madonna del Pozzo (Madonna of the Well) at Capurso, near Bari, is one of the most important sanctuaries in Apulia and still possesses one of best collections of ex-voto in Italy (this collection is discussed in Triputti 1978). According to official histories (like Mariella 1979), the story of the Capurso sanctuary begins in 1705, when Domenico Tanzella, a priest at Capurso, fell ill with a malady that local doctors diagnosed as incurable. While he lay dying, a madonna appeared to him and promised that he would regain his health if he drank some water from a local well, The Well of S. Maria. In return, she asked that

he erect a chapel in her honor. The well in question was more like a cavern with
a hole in its roof than a true well, and it was known as a poor source of water. Still,
Tanzella's relatives extracted some of its water, gave it to him to drink, and he was
cured instantly, just as the madonna had promised.

Toward the end of August in that same year, Tanzella himself descended into
the cavern and found a fresco depicting a madonna. The image detached itself
(miraculously) from the wall, an event we can regard as one of those visual wonders that so often announce the presence of supernatural power in Italy. The
image was installed in the chapel that Tanzella was building at the madonna's
request, and it quickly became known as a source of miraculous favors. The
chapel was completed in early January 1706, six months after the image was first
discovered. On January 12, Tanzella asked Muzio Gaeta, archbishop of Bari, for
official permission to open the chapel to the public.

If Archbishop Gaeta conducted an investigation of the sort implied in the
tridentine decree on images (that is, if he consulted with advisers concerning the
miracles associated with the image or the attitudes of the pilgrims who were
already flocking to the chapel), no record of that investigation remains. In any
event, since Gaeta's decree authorizing the new chapel was issued on February 9,
less than a month after Tanzella's initial request, it seems certain that whatever
investigation took place was conducted quickly. On the other hand, this does not
mean that Gaeta's approval of the new cult was automatic or unthinking. Gaeta
did assess the new cult using criteria that were important to him, and some sense
of what those criteria were emerges from a series of events that occurred a few
years later.

In 1713, several people in the Capurso-Bari area decided to build a larger
sanctuary, to which the miraculous image could be transferred. As part of their
plan, they wanted to bring in a group of Alcantarine friars (the Alcantarines were
a Franciscan splinter group) to administer the new sanctuary. But to bring the
Alcantarines to Capurso, the sponsors of the proposed sanctuary had to petition
the Holy Congregation of Bishops and Regulars at Rome, which they did. This
body in turn asked Gaeta, who was still archbishop of Bari, for his opinion on the
matter. In his response (which was ultimately favorable to the establishment of
the Alcantarines at Capurso), Gaeta reviewed the early history of the sanctuary:

> For the benefit of Your Eminences, I consider it opportune to provide a brief
> report . . . on the state of this chapel. It was erected in February 1706 through the
> efforts of Domenico Tanzella, a priest in this area, and blessed with my consent.
> It had an endowment of twelve ducats annually, which was supplied by Tanzella. So
> greatly has the devotion at this chapel increased, along with the number of the
> faithful who flock there, that in the short space of seven years, three months, the

chapel has accumulated a large number of gifts and offerings, including votive
objects made of gold, silver, and wax, as well animals of various sorts that are now
part of a herd. There is also a farm purchased by the chapel. . . . Overall, my examination of the matter suggests a benefice valued at something like ten thousand
ducats. This chapel is governed by four priests of the community, who were appointed by me and supplied with instructions necessary for the proper administration of the cultic activity at the chapel and for cutting short certain controversies
that arose between the chapel's founder [Tanzella] and the local parish priest over
who should administer the gifts given to the chapel. (Reproduced in Mariella 1979,
179–80)

This report makes it clear that Gaeta had evaluated the new cult at Capurso. His
sole concern, however, had been that the cult be economically viable and that the
funds that flowed to the chapel be administered properly.

The fact that Gaeta mentions "votive objects made of gold, silver, and wax"
in his report means that he was well aware that the image at the sanctuary was
seen by the public to be associated with miraculous cures, and through his letter
the authorities at Rome would have come to know the same thing. Yet at no point
in this report (or in the others that he wrote, all reproduced in ibid.) did Gaeta
raise the matter of these miraculous cures as something to be taken into account
or investigated when assessing the legitimacy of the new sanctuary, nor did the
Roman authorities raise these issues in the letters they sent back to Gaeta over the
next few years. For all parties, these ex-voto were important only because of their
financial implications: they were evidence of the wealth that had accumulated
around the miraculous image at Capurso. In the end, the new sanctuary was not
approved at this time, but here again the reason was financial: Capuchin groups
in neighboring communities objected that their ability to support themselves by
soliciting alms would be undermined if the Alcantarines were brought to Capurso. In the 1740s the Alcantarine friars agreed to limit their solicitation of alms
to a small circle of communities, and the Capuchins withdrew their opposition.
This last (financial) hurdle overcome, the new sanctuary was finally built and the
miraculous image installed there in 1748.

The case of the Capurso sanctuary is interesting for several reasons. First, the
cult organized around the miraculous image of the Madonna del Pozzo emerged
a full century and a half after the Council of Trent. Moreover, within a few months
of its emergence it was being scrutinized by diocesan authorities. Finally, the
involvement of the Alcantarines a few years later ensured that Rome itself would
come to scrutinize the new cult. If there had been any sense of uneasiness among
the hierarchy of the Church over new cults organized around images seen to be a
source of miraculous favors, there was plenty of opportunity for that concern to

have been made manifest. But no such concern emerged. On the contrary, the only concerns expressed (and they were expressed over and over again, by all parties) were purely financial. Did the sanctuary have enough wealth to maintain itself? Who would administer that wealth? Would the new sanctuary undermine the financial stability of other religious groups nearby? These were the important questions. Once they were answered satisfactorily, Church officials were quite happy to authorize yet another cult organized around a miraculous image.

There is no way to know how typical the Capurso case is. There are more than fifteen hundred madonnine sanctuaries in Italy, and most have a miraculous image.[3] For most of these sanctuaries it is difficult if not impossible to get precise information concerning the conditions under which ecclesiastical authorities first approved the cult involved. What can be said is that, in my reading through the local histories associated with the better known sanctuaries, the pattern just described recurs over and over: the bishop who evaluates a new image cult is concerned mainly if not entirely with financial matters and specifically with the question of whether the cult has the revenue needed to function.

There are of course cases in which bishops evaluated image cults using criteria beyond the simple matter of financial viability. A close examination of these cases, however, usually reveals that, here too, there was little concern with stamping out the popular belief that images were the locus of supernatural power.

Miraculous Images in the Age of Enlightenment

Vismara Chiappa (1988) provides an account of the eighteenth-century investigations conducted by the Archdiocese of Milan in connection with nine images that began to dispense miraculous favors. In all these cases, the procedure set in motion by the appearance of a miraculous image (see ibid., 76–77) seems at first sight to conform to the tridentine ideal. Agents acting on behalf of the archbishop would visit the (alleged) miraculous image and seal it in a way that removed it from public view. Generally this was done by hiring a carpenter to cover up the image in the presence of witnesses. A edict was then issued forbidding the image to be uncovered. Any ex-voto or candles in front of the image were removed and turned over to a local cleric for the duration of the investigation. Archdiocesan authorities then questioned witnesses for information relating to the alleged miracles; these were usually people who claimed to have received miraculous cures or the parents of children who had been cured. Eventually, a report was given to the archbishop, who made the final judgment.

3. For an overview of madonnine sanctuaries in Italy, see Carroll (1992, 23–26).

Sealing an image did not end the flow of miraculous favors from an image. On the contrary, testimony taken during these investigations suggests that images continued to attract devotees and dispense favors even after they had been sealed and even while the archdiocesan investigation was being conducted. Vismara Chiappa (78) herself sees this as reflecting the view of the official Church, namely, that the source of the favor was Mary, and not her image. But another possibility, and one entirely consistent with the practice of veiling images (see chap. 1), is that the public saw the supernatural power of these images to be physically present in the image itself and capable of causing miracles even when the image was not seen.

We know the outcome of the investigations—that is, whether a cult was approved or not—for only six of the nine cases studied by Vismara Chiappa. In five of these six cases the archbishop did in the end approve a cult organized around the image involved. In other words, limited as the data are, it would appear that archdiocesan authorities at Milan were generally receptive to new cults organized around miraculous images. One reason for this, at least judging from Vismara Chiappa's account of these cases, is that archdiocesan authorities were easily influenced by local preferences and by the lobbying efforts of local communities.

In two cases, for instance, the local community itself initiated the archdiocesan investigation for the express purpose of gaining a wider legitimacy for an existing cult. Thus in 1731 a group of devout Catholics in the hamlet of Seregno, one of whom was the local parish priest, petitioned the archbishop for an investigation of the miracles that had come to surround a madonnine image in the local oratory.[4] This group made it clear that its request was prompted by a desire to publish a book detailing these miracles and thus to make the cult more widely known. Similarly, in 1746 the trustees for the Church of S. Vittore at Varese solicited an investigation on behalf of a wooden pietà that had been seen as a source of miracles in the local area for more than half a century.

In other cases, local communities actively intervened to secure a positive judgment after an investigation had been initiated by archdiocesan authorities. In 1755, a statue of the Addolorata in the parish church at Casorate began to dispense miraculous favors, and the archdiocesan authorities sealed the image and initiated an investigation. During the course of that investigation, they received a petition to reopen the cult, which was supported by the local clergy at Casorate and by the community's leading citizens. Although the investigating commission decided that none of the alleged miracles associated with this image could be cer-

4. Seregno, like all the communities mentioned in Vismara Chiappa's analysis, is located in the Archdiocese of Milan.

tified, they nevertheless did deem them "notable favors," and they did authorize the reestablishment of this cult.

Perhaps the clearest example of the archdiocesan response to local preferences is that in connection with an image cult that developed at Ornago. Some time before 1700 a chapel dedicated jointly to a madonna and the Souls in Purgatory had been erected in the woods near Ornago on the site of a mass grave for plague victims. The bones of these plague victims had become associated with the souls in Purgatory and were the object of devotion.[5] In April 1715, a spring was discovered near the chapel during the course of a severe drought. Very shortly, the news spread that this water was the source of miraculous favors. Almost immediately (in May) two archdiocesan officials visited the site and conducted a preliminary investigation. This was followed by a second and more elaborate investigation, which concluded in July. This second commission decided to prohibit any cult associated with the chapel and in fact ordered that the chapel be closed. The following September, however, the local community at Ornago sent a request to the archbishop asking that the investigation be continued. The archbishop acceded to this request, and the outcome of this third investigation was quite different: the commission now decided that three miracles associated with the chapel were truly miraculous and authorized a public cult around the madonnine image in the chapel.

Generally, the pattern that emerges from Vismara Chiappa's account of these cases is this: in the face of a clearly expressed desire on the part of local communities for a cult organized around an allegedly miraculous image, archdiocesan authorities at Milan were willing to authorize this cult even when they felt there was no real evidence of miracles and even when they had initially concluded the cult was inappropriate. The cases considered by Vismara Chiappa are the more significant in that they occurred in the Archdiocese of Milan during the eighteenth century. The Archdiocese of Milan, after all, was one area of Italy in which the tridentine reforms were put into place fairly rapidly after the Council of Trent. Further, the eighteenth century was a period during which a number of Lombardy intellectuals—some influenced by Jansenism, some by the Enlightenment generally—spoke out against irrational and superstitious elements in religion. Yet even here and even then, it would appear, Church officials went out their way to accommodate the popular demand for cults organized around miraculous madonnine images.

5. Cults organized around the bones of plague victims are common in northern Italy. The history of these cults and their relation to the souls in Purgatory are considered in chap. 5.

Manufacturing a Madonna

Over the past century or so, a new madonna has risen to prominence in Italy. Being relatively a young madonna, there is often an ad hoc quality to the cult places erected in her honor in older churches. In some churches (and I have seen this often) a simple framed print depicting her image has been placed on a side altar, where it leans against a faded oil painting of some earlier madonna or saint. In other churches a special but decidedly makeshift edicola has been erected and placed along a side wall. But notwithstanding the modest nature of her situation in some churches, she is now one of the most powerful madonnas in the Italian Catholic pantheon.

As with all popular madonnas in Italy, this new madonna holds a child. But her image is definitely not static in the manner of traditional madonnine images; it definitely depicts a scene. The madonna is shown handing a rosary to a Dominican nun kneeling at the madonna's left, while the child in her lap is handing a second rosary to a male Dominican kneeling at the madonna's right. The saints are S. Caterina da Siena and S. Dominic, and the scene is meant to evoke the tradition that the Virgin Mary appeared to S. Dominic and gave him the rosary. Depictions of S. Dominic receiving the rosary from the Madonna del Rosario are common in Italy. But in this particular case the upper body of the madonna is surrounded by a wide circle of large pointed stars. To Italian Catholics it is this iconographical element that most betrays her real identity: she is the Madonna di Pompei.

There are four great supersanctuaries in Italy to which, each year, more pilgrims travel than to any other sanctuary. Three of these—the madonnine sanctuaries at Montevergine (Campania) and Loreto (Le Marche) and the sanctuary dedicated to S. Antonio at Padua—were established in the Middle Ages. But the fourth was established only in the late nineteenth century. It is dedicated to the Madonna di Pompei and is located in the modern city of Pompei, twenty-five kilometers from Naples. The ex-voto left at the Pompei sanctuary indicate that it draws Catholic pilgrims from all regions of Italy and from a number of Italian communities outside Italy as well (Turchini 1990, 109). Yet despite its importance to the history of modern Italian Catholicism, the sanctuary at Pompei is relatively unknown outside the Italian-speaking world.

Most foreign tourists come to Campania mainly to visit the ancient city of Pompei, whose structures were preserved during the eruption of Mount Vesuvius in 79 A.D. Possibly they visit as well the ruins at Herculaneum, preserved by the same eruption. Foreign tourists usually avoid Naples, or rush through it, and so miss one of the most impressive combinations of urban settlement and Mediterranean geography to be found in Italy. There seems to be a vague sense that Naples is unsafe, and certainly this is a view shared by Neapolitans themselves, who often warn well-meaning professors wandering through their older neighborhoods to be careful. For myself, I can only say that, although I have encountered areas that seemed unsafe in both northern and southern Italy, I as yet have no reason to believe that the South is any more unsafe than the North. In any event, if foreigners bypass Naples it is hardly surprising that they bypass the modern city of Pompei, which lies adjacent to the ancient ruins. In this they are aided by the local railway system, which has established separate stations for the excavations (Pompei scavi) and for the city of Pompei.

The official history of the Madonna di Pompei and her sanctuary starts in the 1870s and is dominated by the efforts of a single person, Bartolo Longo. Longo is now on the road to sainthood, having been beatified by Pope John Paul II in 1980. Reading through the story of Longo and the Madonna di Pompei, one may catch sight of other people whose efforts on behalf of this madonna's cult may have been more important than is generally recognized, and it is certainly possible that official accounts chose to focus on Longo's efforts in order to make the story more a typical hero tale, in which a lone figure embarks upon a quest during which he overcomes great obstacles to reach his goal. On the other hand, there is no question that Longo played a central role in causing this madonna to come into existence.

Fortunately, in addition to being a devout Catholic, Bartolo Longo was also a quintessential nineteenth-century bureaucrat who left a detailed account of his efforts to create the new image cult, matter of factly laying out the strategies that he used. His comments (Longo 1981) validate many of the conclusions reached in chapter 1. But Longo did not act in isolation; he had the support of Church officials. The reaction of these officials illustrates particularly clearly what we have been discussing in this chapter, namely, the willingness of the Church to cater to popular beliefs about miraculous images.

Bartolo Longo arrived at Pompei in 1872 to manage the estates of the Countess De Fusco (whom he would marry in 1885). In his account of those first years, Longo (ibid., 33–50) describes the extreme poverty of the local inhabitants, the absence of local governmental structures, and the endemic brigandage. He also calls attention to the superstitions of the local population, in particular to their belief in the evil eye and their use of witches to cast and undo spells. As to religion, he tells us, all they had was a dilapidated local church ridden with vermin and a parish priest who was called upon as a folk doctor.

Longo describes himself as a former freethinker who had dabbled in spiritualism and who had only recently turned to God. He was desperately seeking a way to atone for his past sins when he hit upon the idea of promulgating devotion to the Rosary. To find out how this might best be done, he interviewed people in the local community to determine what activities were popular and discovered what has been mentioned here several times: Italian Catholics are drawn to activities with a strong emphasis upon the concrete and the visible. Longo decided that the best way to begin his campaign on behalf of the Rosary would be to sponsor a combined lottery and festa. Tickets to the lottery would be cheap, and the first five prizes would be items of "gold" jewelry from Naples that were "eye-catching but of little real value" (63). The next eight hundred items would be cheap crucifixes, rosaries, and printed images of the Madonna del Rosario.

Longo is very clear about what he hoped to accomplish: "All the things associated with this festa—the sermon, the artificial fireworks, the popular games, the lottery—would work to impress upon the mind of the people at least the *name* [emphasis in original] of the Rosary and the title Vergine del Rosario." He was, in short, unconcerned with prayer, interior piety, or meditation on the mysteries (events from the life of Christ and Mary) that are associated with the Rosary devotion in the eyes of the official Church. For Longo the first step was to ensure that people came to know the terms *Rosary* and *Vergine del Rosario,* and this was best done by mounting a festa with a strong visual component.

Longo sponsored his festas in 1873, 1874, and 1875. Only then did he seek to promote any real understanding of the Rosary as a devotion. This he did by asking the bishop of Nola (whose diocese included the Valle di Pompei) to send priests to conduct a mission. The bishop was glad to comply. The requested mission commenced on November 2, 1875, and the missionaries paid special attention to the Rosary during the course of their preaching and instruction. The mission lasted for twelve days; the bishop of Nola himself arrived on the final day to administer the sacrament of Confirmation.

For the effects of this mission to be long-lasting, Longo knew that the new Rosary cult would have to have a concrete focus, and this meant an image: "To establish among these people the habit of saying the Rosary in common and to earn the indulgences associated with the Rosary, it seemed to me that an image of the Madonna Del Rosario was absolutely indispensable. It would be before such an image that the people would gather every evening to recite the Rosary" (75). Consequently, on November 13, one day before the 1875 mission was scheduled to end, Longo set off for Naples to purchase an oil painting of the Madonna del Rosario. The sequence of events that follows over the next few years reads like a comedy of errors, but the end result would be a madonnine image that is now one of the most powerful in Italy.

At Naples, Longo met his friend and confessor, a Dominican friar named

Alberto Radente. Together they went to a shop that had a painting of the Madonna del Rosario for sale but quickly left when they learned the asking price was
four hundred lire. Then Radente recalled that he had purchased a painting of the
Madonna del Rosario some years previously for only three lire and had given it
to a nun in the area; he was certain that she would in turn give it to Longo. He
was right. The woman was more than happy to pass on the painting. Unfortunately, when she brought it out, it was not quite what Longo expected:

> Alas! I felt my heart tighten when I saw it. It's not just that it was an old and worn
> canvas, but the face of the madonna, rather than being that of a kindly virgin . . .
> seemed to resemble more a wrinkled old hag. . . . The painting's surface had
> cracked, and bits and pieces of the paint had fallen away. Equally disturbing was
> the ugliness of the other figures depicted. The S. Dominic to the right seemed
> less a saint than a vulgar imbecile, and the S. Rosa to the right, her head crowned
> with roses, had a largish face that was wrinkled like that of a coarse peasant. (79)

Moreover Longo recognized immediately that the painting erred with respect to
its portrayal of (devotional) history: instead of showing the madonna handing a
rosary to S. Dominic, as actually happened, Longo says, she is shown handing it
to S. Rosa. In the picture S. Dominic was being handed a rosary by the child in
the madonna's lap. Nevertheless, Longo was in a hurry and the painting was free;
despite his reservations he felt that it was good enough to become the focus of a
cult. Unfortunately, the priests conducting the mission were less enthusiastic.
Upon seeing the picture Longo had obtained, they decided that it would not be
fitting to expose such an ugly canvas to public veneration. It was set aside and
formed no part of the closing ceremonies of the mission.

Longo subsequently gave the image to a local painter for its first restoration.
This man normally earned his living by making copies of the paintings of ancient
Pompei for the tourist trade. Always the cost-conscious bureaucrat, Longo was
careful to tell the man that the original painting had cost only three lire and that
he would pay only thirteen lire for the restoration.

Meanwhile, Longo was working on two other projects. First, he had secured
official permission for a Rosary confraternity to be erected in the parish church
at Pompei. The formal inauguration of the new confraternity was set for February 13. Second, on the final day of the 1875 mission the bishop of Nola had suggested to Longo that he raise funds for a new church to replace the dilapidated
parish church. Toward that end, Longo and the Countess de Fusco began soliciting donations from members of the middle and upper classes at Naples.

The "restored" painting was returned to Longo in January, and once again
he was disappointed. The madonna was still ungainly and displeasing, and S.
Rosa was still "the same fat and rough-hewn peasant" she had been before. Nev-

ertheless, the blank spots on the canvas had been filled in with new paint and a coat of varnish applied over its entire surface. As bad it is still was, it was now presentable enough to be the focus of a cult. Longo made plans to display the image for the first time on the same day—February 13—that the new Rosary confraternity was to be formally proclaimed.

For an image cult to be popular, it must be seen to be a source of supernatural favors, and so Longo set out to acquire a few miracles for his newly refurbished image. His account of the first miracle associated with this image provides a glimpse into how this could be done. That first miracle, he tells us, was granted to Clarinda Lucarelli of Naples, a twelve-year-old girl who suffered from epileptic convulsions. At the beginning of February 1876, the Countess De Fusco visited the Lucarelli household to solicit a donation for the new church. Clorinda's aunt said that if the Vergine del Rosario would cure Clorinda, she (the aunt) would not only make a large donation but would go from house to house in Naples soliciting even more donations for the new church. In Longo's account, Clorinda was cured on February 13, a date whose significance he was careful to emphasize. "And Clorinda was brought to perfect health [by the madonna] on February 13, that memorable day on which day her Image was exposed to the veneration of the Pompeian people and on which the Confraternity of the Rosary was erected at Pompei" (111).

Taken at face value, the events described here would have seemed to most Italian Catholics an impressive confirmation of the new image's power: on the very day this new image was exposed to the public for the first time, a miraculous favor is granted to someone who had appealed to this particular image. In fact, careful examination of the evidence gathered by Longo in support of this first miracle suggests that the coincidence of these two events might not have been that precise. Later in his book, for instance, Longo (332) suggests that Clorinda's last attack occurred on February 2. Similarly, he reproduces an affidavit from one of Clorinda's doctors, written at the beginning of June 1876, that suggests that her symptoms had disappeared "about four months ago, more or less" (113). All in all, then, it does appear that Clorinda Lucarelli's attacks, whatever they were, ended sometime in February 1876, but there is no particular reason to believe that February 13 was the critical day. Yet this is the precise date cited by Longo because it is the date on which the cure needed to take place. After all, the logic of popular Catholicism in Italy is that madonnas provide miracles in exchange for veneration. Within this logic it makes sense that an image's first miracle be associated with the first act of public veneration offered to that image.

Over the next few years (1876–1878) eleven more miracles would be attributed to the Madonna di Pompei (111). But despite the fact that the image was judged to be a source of miracles, Longo could not resist changing it one more time. In 1879 he turned it over to two Neapolitan artisans adept in modern methods of restoration. Between the two of them they not only transferred the original painted surface to a new (and larger) canvas but also modified the content of the image substantially. At Longo's request S. Rosa became S. Caterina da Siena. This was done by converting Rosa's crown of roses into a crown of thorns, changing her habit into that of a Dominican nun, and painting in the marks of the stigmata on her hands. The faces of the figures, especially that of the madonna, were retouched and made "more refined."[6]

In removing the image for the period of this second restoration (three months), Longo knew he faced a problem: what would serve as the concrete focus of the cult in the meantime? Certainly he had no doubts that the Italian Catholics who came to Pompei needed to have an image as the focus of their cult: "Meanwhile, I realized that it would be unseemly for people to come to Pompei to thank the Most Holy Virgin, or to pray to her, and not find some image there to venerate. After all, popular devotion to the madonna usually proceeds by attaching itself to some particular image or statue . . . and this devotion would certainly weaken [in the absence of an image]. What was to be done?" (98). What he did, in fact, was to install a second painting similar to the one being restored. This second painting showed the Madonna del Rosario handing S. Caterina da Siena a ring to signify Caterina's mystical espousal with Jesus Christ, and it too, for a while, became a source of favors. Eventually, the original image, now remade, was returned (in August 1879) and installed in a chapel in the emerging sanctuary.

The image at Pompei continued to dispense miracles. Figure 2.1 gives the number of supernatural favors attributed to the Madonna di Pompei for the years 1876–87, based on the letters and depositions on file at the sanctuary (see Turchini 1990, 111). Note that the increase in favors over this period was not linear; on the contrary, there was a dramatic increase in favors in 1884, and this increase continued to accelerate in each succeeding year. Here again, we are dealing with a consequence of Longo's efforts at social engineering.

Since Italian Catholics are attracted to image cults when the images dispense favors, the more people who know about the favors, the more that image will attract devotees. The best way to promote a new cult, therefore, is to ensure that news of the miracles reaches the widest possible audience. Implicitly recognizing all this, Longo set out to use the tools of the new industrial age to ensure that the miracles of his new madonna reached the largest possible audience and, in

6. The fullest account of this second restoration is found in Tamburro (1987, 57–60).

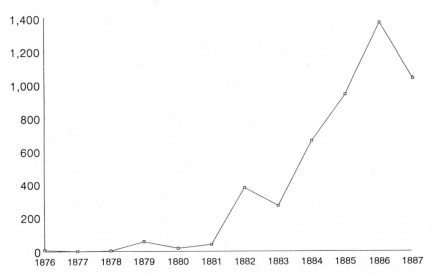

Fig. 2.1. Supernatural Favors Attributed to the Madonna di Pompei, 1876–1887. *Source:* Turchini (1990, 111); graph by Lori Campbell.

March 1884, published the first issue of *Il rosario e la Nuova Pompei*, a monthly periodical devoted mainly to publicizing the favors obtained from the Madonna di Pompei.

According to devotional accounts of the Pompei sanctuary, this periodical was the first mass-market periodical in Italy that openly "talked of miracles" in an age when "talk of miracles was usually greeted with scientific skepticism" (Tamburro 1987, 140). *Il rosario e la Nuova Pompei* started with four thousand subscribers in 1883; by 1887 this number had risen to thirty thousand, and it continued to rise over the next few years (ibid., 141). What the data in the table show is that the inauguration of this monthly periodical did have the effect of making the image at Pompei more powerful: as news of miracles reached a larger and larger audience, more and more people asked for and received miracles. By 1887, the number of miracles had become a torrent. Longo was forced to select only the most important for inclusion in *Il rosario e la Nuova Pompei*, and even then often provided only a very brief summary indicating the place and general nature of the favor obtained (Turchini 1990, 113).

In discussing the miraculous favors dispensed by his twice-remade Madonna di Pompei, Longo was usually careful to stay within the bounds of tridentine orthodoxy: it is not really the image itself that grants the favors, he says, but rather the Virgin, who obtains these favors through her intercession. Nevertheless, in some passages, especially where he is describing how people reacted to the

new version of the madonna's image, he uses the language of a Catholic intellectual to express what is clearly the popular view of powerful images: "This fact
seems uncontestable: to the Neapolitans and other outsiders who come here on
a daily basis, there is something in this image that draws them to admire it. It is
certainly not the workmanship, since this is not one of Raphael's Virgins. Rather
it seems to be a mysterious force [una forza arcana] that imposes itself on people
and leads them, almost without their wishing it, to kneel and pray" (Longo 1981,
105). This, I suggest, is as close as a book published with ecclesiastical approval
(as this one was) can come to saying that miraculous images are infused with
supernatural power.

And what about the Church hierarchy? How did they respond to Longo's
attempt to manufacture a cult around a new miraculous image? Very positively.
As mentioned, it was the bishop of Nola who first encouraged Longo to build a
new church at Pompei, and the bishop was present at the ceremony held to mark
the laying of the first stone for the new structure. Admittedly, the bishop's support for the new cult at Pompei did waver in 1877, but this had nothing to do with
an aversion to image cults. The bishop's concerns were purely financial: he felt
that Longo's project was becoming too extravagant, and he was beginning to
worry that the diocese might be saddled with the debt. "[The bishop] thought,"
says Longo (248), "that I spent twice as much money as I collected." Indeed, as the
bishop's support for the Pompei cult diminished, he began actively promoting a
second image cult that had recently emerged at Boscoreale, four kilometers from
Pompei. His support for this cult quickly soured, and here again the motivation
was financial: the bishop had discovered that the lay administrators at Boscoreale were misusing the money given as votive offerings.[7] At this point, the bishop
of Nola reversed himself and once again became an active supporter of the cult
at Pompei.

The extent to which the bishop was willing to endorse the popular view of
what was happening at Pompei is seen in a pastoral letter he issued in 1878 (reproduced in Longo 1981, 294):

> But are these miracles real?—many people ask—Are the many favors that come
> from the Madonna di Rosario di Pompei real? My beloved children, this I know for
> certain: the people who say that they have received favors from this image of the
> Madonna del Rosario have sent money—a great deal of money—so that a church
> can be constructed in her honor. And it is impossible to believe that people would
> be so stupid as to give money to attest to something that is not true. Moreover, we
> are not just talking of two or three people but of a great many people, from every

---

7. Longo has little to say about the Boscoreale cult except that it drained resources away from the
Pompei cult. An account of what happened at Boscoreale can be found in De Rosa (1983, 346–48).

region of Italy and from every class and condition of life, including the rich and the poor, aristocrats and men of letters. Respectable and powerful people have come to me personally to attest to favors received from the Vergine de Pompei and have given me large sums on her behalf. What must we conclude? Only this: that the Madonna really does work miracles and favors for those who invoke the Vergine del Rosario and who honor her with the Rosary; that the Madonna really does want to be venerated here, in the Valle di Pompei, with a special devotion, and that she gives favors and miracles especially to those who help with the construction of this new church dedicated to her. This is the only true and logical conclusion that we can reach.

At one level, this letter is evidence of the bishop's continuing concern with financial matters; certainly it suggests that the large donations received from wealthy Catholics was one of the reasons for his renewed commitment to the Pompei cult.

But financial issues aside, the letter demonstrates the bishop's willingness to legitimize a number of popular beliefs about powerful images. For instance, he legitimizes the practice of establishing devotions to particular madonnas at particular locations, stating that "the Madonna really does want to be venerated here, in the Valle di Pompei." There is no emphasis in the bishop's letter upon the tridentine Mary-as-intercessor doctrine. On the contrary, he says clearly that "the Madonna really does work miracles and favors" (la Madonna veramente fa grazie e miracoli) for those who invoke her. Undoubtedly the good bishop would have fallen back on the Mary-as-intercessor doctrine if called to task on the matter, but the fact remains that in his letter issued to the churches in his diocese (and thousands of copies of that letter were distributed) the bishop of Nola was quite willing to reinforce the popular view that madonnas have independent power. He also cites the ex-voto (in this modern case, money) brought to the Pompei sanctuary as evidence that the miracles involved are real.

Here again, in other words—just like Athanasio Nelli centuries earlier—a Church official is willing to let the public belief in the miracles dispensed by sacred images stand as evidence that those miracles are real. Finally, in talking of "the people who say they have received favors from this *image* [emphasis added] of the Madonna del Rosario" (la gente che dice di aver avuto le grazie da questa Imagine del Rosario), the bishop is reinforcing the popular belief that has always been central to image cults in Italy: it is the image itself that is the source of the miracles obtained.

The bishop of Nola was not the only important member of the hierarchy to support the new cult. In 1878, Longo met with the new archbishop of Naples, who gave Longo as signed statement saying that as archbishop he "praises, approves and blesses . . . the new church at Pompei." This document was then used over the next few years, Longo says, to overcome unspecified "difficulties" with the local clergy and with various "signori" at Naples. In 1894, Longo offered the still-incomplete sanctuary and all its property to Pope Leo XIII, who willingly accepted the gift. It was at this time that the sanctuary was split off from the Diocese of Nola and put under the direct administration of the Holy See.

Bartolo Longo set out to manufacture a new image cult that would be popular with Italian Catholics by consciously incorporating into that cult those elements that have always been associated with popular image cults in Italy. The Church collaborated in this effect by reinforcing the popular beliefs that coalesced around the image at Pompei, even though some of these (notably the belief that the image itself was source of power) were at variance with official theology.

If there is a Heaven, then no doubt Gregory the Great was for the umpteenth thousandth time smiling his "I told you so" smile to his good friend S. Serenus of Marseilles.

Chapter Three

"Preaching to Their Eyes"

On Good Friday, television stations throughout Calabria present a video clip of the Holy Saturday celebrations that took place the previous year in the hillside village of Nocera Terinese; regional newspapers almost always carry a feature article on these same celebrations. This media blitz is an implicit invitation to attend the current year's version of that same celebration. Nocera Terinese is unreachable by train, and the usual intercity bus service is suspended on Holy Saturday. The only reasonable means of access is by car, and on Saturday morning hundreds, possibly thousands, of cars converge on the village. Specially assigned carabinieri are there to direct traffic and to ensure that visitors park on the surrounding roads. By midday the narrow streets of Nocera Terinese are packed solid with people, most of whom are outsiders. What is it that makes this particular celebration so special? What have so many people come to see? At first, nothing very special.

Around 9 A.M. a man dressed in the white robes of a local confraternity leaves the Church of the Annunziata carrying a large crucifix. He is followed by a priest and a team of fellow confraternity members who carry aloft a platform that holds a life-sized Pietà. This procession begins moving down the hill, stopping at the doorway of each of the shops that line the street. Each shopkeeper hands over a bouquet of flowers, which is placed at the base of the statue. In April 1993, when I saw the festa, these flowers had been delivered earlier in the morning by a professional florist from a nearby town. For most of the rest of the day the Pietà is carried slowly through the streets of Nocera Terinese, stopping at doorway after doorway. Every so often the older bouquets will be taken away to make room for newer ones, and the platform is occasionally set down on special tables set up throughout the village to provide the bearers a rest.

None of this is much different from what happens in hundreds of other festas staged throughout Italy, and this part of the celebration in itself would never draw the crowds to this out-of-the-way village in Calabria. But about an hour after the team carrying the madonna first leaves the Church of the Annunziata, pairs of men suddenly appear here and there in various doorways. One member of each pair is young, usually in his late teens or early twenties, bare to the waist, and with a red skirt wrapped around his lower body. In one hand he holds a cross wrapped in red cloth; in the other, a string that is attached to the waist of the second man. This second man, usually older, is wearing a crown of thorns, a loose-fitting black shirt, and a black loincloth. His legs are bare, and he carries a round slice of cork in each hand. This man is the *vattente* (beater). At particular doorways, the vattente begins slapping his thigh with one of the corks to bring blood to the surface. Then, with the other slice of cork, whose surface contains a layer of wax studded with glass bits, he slaps his thigh until it bleeds. When a sufficient amount of blood appears, a third man (dressed in ordinary clothes and so usually unnoticed until now) comes forward with a plastic jug containing red wine and vinegar. The vattente holds out the first piece of cork, the third man pours some of the wine mixture over it, and the vattente rubs the liquid onto his thigh. The result is a bright red mixture of vinegar, wine, and blood, which covers his thigh and flows onto the ground. The vattente then runs off, his red-skirted partner in tow, to perform the same ritual in another doorway.

Altogether, there are about six pairs of vattenti, and the pairs scurry around the crowded town independent of each other, occasionally stopping in front of the Pietà, who is also moving about. As the day proceeds, the sidewalks in front of the doorways where the vattenti stop most often—which include the doorways of the town's two churches and its major businesses—become drenched with the blood/vinegar/wine mixture. As well, since neither the vattenti nor their partners are wearing shoes, the streets of the village become marked with bloody footprints. These self-flagellations last from midmorning until late afternoon, and it is they that draw the crowds to Nocera Terinese.

It would be easy to see the bloody flagellations at Nocera Terinese as the survival of some archaic medieval practice, possibly a distant echo of the flagellant movement that broke out in Perugia in 1260 and spread to other parts of northern Italy. It would also be easy to see the onlookers who come to the festival (to say nothing of those who watch it at home courtesy of the TV crews on the scene) as interlopers, whose aim is only to observe the bizarre and the unusual and whose presence erodes whatever religious purpose these rituals might originally have served. In fact, both perceptions would be wrong. The bloody rituals at Nocera Terinese, like similar rituals elsewhere in Italy, were almost certainly instituted during the Counter-Reformation, not the Middle Ages. Furthermore, the celebration was purposely made bloody to achieve exactly the same effect that it achieves today: the sight of so much fresh blood creates a striking visual image that attracts and holds the attention of onlookers whose commitment to tridentine Catholicism is either lukewarm or nil.

The Preaching Orders and the Drive for Catholic Reform

By the time the Council of Trent closed in 1563 several religious orders had developed a special commitment to popular preaching, and preachers were particularly effective in reaching large numbers of people. Several of these preaching orders had been around for centuries. The five mendicant orders (the Franciscans, the Dominicans, the Augustinians, the Carmelites, and the Servites) in particular had long been committed to preaching. But a strong commitment to popular preaching was also to be found within several of the newer orders, notably the Capuchins (a breakaway Franciscan group granted the right to exist as an autonomous order in 1528) and the Jesuits (founded by the Spaniard Ignatius of Loyola and formally recognized by the pope in 1540).

These orders also shared a common commitment to moral regeneration, and it was this, most of all, that established an affinity between these orders and the tridentine Church. After all, in the century and a half before Trent, the call for moral regeneration on the part of the preaching orders had always included a call to confession and a "turning to Christ." It was only a short step from here to the view that moral regeneration should include adherence to the full range of Christocentric doctrines and practices endorsed at Trent. The result was that the preaching orders became a key element in the Church's campaign to bring the spirit of Trent to ordinary Catholics.

But in working for moral regeneration in Italy, both before and after Trent, the preaching orders always faced the same dilemma. On the one hand, the members of these orders were themselves personally very much committed to the strongly Christocentric, and often abstract, Catholicism of the official Church. On the other hand, they wanted to win the allegiance of publics very much attached to a variant of Catholicism dominated by madonnas and saints and characterized by an emphasis upon the concrete and the visible. Promulgating the Catholicism of Church elites might satisfy the preachers' own Christocentric predilections but would do little to win over the people; catering to popular tastes might win the allegiance of the people but would do nothing to promote Christocentrism. That was the dilemma.

In confronting that dilemma, the preaching orders adopted a mix of strategies. First, to secure the allegiance and support of ordinary Catholics, they co-opted popular cults. In particular, they actively promoted cults organized around miraculous madonnine images. Even now, for instance, the majority of madonnine sanctuaries in Italy are administered by one of the preaching orders. Second, and more subtly, the preaching orders co-opted that emphasis upon the concrete that permeates popular Catholicism. Most of all, this meant promoting devotions, like the Forty Hours, that have the Eucharistic host as its focus.[1] But they exploited other possibilities, as well. During the fifteenth century, for instance, S. Benardino of Siena developed and promoted devotion to the Holy Name of Jesus. The physical focus of this devotion was the trigram, a tablet (sometimes painted, sometimes made of clay) in the form of a sunburst on which were inscribed the initials IHS. Even now, these tablets can be seen appended to the outside walls of houses in the older sections of Italian towns, especially in northern Italy. In the late sixteenth and seventeenth centuries, the Jesuits began promoting devotion to the Sacred Heart, taken to be the physical heart of Jesus Christ. Although attacked savagely by Jansenist thinkers like Scipione de'Ricci (who called it *cardolatria*— heart worship), devotion to the Sacred Heart of Jesus would become one of the most popular devotions in the Roman Catholic world.[2]

But there was a third strategy used by the preaching orders. To appreciate and understand this strategy, we must remember that most miraculous images in Italy have always been static, that is, they have not been images that evoke scenes from a recognizable narrative. The prototypical miraculous image is a simple Madonna con Bambino that suddenly and spontaneously begins to dispense favors. This static emphasis stands in direct contrast to the dynamic emphasis that pervades the Christocentric Catholicism of the official Church. The Christ of the official Church, after all, is associated with a particular narrative, the core of which is the story obtained by merging the four Gospels of the New Testament. Over time, this core has come to be supplemented by nonbiblical traditions, like the Veronica story.[3] The key events in this narrative (in particular the events surrounding the Last Supper, the Passion, and the Resurrection) have always been central in defining what "Christ" *means* within the logic of official Catholicism.

1. The Forty Hours is a devotion in which a Eucharistic host is placed in a monstrance and "exposed" for public veneration for a considerable period of time (which need not be exactly forty hours). On this devotion, see Carroll (1989, 104–13).

2. On the history of this devotion, see Carroll (1989, 132–53).

3. For several centuries now it has been a widespread belief among Catholics that a woman named Veronica wiped the face of Christ as he carried his cross to Golgotha and that a image of his face was miraculously imprinted on that cloth. No such event appears in any New Testament account. For an account of the historical processes that brought the Veronica myth into existence, see Degert (1913).

This is why dynamic images that evoke a scene from this narrative are especially well suited to promoting the Christocentric Catholicism favored by Church elites.

The preaching orders created a number of devotions that merged the popular emphasis upon visual images with the dynamic emphasis of Christocentric Catholicism. The best known example involves the Stations of the Cross, a devotion promoted most actively by the Franciscans.[4] But other popular devotions also resulted from this merger of the visual and the dynamic, two of which came to be especially important in Italy. Both of these devotions were first popularized during the missions that the preaching orders conducted in the European countryside in the two centuries following Trent.

The Penitential Mission as Theater of Blood

Rienzo (1980, 442) suggests that the missions conducted in Catholic Europe after Trent were of two basic types.[5] First, there were the instructional missions, whose primary goal was to promote a wider knowledge of the doctrines formulated at Trent and a wider practice of those rituals (Holy Communion in particular) favored by the tridentine Church. Second, there were the penitential missions, whose goal was to promote moral regeneration through penitential activity. The distinction Rienzo draws has more to do with emphasis than anything else. All European missions, without exception, were committed to instruction in Catholic doctrine. It was only the penitential element that varied to any significant degree from mission to mission, and this variation was to some extent tied to geography. Although penitential missions were conducted throughout Catholic Europe, they were more common in Spain and southern Italy than in most other areas of Catholic Europe (see ibid., 442). The Jesuits, who conducted the vast majority of missions in southern Italy during the seventeenth century, were strongly committed to penitential missions as a matter of formal policy. But as De Rosa (1983, 196) notes, penitential missions were favored by all the missionary orders active in southern Italy after Trent, including—apart from the Jesuits—

4. The Stations of the Cross consists of a series of fourteen plaques, each depicting a scene from the Passion of Christ. The plaques are usually arrayed along the inside walls of a church, though they can be set up out-of-doors. The devout move from picture to picture (that is, from station to station). At each picture they are supposed to contemplate what is happening in the scene depicted. On special occasions, the congregation remains seated while a priest and his assistants move from station to station and lead the audience in prayer. For a brief history of this devotion and some speculation as to the psychological roots of its widespread appeal, see Carroll (1989, 41–56).

5. Unless otherwise noted, the following account of missionary activity in southern Italy is derived from Di Palo (1992); De Rosa (1983, 195–226); Gentilcore (1994); Novi Chavarria (1982); Rienzo (1980); Prosperi (1980); Rosa (1976, 245–72).

the Pious Workmen (founded in 1602), the Congregation of Apostolic Missions (founded in 1646), the Redemptorists (founded in 1732), and the Passionists (founded in 1737).

A penitential mission was preceded by a period of careful preparation, during which the missionaries sought to familiarize themselves with the history and customs (including the dialect) of the local community. The evening before the actual start of the mission, the missionaries would walk about the streets of the community carrying a crucifix. Stopping at strategic locations, one of them would give a short sermon on sin, divine castigation, and the need for penance and would finish with an invitation to attend the next day's ceremonies. Once it commenced, a mission could last anywhere from six days to eight weeks, although the norm seems to have been seven to ten days (Novi Chavarria 1982, 163).

Scipione Paolucci's 1651 report on Jesuit missionary activity in southern Italy (cited in Di Palo 1992, 24) suggests that the formula for every mission was "instruction, preaching, discipline, and penitential processions." At least in rural areas, instruction referred to catechism lessons given mainly to young children during the afternoons, when the older members of the community were away working. Preaching, by contrast, took place during the evening and involved the entire community.

The evening sermon would be delivered either from a pulpit inside a church or, if the crowds were large enough, from a platform erected in a piazza. To reach the largest possible audience, preachers avoided complicated arguments and fancy language. Indeed, the regulations of the Pious Workmen specifically instructed its preachers not to develop sermons that were "too Tuscan" (that is, too intellectual) in their orientation (De Rosa 1987, 378). Instead, preachers used simple language to rail against the sins of the community (which almost always included concubinage, prostitution, blasphemy, drunkenness, and gambling) and dwelt on the punishments (mainly eternal damnation) that the tridentine Church saw as being the consequence of such sins. In addition, the audience was instructed on the need to make a good confession and to receive Holy Communion. At some point, the missionaries made themselves available to hear confessions.

These evening sermons were not simply aural events. On the contrary, missionary preachers used a variety of theatrical techniques to create strong visual images in the minds of their audiences. The place where the sermon was delivered, for instance, was usually poorly lit, for dramatic effect, and preachers routinely made use of props. They held aloft skulls when they talked of death; they burned their hands with torches when discussing the pains of Hell; they destroyed playing cards, obscene books, and ornamental items of clothing.

The impact of a sermon was also often enhanced by the presentation of a semidramatic skit. Sometimes, while the preacher was speaking, a statue or a living actor representing a Bible character would appear suddenly, and the preacher would engage that character in dialogue. In other cases, statues were carried about within the church to act out a biblical scene. Such minidramas were very much a part of the missionary's repertoire well into the twentieth century. In describing the missions conducted in Apulia during Holy Week, La Sorsa (1925, 228) reports:

> While the preacher was speaking of the Passion of Christ, a knocking was heard at the door of the church. The missionary hesitated for a moment, then resumed preaching as if nothing had happened. A few moments later, the knocking occurred again, but no one came in. When the knocking was heard a third time, and everyone in the church was agitated and puzzled, the doors suddenly swung open and there in the gloomy night, surrounded by candles, was [a statue of] the Virgin . . . The missionary pointed her out to the people and recalled the torments she had suffered [as a result of Christ's Passion]. He talked of the thousand swords that had pierced her heart and invoked her blessing on all the faithful who were present. Overcome by emotion, the people kneeled and cried . . . Some asked forgiveness for their sins, some beat themselves on the chest, others asked for eternal life after death or invoked her blessing for their children. It was a spectacular scene that left a vivid impression on everyone who attended.

Like the dramatic gestures and props used by the preachers, these minidramas not only attracted the immediate attention of the audience but also created a series of striking visual images that could be called to mind long after the missionary had departed and the specific words used in his sermons forgotten.[6]

After an hour or so of preaching, when the emotional state of the audience was sufficiently intense, the women in the audience were led away and the preacher and his assistants subjected themselves to some form of penitential practice, usually flagellation. Rienzo (1980, 455) provides a succinct account of just how dramatic this part of the ceremony could become:

> During the evening sermon, a procession of priests [of the Congregation of Apostolic Missions] would unexpectedly emerge from the back of the church. They were smeared with ashes and each wore a crown of thorns; ropes [scourges] hung from their necks, and they carried human skulls in their hands. Making sounds of lamentation they made their way toward the main altar. When they arrived there the preacher himself also took up a rope and as a group they began to flagellate themselves. In addition, a preacher would sometimes drag his tongue along the ground from the back of the church up to the main altar.[7] The people participated in all this with their shouts and tears, and the psychological climate was often

6. For other examples of the semidramatic skits sometimes incorporated into sermons, see Toschi (1955, 710–12).
7. Tongue dragging is a common penitential practice in southern Italy; see Carroll (1992, 133–35).

sufficiently intense that enemies were driven to make peace and so to redeem themselves.

In many cases during the self-flagellation the men in the audience would begin to "discipline" themselves in a similar manner: "the faithful in the audience were simultaneously spectators and participants in the ritual" (Novi Chavarria 1982, 171). Even the women who had been excluded sometimes participated indirectly. Reports of several seventeenth-century missions (ibid., 172–73) suggest that the women shouted and screamed, struck themselves on their chests, or prayed prostrate, with their mouths touching the ground.

Missions would usually close with several events. If possible, the missionaries would arrange a "peace," a formal ceremony during which the members of hostile factions within the community agreed to reconcile their differences or to submit those differences to binding arbitration, with the missionaries as arbiters (on this aspect of the mission experience, see Gentilcore 1994, 280–81). Missionaries would also arrange for a mass Communion to take place sometime toward the end of the mission. But the one event that most signaled the close of mission was the grand penitential procession.

The penitential procession was a carefully orchestrated event involving all classes in the community and featuring, as the name implies, a variety of penitential activities. In his 1651 account, Paolucci (cited in Di Palo 1992, 28) divides these activities into two categories. The first he calls *mortificazioni* and were practiced, he tells us, mainly by the upper classes. In effect, these were relatively mild penitential activities and included such things as wearing plain and sparse clothing, even in the coldest weather; walking barefoot; and wrapping heavy chains around your body. Paolucci calls the second category *tormenti*. These were more painful activities and were practiced, he tells us, by the lower classes. Activities here included carrying heavy crosses or being lashed to a cross or a cross beam to which heavy weights had been attached. But the most spectacular of the behaviors that fell under the tormenti heading always involved blood. Paolucci says that some participants pushed a crown of thorns into their head, some rubbed thorns across their tongues, some whipped themselves with cords entangled with iron bits, some beat themselves on various parts of their body (thighs and chests in particular) with "pads" studded with pins or bits of glass, some used pinchers on their bodies. The goal here was not simply to draw blood but to ensure that as much blood as possible was displayed to the audience.

Participation in this "theater of blood" (a term suggested by the discussion in Lombardi Satriani 1981) was by no means limited to adults. Paolucci tells us that children as young as three or four willingly beat themselves on the shoulders with knotted cords "happily learning to be penitent before they were able to be sinful" (cited in Di Palo 1992, 29). He goes on to add that older children of seven or eight disciplined themselves with metal scourges or pads studded with pins and were often as adept at shedding blood as the most experienced of adults.

This emphasis upon pain and blood in the penitential procession was legitimated by linking it to Christ's Passion. An official account of a penitential procession staged during a Jesuit mission at Naples in 1631, for instance, indicates that the procession was led by the missionaries themselves, who were bound with chains and whose heads were smeared with ashes. These were followed by

> a great many men dressed in sackcloth and with their faces covered [by a hood]. They were barefoot and bound with chains. Interspersed among these men, but unrecognizable, were many of the city's most illustrious citizens . . . Several of the men in this part of the procession carried large and heavy crosses upon their shoulders. Others wore a crown of thorns on their head. In both cases this was done to commemorate the Most Sacred Passion of Our Lord . . . Following these were a great number of bloody flagellants, among whom appeared various *misteri* [statues] depicting the Holy Passion of Our Lord. (cited in Novi Chavarria 1982, 178)

This procession, like most penitential processions, closed with a statue of the dead Christ and a statue of the Madonna Addolorata.

The strong emphasis upon the visual that permeated all aspects of the penitential mission was not there by accident. Missionary preachers were keenly aware that in creating striking visual images they were making the mission more appealing to southern Italian publics. A section of the constitution of the Congregation of Apostolic Missions, for instance, suggests that "since men are material and sensate beings it is useful to preach to their eyes [as well as their ears], and this is especially true in the case of the illiterate, to whom these holy missions are principally addressed" (cited in ibid., 464). Similar remarks can be found in Jesuit accounts.

Whether the penitential missions sent into the southern Italian countryside were "successful" or not depends entirely on how success is measured. If you take the view of the official Church, which sees doctrine and adherence to official rituals (regular attendance at mass, regular reception of Holy Communion) to be important, then it would appear that the missions were *not* particularly successful. Rosa (1976, 247) suggests that these missions were rather like "meteors exploding on a desolate terrain, resulting in a spectacular but short-lived shows of piety . . . but not inducing a continuing change toward a more Christian life."

Thus while the missionaries might indeed have instructed large numbers of youth on the basics of tridentine Catholicism, the records of pastoral visits in the

centuries after Trent suggest that ignorance of official Catholic doctrine continued to be widespread. True, there might be some short-term gains with respect
to ritual practice. Twelve thousand Communion wafers, for instance, were distributed during a mission held at Naples in 1642, while twenty thousand Communion wafers were distributed during a mission held at Bitonto (Apulia) in
1646 (Novi Chavarria 1982, 183). But here again the records of later pastoral visits suggest that such behavior did not translate into a desire to receive Communion on a regular basis.

Still, though the missions may not have achieved many of the objectives set
by the tridentine Church, this is not to say that they were ineffectual. On the contrary, in some ways these missions did greatly influence the practice of popular
Catholicism. This influence is most evident in connection with the Holy Week
celebrations that sprang up throughout southern Italy in the wake of the penitential missions.

Holy Week Celebrations

Dramatic performances based on the Passion narrative were commonly staged
throughout Catholic Europe during the Middle Ages. By the early sixteenth century, however, Church authorities has turned increasingly hostile to these dramas. In 1539, for instance, Pope Paul III forbid the Archconfraternity of the Gon-
falone at Rome from staging its annual dramatization of the Passion in the
Colosseum, an event that had been attracting large crowds for at least a century
and half (see Toschi 1955, 697–702). Di Palo (1992, 55) lists several attempts by
diocesan authorities in Apulia in the period 1580–1620 to suppress these popular dramas and notes, as well, that in the North no less a figure than Carlo Borromeo, the archbishop of Milan, saw these public dramas as "a hotbed of infec-
tion" for the faithful.

The problem was that popular dramatizations, whether of Passion events or
something else, easily degenerated into licentiousness and rowdiness of the sort
traditionally associated with carnival celebrations. In discussing these sacred dramas as they were performed in Sicily prior to the Council of Trent, Pitrè (1969,
11–12) tells us:

> These dramas were meant to be sacred tragedies, but because they were poorly con-
> ceived and even more poorly performed they were sacred in name only . . . Our
> synods were all in accord with one another in deploring the scandalous things that
> occurred during these performances and in complaining that these spectacles,
> which had originally been staged out of true devotion, had come to provoke smiles
> and laughter from the crowds. These same synods also disapproved of the fact that
> sacred places [churches] were being used to stage ridiculous scenes and stories that

were apocryphal. And more than one synod found it unbearable that the annual commemoration of Christ's Passion was often distorted and profaned by the use of terrifying masks that were so disconcerting to pregnant women and so shocking to young children.

The preaching orders shared this concern over the improprieties associated with these dramas. In a guide written for the benefit of fellow missionaries, the Jesuit Antonio Baldinucci (1665–1717) specifically instructed missionaries to avoid the use of "animated" human actors in staging representations of the Passion, since "the proper decorum is never observed" in such productions (Baldinucci's remarks are cited in Di Palo 1992, 91–92). As a result, missionaries worked to develop new ways of representing the Passion visually that avoided the problems associated with these traditional dramas.

One strategy was to stage processions involving human actors but to regiment and structure the event in such a way that improvisation was unlikely. Often this meant using actors to stage "living pictures" of Passion events with no dialogue and little if any movement (apart from that involved in simply moving in procession). Nevertheless, the use of human actors meant that dangerous improvisations could not be eliminated entirely. At Marsala (Sicily) earlier in this century, for example, the actor portraying Christ in a Passion Week celebration became enraged by the blows he received from onlookers who were acting out the part of "the Jews," especially at the blows delivered by a man who was his longtime enemy. Losing his patience, this "Jesus" responded by killing his tormentor (Lancellotti 1951, 1:507).

A second, and safer, strategy was to eliminate human actors entirely in favor of statues. This is done by carrying in procession a series of statuary groups, called *misteri*, each representing a scene from the Passion.[8] Toschi (1955, 709–10) suggests that the use of such statues in a modern procession almost always means that the procession was initiated subsequent to the Council of Trent in order to avoid the improprieties associated with the use of human actors. In any event, processions involving misteri became increasingly commonplace during the seventeenth and eighteenth centuries.

At first, most misteri were made of wood, but as misteri processions prolif-

8. The term *mystery* has a number of meanings in the Roman Catholic tradition. During the Middle Ages, the label *mystery play* was routinely applied to any play with a biblical narrative. As well, the Rosary commemorates fifteen mysteries, or events from the life of Jesus and Mary; some of these events are derived from the New Testament, but others (like Mary's Assumption or Mary's being crowned Queen of Heaven) are derived from nonbiblical traditions. In connection with Holy Week processions, however, the term *mysteries* (*misteri*) always refers to statues that evoke events associated with the Passion of Christ.

erated other materials came to be used with increasing frequency. Many of the
misteri commissioned for use in Apulia during the late eighteenth and early nineteenth centuries, for instance, were made of *cartapesta* (Di Palo 1992, 93–94).[9]
Whatever material might be used, misteri were always statues and so clearly
different from the two-dimensional images associated with madonnine image
cults in the minds of onlookers.

In many communities, misteri processions were quite elaborate affairs. At
Palermo, the Dominicans sponsored a procession on Holy Tuesday involving
fifteen *bare* (platforms), each holding a Passion scene made of cartapesta (Pitrè
1969, 125). A similar procession, involving fifteen misteri made of cartapesta, was
staged at Caltanissetta (Sicily) on Holy Thursday (Lancellotti 1951, 1:509–10). At
Trapani (Sicily) no less than eighteen misteri, each consisting of several life-sized
wooden statues, were carried in procession on the afternoon of Good Friday
(Mondello 1882, 18–22). For Apulia, La Sorsa (1925, 217) reports that processions involving fifteen misteri were not uncommon. Some idea of just how complex these misteri could be is evident in the following listing (from Lancellotti
1951, 1:510) of the number of life-sized figures in each of the fifteen misteri in
the procession at Catanissetta (Sicily).

1. The Last Supper	13
2. Jesus praying in the garden	2
3. The capture of Jesus	5
4. The Sanhedrin	12
5. *Ecce homo*	7
6. The condemnation of Jesus	18
7. The first fall	3
8. The Cyrene	4
9. Veronica	5
10. Calvary	5
11. The deposition from the cross	9
12. The Pietà	4
13. The transport to the sepulchre	6
14. The sacred urn	2
15. The Desolata (Addolorata)	1

But even in those communities where the number of misteri was relatively
small, every attempt was made to encapsulate the entire sequence of the Passion.

9. *Cartapesta* is usually translated as papier-mâché. While cartapesta is similar to papier-mâché
in that it is a mixture of paper and glue, the final product is more solid and durable—and can be
formed into more subtle arrangements—than the material most North Americans think of as papier-
mâché.

Pitrè (1969, 125) suggests that the procession at Avola (Sicily) was typical of a misteri procession in smaller Sicilian communities:

> First came a representation of Jesus kneeling in the garden under the branches of an olive tree, among whose leaves was an angel offering him a chalice; then came Jesus bound to the column; then the ecce homo with his cloak and reed scepter; then Jesus carrying the cross; then the Crucifixion; then the Virgin at the foot of the cross, with her dead son laying across her knee; then a crystal case within which was arranged the dead body of Christ, and behind this a statue of one of the Marys, said to be Mary Magdalene, dressed in black.

Similarly, in the Good Friday procession at Molfeta (Apulia)—one of the best known of such processions in modern Italy—there are only five misteri: Jesus in the garden, the flagellation, the ecce homo, Jesus carrying the cross, and the body of the dead Christ (see de Marco 1975). Despite the small number of misteri in these two cases (at Avola and at Molfeta), the events depicted are distributed across the entire Passion narrative and so "tell" the Passion story in its entirety.

Sometimes, especially in smaller communities, it was not possible for local confraternities to obtain the elaborate misteri that were characteristic of the larger cities. In these cases, simpler strategies—still using the penitential procession as a model—were used to evoke the Passion narrative. One such strategy was to carry in procession (1) whatever relevant statues might be available (a statue of the dead Christ and the Addolorata, for instance) and (2) a series of symbols. These last were easily available objects similar to objects that had figured prominently in some Passion event.

Di Palo (1992, 28–29) reproduces an eighteenth-century print depicting a Good Friday procession at Cannobio (Apulia) with fourteen clerics, each carrying a single object. Not all the objects are clear enough to be identified, but those that can be identified include a crown of thorns, a hammer, a scourge, a nail, a rooster, a tunic, Veronica's veil, a column, a sponge, a lance, a ladder, and pinchers. The rooster represents the rooster that crowed after each of Peter's denials; the tunic, the one stripped from Christ; the column, that on which Christ was flagellated; the sponge, the one used to give Christ gall to drink; and so on. As with the misteri carried in procession in the larger cities, the number and variety of symbols that could (and can) be carried in procession were not standardized and so varied from community to community.[10]

In a twentieth-century procession, in Castelsardo (Sardinia) the following

10. I do not imply that the use of such symbols was absent in large cities. On the contrary, processions in these areas often involved both the use of misteri *and* symbols. My point is only that misteri were expensive and relatively difficult to obtain, whereas the objects used as symbols were usually

objects were carried (see Sassu 1981): a chalice, a glove, a rope, a chain, a column, a crown of thorns, a cross, a ladder, a hammer, pinchers, a sponge, and a lance.

Flagellation was also popularized by the penitential missions, and it too, like the visual representations of the Passion, came to be incorporated into Holy Week celebrations. There were flagellants, for instance, in the Holy Week processions initiated in Sicilian cities like Catania and Palermo during the 1590s (Naselli 1960, 323; Lancellotti 1951, 1:492), and over the course of the next century and a half, ritualized flagellation became a routine part of such processions throughout the South. In some cases these bloody processions were still being staged in the nineteenth century. In describing the Good Friday procession at Isnello (Sicily), for instance, Grisanti (1895, 80–81) tells us that

> On the morning of Good Friday, members of the Confraternity of the Assumption and other pious congregations march in procession, two abreast, from their oratories to the mother church. They each wear a penitential habit and walk barefoot; every man has a chain around his neck and a crown of thorns on his head. Several carry large crosses; others flagellate their shoulders with iron scourges . . . But it is what used to happen [at this festival] that causes us to shiver. Until the beginning of this century . . . several of these confraternity members . . . just after entering the mother church, uncovered their chests and began to beat themselves on the right and the left with *cardini* similar to those used to card wool and flax . . . The result was a truly pitiful spectacle. Although the wounds that a man opened on his chest using a cardine might not be very deep, they bled profusely. Not only did the blood end up all over the flagellant's chest and hands, it saturated his habit and often dripped onto the pavement as well.

Similar ceremonies were reported by a number of other nineteenth-century commentators (see Bragaglia 1888; Pellizari 1889a; 1889b; Venturi 1901).

Notwithstanding their strong emphasis upon visual imagery—and in particular upon blood—the Holy Week celebrations that emerged in the wake of the penitential missions in southern Italy did evoke the Passion narrative in the minds of onlookers. These popular devotions thus fostered a greater awareness of the dynamic narrative that defines the image of Christ in the official Catholic tradition—and in so doing brought popular and official Catholicism closer together. What sometimes happened, however, is that the link between these bloody rituals and the dynamic Christocentricism of the official Church became obscured over time, and so the achievement of the preaching orders is not always fully appreciated by modern scholars. With this in mind, I return to the bloody ritual described at the beginning of this chapter.

---

easily available. Thus processions using symbols only were likely to occur in smaller communities, with limited resources.

Back to Nocera Terinese

Italian commentators usually interpret the bloody rituals at Nocera Terinese in fairly philosophical terms. Both Lombardi Satriani (1981) and Cardini (1983, 154–56), for instance, see the Nocera Terinese ceremony as a way of ritualizing death, thereby bringing it under control and, in so doing, affirming life. While such an interpretation might be correct at some level, it is ahistorical and, as a result, causes us to overlook several important features of the ritual.

For example, in the case of the two-man teams involved in the Nocera Terinese flagellations, what image does the man in black—the vattente who flagellates his thighs—evoke in the mind of onlookers? Since he wears a crown of thorns, the most likely referent is Jesus Christ during that segment of the Passion narrative when he is scourged and crowned with thorns. But if the vattente is a representation of Christ, then who does the other man, the one in the red skirt, represent? He might be a Roman soldier accompanying Christ—except for the fact that he carries a cross. Just to muddle things even more, this man is called the ecce homo.

Ecce homo is the title given to images depicting Christ as he appeared before Pilate after the scourging and after having been dressed as a mock king (with a "crown" of thorns, a reed "scepter," and a robe) by Roman soldiers.[11] The ecce homo label would suggest that the man in red is also supposed to be an image of Christ. Consistent with this interpretation is the fact that, in the ceremony described by Borrello, this man looked like high-art depictions of the ecce homo; that is, he wore a crown of thorns, he held his wrists joined together, he held a simple reed (not a cross as he does today), and his body was marked with blood on the spots corresponding to Christ's wounds. The fact that he was supposed to be the ecce homo would also explain why this man was wrapped in a scarlet skirt, since scarlet is the color of the ecce homo's robe in many high-art depictions.[12]

In short, as recently as the turn of this century, the man in red was an unambiguous representation of the ecce homo as depicted in the art of Church elites. Over the past ninety years or so, many of the iconographic elements that defined him as the ecce homo have been lost or muted. The reed has become a cross, the

11. The Gospels of Matthew (27:27–31), Mark (15:16–20), and John (19:1–3) all suggest that Christ was scourged and then dressed as a mock king by Roman soldiers, who gave him a crown of thorns and a robe. Only Matthew mentions that Christ was given a reed as his sceptre. The *ecce homo* label derives from the account of this scene in John (19:5) which puts this phrase (which means "behold the man") into the mouth of Pilate when he displays Christ to the assembled crowd.

12. The robe placed on Christ by the Roman soldiers is described as purple in the Gospels of John (19:2) and Mark (15:17) and as scarlet in the Gospel of Matthew (27:28).

crown of thorns has vanished, and he is no longer marked by bloody spots corresponding to the wounds of Christ.[13]

In summary, then, it would appear that both members of the two-man teams at Nocera Terinese (the vattente and the man in red) were originally meant to be a visual representation of a bloody Christ, but at different points in the Passion narrative. The appearance (and actions) of the vattente were meant to call to mind Christ being flagellated, while the man in red was meant to evoke the image of Christ as the ecce homo. Such an interpretation helps us to understand one further (and as yet unmentioned) detail about these teams: the order in which they move. Borrello (1899) tells us that the man in black "tows" the man in red. Certainly, when I observed the ceremony it did appear that the vattente was leading rather than being led. I suggest that this is an attempt to translate a chronological sequence into something visual; that is, in the ceremonies at Nocera Terinese a figure depicting Christ being scourged is followed (literally) by a figure depicting the ecce homo, because in the Gospel narratives the second event follows the first, chronologically.

If we now consider all the images on display during the Nocera Terinese celebration, it becomes apparent that what we are seeing is a series of four images that, collectively, recapitulates the entire Passion narrative. There is (1) an image that depicts the scourging of Christ (the vattente); (2) an image that depicts Christ as the ecce homo (the man in red); (3) an image of the crucified Christ (the large crucifix carried in procession); and (4) an image of the dead Christ with his mother after he has been taken down from the cross (the statue of the Pietà, also carried in procession).

Viewed in this light, the bloody celebrations at Nocera Terinese, whatever their grand philosophical consequences, can be seen as just another application of the strategy popularized by the penitential missions, namely, to made use of striking visual images that capture the attention and the interest of ordinary Italian Catholics while simultaneously evoking the dynamic narrative that defines the Christ of the official Church.

The Addolorata

Holy Week celebrations aside, the penitential missions conducted after Trent popularized a second devotion that became an important part of the pop-

13. Although the men who play the ecce homo role at the Nocera Terinese celebrations are no longer marked with blood in any systematic way, as they were in Borello's day, a remnant of that earlier practice still persists. During the 1993 celebrations, for instance, I noticed that as the day proceeded at least one of the men in red had come to be marked on his chest with a patch of blood that likely came from the plain cork used by his partner.

ular Catholic tradition in Italy. This case is especially interesting because the history of this particular devotion is so often distorted in devotional accounts.

In Italian the word *addolorata* connotes "laden with sorrow," and so the best translation of the madonnine title Addolorata is probably The Sorrowing Madonna. In the view of the official Church, the Addolorata is the Virgin Mary who has suffered because of the things that have happened to her son, Jesus Christ. This intimate association of the Addolorata with the narrative that defines Christ makes her very much a dynamic madonna and, as pointed out in chap. 1, she is the only dynamic madonna who has ever come close to achieving the popularity of the static madonnas that dominate popular Catholicism in Italy.

In most devotional accounts (see Holweck 1913; Cattabiani 1988, 289–92), the history of the Addolorata cult begins in the mid-thirteenth century, when the seven founders of the Servite Order at Florence took the Sorrow of Mary as their principal devotion. Although initially the Servites took the Sorrow of Mary to mean only the sorrow she experienced at the Crucifixion, it became common during the fifteenth and sixteenth centuries for Catholic thinkers and theologians to list a series of events that had caused Mary to sorrow. By the middle of the sixteenth century, the most widely used version of this list included seven specific "sorrows." These were: Simeon's prophecy, the flight into Egypt, losing Christ in the Temple, meeting Christ on his way to Calvary, standing in front of the cross, taking Christ down from the cross, and the burial of Christ.

The iconography of the Addolorata is well-defined but not completely standardized. Most images depict her standing upright and wearing a black mourning dress. In the case of statues, her dress is usually a real dress (that is, a cloth garment fitted over the body of the statue), and it is often embroidered on the front with gold or silver brocade. Usually (again, in the case of statues) she is holding a white "crying towel" in one or both of her hands. In many cases, something sharp (a dagger, a sword, or a lance) pierces her breast in the area of her heart. This iconographical element supposedly derives from the statement made by Simeon to the Virgin Mary when the infant Jesus was brought to the temple in Jerusalem, namely, "and a sword will pierce through your own soul also, that thoughts of many hearts may be revealed" (Luke 2: 21–52). Many Addolorata images have seven objects (seven swords or seven daggers) piercing their breasts, an allusion to the Seven Sorrows of Mary. It is usual to depict the Addolorata standing alone, even in paintings. Paintings or frescoes showing the Addolorata staring at an empty cross, or at a cross draped only with a burial shroud, are common.

Some distinction should be drawn between an Addolorata and a Pietà. A Pietà is any image that depicts Mary near the body of Christ after it has been taken down from the cross. Sometimes Christ's body is resting in her lap, as in the famous Pietà by the young Michelangelo; sometimes Mary is looking upon his body as it lies nearby. Since no such scene is mentioned in any of the Gospels, artists have been free to locate it in more than one context. In some paintings, the Pietà is depicted as occurring at base of the cross at Golgotha; in others, it takes place on the way to the tomb or at the tomb itself. Some commentators use *Pianto* or *Compianto* (terms that refer to funeral laments) to describe images that other commentators call a Pietà. As the number of onlookers in a Pietà increases (say, as the number of apostles or disciples who are depicted standing next to Mary increases), it becomes more likely that a Pietà will be called a Lamentation.[14] From a purely intellectual point of view, a Pietà is a type of Addolorata. Generally, however, at least in the popular Catholic tradition, the term Addolorata is applied to an image that lacks the body of Christ.

Both Pietàs and Addoloratas appear in the paintings and other images created by elite artists during the Middle Ages, and the Servite tradition of the mid-thirteenth century did give a boost to theological discussions on the Sorrows of Mary. But none of this is evidence that either the Pietà or the Addolorata was the focus of a popular cult. In fact, it is not until the early 1600s that we encounter evidence that these madonnas were becoming the focus of popular cults, and even then the evidence suggests that this cult was popular mainly in urban areas and mainly in northern Italy. One of the earliest confraternities dedicated to the Addolorata, for instance, was established at Bologna only in 1598 and received the approval of Pope Clement VIII in 1604 (Di Palo 1992, 129).

Over the next few decades, a few images of this new madonna did become infused with supernatural power, but only a few. There were, for instance, four Pietàs and one Addolorata among the fifty miraculous images at Bologna in the early 1600s (see chap. 1). But in the smaller villages, especially in southern Italy, it took a lot longer for Addolorata/Pietà cults to become established. Looking at altar dedications in churches located in the Diocese of Naples (but outside the city of Naples), Russo (1984, 397–484) finds that a small but consistent number of altars (ranging from 3% to 6% of the total) were dedicated to the Pietà throughout the period 1598–1743. By contrast, there was not a single altar dedicated to the Addolorata prior to 1667, and altars dedicated to the Addolorata were rare prior to 1734. Russo concludes (419) that it was only in the mid-1700s that the Addolorata (as distinct from the Pietà) became the object of a popular cult in this region of Italy.

If we look at sanctuary dedications (as opposed to altar dedications, as in

---

14. For a discussion of the term *Pietà,* as well as for photographs of various paintings of the Pietà executed during the sixteenth century, see Vannugli (1991).

Table 3.1. Italian Sanctuaries Dedicated to the Addolorata and to delle Grazie or dei Miracoli Madonnas, by Century

Century Sanctuary was Established	Sanctuaries Dedicated to the Addolorata	Santuaries Dedicated to the Madonna delle Grazie or the Madonna dei Miracoli
Fourteenth or earlier	1	19
Fifteenth		25
Sixteenth		21
Seventeenth	1	14
Eighteenth	2	5
Nineteenth	9	5
Twentieth	2	
Unknown		10
Total	15	99

Source: Derived from Medica (1965).

Russo's study), the modern nature of the Addolorata cult is even more apparent. Of the 697 Marian sanctuaries in Italy described in Medica's (1965) guide, only fifteen (2%) are dedicated to the Addolorata. The oldest of these is the Servite sanctuary at Florence. Table 3.1 classifies all fifteen of these sanctuaries by century of establishment; the data show that it was only in the nineteenth century that a significant number of Addolorata sanctuaries were established. For comparison, table 3.1 also indicates the century established for the 99 sanctuaries in Medica dedicated to delle Grazie or dei Miracoli madonnas (these being the two most popular madonnine titles in Italy). As is evident, the vast majority of these sanctuaries were founded long before the nineteenth century.[15]

In summary then, while the idea of the Addolorata cult may have been invented by the Servites in the mid-1200s, it took a long time for this madonna to filter down to the popular level. Indeed, the Addolorata did not become the basis of a popular cult until after Trent. The proximate cause of the Addolorata's newfound popularity after Trent is not problematic: hers was one of the cults popularized by the preaching orders during the course of their missions. In his 1651 report, Paolucci (cited in Di Palo 1992, 30) says that Jesuit penitential processions "almost always included a statue of Our Lady clothed in a black mourning dress with a dagger piercing her chest." The fact that the Addolorata was popularized in local communities in the form of a statue carried in procession explains why

15. It would be a mistake to read the data in table 3.1 as indicating that over time Addolorata sanctuaries increased in popularity at the expense of delle Grazie or dei Miracoli sanctuaries. Regardless of when they were established, all the sanctuaries listed in table 3.1 are still extant, which means that in all time periods there were more delle Grazie or dei Miracoli sanctuaries than Addolorata sanctuaries.

she is far more likely than other popular madonnas to be encountered in the form of a statue rather than the more usual two-dimensional image (Russo 1984, 439–40). It also explains why so many of the Addolorata statues now found in southern Italian churches date from the seventeenth and eighteenth centuries, the period of most intense missionary activity in southern Italy (Di Palo 1992, 131).

Why missionary preachers promoted devotion to the Addolorata also seems unproblematic. First and foremost, the Addolorata is a madonna and thus bears a family resemblance to the plethora of madonnas that have always been popular with Italian Catholics. But unlike those traditional madonnas, the Addolorata is intimately associated with the narrative that defines the Christ of the official Church. Promoting devotion to the Addolorata was thus a way of co-opting the madonnine emphasis typical of popular Catholicism and using it to promote Christocentrism. Still, while all this might explain why the preaching orders promoted the Addolorata cult, it does not explain why the cult became popular (at least moderately popular) with Italian Catholics.

Prandi (1983, 174–78) suggests that the popularity of the Addolorata rests upon her appeal to Italian women. Italy has always been a strongly patriarchal society, in which women have been subjected to a wide range of restrictions. Honoring the Addolorata, Prandi argues, is a way of legitimating and coming to accept an unpleasant social status that cannot be effectively challenged.

Prandi's explanation sees the popularity of the Addolorata cults as deriving from the beliefs with which the official Church surrounds this madonna, notably the belief that she is Mary grieving for her son Jesus Christ. But to be a cause of the Addolorata's popularity, this official belief would first have had to be in place, and at least for Italy, there is simply no evidence that this was the case. The missionaries who went into the Italian countryside after Trent, remember, were at pains to document how ignorant the people were with respect to official Catholic beliefs. In this context of ignorance, the more likely scenario is that the Addolorata being promoted by the missionaries would have been seen initially as just another madonna. And madonnas, within the logic of popular Catholicism, were independent and powerful beings and only vaguely associated with the Mary of the official Church.

A second explanation of the Addolorata cult, and one that seems more sensitive to the logic of popular religion (if not popular Catholicism) in Italy, is offered by De Martino in his *Morte e pianto rituale* (1975).[16] For the most part,

16. De Martino's book is a classic work that is widely cited in the Italian-language literature on popular religion and folk practice in Italy. That it has never been translated into English is a measure of the gulf that exists between the Anglo-Saxon and the Italian scholarly communities in regard to the study of these topics. For an English-language overview of De Martino's work, see Saunders (1993).

De Martino's book is concerned with the historic development of the "pagan" Mediterranean funeral, from its roots in classical antiquity to its present forms in southern Italy. These funerals were led by women with dishevelled hair who sang or chanted stereotypical lamentations and whose ritualized movements were governed by set formulas. In the course of their lamentations, it was typical for these women to engage in a range of fairly extreme behaviors; for example, they swooned, pulled out their hair, tore their clothing, and lacerated their cheeks with their nails. At least until the recent past, these women were often professional mourners who were paid for their services. Whether paid or not, they were women who had a special association with death, usually because they had lost husbands or children.

In Italy, Church authorities have always waged a determined campaign against this sort of funeral. Corrain and Zampini's (1970) review of the statutes enacted by Church synods suggest that the Mediterranean funeral was targeted for suppression more often than any other folk practice. Moreover, these statutes leave no doubt as to which aspects of this sort of funeral were considered most offensive by Church authorities:

> A synod held at Lecce [Apulia] c. 1663 prohibits the use of *prefiche* [professional female mourners]. . . . An even older synod held in the diocese of Trani and Salpi [Apulia] prohibits: singing or reciting nocturnal offices and other prayers in the home of the deceased, disorganized lamentations in churches, the funeral chant, and the practice of women pulling out their hair and placing it on the chest of the deceased. The Synod of Castellaneta held in 1595 also talks of disorderly lamentations and of women who pull out their hair in order to put it on the deceased. (183)

> The synod held at Cagliari [Sardinia] in 1628 said that during the *veglia* [vigil] held around the body of the deceased at his or her home . . . there should not be present any of those women who utter lamentations, or scratch their faces, or pull out their hair, or commemorate the deceased with the sort of speech or other actions that provoke a strong lamentation from the assembled group. (313)

In other words, it was the extreme nature of the behaviors exhibited by the women at these funerals, that Church authorities found most objectionable. For De Martino (1975, 322–33) the reason for this is that such extreme displays of grief in the face of death seemed to negate a belief in the eventual resurrection of the body, which has always been central to official Catholic doctrine. He goes on to argue that the Addolorata cult was part of this campaign by the Church to stamp out the traditional Mediterranean funeral.

In the first instance, the popular appeal of the Addolorata lay precisely in the fact that in some ways the Addolorata seemed similar to the women who led the traditional lamentations. De Martino (341) notes that the Addolorata was often depicted as fainting, as being supported by bystanders, as striking her chest, and as scratching her cheeks, all of which are behaviors associated with the traditional funeral. It was also common for traditional mourners to clasp their hands to their chests (see Gigli 1893, 42), and this too, though unmentioned by De Martino, was an attribute given to the Addolorata. Di Palo (1992, 141) points out that this tendency to depict the Addolorata as having the characteristics of the traditional mourner occurred not just in mass-produced images intended for the general public but also in the paintings commissioned to be hung above church altars during the seventeenth and eighteenth centuries.

Unlike Prandi, then, De Martino suggests that the Addolorata was appealing in the first instance because of the popular connotations evoked by her images, not because of the official beliefs that surrounded her. Moreover, in locating the appeal of the Addolorata in her appearance, in what people saw when they looked at an Addolorata, De Martino's explanation takes cognizance of the strong emphasis upon the visual that permeates popular Catholicism in Italy.

Although the Addolorata's similarity to the women who led the traditional funeral may have been the initial basis of her popularity, De Martino goes on to argue that the Church then shaped the beliefs associated with the Addolorata in such a way as to undermine that type of funeral. This was done by stressing the Addolorata's calm acceptance of her suffering and by associating concrete images of the Addolorata with the textual Mary described in John (19: 25–27), who stands silently at the base of the cross. As a result, the Addolorata came eventually to be associated with an attitude in the face of death that was the very opposite of that associated with the women who led the traditional funeral.

De Martino's offers his analysis of the Addolorata cult only in passing and does not deal specifically with the Addolorata cult in the period after Trent. Nevertheless, that analysis can be used to provide insight into the ways in which the Addolorata cult came to be elaborated during this period.

The Incontro

One of the most popular rituals associated with the Addolorata has always been the *incontro* (meeting). An incontro is a special type of procession in which a statue of the Addolorata is brought into contact with a (separate) statue of Christ. Toschi (1955, 708) suggests that this "meeting" between Christ and the Addolorata is the one event commemorated more than any other during the processions staged throughout Italy during Holy Week. Sometimes an incontro takes place on Good Friday, and on these occasions the Addolorata meets an image of the suffering Christ or one of the crucified Christ. But the most common and most popular incontri are the ones that take place on Easter Sunday, when the Addolorata meets the resurrected Christ.

Lombardi Satriani (1979, 75) provides an account of the Easter Day incontro in Calabria (where it is usually called the Affruntata or the Confrunta):

> In a great many communities on Easter Sunday . . . some of the faithful follow a statue of the Madonna Addolorata as she winds her way through the streets enveloped in her dark sorrow. Others follow the statue of the resurrected Christ as it moves toward the incontro with his mother. Still others carry the statue of S. Giovanni, the beloved disciple. When all three processions are near to each other, the statue of St. Giovanni is made to run the distance from Christ to the Madonna so that he can tell her about the Resurrection. He has to run this course three times, because at first the Madonna remains doubtful. But eventually the Madonna runs toward her son and he toward her. At the moment of their meeting, the black mantle that makes her the Addolorata falls from her shoulders and she appears in an azure mantle. The resurrection has now been ratified.

The basic pattern here is repeated on Easter Day in communities throughout southern Italy, though the incidental details can vary from place to place. Pitrè's (1969, 128–35) account of the Easter incontro in Sicilian communities, for instance, indicates that the messenger who runs between the resurrected Christ and the Addolorata is sometimes S. Giovanni but sometimes S. Pietro, Mary Magdalene, or S. Michael the Archangel. Similarly, in some Sicilian communities the messengers run first from Christ to the Madonna, while in others they run from the Madonna to Christ. The "fall of the Addolorata's black mantle" element appears in almost all Easter day incontri, but her new mantle can be variously green, white, blue, and so on. In many communities doves or pigeons are released at the moment the Addolorata is transformed. Finally, in many instances the meeting of the Madonna and the resurrected Christ is marked by a *bacio* (kiss), when the madonna's head is brought into physical contact with the statue of her son.[17]

At first sight, the popularity of the Easter Day incontro is problematic. While the idea that the resurrected Christ appeared to Mary is mentioned in several works written during the Patristic period through to the Middle Ages, this theme never became popular with artistic elites in the way, say, that the Pietà became popular. Nor was this theme ever incorporated into a popular devotion in the period before Trent, in the way that the "Jesus meets his mother" element was incorporated into the Stations of the Cross (which emerged at the beginning of the sixteenth century). Furthermore, the association of the Addolorata and the Resurrection (an essentially joyous event) is not what you would expect given Prandi's

---

17. For detailed accounts of how the Easter Day incontro is staged in communities throughout southern Italy, see Di Palo (1992, 78–95); Pitrè (1969, 128–35); Lancelloti (1951, 2:17–34).

hypothesis that the appeal of the Addolorata rests upon her association with suffering.

Nevertheless, the Counter-Reformation Church promoted the Easter morning incontro at the very beginning of its campaign on behalf of the Addolorata cult, and it did become widely popular. As early as 1601, for instance, an Easter morning incontro was being celebrated in Palermo (Pitrè 1969, 128). In 1650 an especially elaborate Easter Day incontro was staged near the Trevi fountain at Rome. And by 1670 such an incontro was being staged regularly at Naples (Di Palo 1992, 95).

The value of De Martino's analysis is that it helps us to understand why the Easter Day incontro became so popular both with Church elites and the general public. The Mediterranean funeral, remember, was objectionable to Church elites because it seemed to deny the eventual resurrection of the body. A devotion that pairs the Addolorata with the resurrected Christ, as occurs in an Easter Day incontro, undermines that denial of bodily resurrection and so undermines the very thing that made the Mediterranean funeral objectionable. Given that Italian Catholics found the Addolorata appealing because she seemed similar to the traditional mourner, it would thus have been very much in the interests of the tridentine Church to promote this cult while shaping it in such a way as to associate the Addolorata with the Resurrection. This is just what Church authorities did by encouraging the Easter Day incontro.

Spanish and Italian Catholicisms

No one, as far as I know, has yet compared popular Catholicism in Italy with popular Catholicism in Spain in a systematic and precise way. Even so, it is commonplace for scholars to suggest, if only in passing, that these two variants of Catholicism are similar. In this regard, a consideration of the Addolorata cult in both Italy and Spain is useful because it illustrates how apparent similarities can mask important differences.

In his analysis of popular Catholicism in southern Spain, Mitchell (1990, 164–80) argues that southern Spain has long been characterized by nongrowth, lack of autonomy, and a consequent sense of utter hopelessness. In such a society, ordinary Catholics, both male and female, come to be believe that suffering brings redemption from sin. They will thus find appealing those cults that have suffering as their focus. For Mitchell, all this explains why Andalusian Catholics have been so attracted to rituals and devotions associated with the Passion of Christ (hence the title of his book, *Passional Culture*); and it is why they find the figure of the Addolorata, the suffering mother, so appealing.

Consistent with Mitchell's interpretation is the fact that the Addolorata cult in Spain came to be elaborated in a way that made Mary even more of a suffering figure than she was initially. The Addolorata, remember, is supposed to be Mary suffering as a result of the Passion of Christ. But there is another suffering madonna in Spain whose cult parallels that of the Addolorata; she is Nuestra Señora de la Soledad (Our Lady of Solitude). This is meant to be the Virgin Mary who went off into the desert after the death of Christ and lived a cloistered life in a community of nuns. Like the Addolorata, Nuestra Señora de la Soledad also wears a black dress, but in this case the dress is a nun's habit, not a mourning dress. Nuestra Señora de la Soledad suffered more than Christ, Mitchell (173–177) argues, because her suffering did not end with the Passion but continued throughout the remainder of her life. That Nuestra Señora de la Soledad is at least as popular in Spain (and in Hispanic North America; see Wroth 1991) as the Addolorata, and that the two madonnas are not always clearly distinguished (see Wroth 1982, 205) suggests that Mitchell is quite correct in seeing suffering as central to the appeal of both cults in the Spanish case.

But if we transpose Mitchell's analysis to southern Italy, it fails. Although local communities in southern Italy have historically been characterized by the same failure conditions (lack of autonomy, nongrowth, ego-stifling dependence) that Mitchell sees as shaping Andalusian Catholicism, we have already seen that the Addolorata cult developed differently in Italy. The suffering associated with the Addolorata did not become elaborated into anything resembling Nuestra Señora de la Soledad. True, the Madonna della Solitudine (Our Lady of Solitude) does appear here and here (not surprising, given the Spanish influence on Italy), but she is a relatively unimportant madonna. More important, the popularity of the Easter Day incontro between the Addolorata and the resurrected Christ suggests that, in southern Italy, the Addolorata cult came to be elaborated in just the opposite direction, that is, the Addolorata came more and more to be associated with precisely that happy emphasis upon the Resurrection that Mitchell sees as missing from Andalusian Catholicism.

In summary, then, while the Addolorata may have started out as meaning the same thing in both Italy and Spain, those meanings changed dramatically over time as the Addolorata cult was adapted—sometimes by ordinary Catholics, sometimes by Church authorities—to suit different concerns. Specifically, in Italy the Addolorata came to be associated with the Resurrection, on account of the Italian Church's campaign against the Mediterranean funeral. In Spain—for the reasons given by Mitchell—she came to be disassociated with the Resurrection. The general lesson to be learned here is that Catholic images or devotions that might appear the same to outsiders may nevertheless evoke quite different psychological associations in different national traditions. Although such a conclusion may seem banal, it is a conclusion often overlooked in the study of popular Catholicism.

Conclusion: A Tale of Two Images

By the mid-1400s there was a small church at Milan dedicated to the Madonna della Grazie. Like virtually all the other churches in Italy dedicated to della Grazie madonnas, this one contained a image that dispensed miraculous favors. In 1463, work was begun on a much larger church that would incorporate the original structure. In 1495, just a few years after this project was completed, civic authorities commissioned a local artist to paint a picture for the *cenàcolo* (dining hall) of the Dominican monastery attached to the new church. Unlike the original della Grazie image, this new image was to depict some suitably Christocentric theme, one that would turn the thoughts of the Dominican friars who ate there to that dynamic narrative that defines the Christ of the official Church. What the artist painted in the cenàcolo was the Last Supper. Since that artist happened to be Leonardo da Vinci, this particular rendering of the Last Supper has come to be *the* Last Supper for millions of Christians.

Every year, thousands of foreign tourists make a special trip to Milan to see da Vinci's *Last Supper*. Only a very few of those tourists take the time to visit the Church of the Madonna della Grazie itself, and those few give only a cursory glance at the miraculous image that still hangs in a side chapel. Virtually no tourists come to that chapel at night, after the cenàcolo has been closed to the public, to be with the Dominican friars who still lead prayers in front of that miraculous image.

This case, involving the two images associated with S. Maria delle Grazie at Milan, seems particularly useful for thinking about the study of religious images in Italy. Despite the immense importance attributed to Leonardo's *Last Supper* by art historians (and the publics who have acceded to their judgments), it has never been seen as an image that dispenses favors, has never become the object of cultic devotion, and has never become associated with religious celebrations that attract the widespread participation of Italian Catholics. Generally, these same things could be said of almost all the works of high art found in the churches and museums of Italy. This means that the artistic works for which Italy is best known—even though these works often have a religious theme and even though they have generated (and are still generating) a large scholarly literature—have little to do with the images that are important to the experience of popular Catholicism in Italy.

To appreciate the role of images to Italian Catholicism, we have to set aside the scholarly tomes and weighty articles written by art historians and look instead at images that art historians rarely discuss in detail. We must start, as was done in chapter 1, with those images that have come to be invested with supernatural power. These are the images that lie at the core of popular Catholicism in Italy. As we saw in chapter 2, the Church has generally been quite willing to legitimate the cults that form around these miraculous images by giving the behaviors associated with these cults an official meaning, which has little to do with the meanings held by ordinary Catholics. For the Church to have done otherwise would have been to risk alienating its constituency, and that is something the Italian Church has always avoided.

What I have tried to demonstrate in this chapter is that one particular segment of the Church, namely the preaching orders, has been far less passive in confronting the popular appeal of image cults. On the contrary, the preaching orders, in order to create new forms of devotion, have consistently acted to merge the dynamic emphasis that defines the Christ of the official Church with the visual or static emphasis associated with image cults. The result has been a series of images (including the representations of the Passion, which appear in Holy Week processions, and the near-omnipresent statues of the Addolorata) that have achieved a certain measure of popularity among Italian Catholics.

Popularity here does not means that these new dynamic images came to be invested with supernatural power. That, in fact, happened only rarely. What it means, rather, is that these new images came to be confronted and seen on a regular basis and in contexts that the people invested with religious significance. As a result, Italian Catholics became more and more familiar with the Christ of the official Church. This Christ never came close to displacing the madonnas whose images dispensed favors within the logic of popular Catholicism, nor the patron saints who protected local communities, but he did become a more powerful player in the Italian Catholic pantheon.

The veiled image of the Madonna dell'Impruneta being carried in procession (detail). From Giovanni Casotti, *Memorie istoriche della Miraculosa immagine di Maria Vergine dell'Impruneta* (Florence, 1714). Courtesy, the Bancroft Library.

Facade of the sanctuary of the Madonna dell'Impruneta (near Florence) as it appears today. This madonna was one of most powerful veiled madonnas in Italy.

Rural *edicola* just outside Gimigliano (Calabria).

OPPOSITE PAGE

Edicola at Naples. The niche at the top contains a
Madonna con Bambino; the niche at the bottom
holds a diorama of the souls in Purgatory.

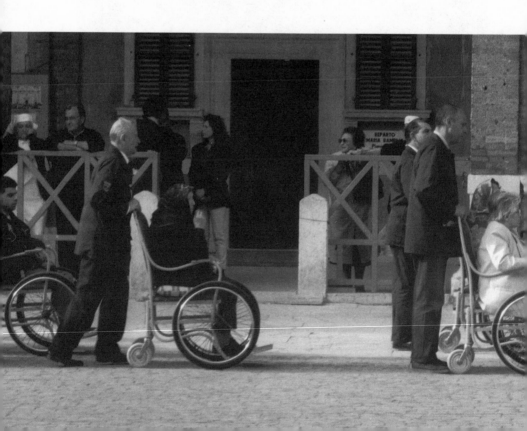

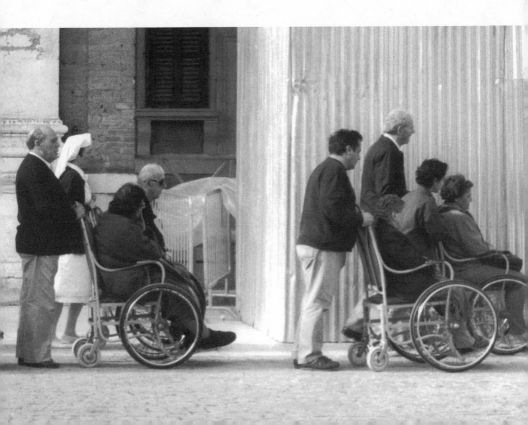

Holy Saturday procession at Nocera Terinese (Calabria).
The Pietà is being carried through the streets.

Flagellation during Holy Saturday celebration at Nocera Terinese (Calabria): the
ecce homo (right) and the *vattente* (left). Note the amount of blood (really blood,
wine, and vinegar) that has accumulated on the steps of the church as a result of
repeated flagellations on this spot.

Facade, Church of Purgatory at Bitonto
(Apulia), depicting the souls-in-a-sea-of-flames
motif associated with the official Purgatory cult.

OPPOSITE PAGE

Sanctuary of the *morti della fosetta*
at Ghedi (Lombardy).

Edicola honoring the beheaded souls at Palermo (Sicily).

OPPOSITE PAGE

The sanctuary of the Madonna di Pompei at Pompei (Campania). Established in the late nineteenth century, this is now one of the three most popular madonnine sanctuaries in Italy.

Perimeter entrance to the area containing the Catacombs of S. Callisto; the catacombs generally were heavily exploited during the Counter-Reformation to satisfy the increased demand for saintly relics.

Chapter Four

The Cult of the Dead, I

J ust outside the entrance to the modern cemetery at Ghedi, in Lombardy, there is a small church hardly distinguishable in its appearance from the thousands of other churches found in small Italian communities. Even so, for more than four centuries this particular church has attracted pilgrims from all over Lombardy. They have come to honor the *morti della fossetta* (the dead from the common grave).[1] The dead, in this case, are victims of the plague that struck Ghedi (and northern and central Italy generally) in 1630–31.

According to the sanctuary's origin legend, nearly half the population of Ghedi died during that plague, and corpses piled up so fast they had to be buried in three large trenches rather than in individual graves.[2] Sometime during the late 1660s, the bones of these plague victims were dug up and deposited in a pit under a small oratory. The pit was left open so that the bones could be seen and touched. These bones quickly become the focus of a popular cult, and in 1683 the oratory was enlarged to accommodate the increasing number of devotees who came to honor the morti della fossetta. By the end of the century, the oratory had its own priest (and so was now, properly speaking, a church), and a confraternity was meeting on its second floor.

At first, Church authorities were unconcerned about the Ghedi cult. They did insist that the oratory be dedicated officially to Saint Rocco, a saint often asso-

---

1. This account of the sanctuary at Ghedi is based upon Chiara (1988) and Riolfi (1980), as well as upon information I gathered at the sanctuary in August 1993.

2. That half the population of Ghedi might have died from the plague is entirely plausible. Del Panta (1980, 151) estimates that the plague of 1630–31 killed about 28 percent of the population in northern and central Italy. In particular areas, mortality was much higher. At Milan, not distant from Ghedi, the number of deaths caused by this plague accounted for approximately 46 percent of the population (ibid., 160).

ciated with plague victims.[3] Even so, they were quite willing to acknowledge the more popular *dei morti* designation. In his report of a pastoral visit to Ghedi in 1683, for instance, Bishop Bartolemeo Gradenigo said that he had visited "the oratory of the Confraternity of S. Rocco, called the oratory of the dead" and that "everything in the oratory was found to be well arranged and in order" (cited in Chiara 1988, 89). But very shortly, the Church's attitude toward the Ghedi cult soured. That the dead were being venerated was not problematic; a church dedicated to the suffering souls in Purgatory in the castle at Ghedi had a strong popular following and the full support of diocesan authorities. What was problematic about the Church of S. Rocco was that its faithful were praying *to* the dead, not *for* the dead. Riolfi's (1980, 384) analysis of testamentary bequests made to the sanctuary demonstrates that in many cases these bequests were being made in gratitude for favors received. In other words, by 1700 the morti della fossetta had become favor-dispensing beings, just like saints and madonnas.

In 1708 the local bishop decreed that the pit containing the bones be covered and that no votive candles be lit inside the church except on November 2, the day designated to commemorate "all the faithful dead." This same injunction was issued by a different bishop in 1722 (suggesting, of course, that the first injunction had not been followed). These restrictions had little effect. In 1770 a Jansenist critic would complain that membership in the Confraternity of the Dead at Ghedi had reached something like 23,000 members, a number he found "frightening" (Piccaluga and Signorotto 1983, 246). Partly, the hierarchy's campaign against the Ghedi cult was undermined by the fact that the cult had the support of the local clergy. Writing to his bishop in 1756, for instance, the archpriest at Ghedi would describe the oratory as "the famous oratory of the Dead, vulgarly called the oratory of the Common Grave" and would characterize it as "a place of great devotion and one that attracts many people" (cited in Chiara 1988, 126). A measure of the cult's popularity during this period can be seen in the fact that most of the ex-voto extant at the Ghedi sanctuary are dated or datable to the second half of the eighteenth century (Riolfi 1980, 785).

It was only during the nineteenth century that the Church finally came to terms with morti della fossetta. Attempts to suppress the cult ceased, and references to the sanctuary in official reports were either neutral or positive. The nearby church dedicated to the souls in Purgatory, the more "official" cult of the dead, was quietly allowed to cease functioning. In 1868 the local archpriest for

3. S. Rocco was routinely invoked for protection against the plague in both France and Italy. For an account of the S. Rocco cult in Brescia and the surrounding region (which includes Ghedi), see Fappani (1980, 371–78).

the very first time used the term *sanctuary* in a report made to diocesan authorities (Riolfi 1980, 385) and, in doing so, gave ex post facto legitimacy to the pilgrimages made to this church over the past two centuries.

By the 1920s every blank space on the walls inside the Ghedi sanctuary was
covered with painted ex-voto in testimony to the continuing power of the dead
who were venerated there. Some of those ex-voto depicted a madonna, some
depicted Saint Rocco, and some the souls in Purgatory in a sea of flames. What
was depicted most often, however, were the skulls associated with the morti della
fossetta.

The Church's attitude toward the Ghedi cult changed once again in 1940,
when the local bishop noted that the pit in front of the altar in the Ghedi sanctuary was sealed only with a glass plate, which could be (and presumably was)
unveiled so that devotees could look at the skulls below. He decreed that this
pozzetto (literally, "small well"; but "hole in the ground" better conveys the dis-
paragement that the bishop intended) be sealed with a locked metal plate and
that it no longer be opened for any reason whatsoever. He also decreed that all
ex-voto be removed from inside the church.

Today, about two hundred painted ex-voto are still conserved at the Ghedi
sanctuary, but they are in a small room off the sacristy and cannot be seen from
the main body of the church.[4] The rest are presumably still stored in some diocesan basement. The pit in front of the altar is sealed with a locked iron plate sten-
ciled with the word OSSARIO. Even so, every so often the custodian still finds an
ex-voto that has been left in the church anonymously (although today an ex-voto
is more likely to be a pair of gold earrings than a painting). It is also common for
devotees to enter the church, kneel next to the iron plate, touch the plate with
their hand, and then bring that hand up to their lips.[5] For some Italian Catholics,
the morti della fossetta continue to have power.

The cult organized around the morti della fossetta at Ghedi demonstrates
especially clearly something that must be kept firmly in mind by anyone who
wants to understand the cult of the dead in Italy: *the* cult of the dead really consists of two analytically separate cults. One of these is organized around the souls
in Purgatory, who are usually depicted as naked human beings swimming in a sea
of flames. But there is a second cult of the dead in Italy, of which the cult at Ghedi

4. The collection of painted ex-voto at Ghedi is one of the very best that I have ever seen in an
Italian church. It is well worth a visit by those who find themselves in the Milan-Brescia area, and we
can only hope that the ex-voto removed in 1940 are being stored under appropriate conditions.
5. This gesture—touching a sacred object with your hand and then bringing that hand to your
lips—is one of the most common gestures encountered in Italian sanctuaries.

is by no means the only instance, and it is always organized around pits or other burial chambers that contain the skeletal remains of a relatively large number of people who have experienced sudden death. The dominant iconographical image associated with this second cult is a skull or a collection of skulls. Although it would be tempting to see one of these two cults as an official tradition promoted by the Church and the other as a popular tradition inherited from some distant pagan past, such an interpretation is not consonant with the historical record.

As we shall see in this chapter and the next, although the origins of these two cults are different, this difference has nothing to do with a Christian-pagan contrast. On the contrary, both cults have impeccably Catholic origins, and both became widely popular around the same time. In considering these two cults it is best (for reasons that will become clear as we proceed) to set aside the skeletal dead cult found at Ghedi and elsewhere and to consider first the cult organized around the souls in Purgatory. We return to the cult of the skeletal dead in the next chapter.

The Souls in Purgatory

In a well-known book, Le Goff (1983) argues that the modern notion of Purgatory was "born" in the late twelfth century, mainly in the works of Parisian scholars and French Cistercian monks. Le Goff does not see the "birth of Purgatory" as resulting from the slow cumulative development of an idea over time. On the contrary he sees it as resulting from a more revolutionary process in which certain preexisting beliefs about the Christian afterlife were shaped and changed by a new *mentalité*, a new way of thinking, that emerged during the eleventh through the thirteenth centuries as the result of changed social conditions. In elucidating this thesis, Le Goff presents a dizzying array of literary evidence drawn from the works of European theologians and clerics whose lives span the first twelve centuries of the Christian era.

By the eleventh century, Le Goff argues, certain ideas about the afterlife had come to be widely accepted among Christian thinkers. First, it was generally agreed that some souls underwent a "purgative fire" after death. Though authorities differed on whether the fully righteous (who were destined for Heaven) or grievous sinners (who were destined for Hell) would experience this fire, most agreed that it would be experienced by the intermediate group, Christians who had sinned but not grievously. For this group, the purgative experience would be painful, but they would ultimately get to Heaven. Another belief current by the eleventh century was that the souls of the dead could be helped by those still living. The various methods for helping the dead were called *suffrages,* and the most commonly mentioned suffrages were prayers, the giving of alms, and—most of all—the celebration of special masses.

Other aspects of the afterlife experience were more ambiguous. Le Goff notes that there was no clear consensus about when souls would experience the purgative fire. Generally, most thinkers believed that it would take place sometime between death and the resurrection of the body, though some thought the experience of painful purgation might begin during a person's life on Earth and some that it would occur entirely on the Day of Judgment. There was even less of a clear idea as to where this fire would be experienced. Gregory the Great (d. 604) had suggested that sinners would experience purgation here on Earth. In the centuries following Gregory, a number of writers described "journeys to the other world," in which purgation was experienced in a nether region near Hell, on a mountaintop, in a Sicilian volcano, and so on. But most writers, Le Goff argues, were vague on the issue of location.

What happened in the twelfth and thirteenth centuries, Le Goff suggests, was that new ways of thinking came into being. One of these new ways of thinking involved a new set of legal principles. Justice came increasingly to be defined as an abstract ideal that should be tailored to particular circumstances, and feudal lords, kings, and bishops were claiming the right to administer this new form of justice over larger and larger jurisdictions. These new legal principles were carried over to discussions of sin and penance, so that theologians now paid more attention to a sinner's intent when deciding upon the seriousness of the sin involved and the penance required in reparation for that sin. Increased contact between Europe and the rest of the world also influenced European thought, Le Goff argues, by inducing an increased concern for topographical exactness.

Finally, changes in the structure of society itself influenced the way people thought. Le Goff argues that the new feudal patterns that had begun to take shape around the eleventh century produced an image of society that represented a revival of the old Indo-European model. This was a tripartite model in which society consisted of those who pray (the clergy), those who fight (the nobles), and those who work (the peasants). This tripartite model undercut the binary patterns that had previously dominated European thought (including the sharp distinction between Heaven and Hell) in favor of trinary patterns.

All these things—an emphasis upon new forms of justice that were both individualized and more expansive, upon topographical precision, upon trinary schemes—were brought to bear upon preexisting notions of purgatorial fire. The result was a "third place," located between Heaven and Hell, where sinners would suffer for their sins for varying periods of time before being released. The precise amount of time each sinner spent there would be determined by the nature of his or her sins and by the suffrages offered by the living. This new place required a new name, and so the adjective *purgatorial* was converted to *Purgatory*, a word that first appeared in the late twelfth century.

Le Goff's analysis has been relatively well received. A few commentators push back by a few decades the first appearance of the word *purgatory*; others argue that the idea of purgatory as a place existed before the word was invented and or at least that ideas about purgation after death were better developed prior to the twelfth century than Le Goff is willing to admit (Edwards 1985). Nevertheless, everyone agrees that Le Goff's is a masterful analysis. The most serious criticisms have been leveled not at what he says but at what he leaves out.

Although Le Goff supplies a near-endless stream of passages written over a thousand-year period that mention something about purgation after death, in almost all these cases the author of the passage related purgation after death to some other concern, and these other concerns are regularly ignored by Le Goff (Bernstein 1984, 182). Other commentators criticize Le Goff for ignoring the crucial role that indulgences played in fostering a popular awareness of Purgatory (Lerner 1982). McGuire (1989) takes Le Goff to task for failing to appreciate the diversity of views on the afterlife that emerged in the late twelfth century. For McGuire, the great change in the thirteenth century was really a "drawing closer" of the natural and supernatural worlds, by which he means that people felt a greater solidarity with the dead and were more likely to see themselves as interacting with the dead. A belief in Purgatory—a place filled with souls who could be helped by the living—was one consequence of this drawing closer of the two worlds, but not the only consequence. The thirteenth century, McGuire points out, also saw a renewed belief in the old idea of an "earthly paradise" as an alternative to Heaven as well as an increase in the number of simple ghosts who came back to talk to the living.

What Le Goff's critics have generally not challenged is the relationship he posits between the emerging doctrine of Purgatory and folkloric tradition. In his introduction, Le Goff (14) tells us that, in the twelfth century, folkloric traditions exerted an especially strong influence on the thought of intellectual elites and that much of what came to be called Purgatory was in fact borrowed from these popular traditions. This claim, that Purgatory reflects the merger of popular tradition with elitist thought, has generally been accepted at face value and is typically seen to be one of Le Goff's most important insights. Davis (1985, 32), for instance, though critical of Le Goff in other regards, nonetheless suggests that

Le Goff "has taken an idea from the confines of theology and 'popular religion' and shown brilliantly that it is at the crossroads of cultural development." Other reviewers make much the same comment (see Boswell 1985; Peter 1987).

Bernstein (1984, 181–82), as far as I can tell, is the only one who points out that Le Goff simply does not do what he promises to do in his introduction. Although Le Goff occasionally talks of Purgatory as a "demand of the masses," most of his discussion, Bernstein notes, is concerned with showing just the opposite, namely, that Purgatory was an idea formulated by learned elites and then subsequently "sent down" to the masses. The whole point of Le Goff's chapter on the "social victory" of Purgatory, for example, is to demonstrate how the preaching orders, the Dominicans and Franciscans in particular, lifted the idea of Purgatory from the realm of abstract theological discussion and promoted an awareness of the idea among the ordinary people to whom they ministered.

The fact is that Le Goff provides no concrete evidence whatsoever to support his contention that folkloric traditions shaped the view of Purgatory that emerged in the twelfth century. Why, then, his introductory claim that it did? The answer, I think, lies in the logic of his theoretical argument. If the changed societal conditions of the twelfth century produced a new mentalité, then this must have been a mentalité that was widely shared. If, for instance, the emerging feudal order predisposed people toward trinary thinking (as Le Goff argues), then the members of each group in this new order (the nobles, the clergy, and the peasants) should have been so predisposed. If this trinary emphasis, along with other aspects of the new mentalité, gave birth to Purgatory, then it had to have been a birth shaped by all levels of society. Not to believe that the peasant classes shared the mentalité that gave birth to Purgatory would undercut the theoretical core of Le Goff's argument.

The fact that the logic of Le Goff's theoretical argument requires the belief that Purgatory be derived from both popular and elite sources probably explains why Le Goff is so cavalier and dismissive about patterns and data that suggest that devotion to the souls in Purgatory was not especially popular with ordinary Catholics for several centuries after the concept first emerged. Le Goff (1983, 293) cites Philippe Ariès as saying that a belief in Purgatory became popular only in the seventeenth century[6] and then dismisses Ariès's claim by pointing to a single study suggesting that at Toulouse (France) bequests for masses of suffrage declined dur-

6. Somewhat surprisingly, given his concern for bibliographic precision in the rest of his work, Le Goff does not provide a citation to the work in which Ariès makes this claim. In fact, it is Ariès (1981, 465–67).

ing the eighteenth century. Quite apart from the fact that a single study proves very little, the study cited by Le Goff is concerned with a decline in devotion to the souls in Purgatory, not with the origins of that devotion. Similarly, Le Goff (289) notes in passing that visual representations of Purgatory on church walls were rare for several centuries following the "birth of Purgatory" in the late twelfth century. He then dismisses this as being the result of "conservatism in iconography" or maybe "the difficulty of representing an intermediary, temporary, ephemeral world." Another possibility, which he ignores, is that Purgatory was a plaything of only the intellectual elites and not the focus of popular devotion.

There seems little doubt that the idea of Purgatory did develop sometime around 1200. The question of just when the souls in Purgatory became the object of widespread cultic devotion, however, is more open.

The Purgatory Cult in Italy

Prior to 1800 (or thereabouts) confraternities played a key role in structuring those organized religious events that were most meaningful to Italian Catholics. The titles chosen by these confraternities, especially in the case of those confraternities established in response to lay initiatives, can reasonably be taken as providing some information on popular religious preferences (or at least on male preferences, since the membership of most of these organizations was exclusively or predominantly male).[7] What the analysis of confraternity titles in Italy suggests is that the souls in Purgatory did not become the focus of a popular cult until the seventeenth century.

In his study of confraternities at Rome, for instance, Paglia (1982, 66) points out that the very first confraternity explicitly associated with the souls in Purgatory, the Confraternity of S. Maria del Suffragio, was founded in 1594 and that the second, La compagnia di Gesù e Maria e di S. Giuseppe per le Anime più bisognose del Purgatorio, was not founded until 1687. Even more revealing, I think, are the results of Grendi's (1976) study of confraternities at Genoa. Grendi provides two lists: the first identifies the 131 confraternities that existed at Genoa in the period 1480–1582, and the second identifies the 124 confraternities that were subsequently established at Genoa between 1582 and 1796. Not a single one of the confraternities on the first list is associated with the souls in Purgatory; by contrast, the second list mentions four Purgatory confraternities, all established

---

7. For a fuller discussion of the pros and cons of using confraternity titles to assess the popularity of various cults, see Carroll (1992, 19–23).

in the seventeenth century. Two of these, dedicated to the *anime purganti*, were founded about 1626 and 1677. The other two, dedicated to the *agonizzanti*, were founded about 1642 and 1646.[8]

Russo (1984, 300–40) provides data on the confraternities existing in twenty-nine villages in Campania at various times between 1598 and 1754.[9] That data indicate that, during 1598–1600, the number of confraternities dedicated to the souls in Purgatory was zero (of thirty-one confraternities in all); during 1601–66, there was one (of sixty-eight); during 1667–1734, there were four (of sixty-seven); and during 1735–54, there were again four (of seventy-five). In short, only a few confraternities dedicated to Purgatory were established in the late sixteenth century; they emerged in significant numbers only during the seventeenth century.

Russo also finds that images depicting the souls in Purgatory were rarely mentioned in pastoral visits prior to the seventeenth century. In addition, she finds that there were no altars dedicated to these souls in the period 1598–1666 and that such altars began to appear only in the period 1667–1754 (483). Further evidence linking the emergence of the souls in Purgatory cult to the seventeenth century can be gleaned from the study of church dedications. D'Engenio (1623) describes the 298 churches then existing in Naples, and not a single one was dedicated to the souls in Purgatory, either directly or indirectly. By contrast, the following century and a half saw the establishment of 3 Purgatory churches at Naples (these churches are discussed in detail at the end of the next chapter).

Sometimes the Purgatory churches that emerged during the seventeenth century were new churches, but quite often they were simply older churches that had been renamed. Granata's (1766, 331) account of one particular rededication in the Archdiocese of Capua (Campania) is typical of what happened all over Italy:

> About a century ago, there was a small church in this district . . . dedicated to S. Maria della Misericordia. Early in the reign of Archbishop Gian Antonio Melzi, several devout members of the *contrada* . . . starting collecting alms, which they used to maintain both the church itself and a chaplain who said a daily mass in support of the souls in Purgatory . . . As the amount of alms collected increased, so did the number of daily masses. [As a result] the name of the church was changed from S. Maria della Misericordia to S. Maria del Suffragio, although the more popular designation was S. Maria del Purgatorio.

8. The two *agonizzanti* confraternities may have been dedicated to the cult of the dead described in the next section, which are often called by this term.
9. Russo was specifically concerned with the twenty-nine villages that lay outside Naples and its immediate environs but within the Diocese of Naples.

Giovanni Antonio Melzi was archbishop of Capua in the period 1661–87, which means the association of this particular church with the souls in Purgatory likely occurred in the 1660s.

Thus several different lines of evidence suggest that a widely popular cult dedicated to Purgatory emerged in Italy only during the seventeenth century. That presents a puzzle. Assuming that Le Goff is correct in asserting that Purgatory was born in the twelfth century and that the preaching orders had been trying to foster a popular awareness of this Purgatory from the thirteenth century forward, why did it take so long for a cult organized around it to become popular? The obvious answer is that the emergence of a truly popular cult required more than just the idea of Purgatory and the transmission of that idea to the public. In retrospect it seems clear that there were in fact three additional developments that contributed to the eventual emergence of a popular cult centered on the souls in Purgatory.

The Papacy and Indulgences for the Dead

Shaffern (1993) points out that by the thirteenth and fourteenth centuries (and possibly even earlier) some preachers were suggesting to European publics that indulgences earned by the living could be applied to the dead. Although this view was strongly opposed by some theologians, it was just as strongly endorsed by many others, including Thomas Aquinas. In the end, Shaffern argues, attitudes toward indulgences for the dead were determined less by theological arguments than by preexisting attitudes toward papal authority. Extending indulgences to the souls in Purgatory was, in effect, a way of extending papal authority into the afterlife. This is why those groups (like the Dominicans) who favored an increase in papal authority tended to favor indulgences for the dead and why those groups (like the Franciscans) who opposed an increase in papal power opposed such indulgences.

The debate over indulgences for the dead was resolved only during the fifteenth century, and here again the critical issue was papal authority. In the decades that followed the Council of Constance (1414–18) and the end of the Great Schism, several popes sought to extend and consolidate the temporal power of the papacy over ever larger areas of central Italy (a process discussed in detail by Prodi 1968; 1987). Given the papacy's efforts to extend its temporal power, it is hardly surprising that it would also favor an extension of papal power into the afterlife by means of indulgences for the dead. That is precisely what it did: the very first verifiable papal indulgence for the dead was in fact granted by Sixtus IV in 1476 (Shaffern 1993, 380).

Almost immediately, the preaching orders incorporated these newly legitimated indulgences for the dead into their campaign to promote the doctrine of
Purgatory, a campaign that (if Le Goff is right) had been ongoing since the thirteenth century. The Carmelites were the first off the mark in this regard, and their
efforts gave rise to what would in time become one of the most popular Purgatory-related devotions in the Catholic world, the Sabbatine Privilege.

According to pious tradition, the Virgin Mary appeared to Pope John XXII
on March 3, 1322, and made a promise to the members of the Carmelite order
that, if any of those who had faithfully observed the rule of the order ended up in
Purgatory, then she herself would descend into Purgatory on the first Saturday
after their death and release them into Heaven. Mary also asked that John XXII
confirm this Sabbatine (from Saturday) Privilege in a papal bull, which he supposedly did. Catholic commentators now agree that this story reflects a tradition
that developed in the late 1400s, more than a century and a half later than the
events it purports to describe. The very first mention of the Sabbatine Privilege
occurs in a work written by a Carmelite author shortly before his death in 1483
(Zimmerman 1904, 333). In other words, the Carmelites first began to promote
a belief in the Sabbatine Privilege during precisely the same period—the late
fifteenth century—when the papacy was beginning to authorize indulgences for
the dead. In fact, the Sabbatine Privilege is a type of indulgence for the dead. Certainly, later commentaries called it an indulgence, and it does benefit the dead in
Purgatory. What makes it special is only that the living person who earns the
indulgence is the same person who, after death, benefits.

The Carmelite campaign on behalf of the Sabbatine Privilege intensified
during the sixteenth century. The Carmelite leadership in Italy, for instance, lob-
bied various popes for a reconfirmation of the supposed bull of John XXII. No
pope actually said that John XXII's bull existed, but Clement VII did confirm the
Sabbatine Privilege in 1528, and Gregory XIII did the same thing in 1577. Moreover, the records of Carmelite General Chapters, held in Italy during the early sixteenth century (see ibid., 335–36), indicate that the Carmelites were raising
money to ensure that these papal decrees would be publicized.

The Carmelite campaign on behalf of the Sabbatine Privilege did much to
make the idea of Purgatory more meaningful to ordinary Catholics. But by the
mid-1500s, there was another reason why Italian Catholics were coming to think
more about Purgatory.

Purgatory as a Rejection of Protestantism

In his account of the sacred and profane events that had occurred in Bergamo, Calvi (1677, 116) reproduces a diary entry written by someone living at Bergamo in 1529:

> On this date [Sept. 28, 1529] the entire city was horrified to find that posters had been put up everywhere that denigrated the pure Catholic faith. These posters challenged the Supreme Pontiff, the truth of Purgatory, sacred images, and the invocation of saints. They were found above the entrance to the Duomo, at the Citadel, at porta pinta, in Pignolo, and in Borgo S. Leonardo. The city was greatly shaken by these impious acts.

The diarist goes on to place the blame for these posters on "heretical" soldiers stationed in Bergamo.

The quoted passage indicates that as far as ordinary Catholics were concerned, even in the earliest stages of the Reformation, the rejection of Purgatory was one of the most salient features of Protestantism, on a par with its rejection of papal authority and image cults. In fact, the doctrine of Purgatory was attacked by all the reformers, including Luther and Calvin. But this gave the Church a weapon in the struggle against Protestantism: it meant that promoting the doctrine of Purgatory became a way of distancing Italian Catholics from the Protestant heresies of the North. As a result, the Reformation, like the earlier papal legitimation of indulgences for the dead, induced an intensification of the campaign by the preaching orders on behalf of Purgatory. Evidence of this intensified campaign can be found in the records of the Council of Trent.

In its earliest sessions, the council had paid very little attention to the matter of Purgatory. In the statement on justification (passed in 1547) there was a passing reference to Purgatory as a place in which the "debt of temporal punishment" occasioned by sin could be discharged, and the statement on the mass (passed in 1562) twice reaffirmed the legitimacy and value of saying masses for the dead. But the escalating attack on Purgatory by the reformers, Calvin in particular, required a stronger reaffirmation. During the twenty-fifth and last session of the council, which met on December 3 and 4, 1563, a Decree Concerning Purgatory was passed. Le Goff's remarks concerning the "social victory of Purgatory" notwithstanding, the decree makes no mention whatsoever of Purgatory as a place of fire; it simply identifies Purgatory as a place where souls are "detained" and where they can be aided by the suffrages of the faithful, notably by the celebration of the mass.

The decree then goes on to talk, very obliquely, of some problems associated with Purgatory, and this section is worth quoting at length:

> The holy council commands the bishops that they strive diligently to the end that the sound doctrine of purgatory, transmitted by the Fathers and sacred councils, be believed and maintained by the faithful of Christ, and be everywhere taught and preached. The more difficult and subtle questions, however, and those that do not make for edification and from which there is for the most part no increase in piety, are to be excluded from popular instruction to uneducated people. Likewise, things that are uncertain or that have the appearance of falsehood they shall not permit to be made known publicly and discussed. But those things that tend to a certain kind of curiosity and superstition, or that savour of filthy lucre, they shall prohibit as scandals and stumblingblocks. (Schroeder 1950, 214)

If one reads through Trent's decree on Purgatory carefully, it seems concerned not with lay practice at all but rather with those who preach to the laity about Purgatory. The implication, then, is that a great many preachers were discussing Purgatory with the people. What the decree also suggests, however, is that some of these preachers were saying something about Purgatory that was inappropriate. What? Here again a consideration of the known history of the Sabbatine Privilege is useful.

In 1609, Spanish authorities at Lisbon sought to ban the publication of the Sabbatine Privilege. The matter was referred to Rome, and an investigation followed. The final decree issued by the Sacred Congregation did not specifically endorse the Sabbatine Privilege, though it did say that the Carmelites could preach its contents. That decree was very precise, however, in specifying what the contents of the Sabbatine Privilege were: "It is lawful for the Carmelite fathers to preach that Christians may piously believe . . . that the Blessed Virgin Mary will assist by her continual intercessions, suffrages, and merits, and also by her special protection, particularly on the Saturday after their death (which day has been consecrated to her by the Church), the souls of such brothers and members of the Confraternity who . . . " and here follows a list of conditions that had to be fulfilled to obtain this privilege (Zimmerman 1904, 337–38). These conditions include having (1) lived a chaste life, (2) worn the habit (scapular) of the order, (3) recited the Little Office of the Virgin or fasted, and (4) abstained from meat on Wednesdays and Saturdays.

Missing from this characterization of the Sabbatine Privilege is the idea that Mary would leave Heaven and descend into Purgatory, a central element in the original Carmelite tradition. In fact, another part of this same decree (cited in Hilgers 1913, 290) specifically forbids paintings and other images that show Mary descending into Purgatory. Presumably, the concern here was doctrinal: to portray Mary as being in Purgatory would suggest (or so Church elites feared) that she would be seen as having sinned during her life, since in the normal course of things the only dead who entered Purgatory were sinners. This ban on painting the Virgin in Purgatory would be reaffirmed during the Counter-Reformation by episcopal directives that specified that the paintings hung above altars dedicated to the souls in Purgatory must locate these souls in Purgatory and the associated flames in a space directly below the Virgin (Piccaluga and Signorotto 1983, 236). In short, Mary and the suffering souls could be associated (within the context of the same devotion or painting) as long as the distinction between them was kept and nothing was done to diminish Mary's stature.

By the early seventeenth century, then, virtually all the important preaching orders of the Counter-Reformation Church were actively promoting devotions involving Purgatory. The Carmelites, of course, promoted the Sabbatine Privilege. The Jesuits in Rome began the practice of sounding an Angelus bell each evening to obtain the liberation of souls from Purgatory (Paglia 1982, 66). During their missions in northern Italy in the late seventeenth and early eighteenth centuries, Jesuit preachers not only encouraged the practice of applying indulgences to the dead but also collected alms to subsidize masses and other public devotions for the dead (Vismara Chiappa 1982, 820). Jesuit missionaries were usually forbidden to collect alms as a matter of policy; that they would set aside this policy in this case (and only in this case) is a measure of their commitment to the cult of the dead. At Naples, by the mid-1600s, the Theatines were regularly preaching on the subject of Purgatory (De Maio 1983, 178). And by the early eighteenth century, Franciscan preachers were actively encouraging people to apply indulgences, through the Stations of the Cross (a favorite Franciscan devotion) to the souls in Purgatory (Signorotto 1983b, 146).

Souls in Purgatory Who Help the Living

It would be a mistake to see the publics targeted in this campaign to promote a cult of the dead as passive, simply absorbing or rejecting what was passed down from on high. On the contrary, we must ask, now, why these publics found such a cult appealing, given the logic of their own variant of Catholicism. For Boswell (1985) the basis of Purgatory's popular appeal is obvious: the idea offers the living some reassurance about their dead relatives. After all, opines Boswell (41), "What comfort would be offered in a religion that suggested that for any sin not properly amended a beloved relative would spend eternity in Hell? Kindly old Uncle Joe, who was so good to me? Just because he didn't have time to make up for that one indiscretion?" Purgatory, for Boswell, became popular because it allowed people to believe that middle-range sinners (like their Uncle Joe) would eventually get to Heaven.

Setting aside the smarmy folksiness of Boswell's presentation, his explanation fails on at least two counts. First, as regards Italy, it does not explain why
devotion to the dead failed to become a truly popular devotion until the seventeenth century. Didn't people in earlier centuries care about their Uncle Joes?
Second, and more important, Boswell's account ignores the logic of popular Catholicism in Italy, in which saints and madonnas are all-important and the relationship that exists between any particular saint or madonna and some particular Catholic is a relationship of strict reciprocity. Saints and madonnas use their
power to benefit ordinary Catholics in a concrete way, either by securing protection from danger or by granting some supernatural favor; these ordinary Catholics, in turn, provide saints and madonnas with public veneration. What this suggests is that the souls in Purgatory could never have become the object of a truly
popular cult in Italy until they acquired the same power that made saints and
madonnas popular: the power to help the living. In other words, it was not
because the idea of Purgatory helped ease anxieties about dead Uncle Joe that
made the cult popular; the dead could become a popular focus only when they
acquired the power to help the living in some material way.

The suggestion that devotion to the dead flows from less-than-altruistic
motives is hardly novel. Writing in the early 1700s, Neapolitan historian Pietro
Giannone (1676–1748) made much the same point:

> What could be more holy and meritorious than to pray for the souls of the dead,
> and by means of the sacrifice of the mass to ask that they be liberated from the pain
> they suffer in Purgatory? And yet superstition and dangerous delusions can creep
> into this devotion, with the result that bringing relief to the souls of the dead causes
> the souls of the living to be lost. It is one thing, for instance, to work for the salva-
> tion of your soul by holding it aloof from the corrupting influences of the century
> or by providing some relief to widows and the oppressed. But how many people go
> beyond this and come to believe that building sumptuous chapels, multiplying
> masses, and having masses said at every altar is a way of settling all their accounts
> with God? (Giannone 1821, 193)

Clearly, the Catholics whose behavior is being criticized by Giannone were less
interested in benefiting the dead (dear old Uncle Joe included) than in benefiting
themselves. Toward the end of his book, Le Goff (1983, 356) makes a passing reference to this issue by saying that "at some point these souls [in Purgatory] begin
to acquire not only merit but the power to transfer their merit to the living, to
return service for service, to give assistance to men and women on earth." Unfortunately, he—along with most other historians who discuss Purgatory—offers
no precise suggestion as to just when or how the dead acquired such power.

As a matter of abstract theological discussion, the issue of whether the dead could help the living was addressed almost immediately after Purgatory's birth. Thomas Aquinas (d. 1274), one of the most influential of all medieval (and Italian) theologians, addressed the issue and concluded that they could not, on account of the intense pain they were suffering. Aquinas's view was shared by most other medieval theologians. More important, it was a view shared by the preachers trying to promote the doctrine of Purgatory with the public. That medieval preachers did not attribute the "power to help the living" to the dead is most easily established by considering the *exempla* they used in their sermons.

Exempla are stories told in the course of a sermon or religious treatise to convey some point of doctrine or theology, using situations or settings familiar to the audience. Using a variety of medieval texts, Tubach (1969) summarizes 5,400 different exempla, 31 of which mention Purgatory. Several of these exempla are about souls in Purgatory who appear to the living to solicit prayers or masses. Other exempla are about souls who appear to the living in order to describe their sufferings in Purgatory or to indicate the particular sins that caused them to end up there. In still other exempla living people are granted a vision of Purgatory and its horrors (usually in a dream). But in none of these medieval exempla are the dead portrayed as being able to grant material favors to the living.

Zarri (1982) examines the ways in which the dead in Purgatory are portrayed in exempla and other vernacular texts published in the early sixteenth century. Two images emerge. On the one hand, the dead are often bothersome ghosts who return to hector the living into offering suffrages. A religious treatise published by an Augustinian at Venice in 1521, for instance, tells the story of a man at Vicenza who earns a plenary indulgence for himself by visiting the Franciscan church at San Lorenzo. A few days later, strange noises begin to be heard in his house during the daylight hours. Eventually, his wife concludes that the noises are being made by dead relatives—her mother and a daughter—who are asking for suffrages. The wife earns a plenary indulgence for these two souls, and the noises stop.

In other stories mentioned by Zarri, a soul inhabits a house at Andria in order to serve out his time in Purgatory; a soul at Pavia comes to a couple at night and removes their bedcovers in order to get their attention; at Mantova the souls of three noblemen confined to a palazzo attract the attention of a cobbler and convince him to make a pilgrimage to a sanctuary to obtain suffrages for them; and so on. In short, the dead are often portrayed as bothersome ghosts with no more powers than the other bothersome ghosts that regularly appear in Italian folk tradition. The one big difference between the souls in Purgatory and other bothersome ghosts is that these souls can be mollified if the living engage in certain religious practices (sponsoring a mass, visiting a particular sanctuary, etc.) and apply the benefits of these practices to the dead.

A second type of soul from Purgatory who emerges in the stories and texts considered by Zarri (477–78) appears to the living to ask for suffrages and to provide the living with moral instruction, that is, with warnings about the sinful activities that cause someone to end up in Purgatory. There is an exchange evident here, in the sense that these souls are exchanging moral instruction for suffrages. Still, in such an exchange the the dead are little more than surrogates for the official Church. What they do not offer are supernatural favors that benefit the material well-being of the living and that are the sort of favors that Italian Catholics routinely sought from saints and madonnas. In short, Zarri's analysis suggests that as late as the early sixteenth century the dead in Purgatory were still not generally credited with the ability to grant material favors.

On the other hand, there is no doubt that a definite shift in opinion on this issue took place as that century progressed. For example, in 1529 a friar named Tomaso Spagnolo (Thomas the Spaniard) preached a number of sermons in the Duomo at Milan and recommended a variety of devotions that might safeguard Milan from an impending invasion. A contemporary commentator indicates that Tomaso was "an eloquent speaker and a subtle theologian" and that in one of these sermons "he exhorted the citizenry to pray for the dead, saying that good things have happened as a result of their help" (Burigozzo 1842, 486, 491). The implication, in other words, is that the dead could help the living.

Toward the end of the sixteenth century, the eminent Jesuit theologian Roberto Bellarmino (d. 1621) said much the same thing. Bellarmino considered the issue of whether the dead could help the living and explicitly rejected Aquinas's argument, arguing that because the dead were closer to God than the living they could intercede with him on behalf of the living. Bellarmino stopped short of affirming as a certainty that prayers to the dead were useful to the living, since he felt that the dead would usually be ignorant of our particular situations. Nevertheless, he did think that it was probable.[10] Alphonso Liguori (d. 1787), another influential Italian theologian, would eventually eliminate the one objection that had made Bellarmino hold back, by suggesting that God would make the particulars of our earthly condition known to the dead.

All Catholic theologians who discuss the powers of the dead take care to cast their discussion in proper tridentine terms, saying that these souls (like Mary and

---

10. For a more detailed consideration of Bellarmino's views, see Hanna (1913, 579–80); Signorotto (1983, 309–11).

the saints) have no independent power and can only intercede with God on our behalf. Furthermore, even though Church authorities permitted the faithful to believe that the dead can intercede on behalf of the living, this was never proclaimed a doctrine of the Church, something that modern Catholic commentators are still quick to point out whenever Purgatory is discussed (see, for instance, Peter 1987). Nevertheless, it seems clear that, in the sixteenth century, there was a decided shift in theological thinking away from Aquinas's definitive view that the souls in Purgatory can be of no use to the living and toward a more diffuse formulation that suggests that the dead can help the living.

In his account of the parables that Sicilians used to justify their actions, Guastella (1968, 46–47) provides a good example of just how thoroughly the dead came to be seen as "the same" as saints and madonnas. In a parable about a man brought home sick from the fields, we are told:

> Poor Biagio lay sick for eight days. The doctor came and went, and Biagio was no better off than he was at the beginning. . . . His poor wife no longer knew what saint she should appeal to. She had already lit a lamp for the ecce homo [an image of Christ] at Spaccaforno, had already promised earrings to the Madonna Addolorata at Modica and plaits of her hair to the S. Sebastiano at Melilli, something that she would bring to him walking with bare feet. She had also promised to make a *trapasso* [a type of long fast] on the vigil of S. Giovanni and to pay for a mass in support of the holy souls of Purgatory. But as luck would have it, neither the Madonna nor the saints nor the blessed souls [le anime benedette] seemed in the mood to accept these offers.

The wife turns next to various folk remedies and then, when these fail, to a witch, who discovers that the husband had been put under a spell by a woman to whom he had at one time been engaged.

At one level this parable is interesting because it suggests that Italian Catholics were eminently pragmatic individuals who turned to a variety of sources—Christ, madonnas, saints, medical doctors, supernatural beings, folk healers, witches—in search of what might relieve suffering and pain. But it also illustrates the point made above: in the minds of Italian Catholics, the dead were supernatural beings who, like saints and madonnas, could be petitioned for miraculous favors.

In the end, then, we arrive at a solution to the question of why a widely popular cult centered on the suffering souls in Purgatory emerged during the late-sixteenth and early-seventeenth centuries. That efforts to promote a belief in Purgatory had been intensifying over the preceding two centuries is only part of the answer. Mainly, the cult grew during this period because it was not until then that these dead souls acquired the power to grant favors. On the other hand, the elaboration of the cult did not stop here. As it increased in popularity and became more familiar it came to be shaped and modified even further by the logic of popular Catholicism, leading to still more popular beliefs about the dead in Purgatory.

Two Types of Soul in Purgatory

Purgatory is mentioned several times in the decrees of the Jansenist Synod of Pistoia held in 1786 (see chap. 1). Generally, the decrees endorse all those doctrines about Purgatory that had been promulgated at the Council of Trent. Nevertheless, they also argue that various errors had arisen in connection with the idea of Purgatory. They specifically reject, for instance, the idea that indulgences could be applied to the dead (see Stella 1986, 152–53), even though this had come to be endorsed by the papacy. But perhaps the most interesting of Pistoia's remarks relating to Purgatory appear in its decree on public prayer (ibid., 203–11).

That decree acknowledges that Purgatory is a place in which the dead who died in a state of grace would suffer for their sins in order to satisfy divine justice. It also recognizes that there is "an intimate union based on charity between the members of the Church on Earth [la Chiesa militante] and the members of the Church in Purgatory [la Chiesa purgante]." For this reason, it says, prayers for the dead should be sung in every parish on the first Sunday of each month, and a mass for the dead should be said in the same parish the following morning. Still, although the decree endorses the view that the dead can be helped by prayers and masses, it goes on to say:

> But it seems that various and pernicious errors are spreading among the people in this regard. One such error is the belief that Purgatory contains some abandoned souls [anime abbandonate], for whom nobody prays and who for this reason might be deprived of relief . . . Therefore this Holy Synod exhorts pastors to make every effort to prudently instruct the people, making it clear to them that ideas like these are entirely contrary to the doctrine of the Church. (Ibid., 204)

From the point of view of official doctrine, the suggestion that certain of the dead are abandoned and deprived of relief makes no sense whatsoever. After all, the whole point of Purgatory in the logic of the official Church is that it is a place of temporary punishment for souls destined to eventually get to Heaven. On the other hand, if we assume that Italian Catholics were actively working to make sense of Purgatory in light of both the logic of popular Catholicism and the logic of official doctrine, then other possibilities emerge.

Among the living, an indulgence is always associated with a single, identifiable person, that is, the person who does what is required to earn the indulgence.

Generalizing this to the dead leads to the conclusion that indulgences for the dead, to be effective, must also be associated with an identifiable individual. I grant that this does not follow as a strictly logical consequence. Furthermore, it is definitely not the view of the official Church, which allows indulgences and other suffrages to be applied to the dead collectively, with the understanding that individual dead souls will partake of the benefits involved in proportion to the merit acquired in life.

Strict logic and official doctrine aside, ordinary Catholics did (I argue) generalize the one-to-one relationship that characterizes indulgences for the living and so did come to believe that an indulgence—or any other suffrage—for the dead could be effective only for some particular soul in Purgatory. But this in turn suggests that, if the identity of some particular soul in Purgatory were forgotten, then that soul could never be targeted for indulgences or other suffrages and so would never be released from Purgatory. As alien and as nonsensical as this conclusion might seem to theologians of the official Church, it falls naturally from the cluster of popular Purgatory-related beliefs that we have been examining here. In the end, then, Italian Catholics came to believe that the souls in Purgatory fell into two categories: those who were remembered by the living, who could be targeted for indulgences or other suffrages, and whose stay in Purgatory was temporary; and those who had been forgotten by the living, who could not be targeted for indulgences or other suffrages, and who were destined to remain forever in Purgatory. Those in this latter category are the abandoned souls mentioned in the Pistoian decree.

Although very little has been written about these abandoned souls in Purgatory, the material that is available suggests that they were seen to be especially powerful. During his fieldwork in a neighborhood in modern Naples, Pardo (1981) found that his informants clearly distinguished between the souls of their dead relatives, whose stay in Purgatory will be temporary because of the suffrages offered by the living, and "the forgotten souls, those that no one paid attention to" and who were thereby consigned to Purgatory for "eternity" (105). He also finds that the forgotten souls are seen as being especially powerful, and it is to these souls that Neapolitan Catholics turn for favors and protection.

Here again, however, we encounter a puzzle. The logic of popular Catholicism dictates that favors from supernatural beings are obtained in exchange for something else. In the case of saints and madonnas, that "something else" is veneration; in the case of the remembered souls in Purgatory, it consists of indulgences or other suffrages that lead to their release. But what is that "something else" in the case of the forgotten souls, who (precisely because they are forgotten) cannot be targeted for indulgences or prayers and so will never be released?

Neapolitan Catholics responded to this puzzle by creating a category that has no counterpart in official theology: in daily life, relief from the discomforts of excessive heat is obtained by drinking something cool; so Neapolitan Catholics have come to believe that the suffrages on behalf of the forgotten souls in Purgatory can provide those souls with a *refrisco* (ibid., 105), that is, a temporary relief from the terrible thirst they suffer as a result of the purgatorial fire in which they are immersed.

The emergence of concepts like the abandoned souls of Purgatory and the refrisco was the result of applying the logic of popular Catholicism to the ideas about Purgatory being handed down by Church elites. But creative processes, by their nature, lead to variation, not standardization. In the usual case, the application of the reciprocal exchange model to the dead has resulted in cults in which the dead were seen to exchange favors in return for relief from suffering (either permanent or temporary). In a few cases, however, the application of this model has produced cults in which the dead grant favors in exchange for the very thing that saints and madonnas want: veneration.

Mummies

Well into the 1960s there was a mummified nude body on display (in a crystal urn) in the Church of S. Cresenzio at Bonito (Campania); the cult that developed around this body is described by Rossi (1969, 49–54).[11] The pious belief is that this body was found during a restoration of the pavement in the church sometime in the distant (and unspecified) past and that it belonged to someone called Vincenzo Camuso. There are no clear and unambiguous traditions that tell us who Vincenzo Camuso was, when he died, or even how people came to know his name. But in death there is no question about his identity: to the Italian Catholics who made pilgrimages to the church at Bonito, Vincenzo Camuso was a soul in Purgatory.

There are many stories in oral circulation describing how Vincenzo Camuso has appeared to the living. In one of these stories he is said to have visited a patient in a hospital in the guise of a doctor and performed a surgical operation that healed the patient, much to amazement of the real doctors who saw the patient the next day. In other stories, he appears to patients and heals them without making use of the operation for which they were admitted to the hospital. Most of the stories about Vincenzo Camuso suggest simply that he grants favors when called

11. Unless otherwise noted, all the descriptive material dealing with the Vincenzo Camuso cult in this section is taken from Rossi's account.

upon. Sometimes these favors are for the living, sometimes they are for his fellow dead. One devotee reports that Vincenzo Camuso showed her a vision of the souls of Purgatory amid flames and told her they were suffering because she had forgotten to say prayers on their behalf the night before (53).

And what does Vincenzo Camuso ask in return? The same thing demanded by saints and madonnas: veneration. He seems particularly concerned with obtaining oil for the lamps that burn in his chapel, and several people who have found themselves in front of the church at night report hearing his voice asking for oil. One devotee provided this account of her attitude toward Vincenzo Camuso:

> If you have faith and ask him for a favor, he will grant you that favor. Don't you see that he has more gold [ex-voto] than S. Antonio? He shows himself to people who had never heard of him before, saying "I am Vincenzo Camuso and I can be found at Bonito." . . . In 1955, he cured my son of pleurisy. I had invoked him because he is a holy soul of Purgatory [un'anima santa del Purgatorio]. We invoke him just as we invoke the Madonna di Pompei. . . . One day when I was passing by [the church] he called to me and said: "Come here—tell your husband that he should bring me a bit of oil." He wanted oil for his lamp. I brought the oil and I heard his voice . . . he told me many sweet things. He has given sight [to the blind]. Women invoke him when they give birth. If someone has to make a long journey, they invoke him, saying, "My Vincenzo Camuso, accompany me." (52).

Notice that, although this woman explicitly suggests that Vincenzo Camuso has the same powers normally associated with particularly powerful saints and madonnas (like S. Antonio and the Madonna di Pompei), she goes out of her way to make it clear that he is a soul in Purgatory and not a saint. His devotees seem to make this disclaimer as a matter of course. Rossi (51) tells of meeting several women during a pilgrimage to the madonnine sanctuary at Montevergine "who said to me that even if Vincenzo Camuso was not a saint but only a soul in Purgatory he was [still] more of a miracle worker than them all, even the Madonna di Montevergine."

Conclusion

The idea of Purgatory may have been born in the twelfth century, but it took several centuries for it to become the object of a popular cult. The emergence of this cult had to await several developments, but the most important of these was the ability of the dead to dispense favors, just as saints and madonnas do. Once they had that power (in the popular imagination), it became possible to apply to the cult of the dead the logic of the reciprocal exchange model so central to popular

Catholicism in Italy. This in turn led to the creation of categories, like the abandoned souls and the refrisco, and even to the occasional supernatural being, like Vincenzo Camuso (the soul in Purgatory who thinks he's a saint) that have no place in the ideology of the tridentine Church. Even so, for Italian Catholics these things formed part of worldview that was logically consistent and useful.

The creative impulse that led Italian Catholics to merge the logic of popular Catholicism with ideas about Purgatory handed down from on high did not evaporate with the establishment of the cult of the dead. On the contrary, once established the cult of the dead merged with other popular traditions, and the result was a second cult of the dead. This second cult was dedicated to the skeletal dead, mentioned at the beginning of this chapter, and it is time to tell their story.

Chapter Five

The Cult of the Dead, II

The sanctuary at Ghedi, described at the beginning of the last chapter, is only one of many cults in Lombardy whose physical focus is a large collection of bones belonging to people who died en masse from plague or some other contagious disease. Each May, for instance, the inhabitants at Cerveno make a procession to the ruins of a chapel dedicated to S. Rocco in order to honor the people who died in an epidemic and who are supposedly buried nearby (Sordi 1983). A cult dedicated to the *morti del colera* (the colera dead) exists at Lozio and another dedicated to the *morti della selva* (the dead of the woods) at Drugolo (Riolfi 1980, 380). Similarly, in the region around Brescia alone there are over three dozen edicole associated with the victims of some epidemic, and many of these were still the focus of cultic activity well into this century (Fappani 1980, 366–69).

Whereas the souls in Purgatory are usually represented as human beings swimming in a sea of flames, the imagery most associated with the dead who lie at the center of the cults just mentioned is dominated by skulls and bones. At Ghedi, for instance, the marble tablet above the sanctuary's entrance is surmounted by a carved skull.[1] More important, the painted ex-voto at Ghedi make it clear that devotees once prayed in front of real skulls. Several of these ex-voto depict people praying before an edicola crammed full with a dozen or so skulls; others depict devotees praying before a table or altar on which a number of skulls have been arrayed. Edicole crammed with human skulls appear as well in painted ex-voto found at other sanctuaries in Lombardy (see for instance plates 206 and 209 in Barbi 1980).

1. It seems likely that this marble tablet and its associated skull were part of the original oratory to the dead at Ghedi; chap. 4.

In some cases, the skulls associated with these cults were used in ritual activities that went beyond simple prayer. For instance, during periods of drought or when the Livrio river threatened to overflow its banks, people living in the Valtellina (Lombardy) took the skulls kept in the Church of S. Salvatore down to the river to be washed. They believed, Marchesi (1898, 422) tells us, that such washing of the skulls would propitiate the souls of those who had died and so end the drought or the threat of flooding. Given the emphasis upon human skulls in both the iconography and the devotional practices associated with the cults discussed here, it is convenient to call the souls at the center of these cults the skeletal dead.

Skeletal imagery per se, of course, is not alien to the official Catholic tradition. The triumph of death has long been an iconographic theme favored by artistic elites in Catholic Europe, and it became especially popular during the early modern period (see Strocchia 1992, 31).[2] In a typical Triumph of Death depiction, a skeletal figure representing Death—and usually holding a scythe or an hourglass—is seen in the midst of people from widely varying social strata. Often there are several skeletal figures, each wearing some distinctive item (a crown, a bishop's mitre, etc.) representative of a specific social category. The underlying message in these images is that death is inevitable and strikes down both rich and poor. Such a message is obviously supportive of official Catholic doctrine, which has always emphasized that social inequalities in this world are less important than whether a person's soul ends up in Heaven or Hell in the next. But the skeletons who appear in high-art depictions of the triumph of death have little or nothing to do with the skeletal dead. The human skulls in the burial pits and edicole at Ghedi and elsewhere were the objects of cultic activity; that is, people prayed *to* these skulls, and the purpose of these prayers was to secure some benefit in this world, not the next.

Some of the earliest references to skeletal dead cults in Lombardy can be found in Donato Calvi's (1613–78) three-volume work, published in 1676–77: *Almanac of the Memorable Events, Both Sacred and Profane, that have Occurred in Bergamo, its Diocese, and Territory, from Their Beginnings to the Current Year.* Calvi's work has always been a valuable source of information about Catholic practice in Lombardy, for two reasons. First, he cites extensively from published and unpublished documents that are now lost or at least not easily accessible; and second, he often reports on his own observations of religious practice in the Bergamo region during the mid-1600s.

Under his entry for May 7, Calvi (1676b, 34–35) describes a "chapel of the

2. For a good example of these triumph-of-death depictions, see the frontispiece to Strocchia (1992).

dead" built in 1670 near the Church of S. Antonio dell'Ospedale maggiore at Bergamo. The event was sufficiently important, he tells us, that the first mass in the new chapel was celebrated by the vicar-general of the archdiocese.[3] A painting of the souls in Purgatory being liberated by angels was later installed in this new chapel, which suggests that Church authorities were trying to associate the devotion there with the souls-in-Purgatory cult. But Calvi ends his account with an extract from his personal diary, which suggests that the skeletal dead, not the souls in Purgatory, were at the center of the popular devotion that gave rise to this church: "Up until the preceding year [1669], a small chapel without an altar had stood on this same spot. A large number of skulls and bones belonging to the dead [gran numero di calvarie, & ossa de Defonti] were exposed to view within that small chapel, and it was the alms gathered here that subsequently gave rise to the building of the new oratory" (35). What Calvi is describing is almost certainly one of those edicole crammed with skulls depicted on so many ex-voto in Lombardy.

Calvi mentions several other churches associated (or likely associated) with devotion to the skeletal dead. Thus, he tells us (1677, 352) that in 1660 the bones of several thousand plague dead were removed from a cemetery outside Bergamo and installed in a specially prepared place at the nearby Church of S. Maria in Val Verde. Calvi is quite clear that it was the "piety of the citizens" that persuaded the Augustinians who controlled this cemetery to allow the bones to be removed. The cult, in short, arose spontaneously among ordinary Catholics and was only subsequently legitimized by Church authorities. Similarly, in 1665 the bones of several thousand plague dead were removed from a field at San Fermo, outside Bergamo, and carried in procession to the nearby Church of S. Mauritio. Here again, Calvi (1676a, 407) is careful to note that this occurred in response to the "piety of the faithful." Finally, Calvi (ibid., 444) says that the faithful regularly traveled to the country Church of S. Martino, near Vignano, where a great number of people struck down by plague had been buried.

All of the skeletal dead cults identified by Calvi, at least in those cases where he supplies the year involved, emerged in the latter half of the seventeenth century, the same period during which the Ghedi cult emerged. This is true even though in other contexts Calvi routinely describes events that date from the fifteenth and sixteenth centuries.

3. A vicar-general was the highest official in an archdiocese, apart from the archbishop himself, and assumed many of the archbishop's administrative duties.

Devotion to the Beheaded Souls in Sicily

Interestingly, Lombardy was not the only region of Italy that saw the emergence of skeletal dead cults during the latter half of the seventeenth century.[4] They also existed in Sicily, although here the bones and skulls that lay at the center of these cults belonged to executed criminals, not plague victims.

Pitrè (1978c, 4–25) reports that devotion to *le anime dei corpi decollati* (the souls of beheaded bodies) was one of the most widespread religious devotions in Sicily. The "beheaded" in this case were people executed by state authorities whose bones and skulls were subsequently deposited at special churches. According to Pitrè, the beheaded souls were usually distinguished from the *anime sante*, the souls in Purgatory, but the distinction was fluid, and the two groups were often merged in the popular imagination.

In Pitrè's account, the earliest of the churches dedicated to the beheaded souls was the Church of the Agonizzanti, established at Palermo in 1630. The most famous of the churches associated with the beheaded souls cult, however, was La Chiesa delle Anime Dei Corpi Decollati at Palermo, and "it is on this church that we must linger," says Pitrè (ibid., 7), "if we want to come to get into the spirit, so to speak, of this devotion" (the pun is in Pitrè's italian text).

In 1113, Admiral Giorgio Anticheno built a bridge across the Oreto River, which runs along the southern edge of Palermo. The Ponte Ammiraglio (Bridge of the Admiral), with its sharply pointed and distinctive arches is still there, although the course of the Oreto was shifted in this century and the bridge now stands alone. Sometime during the seventeenth century a small church was built near the Ponte Ammiraglio. It was originally dedicated to a madonna, variously called the Madonna del Fiume (of the river), the Madonna delle Grazie, and the Madonna del Ponte (of the bridge). In 1785 a cemetery adjacent to the church was formally consecrated as a cemetery for executed criminals.

Beginning in 1799 all prisoners executed at Palermo, beheaded or otherwise, were buried there.[5] This "cemetery" was really nothing more than a large pit under the piazza. Bodies were thrown into the pit by opening a trapdoor located in the piazza. Somewhere in or near this cemetery was a "pyramid" (apparently a type of ossuary) containing the skulls of these executed prisoners. The skulls were *spolpati e bianchi* (Franzonello 1946, 47), that is, "picked clean of flesh and pure

---

4. This account of devotion to the beheaded souls in Sicily is derived from Pitrè (1978e, 4–25; 1978d, 185–88); Franzonello (1946); and Hartland (1910), as well as from information obtained at the Sanctuary of the Corpi Decollati at Palermo during a visit in August 1993.

5. Beheading was originally accomplished using a sword; in 1771 authorities at Palermo started using a mechanism similar to the guillotine (Franzonello 1946, 31).

white," and could be viewed through openings in the pyramid. The souls associated with these skulls came increasingly to be the object of cultic devotion, and the church came to be called La Chiesa delle Anime dei Corpi Decollati (The Church of the Souls of the Beheaded Bodies). Apparently, "beheaded" referred less to the mode of execution—since many people executed by hanging were also buried at the church—than to the practice of separating the skulls of those executed from the rest of their bodies.

In response to its increasing popularity the church was rebuilt and enlarged in 1857–65. It was during this period, apparently, that Church authorities decided to sanitize the devotion by closing in the openings in the "pyramid" so that the skulls inside could no longer be viewed. By the time Pitrè observed the sanctuary in the latter half of the nineteenth century, the focus of the cult had become a small side chapel, which opened onto the piazza containing the cemetery. Devotees would start their journey to the sanctuary on a Monday or a Friday, often walking most of the distance barefoot. Along the way they would pray a special Rosary that incorporated prayers mentioning the *corpi decullati*.

Reaching the sanctuary, the devout would first pray in front of the altar consecrated to S. Giovanni Battista Decollato (St. John the Baptist Beheaded) and then move to the chapel on the right. Here they would begin whispering to a memorial tablet set in the floor. Having completed their request, devotees would bend their ears to the tablet in hopes of hearing a response. If they did hear a sound from behind the tablet (and, Pitrè notes, it was inevitable in this situation of heightened emotion that they would), it was a sign that the favor they had requested would be granted. At this point, the faces of the devout "would be flushed with joy and their eyes would gleam brightly" (Pitrè 1978c, 17). The scene was sufficiently moving that Pitrè could not resist a bit of hyperbole: "Even people who are not much concerned with popular traditions should see this particular scene. When my foreign friends come to Sicily, I take them to this church and this chapel. When they see what happens there, they're dumbfounded, unable to comprehend the nature of the world they've wandered into" (ibid.).

The sanctuary was especially popular with the women of Palermo, but it drew Catholics from the entire province, especially from those communities in which executions rarely or never took place and which for this reason lacked their own church dedicated to the beheaded souls.

Although Church authorities had ensured that the skulls of the dead at this sanctuary were no longer on public view, they could not purge skeletal imagery from the popular traditions surrounding this cult. The beheaded souls, for instance, were believed to be especially protective of devotees who were attacked by thieves while traveling. In one particularly well-known story, a devotee traveling on horseback near the sanctuary was set upon by brigands who had heard he was carrying lots of money. He called upon the beheaded souls for help. Almost immediately skeletons armed with bones rose from the burial pit and rushed to his aid, attacking the thieves and driving them off. Pitrè (13) says that lithographic prints showing this scene were in such great demand that they had to be reprinted every year.

Devotion to the beheaded souls was not limited to the Oreto sanctuary. People who had need of a favor but who were unable to go to the sanctuary itself could and did pray in front of home altars dedicated to these souls. Sometimes the images placed on these home altars showed figures in the midst of fire and were little different from standard representations of the suffering souls in Purgatory, but quite often these images depicted bodies hanging from a gallows. As with the sanctuary devotion, prayers addressed to the beheaded souls in domestic settings were usually said at night. There was also a domestic analogue to the practice of listening for an "echo" at the sanctuary. After saying a variety of prayers and making a request of the beheaded souls, a devotee would stay silent and listen for a "sign." Signs could be either "good" (signifying that the favor was or would be granted) or "bad" (signifying that it would not be). Good signs included a cock's crow, the barking of a dog, a pleasant-sounding whistling, a love song, or the rapid passage of a carriage. Bad signs included a cat's meowing, an ass's braying, a funeral lament, a fart, and worst of all, the sound of water being thrown onto the ground.

In Pitrè's day, there were several hundred painted ex-voto appended to the walls enclosing the sanctuary. The favors represented in these ex-voto (soldiers escaping injury during war, sailors being saved from a shipwreck, people surviving attacks by bandits or thieves or recovering from injuries sustained from overturned carts, etc.) are exactly the same as those represented in the ex-voto given to saints or madonnas. A great many of the ex-voto at the sanctuary were dated 1860 and were from the partisans who had fought against the Bourbon regime for an new Italy. Because these men had seen their cause to be holy, says Pitrè, it was inconceivable to them that the beheaded souls would not come to their aid.[6]

Just after the turn of this century, the English folklorist E. S. Hartland visited the sanctuary after reading about it in Pitrè. Hartland (1910) tells us that the structure was a bit dilapidated, although the entrance to the chapel that was the focus of the cult had been restored. He also mentions that the chapel contained

---

6. Although Pitrè does not mention it, the first clash between Garibaldi's men and the Bourbon army occurred near the Ponte Ammiraglio and thus near this sanctuary.

a number of body-part ex-voto, in addition to painted ex-voto on the walls surrounding the piazza.

In the early 1940s, Franzonello (1946, 79–80) found that the small chapel off to the right in the sanctuary was well lit on a daily basis by votive candles and was still adorned with body-part ex-voto (legs, heads, feet, etc.) as well as with photographs of Italian soldiers at war. The sanctuary, however, was virtually destroyed in the bombing at the war's end. It was rebuilt in 1955, at which time it became a parish church dedicated to Our Lady of Mount Carmel at the sanctuary of Beheaded Bodies.

The present sanctuary is small, nondescript, and entirely unmentioned in tourist guidebooks. Whereas it was once located some distance from Palermo in a forest setting, it is now lost amid a mass of modern and often decrepit buildings. There are no visible reminders that a cemetery once bordered the church, except for some marble slabs in the church's courtyard that give the names of patriots executed by the Bourbon regime in the early 1800s. The painted ex-voto mentioned by Pitrè and Hartland are gone, presumably lost in the confusion and destruction that occurred at the end of World War II. As you enter the church there is a small, shallow chapel just off to the right with a small altar. Hanging above this altar is a large painting of S. Giovanni Battista about to be beheaded. A diorama of the souls in Purgatory in their traditional sea of flames is set up in the space beneath the altar, and a dozen or so body-part ex-voto are attached to the backdrop of this diorama. Sitting on the altar itself are a number of electrified votive lights. The newest bank of lights carries an inscription identifing it as an ex-voto donated in 1993 and offered to the *anime decollati* (not the souls in Purgatory).

Perhaps the strongest continuing link to the old devotion is not the sanctuary itself but an edicola that stands a block away, where the Via Decollati (the street on which the sanctuary is located) meets with the wide Corso dei Mille. This edicola is a free-standing pillar with a brass plaque on one side showing the Madonna con Bambino being crowned by angels. She is flanked by S. Giovanni Battista on one side and the adult Christ on the other. Below and off to one side is a representation of the original sanctuary. Directly opposite this is a representation of the distinctive Ponte Ammiraglio. The bottom of the plaque shows the souls in Purgatory in their familiar sea of flames. But right in the middle of the plaque is a gallows from which a poor soul, his hands bound, hangs by his neck. When I saw this edicola in August 1993 its top was crammed with red votive candles and small vases holding fresh flowers. The beheaded souls at Palermo are down, but not out.

In addition to the cult at Palermo, beheaded souls cults existed in several other Sicilian communities. At Messina the bones of executed criminals were deposited in a church dedicated to San Giovanni decollato; the souls of these criminals were called *mpillusu*, a word that suggests that these souls were asking for the suffrages of the living. Pitrè (1978d, 185–88) indicates that the women of Messina made nocturnal processions to this church to ask favors of the mpillusu. At Trapani, the beheaded souls were called *armiceddi* (little souls) and were venerated at a church near to where executions were carried out (Pitrè 1978c, 8; Serraino 1968, 293–94). Pitrè indicates that beheaded souls cults were also to be found in Arcireale, Marsalla, Paceco, Sambuca, Noto, and Mineo. If one plots on a map all the communities known to have had a beheaded souls cult, it becomes clear that the devotion was found in all regions of Sicily.

Souls That Fail to Make the Journey to the Otherworld

There is no denying that the cult of the skeletal dead in Italy, whether organized around plague victims or executed criminals, was shaped partly by folkloric traditions that have little to do with Catholicism. Like many other peoples, Italians have long believed that at death a person's soul detaches from the body and tries to make its way to the otherworld, which is parallel and very similar to this one. Part of this journey involves crossing a narrow bridge that links this world and the next (a belief found in a great many Indo-European cultures). In Sicily and other parts of the Mezzogiorno this bridge is called the Ponte di San Giacomo and is conceptualized as paved end to end with sharp objects. Usually, these objects are swords placed sharp edge up, but they can also be knives, daggers, nails, or thorns. If a soul fails to make a successful transition to the otherworld, it will either remain in this world or be trapped in a transition zone from which it can occasionally enter this world.

Although beliefs about the Ponte di San Giacomo were not part of the official Catholic tradition, they were often endorsed by the local clergy. Pitrè (1978a, 249) reports that in some Sicilian communities doubting the existence of the Ponte di San Giacomo was considered a sin, and anyone who confessed this sin to a priest was required to drag their tongue along the floor of a church as penance.

A number of folk practices in Italy aim to ensure that souls make a successful transition across the Ponte di San Giacomo and so do not return to interfere in the world of the living. In a pastoral letter written in 1530 (reproduced in Prosperi 1965, 393–402), Gian Matteo Giberti (1495–1543), bishop of Verona (in the Veneto), instructed his priests to root out superstition, and singled out in particular "the practice of uncovering the roof so that the soul [of the dead] can get out, something that suggests that the soul could be held back by a roof." In fact, Italians have long believed that the human soul does have physical substance and so can be blocked by physical barriers like a roof.[7] This is why those present at a death leave an exit for the soul of the dead person by removing a slat from the roof or by opening a window (see Lombardi Satriani and Meligrana 1982, 122–23). The fact that diocesan synods throughout Italy continued to condemn these practices into the modern era (see Corrain and Zampini 1970, 52, 182) is an indication of just how rooted and widespread this view was. In some Italian communities it was common practice well into this century to remove a slat or open a window (see the examples cited in ibid.) and it is likely that the practice still persists in some areas.

The walls and roofs of a house are not the only physical barriers of concern to those gathered around a dying person. Metal chains around the neck can impede a soul's exit from the body, and so such objects are typically removed from the dying person. Even the body itself can block the soul's exit. The location of a soul, for instance, is assumed to be at the mouth of the stomach, but occasionally a soul is "off to the side" and so has a difficult time exiting.

The soul's journey across the Ponte di San Giacomo begins when the dying person loses consciousness. Nevertheless, the separation of a soul from its body is a slow, gradual process, and the soul retains a link with the body even after its journey has begun. For this reason, the suffering of the unconscious person just prior to death is often interpreted as reflecting the pain and effort of having to walk across the sharp edges of the Ponte di San Giacomo. A lingering connection between body and soul is often assumed even when a person seems dead to onlookers. Because of this continuing link between body and soul, changes made to the body can affect the soul's journey. The legs of the corpse, for instance, might be bound so that the soul can more easily fit through a window or a hole in the roof; subsequently, the legs might be unbound so the soul can better negotiate the Ponte di San Giacomo. Other actions designed to facilitate the soul's transition include washing the corpse, putting food and water nearby so the soul can maintain its strength on the journey, and talking to the corpse in a reassuring manner.

But the greatest impediments to a successful transition are psychological, not physical. To reach the otherworld, a soul has to detach completely from its body, and a complete detachment depends most of all upon the dying person's

7. The discussion that follows, concerning Italian folk beliefs about the soul and its relation to the body, is derived from a number of sources, but principally from Pitrè (1978a, 201–52); Lombardi Satriani and Meligrana (1982, 121–48); Pardo (1982).

state of mind. Unless a person's experience of impending death is "gentle, gradual, and most of all, *accepted*" (Pardo, 1982, 536; emphasis in original), the soul
will not fully detach from the body and so will not make a successful transition.
This is why the souls of people who die a sudden and violent death, where there
is no time for a detachment that is "gentle and gradual," are seen as likely to
remain in or near this world as ghosts. This is also why the souls of people who
feel they still have much to do in life, such as a mother with young children (see
ibid., 559n)—and who for that reason cannot accept death—are unlikely to make
a successful transition. Given the importance of this acceptance of death, the relatives and friends of a dead person often use magical means (consulting a witch
for instance) to find out if the deceased person has in the end come to accept their
death (La Sorsa 1925, 75).

In the context of these folk traditions, it is not surprising that Italians came
to see the souls of executed criminals and plague victims as being especially unlikely to have made a successful transition across the Ponte di San Giacomo. In
the case of executed criminals, the fact that they knew in advance the exact moment of their death was the critical element, because knowing the exact moment
of your death produces an increased desire to continue living (see Pardo 1982,
559). But this increased desire for life runs directly counter to that calm acceptance of death that more than anything else facilitates the smooth and complete
detachment of a soul from its body. Also working against the calm acceptance of
death in the case of executed criminals was the knowledge that their lives were
being unjustly ended, since in many cases (especially in southern Italy prior to the
late nineteenth century) they were political prisoners being executed by a repressive regime.

In the case of plague victims, it was the social disruption caused by a sudden
and dramatic increase in the proportion of people dying in a single community
that made the successful transition to the otherworld unlikely. One of the conditions that facilitates a good death—that is, one in which the soul detaches easily—is dying at home surrounded by family and friends. This experience not only
makes it more likely that the dying person will accept death but it ensures that
there will be people around the dying person to perform the magical procedures
that facilitate the journey to the otherworld. When plague strikes, people die so
fast that it becomes impossible to keep up—that is, to organize the experience of
death in the usual manner and so to facilitate the voyage across the Ponte di San
Giacomo. Remember that prior to the mid-seventeenth century, in communities
hit by plague, it was common for 30–60 percent of the population to die in a relatively short period (Del Panta 1980). Simply getting the dead buried was a problem (hence the use of common graves at Ghedi and elsewhere); performing the
usual rituals was impossible.

Still, we must be careful. Although Italian folk traditions would lead us to the conclusion that the souls of executed criminals and plague victims were unlikely to make a successful transition across the Ponte di San Giacomo, this in itself does not help us to understand why souls in these two categories became the object of cultic devotion. There are other categories of people whose souls are also unlikely to make a successful transition to the otherworld, and who do return regularly as ghosts, who have not become the object of cultic devotion. Pitrè (1978c, 26–27) reports that the souls of people who die a violent death away from home—people, for instance, who are attacked and killed by robbers—are thought to wander in and around the place where their body fell. Similarly, the souls of thieves and the souls of their descendants are condemned to return to the world of the living at night until the items stolen are restored to their rightful owners (ibid., 28). Also likely to return as ghosts are the souls of priests who accepted money for saying masses but who did not say those masses (ibid., 29–30). The souls of such priests are said to return at night to particular churches to say special masses, attended by the souls of other dead. Stories about living persons accidentally coming upon such masses are found in many regions of Italy (De Martino 1975, 106–7).

Although the souls of the dead in all these categories—murder victims, thieves, dishonest priests—are often seen as dangerous to the living, they have not become objects of cultic devotion like the souls of executed criminals and plague victims. What made these latter two categories special? The answer partly depends on recognizing that for a long time these two categories were *not* special. This can be demonstrated most clearly in connection with the souls of executed criminals. Between 1350 and 1550, *del morte* (death) confraternities were established in most of Italy's major cities, including Siena, Florence, Genoa, Rome, and Naples, with the goal of providing spiritual guidance to condemned prisoners, both in their cells and on the way to the place of execution.

The documentary records left by these confraternities suggest that they were most concerned with getting the condemned person to accept their death (Fineschi 1993, 815; see also Paglia 1982, 81–84; Prosperi 1982, 971f; Di Bella 1994). Church elites have always insisted that an acceptance of death would ensure that the condemned person had acknowledged their sins (especially the sin that led to their being sentenced to death), which would allow them to have their sins forgiven and so would allow them to enter Purgatory (see for instance the discussion in Mondello 1874, 267–81). But Fineschi's (1993) analysis of the statutes and origin legends associated with these del Morte confraternities indicates that the driving force behind the establishment of these organizations was the widespread fear that the souls of these executed criminals might return to invade the world of the living. These confraternities, he argues, were established to prevent this from happening. Although Fineschi does not mention it, it was likely a desire to prevent the return of dead souls that explains why these confraternities placed so much emphasis upon inducing a calm acceptance of death in the condemned prisoner. As noted earlier, a calm acceptance of death is the one thing that most facilitates a successful transition across the Ponte di San Giacomo and thus is the one thing that most guarantees that a soul will not return to the world of the living.

On the other hand, there is nothing in the records of these death confraternities prior to, say, 1600 that suggests that the corpses of the prisoners they counseled became the object of special devotion. There is certainly nothing to suggest that the members of these confraternities (or anybody else) prayed to the skulls of these people in order to obtain favors. In other words, it would appear that up until the late sixteenth century the souls of executed criminals were seen as a potential danger but they were not seen as favor-granting beings and were not made the object of cultic devotion. They were simply bothersome and dangerous ghosts and had no special status relative to the souls associated with other categories of people (like dishonest priests and murder victims) whose souls were also likely to become bothersome and dangerous ghosts.

Something happened between the mid-sixteenth and mid-seventeenth centuries that transformed the way in which Italian Catholics saw the souls of executed criminals and plague victims. For some reason, souls in these two categories moved from being simply bothersome and dangerous ghosts to being akin to saints and madonnas. In fact, we have already discussed the event that set this transformation in motion: it was (I want to argue) the rising popularity of the official suffering souls in Purgatory cult.

On Popular Creativity (Again)

Italian Catholics took the reciprocal exchange model associated with saints and madonnas and applied it to the souls in Purgatory, with the result that these souls became favor-granting beings and the object of cultic devotion. What happened next, I suggest, is that the logic of this cult was merged with preexisting folk beliefs about death. The official Church, for instance, was very clear in saying that the souls in Purgatory were trapped in between Heaven and Hell. In the minds of ordinary Italian Catholics, this would have made the souls in Purgatory similar to other souls trapped "in between," namely, those who for one reason or another had failed to negotiate the Ponte di San Giacomo and who were now trapped in between this world and the next.

But the official Church had also consistently portrayed the souls in Purgatory as an undifferentiated mass of individuals who were gathered together in single geographical location (Purgatory). This would have made these souls especially similar to other souls trapped in between this world and the next and whose bodies had been (for one reason or another) systematically gathered together and deposited in special cemeteries. While there were no special burial sites for dishonest priests, for people waylaid by thieves, for thieves who failed to make restitution, and so on, there were special burial sites for the bones of plague victims and for executed criminals. At least until the early nineteenth century, executed criminals were usually buried in or near the churches associated with the del Morte confraternities (Prosperi 1982, 992), and plague victims were often buried in common graves. What happened next (I suggest) is that the souls of executed criminals and plague victims came to acquire the power associated with the souls in Purgatory—namely, the power to grant favors. This is why the souls of executed criminals and plague victims became the object of cultic devotion.

The hypothesis—that skeletal dead cults were a popular response to the official cult organized around the souls in Purgatory—runs counter to the interpretation offered by most Italian investigators, who prefer to see skeletal dead cults as archaic forms deriving from a distant agricultural past (see for instance Rivera 1988, 65–123). Quite apart from the fact that this more usual interpretation cannot easily account for the fact that skeletal dead cults emerged in the seventeenth century, it seems at variance as well with the fact that these cults were so popular in urban areas and among social groups that were least involved with agricultural pursuits. In Sicily, for instance, the most popular cults organized around the beheaded souls were found in the larger cities, like Palermo, Messina, and Trapani, and not in smaller agricultural communities. Furthermore, the available information suggests that this devotion diffused from these larger urban areas to smaller communities, and not vice versa, as the agricultural past hypothesis would suggest. For instance, although devotion to the beheaded souls was well established at Palermo by 1800, the church dedicated to these souls in the nearby community of Monreale was not established until the 1860s (Franzonello 1946, 74).

But perhaps the best example of just how far removed from the agricultural world the skeletal dead cults were is to be found not in Sicily but in Lombardy and, in particular, in Milan.

Devotion to the Skeletal Dead in the Age of Enlightenment

Sometime during that the late seventeenth century bones from several suppressed cemeteries at Milan were relocated to the Church of S. Bernardino, a short distance from the Duomo. There, these bones were arranged into various designs and appended to the walls of a chapel. The chapel came to be called the Cappella Ossario and the church itself San Bernardino alle Ossa (San Bernardino at the bones). Over time, the bones in the Cappella Ossario came increasingly to be the focus of a popular cult.

The "flavor" of the devotion that developed at S. Bernardino alle Ossa is best conveyed by considering an incised rectangle of plaster still visible on the outside of that church, just where the main building joins the Cappella Ossario. The lower half of this rectangle contains a well-worn niche through which coins can be dropped and a lightly incised line that reads "Restored 1776." The incising in the upper half of the rectangle is hard to make out, mainly because of the spray-painted graffiti added by some modern vandal, but close inspection reveals two large skulls set against a long bone, all of which are set above a Latin phrase that translates as "Give and it will be given to you." However the official Church might interpret this, Milanese Catholics were coming to the Cappella Ossario to solicit favors from the skeletal dead whose bones resided there. On the other hand, by the late eighteenth century, when this plaster engraving was restored, S. Bernardino alle Ossa was only one of several churches at Milan associated with the skeletal dead—and not at all the most important.

The history of skeletal dead cults at Milan during the eighteenth century has been well described by Signorotto (1983c), and unless otherwise noted, the descriptive material in this section is derived from his account. Signorotto in turn obtained much of his information from the diary of Giambattista Borrani, a Milanese priest who describes a number of the religious processions held at Milan in the period 1737–84. Borrani's diary makes it clear that these processions were often staged to solicit favors. Most commonly, the favor sought was an end to a period of drought or excessive rain or an end to some epidemic that was killing animals. The dead were always the ones whose aid was solicited first. Although Borrani often uses the term *le anime purgante* to describe the dead to whom these appeals were made, he also tells us that these processions took place "above all in the cemeteries for the plague dead, the so-called *fopponi*" (cited in Signorotto 1983c, 305).

In his first notebook (he left forty-two notebooks in all) Borrani writes: "In the month of September (1738) public suffrages for the souls in purgatory were ordered in order to obtain an end to the deaths that were occurring among the animals in the city. These suffrages took the form of a procession of the Company of the Holy Cross and all the clergy to the foppone of S. Gregorio" (cited in ibid., 306). The church of S. Gregorio was situated next to the lazaretto at Milan, located at what was then the northeastern outskirts of the city. The foppone associated with the lazaretto had been an important burial site during the great plague that struck Milan in 1630 (Staurenghi 1916, 579). In short, once again, as at Ghedi, we are dealing with a popular devotion that had as its physical focus a site containing a mass of bones belonging to plague victims.

There was a second skeletal dead cult associated with the Church of S. Michele at the *foppone dei nuovi sepolcri*. At first sight, the devotions held at S. Michele would seem an exception to the pattern of organizing these devotions around the plague dead, since the foppone dei nuovi sepolcri was built in 1697 to receive bodies from the Ospedale maggiore at Milan. But history is less important in these matters than public perception, and during the eighteenth century it was widely *believed* that victims of the 1630 plague had been buried in this burial ground (ibid.).

Signorotto provides photographic reproductions of some of the printed notices that advertised these processions to locations containing the bones of plague victims. One of these notices (see Signorotto 1983c, 333) reads:

> During the morning of S. Matteo's day, which will be the 21st of the present month, a Thursday, the Company of the Holy Cross of the City of Milan will go in procession from the Piazza of the Holy Sepulchre to the foppone of S. Rocco at Gentilino, just outside the Porta Ludovica, in order to offer assistance in the usual manner to the souls of the faithful dead who are buried there. And if the weather is bad on S. Matteo's day, then the procession will be held the following Sunday. At the foppone, those who attend will have the comfort of the mass and will be able to confess and receive communion; as well, they will have the benefit of a spiritual discussion and other things. For these reasons every faithful Christian is invited to attend and to offer prayers and alms in aid of those poor souls, being assured that in due course favors will be given in return [assicurandoli del contracambio à suo tempo].

Directly beneath this text is a grim-looking skull set against two crossed bones: the foppone associated with the Church of S. Rocco had also been a burial site during the 1630 plague (Staurenghi 1916, 579). The final line of the notice provides a clear expression of the reciprocal exchange model central to all popular cults in Italy: by offering prayers and alms to the skeletal dead (or to the souls in Purgatory, or to the saints and madonnas), we obligate them to reciprocate by granting favors to us.

The exact origins of these skeletal dead cults at Milan is unclear. Signorotto (1983c, 311–12) himself recognizes that the skeletal dead are quite different from the suffering souls in Purgatory but, like most Italian investigators, sees the skeletal dead as an inheritance from some nebulous agricultural past. But as far as I know, there are no examples of popular devotions centering on a large mass of bones prior to the devotion developed at S. Bernardino alle Ossa during the late 1600s. Unfortunately, it is not known if the bones in the Cappella Ossario were explicitly associated with the plague dead in the popular imagination. Devotion to the souls of the plague dead was certainly well established by 1737, when Borrani began his diary. It seems likely that the Milanese devotion to the plague dead emerged some time during the late seventeenth or early eighteenth centuries, which would make it roughly contemporaneous with the plague dead devotions that emerged at Ghedi and elsewhere in Lombardy.

By the latter half of the eighteenth century the cult of the skeletal dead was sufficiently popular at Milan that public order was sometimes threatened. In 1750, for example, the crowds attending a mission organized by the Capuchins at the foppone of S. Gregorio could not be contained within the limits of the cemetery, and in 1754 soldiers from the castle had to be called in to manage the crowd that attended the newly enlarged Church of S. Bernardino alle Ossa (ibid., 318).

But such threats to public order notwithstanding, these devotions had the approval of both civil and religious authorities. Civil authorities at Milan quite often requested from the archbishop public processions in honor of the dead and then facilitated public participation by requiring artisans to close their workshops or be fined (ibid., 313). Archdiocesan authorities not only acquiesced in these requests but made their own contribution to skeletal dead cults by allowing the churches (or chapels) associated with these cults to be enlarged and their staffs to be enlarged in order to handle the ever increasing number of devotees.

In summary then, popular devotion to the skeletal dead at Milan increased dramatically during the eighteenth century, and it was a devotion supported both from below and from above. It is difficult to see it as merely the survival of some distant agricultural past. Undercutting the agricultural survival interpretation even further is evidence suggesting that urban-based artisans and merchants were the segments of the population most committed to the skeletal dead.

The license accorded the Ospedale maggiore at Milan during the 1690s specified that cadavers from the hospital would be transported to the foppone dei nuovi sepolcri late at night and in a covered wagon whose wheels had been silenced. Hospital officials also promised that the burials themselves would be conducted out of public view. The purpose of these arrangements was to avoid spreading apprehension about death among the general public. It was presumably this same desire—to keep the funerals at the foppone out of public view—that led to the construction (in 1725) of the Rotunda, a high-perimeter wall with interior porticos that completely surrounded both the foppone and the associated church of S. Michele (which had been built in 1713).

During the late 1760s the members of an all-male confraternity began seeking out these death wagons in order to accompany the cadavers on their nocturnal trip from the hospital to the foppone. Very shortly, the number of those involved in this practice grew considerably; Borrani estimates that at one point two thousand men were involved. After reaching the cemetery, the men would subdivide into small groups and move about the city, praying. Signorotto (1983c, 319) sees these nocturnal processions as a spontaneous and logical offshoot of the public procession that appealed to the dead of the fopponi for favors.

What is most interesting (to us) is the social background of the leaders involved in this devotion. One government report (cited in ibid., 319) identifies them as *artisti* and *artigiani* and suggests that "a certain cabinetmaker named Fontana" was a central figure in organizing this particular devotion. Records of the confraternity itself define its membership as consisting of "merchants and artisans" under the patronage of S. Giuseppe. Some further sense of the social standing of the men involved in the confraternity can be gleaned from the fact that an inspector whose report calls attention to the activities of this group suggests that the matter is a "delicate" one and that the investigation should be conducted "prudently" and out of public view (see ibid., 319). These men, in other words, were not simple laborers; they were semiprofessionals, whose occupations made then a central element in the distinctively urban culture of Milan. Yet it was in this stratum of the population that devotion to the skeletal dead at the foppone seems to have taken deepest root.[8]

Toward the end of the century, Austrian government authorities (Milan being under Austrian control at this time) came more and more to be influenced by Jansenist and Enlightenment critiques of the "superstitious" elements in popular religion. In such climate it is hardly surprising that skeletal dead cults came under close scrutiny. In 1779 a French Jansenist periodical noted that it was common in Austrian Lombardy for Catholics to pray for rain in chapels located in cemeteries and specifically ridiculed one particular Italian bishop who authorized a triduum in a chapel dedicated to S. Rocco in which executed criminals had been buried. A few months later, Prince Kaunitz, the Austrian chancellor, ordered Count Firmian, the Austrian governor for Lombardy, to investigate the practices at the chapel of S. Rocco mentioned in the Jansenist critique. Firmian sent back reassurances designed to allay Kaunitz's concerns. Although Kaunitz was somewhat mollified, his response provides a succinct description of the Italian cult organized around the skeletal dead: it cannot be denied, he said, that "in times of both public and private need . . . the [Italian] people place more confidence in the invocation of the souls in purgatory than of the saints, and most of

8. This would not be the only time that merchants and artisans at Milan would be associated with devotional excess. In 1790, a number of complaints would be made against individuals who engaged in public prayers in front of "hastily set-up images and small altars" (Signorotto 1983c, 319). Although the exact nature of these images and altars are not specified, the occupations of those involved are, and they include a grocer, an archivist, a printer, a pharmacist, and a hairdresser.

all they prefer [to appeal to] the souls of those who have been executed by the authorities" (cited in ibid., 324).

Notice that both the original Jansenist critique and Kaunitz's reply refer to cults organized around executed criminals. One such cult at Milan persisted into the nineteenth century: Cusani (1865, 29) describes a chapel in the Church of S. Giovanni alle Case-rotte that had at one time been associated with a del morte confraternity.

> Hanging [on the wall] was a large painting that showed the members of this con-fraternity accompanying a condemned prisoner to the place of execution . . . Two skeletons hung beside the painting, one on each side. One skeleton had a noose around its neck, while the other was holding its own skull in its hands. These sym-bolized hanging and decapitation, the two ways of meting out capital punishment. Underneath were reliquaries containing sixteen skulls and one bony torso, placed there to collect alms in support of the executed criminals buried in this church over the course of three centuries.

In summary, cults organized around the bones and skulls of plague victims and executed criminals flourished at Milan during the late seventeenth and early eighteenth centuries and continued to exist well into the nineteenth century. Such a pattern accords well with the hypothesis being offered in this chapter, namely, that skeletal dead cults were not remnants of a fading agrarian past but were a popular and creative response to the success of the more official cult of the souls in Purgatory.

And what of these cults in today's Milan? For the most part they seem to have died out. The church of S. Michele is still there, along with the surrounding Rotunda, but the adjacent cemetery was closed in 1783. By the early twentieth century, S. Michele had been converted into a laundry for the Ospedale maggiore (Arrigoni and Bertarelli 1936, 64). The area inside the Rotunda is currently used as a civic garden, with the old church as a backdrop. When I visited Milan in the summer of 1993, crowds were still traveling to the Rotunda at night, but they were coming for the free outdoor movies sponsored by Milan's municipal government, not to venerate the dead as their ancestors had done two centuries earlier.

The Church of S. Gregorio in the foppone of the lazaretto, which was the focus of so many of the services dedicated to the dead in Borrani's account, was converted into a private house in the early nineteenth century and later fell into disrepair.[9] Most of the old lazaretto was torn down in the 1880s to allow for

9. A church dedicated to S. Gregorio still exists near the site of the old lazaretto; this church, how-ever, was erected around the turn of this century. On the history of the Church of S. Gregorio at the foppone, see Arrigoni and Bertarelli (1936, 32).

urban expansion. All that remains is a small section of the porticoed perimeter (which now houses a Russian Orthodox church) and the octagonal Church of S. Carlo that originally sat at the very center of the lazaretto.[10] As far as I know, the only traces of anything resembling the old devotion are to be found at S. Bernardino alle Ossa. Small floral bouquets are occasionally tied with wire to the metal grillwork that covers the two street-level windows of the Cappella Ossario. It seems likely that these are ex-voto offered in exchange for favors received, which would mean that the bones in the cappella Ossario and the souls associated with these bones in the popular imagination have not completely lost their power.

Del Latte Madonnas

One of the strengths of this book, I hope, is that it will open up interpretive possibilities overlooked by previous research and that, as a result, readers will be able to see Italian Catholicism in new but entirely plausible ways. It is with this goal in mind that I now consider a madonnine image, familiar to many readers, that at first sight seems far removed from devotion to the skeletal dead—but that possibly was once linked to the skeletal dead in the popular imagination, at least in Italy.

Anglo-Saxon scholars, feminist scholars in particular, have a soft spot in their hearts for the Madonna del Latte, a designation routinely given to any madonnine image that shows a madonna nursing her child. Two analyses in particular have had wide visibility: Warner (1976, 192–205) devotes an entire chapter to the Madonna del Latte in her popular book dealing with the history of the Mary cult, and Bynum (1987) discusses Madonna del Latte images at length in her well-known study of female mystics. Unfortunately, both of these analyses are flawed if our goal is to understand what these madonnas might have meant to ordinary Catholics.

Warner (1976) concedes that Madonna del Latte images evoked a variety of different meanings over the centuries but argues that by the late fourteenth century one of the most important of these meanings had to do with Mary's role as intercessor. Nursing, Warner suggests, was seen to establish an especially strong bond between mother and child. Madonna del Latte images thus reminded people of the especially strong bond between Christ and Mary, which in turn reinforced the view that Mary was the most effective of all possible intercessors with

10. Originally, the exterior of the Church of S. Carlo consisted of open porticos, and its octagonal shape allowed the sick in the lazaretto to view the celebration of the mass without having to leave their cells along the perimeter. For a brief account of this area of Milan, see Ciocia (1985).

her divine son. Although Warner presents several random bits of information linking nursing with the Virgin Mary (such as the fact that Virgin's milk relics began to proliferate in the thirteenth century, that legends about unicorns nursing at the breast of a virgin were used in discussions about Christ, or that paintings and plays show Mary exposing her breast to the adult Christ), she presents no evidence for her central assertion, namely, that European Catholics associated the image of Mary nursing with the idea of Mary as intercessor.

On the contrary, Warner's seems prototypical of arguments constructed by projecting modern attitudes onto the past. The view that nursing establishes a close tie between mother and child was very popular in the 1970s (though it seems to have lost ground since then), when Warner was writing her book, but there is no particular basis for believing that it is a view that predominated in all European cultures in all time periods. Similarly, that Mary is an intercessor with Christ may be the view of the modern Catholic Church, and it may have been the view of certain religious elites in the past, but Italian Catholics have traditionally seen their madonnas not as intercessors but as supernatural beings with independent power. In short, Warner attributes a modern view of breast-feeding and an elitist view of Mary to ordinary Catholics of centuries past to determine what the Madonna del Latte meant for those Catholics.

Bynum (1987) presents a more sophisticated interpretation of the Madonna del Latte, and one that is less easily dismissed. Female mystics in the later Middle Ages, Bynum argues, used food metaphors to express their desire for mystical union with Christ. In particular, they established a metaphorical correspondence between the milk that issued from the Madonna's breast and the blood that issued from the wound in Christ's side. Since Christ's blood was seen by Christian theologians as a source of spiritual nurturance, this correspondence allowed female mystics to see Mary's breast milk in the same way. Identification with the nursing Madonna was thus not only fully legitimate in the eyes of the Church but also a way they could see themselves as Christ, that is, as dispensers of spiritual nourishment, something otherwise at variance with the Church's insistence that Christ had intended his priestly functions to be reserved to males alone.

Bynum adduces two types of evidence in support of her interpretation. First, she scoured museums for paintings that seemed to show an equivalence between Christ's side wound and the Madonna's breast. Many of the paintings she found are reproduced in her book. In some of these paintings, Mary and Christ both appear, and Christ is clearly holding his breast wound in a manner similar to the way Mary is holding her breast. In other cases, Bynum compares separate paintings of Christ and Mary. Even though the two paintings are often from different societies and different centuries, the gestures, again, appear similar. Considering only the paintings reproduced in Bynum's book, there would appear to be support for the equivalences that she posits. Nevertheless, the paintings were selected precisely because they seem to exhibit the equivalences that Bynum proposes; if however we compared all extant paintings of Christ showing his side wound, the vast majority would certainly bear no resemblance to a nursing madonna. The striking parallels evident in Bynum's sample of paintings, in other words, are to some extent an artifact of the way the sample was selected.

Paintings aside, Bynum also scrutinizes the written work left by female mystics, and here her evidence is more convincing. The passages cited leave no doubt that these women did make extensive use of food metaphors when writing about their sought-after union with Christ and that they were particularly fond of the nursing metaphor. Unfortunately, Bynum too often slips from her initial focus on female mystics and writes of medieval women in general. The problem is that female mystics were in many ways atypical of women in general. Female mystics usually removed themselves from mundane affairs by shutting themselves behind convent walls; ordinary women were very much part of the world. Female mystics often (as Bynum demonstrates) rejected food, whereas obtaining food was often the focus of religious rituals for ordinary women. But most important, perhaps, female mystics were intensively Christocentric, and when they referred to the Madonna, they were clearly talking about the Mary so favored by Catholic theologians. Their religiosity was thus quite different from popular Catholicism, in which Christ was less important than saints and madonnas and in which madonnas were differentiated from one another in terms of power and prestige. In short, Bynum's analysis may help us to understand what del Latte Madonnas may have meant to a few dozen female mystics but not what they meant to the vast majority of Italian Catholics, women or men.

One way to figure this out would be to scrutinize Italian folk traditions to identify the psychological associations that would have been activated in the minds of Italian Catholics when they looked upon a Madonna del Latte image. Piccaluga (1983) has done something very much like this. Her concern is with images showing the Virgin above showering the faithful down below with milk that pours from her breast.

Piccaluga (97) argues that such pictures, whatever meaning they might have had for upper-class audiences, would likely have been read by popular audiences as being concerned with the voyage across the Ponte di San Giacomo. She bases this claim on Pitrè's report (see Pitrè 1978a, 246; 1978b, 10–11) that the Ponte di San Giacomo is often called the Via Lattea (the Breast Milk Way). The *Via Lattea* label derives from a folk tradition that says that the Ponte di San Giacomo was formed by drops of the Virgin's breast milk which fell while she was on earth. This view of the Ponte di San Giacomo seems to coexist with the view that it is covered with rows of sharp objects like swords, knives, daggers, nails, and thorns. But if Piccaluga is correct, then an Italian Catholic looking on a Madonna del Latte image could have been led (by virtue of the Virgin's breast milk = Via Lattea = Ponte di San Giacomo) to think about the voyage of the soul across the Ponte di San Giacomo after death.

Something else that always appears in Madonna del Latte images would also have led Italians to think about the dead, and that is the infant. Lombardi Satriani and Meligrana (1982, 107–16) point out that a number of folk practices and beliefs in Italy, southern Italy in particular, attest to the existence of a strong psychological association between "young children" and "the dead." Thus in the Basilicata, baptizing a child within twenty-four hours of its birth was seen to liberate one soul from Purgatory (a belief that Pitrè documents as well for Sicily; see Pitrè 1978a, 158). In Sicily the most important time of the year for young children is the night before the Day of the Dead, on November 2, since this is the night the dead return to reward or punish young children for their behavior during the year. In Campania, young children are given prominent roles in carnival celebrations involving mock funerals or personifications of death. Folk practice aside, Lombardi Satriani and Meligrana (1982) also present a number of legends that show evidence of this same association between young children and the dead.

Why young children were so strongly associated with the dead is unclear. Lombardi Satriani and Meligrana (108) suggest that the association exists because young children are so close to the dividing line that separates life from the vague condition that is not-life. Whatever the reason, the fact that this psychological association existed means that the presence of a young child in a Madonna del Latte image would have reinforced and strengthened any thoughts about the dead that might have been brought to mind by means of the association between breast milk, Via Lattea, and Ponte di San Giacomo.

In summary then, psychological associations evident in Italian folk tradition make it plausible that Italian Catholics looking upon a Madonna del Latte image might have been led to think about the journey of the soul across the Ponte di San Giacomo after death. This could easily have led them to think about the skeletal dead, those souls who failed to make that journey successfully and who were the object of cultic devotion in other contexts. Did things happen this way? It is unlikely that we will ever know. But it is an interpretation to consider, alongside those developed on the basis of modern attitudes projected backward or those developed on the basis of writings left by religious elites.

Churches Associated with the Dead at Naples

Most churches in Italy with a special association with the dead end up being dedicated to the suffering souls in Purgatory or to the Virgin Mary. Nevertheless, the popular devotion that gives rise to such churches can in the first instance be centered either on the souls in Purgatory or on the skeletal dead. The history of the three churches associated with the dead at Naples provides an especially clear example of both processes and how they eventually converge.

As mentioned in the last chapter, there were no churches dedicated to the dead in Purgatory among the 298 Neapolitan churches described in D'Engenio (1623). But one Purgatory church is listed in two other accounts of Neapolitan churches written just a few decades later (see De Lellis 1977, circa 1666, 301–2; D'Aloe 1883, circa 1660, 689). These two later accounts suggest that in 1604 (or thereabouts) a confraternity was established in the Church of S. Angelo a Segno whose purpose was to finance masses and other pious works on behalf of the souls in Purgatory. Membership in this confraternity was limited to seventy-two deputies (seventy-two being the number of years the Virgin Mary was supposed to have lived on Earth), and each deputy pledged to contribute a perpetual income to be used to subsidize these suffrages. The confraternity was directed by three governors, elected from among the deputies on November 2, the Day of the Dead.

As might be expected, given the financial obligations of membership, the members of this confraternity were drawn disproportionately from the upper classes. In 1606 Pope Paul V confirmed the constitution of the confraternity and granted it a number of privileges and indulgences. By the 1620s, the confraternity had prospered sufficiently that it could sponsor the building of a new church. That church, dedicated to S. Maria dell'anime del Purgatorio, was officially opened on November 2, 1638, and still exists at Naples.

The other two churches at Naples dedicated to the dead derived ultimately from the same event—the plague that struck Naples in 1656.[11] Here again, the large number of deaths necessitated the use of common graves; one of these was an underground grotto on the outskirts of the city. Celano (1860, 467) reports that this grotto quickly filled up with something like fifty thousand bodies and had to be sealed. Some years later, he tells us, the presence of so many bodies there led Neapolitans to erect a church over the grotto. That church was dedicated to

---

11. This plague was one of the last major outbreaks of plague in Italy. The cities hardest hit—including Genoa, Rome, Naples, and Bari—had been spared in the plague of 1630–31 (see Del Panta 1980, 118, 163).

S. Maria del Pianto, *pianto* in this case denoting the weeping and lamentation associated with funerals.

Also pressed into service as common graves during the 1656 plague were four large trenches in the Carmine market, normally used to store grain. Galante (1985, 110) reports that the largest of these pits eventually contained forty-seven thousand bodies, most of which had been burned before being thrown in. When the plague had passed, the "superstitious citizens" of Naples (Galante, 187) erected a column within an enclosure on the site of these mass graves. Alms collected among the citizenry were used to ensure that lamps were kept burning within the enclosure both day and night.

Over time, the enclosure containing the column was increasingly used for "games and other irreverent activities" (ibid.). In 1774 a group of pious men sought to revive the original devotion by erecting a small chapel on the site, called Santa Croce, after the cross that had surmounted the original column. In 1780 the chapel was converted into a large church with seven altars; it stood in the middle of the market. Five years later, this church was demolished and a new church built on the market's edge. One effect of this shift was to ensure that the new church was no longer sitting atop the trench containing the bones of the victims of the 1656 plague. Furthermore, Church authorities expanded its dedication from Santa Croce to Santa Croce del Purgatorio al Mercato (the Holy Cross of Purgatory at the Market). Consistent with this new dedication, the painting installed above the main altar of the new church showed the Addolorata with the souls in Purgatory in a sea of flames.

Naples' three churches associated with the dead did not proceed from the same roots. S. Maria dell'anime del Purgatorio derived directly from the efforts of a few individuals, mainly from the upper classes, who were clearly promoting devotion to the souls in Purgatory and whose understanding of what Purgatory and these souls were derived directly from Church doctrine. The other two churches—Santa Croce del Purgatorio al Mercato and S. Maria del Pianto—sprang from popular devotion to the bones of thousands of plague victims whose corpses had been gathered together in one spot. The devotion in these two cases, as at Ghedi, Milan, etcetera, was clearly devotion to the skeletal dead.

Incidentally, the fact that in this case the official Purgatory church emerged first and was followed by two churches associated with devotion to the skeletal dead is entirely consistent with the general hypothesis advanced in this chapter, namely, that skeletal dead cults were a creative popular response to the official cult of the suffering souls in Purgatory during the early years of the Counter-Reformation.

Chapter Six

Relics

Once upon a time, in the year 594, the Empress Constantina asked a small favor of Pope Gregory the Great. Would he please open the crypt containing the body of S. Paul and send her the saint's head, so she could install it in a church she was building in this saint's honor? She also asked for the burial shroud that covered Paul's body. In his letter of reply (cited in Dudden 1905, 280–82), Gregory expressed his general willingness to comply with almost any request the empress made but said that in this particular case she was asking something that he simply could not do, and he went on to explain why.

Gregory's justification for his refusal was simple, direct, and entirely pragmatic: we know that touching saintly bodies is wrong because when we try to do this it elicits visible and unambiguous signs of supernatural disapproval. As an example, Gregory says that when one of his predecessors wanted to change the silver covering over the body of S. Peter, a "most alarming portent" appeared as he approached the saint's body. Gregory himself had once authorized some improvements to the tomb of S. Paul. During the excavations the sacristan found some bones near the saint's tomb. As he began to move those bones, certain "portents of evil" appeared, and the man died suddenly. In another case, Pelagius II (Gregory's immediate predecessor) ordered improvements to the place where the body of St. Lawrence was entombed. Quite by accident, Gregory says, the workers uncovered and opened the sarcophagus containing the saint's body. Even though the workers had been careful not to touch that body, every single one of them died within ten days.

In light of these and similar events, Gregory argued, he could not possibly open the tomb of S. Paul, not even to send the empress his burial shroud. He went on to say that Romans like himself prefer to create saintly relics by placing objects in proximity to holy bodies. Thus it is common practice, he says, to place a piece of cloth in a box and to place that box near a saint's tomb. When that piece of cloth is subsequently enshrined in a church, "the miracles wrought by it [the cloth] are as great as if the very bodies of the saints had been brought there." As evidence that these pieces of cloth—called *brandea*—were just as good as the original saintly body, Gregory offered yet another anecdote. At the time of Pope Leo, he says, certain "Greeks" (Eastern Christians) had doubted the efficacy of these brandea. To demonstrate their error, Leo cut one with a pair of scissors, and blood flowed from the cut just as if it had been a human body.

In the end, Gregory promised to send the empress some filings from the chain that had bound St. Paul. This was a favorite sort of relic with Gregory, and his correspondence indicates that he often gave away filings from the chains that had bound St. Peter and St. Paul, usually enclosed in a reliquary. Writing in 603 to a friend with weak eyes, Gregory said, "I have sent you a little cross, in which is inserted a gift of the chains of the Apostles St. Peter and St. Paul . . . Let them be continually applied to your eyes, for many miracles have often been wrought by this same gift" (cited in Dudden 1905, 279). Another relic favored by Gregory was oil from the lamps that burned before the tombs of martyrs in the Roman catacombs (Mioni 1908, 86–87).

Gregory's letter to Constantina, as well as other writings in which he mentions relics, tells us several things. First, official theology aside, it seems clear that Gregory saw saintly bodies as infused with supernatural power. Second, he believed that this supernatural power could be transferred to other objects (like brandea, chains, oil) and that physical contact with these secondary relics could be a source of miracles. Finally, he clearly felt that breaking apart saintly bodies was wrong.

We know from other sources that this last view was not universally shared in the Christian world. On the contrary, in Gregory's time saintly bodies were being dismembered in the Eastern Church (Thurston 1913, 736). Nevertheless, all commentators agree in suggesting that Gregory was expressing a view that was widely shared by Western prelates. As Petersen (1984, 122–50) points out, this does not mean that Western prelates were unwilling to accept relics that had been split off from saintly bodies elsewhere—only that they themselves were reluctant to engage in the practice.

Over the next two centuries, however, this Western bias against saintly dismemberment weakened and then reversed itself. By the early ninth century the dismemberment of saintly bodies had become commonplace in the West. Perhaps the one incident that best epitomizes this shift in attitude occurred in the late ninth century, when the head of St. Paul, which Gregory the Great had so categorically refused to give to the Empress Constantina, was removed from its body and installed in the private chapel of the popes (Mioni 1908, 134).

What caused this change in Western attitudes toward saintly dismemberment is problematic. Both Geary (1984, 267) and Mioni (1908, 132) suggest that it was a political move. The dismemberment of saintly bodies at Rome and the distribution of these relics outside Italy established a closer tie between Rome and Christian churches in other parts of Europe. In fact, it seems likely that the distribution of body-part relics did bind the Christian periphery in Europe more tightly to the Roman center. Nevertheless, the fact remains that the distribution of body-part relics could have served this same political function for Gregory the Great had he viewed saintly dismemberment as legitimate. What the Geary-Mioni argument leaves unexplained, in other words, is why attitudes toward saintly dismemberment changed sufficiently that such dismemberment became a viable political option in the eighth and ninth centuries.

Nolan and Nolan (1989, 164) propose a more matter-of-fact explanation for the change in attitude toward saintly dismemberment: "Possibly the reduction of many early saints to piles of disarticulated bones and dust through purely natural processes made the dismemberment of saints' bodies seem less distasteful." Possibly, but many of the bodies that Gregory had dared not look upon, let along touch, had lain around for over four centuries; it is difficult to imagine that another three centuries would have produced a drastic change in their appearance.

In the end, we know that during the seventh and eighth centuries the Western Church did reverse its earlier bias and did come to promote the dismemberment of saintly bodies. Why this policy shift occurred is a puzzle that historians of the early Church still need to solve.

Relic Cults in the Middle Ages

During the Middle Ages the most important relic sanctuaries were still those that contained (or at least were believed to contain) the entire body of some particular saint or, better yet, the entire bodies of several saints. Nevertheless, body-part relics—usually, bits of bone from the body of a saint—were the focus of many popular cults. The demand for saintly relics was sufficiently intense that relic theft (stealing a relic and bringing or selling it to another community) was routine.[1] Often these thefts were regarded as an act of patriotism for which the

---

1. For an extended discussion of medieval relic theft, see Geary (1978); Mioni (1908, 154–56).

thieves earned a place in history. To this day, for instance, tourists visiting the cathedral of S. Nicolà at Bari (Apulia) can buy a reproduction of the parchment listing the merchants who stole the body of S. Nicolà from Mira (Asia Minor) and brought it to Bari in 1087.

As popular as they were, however, relic cults did not go unchallenged. Quite apart from those explicitly heretical groups (like the Waldensians) that devalued everything connected with the cult of the saints, there was an identifiable countertradition well within the bounds of Catholic orthodoxy that was strongly critical of relic cults. Cults organized around body-part relics, in particular, attracted criticism.

One of the most widely read books of the Middle Ages, for instance, was the *Legenda aurea* (Golden Legend) by the Iacopo da Voragine (circa 1230 to circa 1298), the Dominican archbishop of Genoa.[2] The *Golden Legend* consists mainly of stories about saints. Redon (1983) points out that the implicit emphasis in many of these stories promotes a concern for maintaining the integrity of saintly bodies. In one of da Voragine's stories, the body of St. Paul was buried separately from his head. One night miraculous signs lead to the discovery of the head, and it is placed at the feet of the body. As a bishop prays nearby, the body "recognizes" its head and turns around to align itself properly with that head. In another story, the bodies of St. Paul and St. Peter are stolen and the bones mixed together, making the two bodies indistinguishable. A divine revelation, however, provides the key that allows them to be separated: the large bones belong to Paul, the smaller bones to Peter. In another story, the bones of S. Bartolomeo are dispersed by Saracens on the Lipari islands and mixed with a variety of other bones. The saint appears to a monk and tells him to gather his bones together; the monk will know which bones are Bartolmeo's because they will shine like fire in the dark. In still other stories, saintly bodies are torn apart while the saint is still living (usually during the saint's martyrdom) and the pieces are miraculously rejoined after death.

In short, Redon (196) concludes, the emphasis in da Voragine's *Golden Legend* (the dismemberment of a saintly body before death, the unification of the saint's body parts after death) is very much the reverse of the by-then-common devotional practice, which was to dismember saintly bodies after death in order to create relics.

Other authors in medieval Italy launched a more direct attack on relic cults.

2. The original title of da Voragine's work was *Legend of the Saints.* Ott (1913, 262) suggests that it came to be called *The Golden Legend* because medieval Christians "considered it worth its weight in gold."

In the *Decameron*, written about 1350, Boccaccio (1982, 471–79) satirizes relic cults in the tenth story told on the sixth day.[3] The protagonist in this particular story is Fra Cipolla (Brother Onion), a friar who solicits alms from simple folk by his eloquent preaching and by his willingness to display a great relic, namely, a feather shed by the Angel Gabriel when he announced to Mary that she was to be the mother of Jesus. The feather, Boccaccio tells us, was really a parrot's feather. One day, as a practical joke, two men sneak into Fra Cipolla's room, remove the feather from its case, and replace it with a bit of coal that happens to be nearby. Fra Cipolla does not discover the switch until he's in the middle of his sermon, at which point he quickly improvises. He tells his audience that he once went on a pilgrimage to Jerusalem. There he met with the patriarch of that city and was shown a wondrous collection of relics: the finger of the Holy Ghost, fingernails from one of the cherubim, rays of the star that guided the Wise Men, sounds from the bells from Solomon's temple, etcetera. The patriarch gave him several of these relics, including Gabriel's feather and some of the coal used to roast S. Lorenzo.[4] By chance, he continues, he has mistakenly brought the coal not the feather, and with that he opens the case and displays this relic to the people. As they crowd around him, giving him more alms than usual, the good friar uses the coal to mark crosses on their vestments.

Franco Sacchetti (1330–circa 1400) also ridicules the public credulity so often associated with relic cults. He (Sacchetti 1970, 152–54) begins one of his short stories by noting that relics are often not what they seem to be. The people of Florence, he says, received an arm of S. Reparata from Apulia. For the next several years, the relic was solemnly displayed on this saint's festa. Unfortunately, they later discovered that it was made of wood.[5] Later in this same story, Sacchetti tells us that Taddeo Dini, a Dominican, once found himself preaching at a convent dedicated to S. Caterina on the festa of that saint. At the end of his sermon, just before he could come down from the pulpit, some priests brought him a reliquary containing an arm of S. Caterina and asked him to show it to the people.

---

3. In Boccaccio's narrative, seven women and three men escape to a villa outside Naples to avoid the plague. To pass the time, each member of the group tells one story on each of ten days, for a total of one hundred stories.

4. According to tradition, S. Lorenzo (St. Laurence) was martyred in 258 A.D. by being roasted on a gridiron.

5. This incident actually occurred. Florence obtained S. Reparata's arm in 1352 and discovered that it was made of wood in 1356. A history of Florentine churches published in 1757 (cited in Delehaye 1934, 102–3) says that S. Reparata's arm was originally kept at a convent in southern Italy. The Florentines requested the relic from the king of Naples, and he in turn ordered the abbess of the convent to send it to them. Unwilling to comply with the request, the abbess resorted to a ruse and substituted the wooden arm for the real arm.

But Dini was no fool, Sacchetti tells us, and he told the priests carrying the relic that he had in fact been to Mount Sinai and seen the body of S. Caterina, with her two arms still attached. "No," said the priests, "we consider *this* truly to be the arm of the saint." When Dini still refused to display the relic, the abbess sent a message begging him to show the relic lest devotion at the convent diminish. In frustration, he took the relic from the casket and showed it to the crowd, saying: "Ladies and gentleman, the sisters of this convent say that the arm you see before you is the arm of S. Caterina. I have been to Mount Sinai and have seen the body of S. Caterina, fully intact and with at most two arms. [But] if she possibly had a third, this is it" (ibid., 153). With that, he made the sign of the cross. Some listeners laughed at Dini's sarcasm, but others, says Sacchetti, either because they did not hear his remarks or because they did not understand his remarks, simply and devoutly made the sign of the cross themselves. Sacchetti's story is less critical of the regular clergy than Boccaccio's, but in the end he too is giving vent to a strong skepticism concerning relics.

Nevertheless (the reservations expressed by writers like da Voragine, Boccaccio, and Sacchetti notwithstanding), the central sociological fact about relic cults is that they were immensely popular with ordinary Catholics, and that fact needs to be explained.

The Meaning of Relics

Central to any explanation of relic cults in Italy is an understanding of what relics meant to ordinary Italian Catholics, and here we must avoid the common mistake of conflating official doctrine and popular belief. For example, in discussing the sack of Constantinople by Western crusaders in 1204, Andrea and Rachlin (1992, 152) advance the following argument to explain why the crusaders seized so many of Constantinople's relics: "The remains of saints possessed a powerful attraction for the medieval mind. Relics were not seen as inanimate objects. Rather, sacred relics mediated the power of God through the holy person whose remains were enclosed in a reliquary. It was believed that a saint . . . watched over his relics, traveled with them, and protected those persons who legitimately possessed them."

Although these authors claim to be speaking of the "medieval mind," their description here has a suspiciously tridentine feel about it, notably when they assert that relics were important because they "mediated the power of God." The fact is that neither these authors nor anyone else can bring forth any evidence that this was the view held by the majority of medieval Catholics. At best, Andrea and Rachlin are describing the way relics were viewed by medieval theologians and their close associates; at worst they are simply projecting post-Trent Catholic doctrine onto the past. Official theology aside, saints—like madonnas—have always been seen by ordinary Catholics to have independent power. This means that, if saintly relics were seen to have power, it was the power associated with the saint from whose body the relic was taken, not the God of the official Church.

We must also be careful in talking about the relationship between saint and relic. To most readers it will seem obvious that these two things are analytically and substantively separate. A saint is a supernatural being who resides in Heaven, and a relic is a material part of the body that once belonged to the saint. This is why it makes sense for Andrea and Rachlin to say that saints "watched over" their relics. But this clear separation, so obvious to the modern mind, is absent from popular Catholicism in Italy. Within the logic of popular Catholicism, there is no clear separation between a saint and that saint's relic, in the same way that there is no clear separation between a madonna and her image (see chap, 1). As a practical matter, this means that (1) the relic is seen as much a source of supernatural power as the saint himself or herself and (2) relationships of reciprocity (mainly, exchanging veneration for favors) established with the relic are, ipso facto, established with the saint.

The suggestion that Italian Catholics saw relics as infused with supernatural power is hardly novel. On the contrary, it is a suggestion that Church authorities themselves have made over and over again. The Jansenist Synod of Pistoia (see chap. 1), for instance, took explicit note of the popular view:

> Finally, we must remember that in honoring relics we are honoring the saints, and that the miracles that it pleases God to work in the presence of sacred relics are only an invitation to us to appeal to these holy souls for intercession. *Far from believing that there is any special power that resides in these relics* [emphasis added], the Faithful must be reminded that all our hope should be founded on the power and bounty of God. (Stella 1986, 201)

Similarly, a directive issued by diocesan authorities at Bergamo in 1782 instructed parish priests "to explain to the faithful that the veneration due to relics does not derive from an energy that they possess [un'energia da esse possedute] but rather is veneration being offered to the saints that the relics call to mind" (Zanchi 1988, 205). This same call—to stamp out the popular belief that relics possess an inherent power—continued to be issued by Church authorities, in both northern and southern Italy, right up to the late nineteenth and early twentieth centuries (see the examples cited in Cattaneo 1981).

In the first instance, then, relic cults were popular because saints were a source of supernatural power and because the distinction between relic and saint was not clearly drawn. As a result, contact with a relic provided a simple and direct way of accessing saintly power. The belief that saintly power was physically present in a relic also explains why the power associated with a relic was seen to diminish as physical distance from the relic increased (Boesch Gajano 1990).

Two Types of Power

Elsewhere (Carroll 1992, 36–40), I point out that the saints and madonnas of Italy have two distinct types of supernatural power. The first is the power to heal or, more generally, to improve some aspect of the current situation; the second is the power to protect from future dangers. Any given saint or madonna is capable of exercising both types of power. Nevertheless, there is a rough and loose division of labor among saints and madonnas. Generally, individual Italian Catholics who have immediate need of some supernatural favor (a miraculous cure for instance) are more likely to appeal to a madonna than to a saint. On the other hand, when a social group (a city, a village, a neighborhood, etc.) seeks collective protection from dangers that might strike during the upcoming year, it will usually turn to a saint. This is why statistical studies of community patrons in Italy (reviewed in ibid., 15–17) find that saints are far more likely to be chosen as community patrons than madonnas.

Saintly relics, like saints themselves, are also most often associated with the power to protect. This is why it so important for a community to have a relic of its supernatural patron in a local church. Such a relic, as the physical reservoir of the saint's supernatural power, can be can be carried in procession throughout the community, thus ensuring that the community as whole comes into physical contact with that power and so partakes of the saint's protective mantle.

Let me be clear: relics do sometimes have the power to cure. Saintly relics in Italy specialize in exorcising the possessed, in curing hernias, in counteracting the bite of rabid animals, and so on (see Rivera 1988, 265–334 for specific examples). My point is only that the more common pattern is for both saints and saintly relics to be associated with the power to protect groups from this-worldly dangers, and it is this power—the power to protect—that more than anything else explains the popularity of relic cults in Italy.

Strange Histories

In a careful consideration of relic cults, the Bollandist Hippolyte Delehaye (1934, 79–116) argues that there was a dramatic surge in the number and popularity of these cults at three distinct points in the history of the Western Church. The first occurred during the late eighth and early ninth centuries, when several popes transferred ("translated") the remains of saints buried outside Rome. Sometimes these bodies were transferred to churches located within the city of Rome itself, sometimes they were shipped to churches in northern Europe. The second surge occurred in the years following the sack of Constantinople by European crusaders in 1204, when these crusaders brought back and distributed many of the relics that had accumulated in Constantinople over the centuries.[6] The third surge took place in the century and a half following the Council of Trent.

Delehaye's assertion (103) that relic cults enjoyed a "renaissance" during the Counter-Reformation might surprise some readers, since most accounts of relic use in the Western Church create a quite different impression. Mioni (1908), for instance, devotes more than three hundred pages of text to the emergence of relic cults in the early Church and the elaboration of these cults during the Middle Ages. Only in his last chapter does he consider relic cults in the modern period, and his discussion here is concerned mainly with rebutting Protestant critiques; the matter of popular practice during the modern period is ignored.

Later histories, especially if addressed to the general public, tend to follow the same formula. For example, most of the text for the "relics" entry in the *New Catholic Encyclopedia* (see Chiovaro 1967) is concerned with relic use in the early Church and during the Middle Ages; only a relatively brief concluding section deals with the modern period, and the concern here is entirely with the regulations and restrictions that the Church established in regard to relics, not with popular practice. Strong (1987, 277–80) simply ends his discussion of relic cults with the Middle Ages and ignores entirely relic use in the modern period. It would be easy to conclude that relic cults were a devotional form that flourished during the Middle Ages and declined in popularity in the modern period. Nevertheless, Delehaye is absolutely correct: cults organized around saintly relics proliferated during the Counter-Reformation.

In northern Italy there was an increased emphasis on saintly relics immediately following the close of the Council of Trent in 1563. Carlo Borromeo (1538–84), for instance, archbishop of Milan and often regarded as the prototypical Counter-Reformation bishop, was an avid promoter of these cults. Between 1571 and 1582, Borromeo oversaw nine separate translations of saintly relics, which brought relics associated with over two dozen different saints into Milanese churches. His concerted efforts on behalf of relic cults gave rise to the saying

6. For a succinct account of how a European Christian army that had set out to liberate the Holy Land (Palestine) ended up sacking a Christian city like Constantinople, and how they justified the assault, see Andrea and Rachlin (1992).

"Cardinal Borromeo doesn't leave either the living or the dead in peace" (Signorotto 1985, 409). A passion for relics also characterized Federico Borromeo
(1564–1631), Carlo's cousin, who himself became archbishop of Milan. As we
shall see later in this chapter, Federico Borromeo would oversee the importation
of several thousand relics into Milan and the surrounding area. The Borromeos
aside, a passion for relics was widespread in Lombardy generally, and Lombar-
dian relic collections during the seventeenth century grew rapidly (Zanchi 1988,
204–5).

The Counter-Reformation zeal for relics is neatly encapsulated in the history of what happened to Carlo Borromeo's own body. Shortly after his death in
1584, parts of his heart and his intestines were removed from his corpse and sent
as relics to the Church of S. Carlo al Corso in Rome. At the same time, pieces of
his clothing were sent to other churches throughout Italy. In 1611, Federico Borromeo authorized a surgeon to remove two ribs from his cousin's corpse, one of
which was sent to Pope Paul V, the other to Philip III of Spain. Some time later,
another piece of Carlo Borromeo's heart, along with a bit his flesh and some of
his blood, ended up at a church dedicated to (another) S. Carlo at Naples (De Lellis 1654, 296), and a bit of his liver ended up in the relic cabinet of the sacristy of
the Duomo at Naples (Celano 1856, 154). Carlo Borromeo, who in life had done
so much to promote the cult of relics in northern Italy, continued after his death
to be consumed, literally, by a passion for relics.

In southern Italy, the upsurge in relic use occurred a little later than in northern Italy but was nevertheless well under way by 1600. De Maio (1983, 218) suggests that at Naples the "frenetic importation of relics" began in the 1590s, when
several especially large relic collections were donated to Neapolitan churches. In
this particular case, we can assess the Counter-Reformation surge in relic use with
some precision, because of two accounts, one published just a few years before
the close of the Council of Trent (de Stefano 1560) and one published a little more
than sixty years later(D'Engenio 1623). Each tried to do the same thing: survey
all the churches in Naples and provide a brief description of the important things,
including relics, found in each. In addition to these two sources, we have for some
churches a third source: a supplement to D'Engenio's work published in 1654 (De
Lellis 1977). None of these three sources provide an exhaustive and absolutely
accurate account of all the relics in Naples; some were undoubtedly missed or
simply not recorded. Still, all three authors pay special attention to the important
relics in the churches they survey. If our concern is only with assessing change (as
it is), then the data extractable from these accounts are likely adequate.

One pattern that emerges from a comparison of these three accounts is that
following Trent there appears to have been a modest increase in the proportion
of churches possessing important relics. In 1560, De Stefano discussed 251 churches

and identifies 32, 13 percent of the total, as having important relics. In 1623, D'Engenio described 298 churches, and indicated that 70, 23 percent of the total, had important relics. But the more striking change is that there was a fairly dramatic increase in the size of relic collections held at any one church. Consider the relic collection held at S. Giovanni Maggiore, one of the four "ancient parishes" of Naples. In 1560 (De Stefano 1560), it had three relics:

—the head of S. Matteo the Apostle,
—a rib of S. Giovanni the Apostle, and
—the eyes of S. Lucia, Virgin and Martyr.

In 1623 (D'Engenio 1623), this collection had increased to seven important relics:

—a piece of the Most Holy Cross,
—a thorn from Our Lord's Crown of Thorns,
—a rib of S. Giovanni Battista (not "the Apostle," as in De Stefano's list),
—a vial of S. Zaccaria the Prophet's blood,
—part of the head of S. Matteo the Apostle,
—an eye of S. Lucia, Virgin and Martyr, and
—an arm of S. Pomponio, bishop of Naples.

By 1654, according to De Lellis's account (see De Lellis 1977), this collection had expanded dramatically and now included:

—wood from the cross,
—a thorn from the Crown of Christ,
—part of the sponge used to give gall and vinegar to Christ,
—the upper part of the head of S. Matthew the Apostle,
—a rib and a molar tooth of S. Giovanni Battista,
—an eye of S. Lucia, Virgin and Martyr,
—bones of S. Lorenzo, Martyr, S. Elisabetta, S. Leon, pope, and S. Sabino,
—blood of S. Zaccaria,
—a relic of S. Simone,
—blood of the Prophet Isaiah,
—relics of Pope S. Giovanni I, S. Cosma, S. Damiani, S. Antonio abate, S. Bonifacio, S. Christoforo, S. Vicenza Donati, S. Zenone, Martyr, S. Pancratio, Martyr, and S. Festo, Martyr,
—a stone used to stone S. Stefano,
—a bit and reins belonging to S. Giorgio,
—a veil used by S. Margarita, and
—a tooth of S. Fortunato, Martyr.

Table 6.1. Relic Collections, Selected Neapolitan Churches during the Late Sixteenth and Early Seventeenth Centuries

Church	Christ Relics	Marian Relics	Saintly Body Relics	Other Saintly Relics	Number of Saints in Collection
S. Maria Maggiore					
1560	0	0	1	0	1
1623	2	1	1	37	35
S. Giorgio Maggiore					
1560	0	0	1	0	1
1633	0	0	1	4	3
1654	0	0	1	173	162
S. Gaudioso					
1560	0	0	1	1	2
1623	4	2	40	21	58
S. Paolo Maggiore					
1560	0	0	0	0	0
1623	7	1	1	124	122
S. Patritia					
1560	1	0	1	1	2
1623	10	2	1	36	22
S. Martino					
1560	1	0	0	0	0
1623	4	0	0	39	36
S. Pietro à Maiella					
1560	0	0	0	1	1
1623	1	0	0	9	4
1654	1	0	0	10	5

Sources: Derived from de Stefano (1560); D'Engenio (1623); De Lellis (1654).

As dramatic as the growth of this relic collection was, it was not at all unusual. On the contrary, the relic collections at several other Neapolitan churches expanded even more dramatically. Table 6.1 shows the increases in relic collections at seven Neapolitan churches. Some of the increase was due to the acquisition of Christ relics, usually items associated with the Passion (a piece of the cross, one of the nails used to crucify Christ, a thorn from the Crown of Thorns, etc.). There was also a modest increase in Marian relics, such as bits of Mary's hair, some of her breast milk, items of her clothing. But the biggest portion of the increase was in saintly relics. Sometimes, as with the Church of S. Gaudioso, the entire body of a saint (or a set of entire saintly bodies) was added to the collection. The more common pattern, however, both for the churches listed in table 6.1 and for all cases where relic collections increased, was for these collections to increase through the addition of body-part relics (usually small bits of bone).

If the size of Italian relic collections increased dramatically during the

Counter-Reformation, that raises an obvious question: Where did the relics that flowed into these collections come from? In some cases, new relics were created simply by breaking apart older relics. In other cases, the new relics were retrieved from areas of Europe that had fallen into Protestant hands. In still other cases, relics were extracted from especially large existing collections and distributed in small batches to new locations. The relic collections at Cologne, in particular, which included (among other things) the bones of St. Ursula and her eleven thousand virgins, were a common source of relics for Italian churches during the Counter-Reformation. But the lion's share of the new relics that appeared during the Counter-Reformation came from a source that had not been exploited for more than seven hundred years.

Down to the Past

In June 1578, workers digging in a quarry outside the Porta Salaria at Rome came upon a maze of subterranean passageways. Carved into the stone along these passageways were rows of large niches, obviously burial places. The frescoes and inscriptions associated with these niches made it clear that this was a Christian cemetery dating from the earliest years of the Church. Other such cemeteries would be discovered in the years that followed. In 1593, Antonio Bosio (1576–1629) made his first descent into this subterranean world and began the systematic explorations that would earn him the label Columbus of the Catacombs. Bosio's massive *Roma sotteranea*, published in 1629, would introduce the catacombs to the world.

In retrospect, it seems clear that the "discovery" of the catacombs in 1578 was not really a discovery at all. Church officials had known for some time that cemeteries existed under certain Roman churches, including those dedicated to S. Sebastiano, S. Pancrazio, and S. Agnese. The catacombs under S. Sebastiano, in particular, were both known and accessible, and Filippo Neri (1515–95) often went there for contemplation. Moreover, exploration of the catacombs by Bosio and others would reveal graffiti left by much earlier visitors. Someone, for instance, seems to have explored the catacombs of S. Callisto as early as 1432 (Hertling and Kirschbaum 1949, 3). Broken pieces of marble from the catacombs would also be discovered in Roman churches built before 1578, suggesting that the catacombs had often been entered and plundered for building materials.

What made the discovery outside the Porta Salaria significant was that it occurred during the late sixteenth century, when the Church was searching for ways to counter Protestantism and to maintain a hold on the allegiance of Catholics not yet infected by this heresy. With regard to these goals, the catacombs were valuable in a number of ways. First, Church officials could and did point to the frescoes found in the catacombs as evidence that images had been used in the early Church and therefore that the Protestant attack on image cults was wrong. Modern scholars, both Catholic or Protestant, point out that the catacombs were cemeteries, not places of worship, and that there is no basis for believing that the images in the catacombs had been the object of cultic veneration. But this is a tempered and reasoned scholarly judgment that would have been unsuited to the needs of the Catholic propagandists of the Counter-Reformation, and so it was ignored.

The catacombs were also useful to the Church for the simple reason that they were located in Rome. A key element in all Protestant formulations was the contention that the Roman Church had moved away from the purity and simplicity of the early Christian experience. To a large extent, the Church accepted this privileging of "early Christian experience," and the fact that the catacombs were located at Rome established a direct physical link between the early Christian experience and the Roman Church that could not be matched by any of the Protestant denominations.

But in retrospect, what made the catacombs most valuable to the Church was that they were believed to contain the bones of several thousand early Christian martyrs. Being martyrs, they were automatically saints, and so their remains were relics. True, here again, as with the frescoes in the catacombs, what Church officials "found" owed more to their preconceptions than to what was actually there. The Church hierarchy obviously wanted a new supply of saintly relics, and so these burial grounds were assumed to date from the period when Christians were persecuted and to contain the bodies of martyrs. As a result, signs of martyrdom were seen everywhere. Vials embedded in the plaster surrounding the burial niches were assumed to contain blood gathered at the time of martyrdom; every shorthand inscription was stretched out into a Latin phrase that connoted martyrdom; and so on. In fact, it is now recognized that most of the burials in the catacombs date from the fourth century A.D. or later (and thus from a period subsequent to the persecutions of Christians at Rome) and that the signs originally taken as evidence of martyrdom have other interpretations. To understand why the Church wanted to see the catacombs as a source of saintly relics, we need to remember that Protestant leaders had attacked relic cults as vehemently as they had attacked image cults. Calvin (1921), in particular, had in 1543 written a scathing critique of relic cults.

In the first part of his critique, Calvin considers relics associated with Christ and the Virgin Mary, and here his core objection is that most of these relics are inherently implausible. How, he asks rhetorically, could the prepuce of Christ, removed at his circumcision, have possibly ended up in a church in the diocese of Poitiers? How could items from the Last Supper (the table, a knife used to cut the paschal lamb, etc.) have ended up in various European churches several centuries after Jerusalem was destroyed? As to Marian relics, Calvin suggests that the Holy Virgin would have had to have been a milk cow all her life to produce the quantity of "Virgin's milk" found in Christian churches.

But it is in the last section of his critique, where he considers saintly relics, that Calvin's criticism becomes most deadly, as he piles up physical impossibility upon physical impossibility. How could so many different churches claim to have the head of John the Baptist? How could the body of the same saint be found in two, three, four, five, even six different churches? How could many churches claim to have an arm belonging to the same saint? From a purely intellectual point of view, the cumulative weight of Calvin's examples submerges any possible compromise with the Church on the matter of cults organized around saintly relics. It is thus hardly surprising that relics were destroyed, along with images, in the iconoclastic frenzies that swept through the areas outside of Italy where Calvinism became popular.

But Calvin's unconditional rejection of relic cults made it possible for the Counter-Reformation Church to use relic cults in the fight against Protestantism. As we have seen, ordinary Italian Catholics saw relics, like sacred images, to be infused with supernatural power, and it was this perception that made relic cults popular. By promoting relic cults in Italy (and elsewhere), where they had wide popular appeal in spite of the purely intellectual considerations enunciated by Calvin, the Church co-opted a popular devotion that entailed a clear rejection of Protestantism. Promoting relic cults, in other words, was a way of giving ordinary Catholics what they wanted while simultaneously distancing them from heresy.

The procedures surrounding relic cults, especially as they concerned catacomb relics, were also used to reinforce a number of organizational principles established at Trent. Roman authorities, for instance, very quickly acted to ensure that they had a monopoly on the extraction of relics from the catacombs. Urban VII (r. 1590) stationed authorities at the gates to Rome search purses and other containers to make sure they did not contain relics. In 1603 an edict issued on the authority of Clement VIII forbade the removal of relics from the catacombs and gave property owners ten days to seal any entrances to the catacombs that might exist on their land. A few years later, Paul V (r. 1605–21) ordered that unauthorized removal of relics would result in excommunication, a penalty that would be reconfirmed by Benedict XIV (r. 1740–58).[7]

Collectively, these measures meant that all requests for catacomb relics had

7. All of the measures mentioned here are discussed in Signorotto (1985, 414–15); Mioni (1908, 153).

to be made to Roman authorities. If the request was granted, the relics were transported to the requester's home community, where they had to be "recognized" in a formal ceremony attended by the local bishop or his representative. These procedures reinforced the hierarchical principle that was in many ways the organizational cornerstone of the Counter-Reformation Church: the pope at Rome was to have authority over the bishops, and bishops were to have authority over the people in their dioceses.

There is no way to know with certainty how many requests for relics were approved and how many rejected. Still, given the number of catacomb relics that were exported to various areas of the Catholic world, it seems likely that most such requests were approved. Delehaye (1934, 114), for instance, notes that, in Switzerland alone, more than 400 "catacomb" saints became objects of cultic devotion, while a single Italian monastery at Forli (Emilia-Romagna) had the bones of no fewer than 155 catacomb saints.

Partial Answers, New Puzzles

That relic cults served the political interests of the Counter-Reformation church only partly explains the renaissance of relic use during the late sixteenth and early seventeenth centuries. While the fact that relic cults served the political interests of the Counter-Reformation Church might explain why members of the Church hierarchy worked to increase the number of churches with important relics, how does it account for one of the central features of relic use during the Counter-Reformation, namely, the dramatic increase in the size of individual relic collections?

Generally, Counter-Reformation relic collections did not grow slowly as single relics were added over a period of years. On the contrary, the common pattern was for a set of new relics to be added all at once to an existing collection. In the usual case, these new relics had been gathered by one person, who then donated them to a church. The individuals who made these relic donations are always singled out and identified by name in contemporary accounts. For example, in his updating of D'Engenio's work, De Lellis (1654, 314) tells us how the relic collection at S. Giorgio Maggiore came to be enlarged:

> In addition to the relics that have been in this church since time immemorial, a great many other relics have recently been acquired from diverse sources by Padre Domenico Cenatempo, a man of good will and sound doctrine who is rector of the Pious Workmen who staff this church . . . and my own spiritual adviser. These relics were acquired to enhance the dignity and beauty of this church and have been installed in a specially prepared treasury. They have all been authenticated, recognized, and approved by the Archdiocesan Court of Naples.

There follows a list of relics belonging to 147 different saints. The vast majority of these saints (approximately 90% of the total) are identified as "martyrs," which almost certainly means that Cenatempo obtained them from the catacombs.

This same concern with naming names, that is, with precisely identifying the donors associated with important relic collections, is also evident in the accounts of relic collections given in Donato Calvi's "almanac" of important events in the Bergamo region. The following entry, for instance, is typical:

> The bodies of two saints, S. Bonifacio, Martyr, and S. Felicita, Martyr, were donated to parish church of Alzano maggiore. On this day today [Nov. 18, 1673] these relics were presented to the bishop and approved and recognized using the appropriate formulas. These relics were obtained through the efforts of Monsignor Reverend Giovanni Alviani, Signor Francisco Barizza, and Signor Dionisio Agnelli. With the collaboration of Signor Tranquillo di Negro at Rome . . . these men obtained the body of S. Bonifacio from Cardinal Altieri on August 2, 1671, and the body of S. Felicita from Cardinal Carpegna on July 29, 1672. These holy relics are now conserved in two beautiful silver caskets adorned with statues, crosses, and palms . . . Sixty ounces of silver were used in the construction of these caskets, which now reside in two distinguished chapels that were specially constructed to hold them. (Calvi 1677, 315)

I might add that Calvi does not usually identify donors when discussing relics that were part of a church's collection prior to Trent.

What purpose was served by identifying donors so precisely? The obvious answer is that donors thus received public recognition for their acts of generosity, suggesting that donating relics to a church was a way of securing social status in the larger community. This establishes a similarity between the donation of relics to a church and other activities that also became common during the Counter-Reformation. Burke (1987) argues that the mid-sixteenth century witnessed a dramatic increase in conspicuous consumption on the part of the urban upper classes in both northern and southern Italy. Members of these classes began to spend large sums of money in ways that could be observed by others in order to gain or maintain social status. "Established families," Burke argues (135), "had to engage in conspicuous consumption in order to maintain their position [and] new families had to do so in order to acquire one, to gain admittance to the upper circle." Although there were any number of projects or objects on which money could be spent in this competition for status, Burke singles out the following:

> —building expensive palaces, stuffed to the brim with tapestries, velvet curtains, artwork, inlaid tables, cabinets, etc., and staffed with armies of servants;

—building new churches, even in cities already crowded with churches, or remodeling the facades of existing churches;

—purchasing and using elaborate carriages (in Venice, gondolas) or sedan chairs; and

—sponsoring highly theatrical festivals, either secular or religious.

He also mentions (if only in passing) that giving alms, which often constituted a significant portion of the household budgets of patrician families, should be regarded as a form of conspicuous consumption.

Burke nowhere mentions relics, but it seems unlikely that relics would be overlooked in this frenzy to engage in conspicuous consumption. In the eyes of the general public, relics were infused with supernatural power and a source of supernatural protection for the entire community. On the other hand, obtaining new relics was time consuming and costly. In donating relics to a church, then, individuals were in a very real sense distributing an extremely valuable and relatively scarce commodity to the members of their community. For this reason, such donations were every bit as likely to generate status as building churches or giving alms.

But how could a person be as conspicuous as possible in donating relics? In other contexts, conspicuousness was measured in a purely quantitative way: in terms of the amount of money spent. This is why the costs associated with most patterns of conspicuous consumption were well advertised (see Burke for examples). To a certain extent, relic donors could do the same, by commissioning lavish and expensive reliquaries to hold the relics they donated. Often, they went so far as to advertise just how expensive these reliquaries were, which is presumably how Calvi (see above) came to know the exact amount of silver used to construct the reliquaries that housed the bodies of S. Bonifacio and S. Felicita. But in the case of relics, there was a second quantitative measure (apart from amount of money spent) that could be used to assess conspicuousness and that was the number of different saints represented in the collection. Simply put, measuring the worth of a relic collection in terms of the number of saints represented allowed relic collections to be evaluated against a common standard, just as an emphasis upon cost allowed palaces, festivals, and carriages to be evaluated against a common standard. This meant that the most valuable donations, and thus the donations that would earn the most status for the donor, were those that contained the bones of many saints. It was this (I suggest) that drove individuals to acquire and donate large relic collections and so it was this that was most responsible for the dramatic increase in the size of relic collections during the Counter-Reformation.

The suggestion that the accumulation and donation of relics was a method used by the urban upper classes in Counter-Reformation Italy to secure and maintain social status has two advantages: (1) it links relic donations to the general processes of conspicuous consumption and status striving that (if Burke is correct) emerged during this same period, and (2) it explains the data, namely, the fact that the size of relic collections increased dramatically during this period.

Still, it would be useful to have more direct evidence in support of my contention that relic donors were motivated by a desire for social status. Such evidence can come only from case studies of particular donors. Fortunately, just such a case study is available for one of the most important figures in the history of relic donation in Italy.

Giovanni Giacomo Castoldi, Relic Hunter Extraordinaire

On May 14, 1609, Federico Borromeo, the archbishop of Milan, opened a provincial synod in the cathedral at Milan. Two weeks later, the synod closed, an event marked by a grand procession in which all of Milan's clergy, both regular and secular, as well as the members of the city's Senate, participated. But the human participants in the procession were less important than the eighteen floats that carried the "Sacred Treasure," a collection of more than 3,500 relics. This collection had been gathered and brought to Milan largely through the efforts of a single man, a Milanese merchant named Giovanni Giacomo Castoldi.

The story of how Castoldi put together the Sacred Treasure is told in a manuscript written circa 1615 by Gierolamo Bennardini; the manuscript also contains an introduction written by Castoldi himself. Using this manuscript and other sources, Signorotto (1985) has published a modern account of Castoldi's career as a relic hunter. The account that follows is based entirely on Signorotto's account, and it is to Signorotto that all credit is due for bringing Castoldi's story to light.

Giovanni Castoldi was born in the parish of S. Tommaso at Milan in 1560. As a young man he took an active role in lay religious activities. He was, for instance, prior (director) of the Confraternity of the Santissimo Corpo di Cristo at S. Tommaso. But it wasn't until 1585, when he was twenty-five, that Castoldi embraced the avocation that would enable him to influence religious practice at Milan in a grand manner. In that year, Castoldi found himself at Rome and decided to visit the catacombs of S. Lorenzo and S. Sebastiano. (This was, remember, only seven years after the Roman catacombs had been discovered.) This visit engendered in him a burning desire to "obtain some part of these sacred relics by whatever means necessary" (Bennardini, cited in ibid., 384) and to bring them to Milan. Before the pressures of business forced Castoldi's return to Milan, he enlisted the aid of Silvio Cappi, a priest living at Rome, as a collaborator.

For reasons that are unclear, Castoldi and Cappi's quest for Roman relics did not come to fruition until 1596, more than a decade after Castoldi's epiphany in the catacombs, when Clement VIII conceded Cappi the right to procure a few relics found at three Roman churches. These relics were sent to Milan and formally recognized by archdiocesan authorities in a ceremony at S. Tommaso, with Castoldi in attendance. Unfortunately for Castoldi's self-esteem, that evening he fell into conversation with an archdiocesan official who related the story of an earlier shipment of relics. It seems that Carlo Borromeo had prevailed upon a citizen of Milan residing in Cologne to obtain some of the many relics in that city. His efforts were successful, and the relics from Cologne were eventually installed in an elaborate reliquary in the duomo at Milan. Castoldi was crestfallen; the comparison with his own effort was obvious, and he realized that he had obtained "only a very few relics, none of which were of any great importance" (Bennardini, cited in ibid., 389). Castoldi resolved to renew his efforts to extract relics from the Roman catacombs and also to try to obtain relics from Cologne.

In 1600, Cappi obtained permission from various authorities to enter two catacombs and extract some relics. These were sent to Milan and, as before, were formally recognized by archdiocesan authorities in a ceremony at S. Tommaso. Somewhat later, a team of eighteen or so persons explored the S. Lorenzo catacombs on two occasions and on each occasion extracted a variety of relics. Perhaps surprisingly, Castoldi himself did not enter the catacombs on either occasion: on the first, he was present but stood guard at the entrance, while by the time of the second exploration he had returned to Milan on business.

The relics obtained during these descents into the catacombs were only a halfway point in Castoldi's career as a relic hunter. While in Rome he had visited a relative who was abbot of the Cistercian monastery attached to the Church of S. Croce in Jerusalem. There Castoldi saw a reliquary containing a part of the cross on which S. Dimas (Dismas, in English), the "good thief," had been crucified.[8] He made arrangements to have a piece of this relic sawed off and turned over to Cappi. During his return trip to Milan, Castoldi met and formed a friendship with a priest who was a member of the aristocracy at Cologne and who promised to help Castoldi obtain some relics from that city.

---

8. According to New Testament mythology, Christ was crucified along with two thieves (Mark 15:22–32; Matthew 27:33–44; Luke 23:33–43; John 19:18). The versions of the Crucifixion myth in Mark and Matthew suggest that both thieves mocked Christ. Luke's Gospel, however, says that, while one thief mocked Christ, the other recognized that Jesus was innocent of any crime and that Jesus promised this "good thief" that he would be with him, Jesus, in paradise. Although Luke does not supply a name for this good thief, he has traditionally been called Dismas.

The relics collected at Rome by Cappi arrived at Milan in August 1603 and were formally recognized by the vicar-general of the Archdiocese of Milan, who was astonished to see such a great abundance of "legs, arms, ribs, jaws, fingers, teeth, and other parts" (Bennardini, cited in ibid., 395), not to mention the fragment of S. Dimas's cross.

Castoldi now turned his attention to Cologne. With the help of his contacts there, including the priest he had met on his trip back from Rome, he was successful in having a large shipment of relics sent to the Church of the Concezione at Milan. These relics were formally recognized on January 12, 1606, in a ceremony presided over by Federico Borromeo himself and attended by a great crowd. Signorotto (1985, 396) sees Borromeo's presence at this ceremony as significant. Although Castoldi's relic collecting was by now well known to the public, Borromeo's personal involvement in the ceremony was a way of bestowing official approval on those activities and legitimating Castoldi's growing reputation in the eyes of the public.

During this recognition, each relic was carefully and reverently removed from the chest in which it had been shipped and placed on a large table. Twenty-two skulls, some partial and some complete, were removed first. These included the skull of S. Eulalio, two skulls belonging to the Holy Innocents (the children slain by Herod the Great around the birth of Christ), and the heads of S. Valbina and S. Cordula. Removed next were "many legs, arms, entire jaws with their teeth intact, and various other parts of the holy bodies of the ten thousand virgins" (Bennardini, cited in ibid., 397). Other relics followed. Over a four-hour period 1,700 relics were formally recognized as authentic.

In June of that same year Borromeo made a second visit to the church, by which time the collection (with the addition of the relics from Rome) included approximately 3,500 pieces. At this time he requested for his personal use one of the skulls of S. Orsola's virgins as well as twenty-four teeth "in order to make a corona of gold" (Bennardini, cited in ibid.). *Corona* in this case might refer to either a necklace or a rosary. The fact that modern audiences might find it hard to imagine the highest-ranking religious official of Milan wearing a necklace or using a rosary made of human teeth is an indication of how different our attitudes have become from those that prevailed in the Counter-Reformation Church. These 3,500 relics were the Sacred Treasure that would be paraded through Milan at the close of the provincial synod in 1609.

Although Castoldi was well connected at Rome, it is hard to see behind his actions some deep-seated desire to promote the political interests of the papacy. On the contrary, he seems driven most of all to serve local interests, which meant first serving the interests of Milan and then interests that were (literally) closer to home. In the years following 1609, the Sacred Treasure was divided and installed in 212 reliquaries, which were distributed to 120 churches at Milan and the surrounding area. Most of these churches received only one or two reliquaries. The major exceptions to this pattern were the Church of S. Tommaso (Castoldi's parish church), which received twelve, the oratory of S. Spirito (of which Castoldi was a member), which received seven, and the private oratory that Castoldi had built in his own house, which received eight (ibid., 403n).

What drove Castoldi to go to so much effort and so much expense over so long a period to amass the relics? Castoldi was a merchant, whose major activities were the sale of perpetual leases, often to religious groups, and the loaning of money (ibid., 387). He was thus someone very much at ease with numbers and with the use of numbers to measure success. Suddenly confronted during his 1585 visit to the catacombs that they contained innumerable saintly bones, it would be entirely natural for such a person to see the translation of a great many of these relics to Milan as a way to benefit Milan—and thus to impress both Church authorities and the general public in that city.

Certainly, Castoldi's activities did earn him a great deal of status. During the recognition of 1603, Castoldi was right there beside the archbishop and took an active role in the ceremonies. When the archbishop gave him a box of relics during the ceremony, Castoldi assured the prelate that these would be installed in an oratory that he was building "at great expense" in his house (Bennardini, cited in ibid., 397). Castoldi also took steps to ensure his visibility during the parade of the full Sacred Treasure in 1609, by designing a giant standard that was carried during this parade (ibid., 400). One side of this standard depicted the three crosses of Golgotha, and below the cross of the "bad thief" was an image of Hell that is said to have inspired awe and terror in the crowds. On the other side of the standard, surrounded by saintly effigies, was an inscription that referred to Popes Clement VIII and Paul V and, at the bottom, another inscription that referred to Castoldi himself. The standard, in other words, was constructed to attract the attention of the crowds and to place Castoldi in the company of popes.

In the years following the procession of the Sacred Treasure, a great many important visitors came to Castoldi's house to see the relics he had installed in his private oratory. Finally, Bennardini's account of the Sacred Treasure, on which Signorotto relies so heavily, was addressed to King Philip III of Spain, and Castoldi's introduction makes it clear that this account was written precisely because Philip had heard of the Sacred Treasure and had wanted to learn more about it (ibid., 384).

In short, Castoldi's relic hunting was a very visible activity (he made sure it was visible) and earned him the respect not only of his fellow citizens at Milan but also of archbishops, nobles, and even a king. Such social standing was precisely that sort of return on investment that other members of the urban upper classes were seeking through other patterns of conspicuous consumption.

Conclusion

In the period following Trent, the Church encouraged relic cults in order to realize a number of essentially political and organizational objectives. Further, many donors whose efforts enlarged the relic collections were driven by a desire for social status that led to so many other forms of conspicuous consumption during same period. Does such an interpretation mean that we should view the dramatic increase in relic use during the Counter-Reformation in a purely cynical way, as something that had little or nothing to do with honest religious sentiment? Not at all. Relic cults were useful to the Church and to relic donors only because relics were seen by ordinary Catholics to be infused with supernatural power. This popular belief preexisted the activities described in the last few sections and was a necessary precondition for the development of those activities.

Just as important, perhaps, there is no reason to believe that Church officials and relic donors, themselves, did not share the popular view of relics. During the exposition of the Sacred Treasure at Milan in 1606, the bishop of Casale said that "wherever you find the bodies or the relic of saints, you also find great and potent means for defending this city" (Bennardini, cited in ibid., 401). Other preachers said the same thing. They were expressing the popular view of relics, to be sure, but almost certainly it was a view that they shared. This is why Federico Borromeo, during the recognition of the relics from Cologne, took the head of S. Eulalio, kissed it, and then stared at it for so long that bystanders thought he was in rapture (ibid., 397); why he used tooth relics to make a rosary or necklace; and why he would preside so coolly at the surgical removal of relics from the corpse of his cousin Carlo.

What was true of Frederico Borromeo was almost certainly true of other Counter-Reformation prelates and of such lay donors as Castoldi. Assembling and donating relics may have served the Church's political interests and it may have conferred status, but in the minds of all parties involved—prelates, urban upper- and middle-class donors, the general public—these activities also worked to build a shell of supernatural protection over the communities in which they all lived.

Chapter Seven

Reformation and *Ricettizie*

B y 1600 it was clear that the Reformation had failed in Italy. The Inquisition had been ruthlessly effective in suppressing the dissemination of Protestant literature. It had also worked to ensure that individuals who openly expressed Protestant views had been executed, made to recant, or forced into exile. The net result was that Italy remained solidly Catholic. But the eventual failure of the Reformation in Italy must not blind us to Protestant successes on the peninsula earlier in the century. While Protestantism nowhere won over local majorities, it did win over substantial minorities in a number of Italian communities, at least in northern and central Italy.[1]

Throughout the 1520s and 1530s, for instance, Protestant materials of every sort flowed into Venice, and the city became a node for the diffusion of Protestant ideas throughout the entire peninsula. One contemporary observer (cited in Caponetto 1992, 261) suggests that there were six thousand Protestants in Venice alone by the early 1550s. Organized Protestant groups also sprang up in a number of cities under Venetian control, including Bergamo, Brescia, Padua, Vicenza, and Verona. More so than in most other regions of Italy, Protestantism in the Veneto included a mix of Lutherans, Calvinists, and Anabaptists.

Protestantism was also successful in northwestern Italy. In Piemonte, the Reformation scored a major victory in 1532 when the Waldensians voted to unite

---

1. For English-language accounts of the Reformation in Italy, see McNair (1981); Cameron (1992). For Italian-language materials, see Caponetto (1987; 1992); Firpo (1993); Ganzer (1993); Olivieri (1979); Welti (1985). In discussing the geography of the Reformation in Italy, I have relied on Welti (1985) and Caponetto (1992). Caponetto is especially useful, since he lists the cities and communities in which organized Protestant groups are known to have existed.

with the Calvinists in Geneva.[2] But support for Calvinism was strong even outside Waldensian circles, and Protestant groups emerged in Turin and other major
Piemontese cities. In Lombardy and Liguria, Protestant groups—mainly Calvinist—formed at Milan, Pavia, Como, Cremona, and Genoa.

In central Italy, Protestant groups, again mainly Calvinist, emerged at Lucca,
Florence, Siena, Ferrara, Faenza, and Modena. The Protestant successes at Ferrara
and Faenza are especially interesting in that these cities were part of the Papal
States at the time. Central Italy also provides evidence that Protestantism in Italy
had an appeal that went beyond the urban middle and upper classes. In the
Lunigiana and the Garfagnana, for instance, two areas north of Lucca, Protestantism drew support from among peasants and the urban poor (Caponetto
1992, 337f).

By contrast, the Italian South was relatively immune to Protestantism. Only
at Naples, and possibly in Palermo and Messina, was there any substantial support for Protestantism, and even there it seems limited to educated elites. There
are traces of Protestant activity in Apulia and Calabria, but this mainly involves
Waldensian communities that had been transplanted from the North centuries
earlier. There is no evidence suggesting that Protestantism enjoyed any measure
of success whatsoever in the Abruzzi, Molise, and Basilicata.

Turning Point

Schutte (1989) points out that until recently it was common for historians
to see a single year—1542—as marking the end of the Reformation in Italy. There
is no denying that several things happened in 1542 that undermined the Reformation forces. In July, Pope Paul III reconstituted the Roman Inquisition. This
was a new and centralized Inquisition, which replaced the various local and regional inquisitions run by bishops or by Dominicans or Franciscans operating
under papal authority. Almost immediately this new Inquisition proved sufficiently threatening to provoke the flight of two of the most influential leaders of
the pro-Protestant faction within the Italian Church. In August 1542, Bernardino
Ochino (1487–1564), vicar-general of the Capuchins and one of most popular
preachers in Italy, fled to Geneva. In that same month Pietro Martire Vermigli
(1500–62), a prominent member of the Augustinian order, also bolted and fled

---

2. The Waldensians were a Christian group founded during the twelfth century by Peter Waldo
of Lyons (France). Although their settlements were first established on the French side of the Alps,
they quickly spread to the alpine valleys of Piemonte.

to Zurich. Ochino and Vermigli became the first and best known of a series of "fliers," to use McNair's (1981, 164) term, who left Italy just a few steps ahead of the new Inquisition. This same year also saw the death of Cardinal Gasparo Contarini, who had worked to forge a doctrinal compromise with Protestants at the Ratisbon Conference of 1541.

But an increasing number of scholars (whose work is reviewed in Schutte 1989) caution against interpreting the events of 1542 in light of hindsight. Both Firpo (1988) and Fragnito (1989, 28f), for instance, remind us that several things occurred in 1542 that would have seemed (at the time) to augur well for the Reformation forces. It was in 1542 that Giovanni Morone (1509–80), a prelate sympathetic to Protestantism, was made a cardinal. This was also the year in which both Morone and Reginald Pole (1500–58), another prelate sympathetic to Protestantism, were appointed by the pope to preside over the first session of the Council of Trent, which had been scheduled to open in 1542.[3]

The Reformation forces in Italy suffered a blow in 1547, when the hard-liners, who by then controlled the Council of Trent, caused the council to pass a decree on "justification," which stated that both faith and good works merited salvation. Such a position left no room for compromise with the view, common to all Protestant traditions, that good works could not merit salvation. Yet even at this point it is possible to argue that the Reformation had not yet failed completely. Just two years later, in 1549, it was generally expected that Reginald Pole would be elected pope in the conclave that followed the death of Paul III. Most historians (see, e.g., Fenlon 1972, 226–32) suggest that Pole would have become pope had he been willing to accept election by acclamation. Instead, he insisted upon winning by ballot and ended up a single vote short.

In 1555, Gian Pietro Carafa (1476–1559), the man who had reorganized and headed the Roman Inquisition and who was very much a hard-liner against Protestantism, was elected to the papal throne as Paul IV. Even this did not bring the Reformation in Italy to a complete stop. Bozza (cited in Schutte 1989, 279) points out that Swiss and French publishers continued to publish Italian translations of Calvin's works, indicating that Calvinist groups probably continued to exist in Italy through to the 1560s. In some cases, we have documented evidence that such groups did persist. Bracessi (1988) has found evidence of Calvinist groups func-

---

3. Reginald Pole was born in England and had ties to the English royal family. His studies at Padua put him in contact with the Italian humanist tradition of the Renaissance. He was made cardinal in 1536 and in 1541 was appointed papal legate at Viterbo (Lazio), where he was part of an intellectual circle that included Michelangelo and the poet Vittoria Colonna.

The first scheduled session of the Council of Trent failed to materialize, and the council did not formally convene until December 1545.

tioning in Lucca through to the early 1570s. Other investigators (see Schutte 1989, 279–80, for a review of the literature here) document Protestant activity in central Italy, Lombardy, the Veneto, and Friuli throughout the period from 1550–80.

Still, although it is now less common to suggest that 1542 (or 1547, or 1555, or any single year) marked the defeat of Protestantism in Italy, there is no denying that after, say, 1560, Protestant activity was definitely on the wane. Protestant groups were still functioning after this date, but usually the only reason we know this is because they were detected and suppressed by the Inquisition or by local governments acting under pressure from the Inquisition.

Most attempts to explain why the Reformation failed in Italy are still very much in the religion-proceeds-from-the-top-down tradition. Welti (1985, 157) suggests that the Reformation in Italy failed because ecclesiastical authorities there exerted an especially strong influence over everyday life. Cameron (1992, 200) argues that the Reformation failed because influential members of the pro-Protestant faction within the Church (Contarini, Morone, and Pole) were sympathetic to Protestant doctrine but chose to resist "that logical and cultural drift, which everywhere else in Europe, pushed on from theological discussion to . . . the reworking of Church structures." In other words, prelates like Contarini, Pole, and Morone hesitated in pursuing a thoroughgoing reform of the Church along Protestant lines, and in the interim hard-liners like Carafa took control and closed off all chance of compromise with the Protestants.

But if we take seriously one of the central claims being advanced in this book, namely, that the Italian Church has always adapted itself to the broad outlines of popular preference, then it seems obvious that the machinations and intrigues among Church elites, whether hard-liners or moderates, would have turned out quite differently if Protestantism had become widely popular during the first few decades of the Reformation. Stated differently, the failure of the Reformation to win over local majorities in any region of Italy produced a context in which the leaders of the Italian Church could eventually suppress Protestantism. It is, therefore, this initial failure to win over local majorities that more than anything else accounts for the ultimate failure of the Reformation in Italy, and so it is this initial failure that needs to be explained first if we want to understand why the Reformation failed in Italy.

The Reformation as Urban Renewal

The scholarly literature on the Reformation constitutes thousands of articles and books written by hundreds of Reformation specialists who stand ready to challenge any generalization made by unwary commentators. Still, over the past few decades Reformation scholars have increasingly come to favor one particular hypothesis. Stated in its most general terms, that hypothesis is this: Protestantism in all of its variants was an ideology that liberated individuals from tradition and from existing institutional arrangements and so appealed to individuals or groups who could derive some advantage from such liberation.

A variety of things have been mentioned in connection with Protestantism's liberating quality. Some authors point to the Protestant emphasis on Biblical authority, which entails the rejection of traditional religious practices not clearly rooted in Biblical text. Others argue that the Protestant view of the priestly role had the effect of undercutting the elaborate system of hierarchial authority associated with the Roman Church. Still others suggest that the emphasis on faith, central to many Protestant formulations (notably those with a Lutheran bent), led naturally to a deemphasis upon the external rituals inherited from the Middle Ages. But the one thing that all authors see as being liberating is the Protestant willingness to break away from the organizational structure of the Roman Church. Such an organizational break not only liberated local populations from the authority of Rome, it legitimized the rejection of all those religious traditions and practices that had been sanctioned and promulgated by the Roman Church over the centuries.

In an influential and well-known work, Ozment (1975) uses the Protestantism-as-liberation hypothesis to explain one of the most important social patterns associated with the Reformation: its distinctively urban character.[4] Protestantism achieved its greatest success in urban areas, Ozment argues, because the transformation of urban economies during the fifteenth and sixteenth centuries ensured that the costs of tradition were higher in urban areas than elsewhere. It was thus very much in the interest of people living in urban areas to embrace a religious ideology (like Protestantism) that allowed tradition to be set aside. Ozment uses much the same argument to explain why the merchant classes in European cities were drawn to Protestantism.

Other investigators reject the view that social transformation was always the root cause of Protestant success in urban areas, but in the end they still make use of the Protestantism-as-liberation hypothesis. Meyer (1993), for instance, examines the case of La Rochelle, a French city that had a Protestant majority until the first half of the seventeenth century. He points out that La Rochelle had a cultural tradition of independence from clerical authority that predates the Reformation. What Protestantism offered the inhabitants of La Rochelle, however, was an ideology that allowed them to justify and reinforce this long-standing tradition.

---

4. For an overview of the evidence establishing the urban character of the Reformation, see the introductory section of McGrath (1990).

Protestantism appealed to the people of La Rochelle, in other words, because it justified and reinforced a liberation from Roman authority to which they were already predisposed.

Finally, still other investigators use the Protestantism-as-liberation hypothesis to explain why Protestantism was appealing to particular kings and princes. The simplest form of this common argument suggests that by undermining the authority of Rome such rulers were better able to consolidate their own power. Wuthnow's (1987, 311–30; 1989, 25–156) account of the Reformation in England and France can be regarded as a recent example of this sort of argument.

For all its current popularity, we should keep in mind that the Protestantism-as-liberation hypothesis was developed mainly in connection with the study of Reformation success in northern Europe. What happens if we use this hypothesis to explain the history of the Reformation in Italy? At first sight, the geographical pattern associated with Protestant successes in Italy would seem to support the hypothesis. After all, Protestantism was most successful in the urban centers of northern Italy, especially in commercial cities, like Venice, Florence, and Lucca. In other words, as in northern Europe, Protestantism was most successful in those areas that had the most to gain from an ideology that liberated them from the costs of tradition. By contrast, Protestantism had little or no appeal in those areas of Italy that were least urbanized and commercialized.

There is, however, a body of evidence that suggests that a desire for liberation was not central to Protestantism's appeal in Italy, or at least not as central as it may have been in northern Europe. That body of evidence has to do with what is usually called Italian evangelism.

The Problem of Italian Evangelism

Some time ago Jung (1953) called attention to what she terms "Italian evangelism," a tradition of Catholic reform that (she argues) is distinguished both from Protestantism and from the Catholicism of the Counter-Reformation. Jung's article gave rise to a large critical literature. Unfortunately, as that literature has developed, the meaning of Italian evangelism has become less, not more, precise.[5] In some cases, the label is attached to those Italian Catholics who argued that individuals should have a direct relationship with Christ and who consequently came (like Luther) to emphasize the centrality of faith, and faith alone, to salvation. Other commentators suggest that evangelism is nothing more than the various traditions that developed from the work of individuals like Savonarola, Erasmus,

---

5. For an overview of the literature on Italian evangelism, see Fenlon (1972; 1974); Martin (1988; 1993); McNair (1967, 1–50); Schutte (1989); Welti (1985, 10–23).

and Juan de Valdés (for an overview of this position, see Schutte 1989, 274–75).[6] Everyone agrees that evangelism (if it existed at all) was a diffuse movement.

Still, all the individuals associated with the evangelism label in the scholarly literature did share one element in common: they promoted a type of religiosity that privileged interior experience. This experience meant, variously, (1) salvation by faith and faith alone, (2) personal inspiration, as with Valdés and his followers, (3) a vaguely defined notion of interior piety, involving private prayer and contemplation, or (4) what Seidel Menchi (1987, 100–122) calls "the freedom of the Gospel," the belief that the only obligation imposed on Christians was to internalize the precepts of the Gospels, especially the injunction to love God, to love their neighbors, and to live a life guided by these internalized precepts. This emphasis was common to all the reform traditions that emerged in Italy during the early decades of the sixteenth century.

However it was expressed, this emphasis upon interior experience established an affinity between the religiosity espoused by Italian evangelists and the religiosity associated with the Protestant theologies being developed north of the Alps. This is one reason Italian evangelists actively sought out and used Protestant works in developing their thought. It is now generally recognized, for instance, that some passages in the *Benificio di Cristo* (published in the early 1540s and long regarded as one of the most influential works in the evangelism tradition)[7] were taken from the first edition of Calvin's *Institutes of the Christian Religion*. Similarly, Valdés made use of early Lutheran texts (Caponetto 1992, 83).

But these undeniable links between Italian evangelism and northern European Protestantism notwithstanding, the evangelistic emphasis on interior expe-

6. Most readers will likely already have some familiarity with Savonarola (1452–98) and Erasmus (1466–1536). Juan de Valdés (circa 1498–1541) may be less familiar. Valdés was a Spanish theologian who settled in Naples in 1534. Central to his theology was the contention that individuals should seek to know God's will by an illumination of the spirit rather than by scriptural texts. Valdés influenced intellectuals in every part of Italy. For an overview of his work and an assessment of his influence in Italy, see Firpo (1993, 115–27); Nieto (1970). Unfortunately, Valdés's followers, called Valdesians in English, are often confused in English-language scholarly discussions with the Waldensians (see n 2).

7. This short book, whose full title was *Trattato utilissimo del benificio di Giesù Christo crocifisso, verso it christiani*, was first published in 1543. Its central message was that faith in the benefits that flowed from Christ's sacrifice on the cross—and that faith alone—brought salvation. It was a popular message. One Italian bishop estimated that between 1543 and 1549 forty thousand copies of it were sold in Venice alone (McNair 1981, 157). It was quickly translated into French, English, Spanish, and Croatian. In 1559, Rome placed it on the "Index of Prohibited Books." It is a testament to the efficiency and effectiveness of the Italian Inquisition in suppressing banned material that by the early nineteenth century not a single copy of the Italian edition of this book was known to exist. It was not until 1843 that a copy was discovered in the library of St. John's College, Cambridge; it apparently had been donated in 1744 by an Italian exile living in London. For more on the *Benificio*, including the original Italian text and two early (1545 and 1573) English translations, see Caponetto (1972).

rience predates the importation of Protestant ideas. At least for northern Italy, a number of documentary sources indicate that calls for a renewed emphasis upon the figure of Christ, upon the Gospels, upon the writings of St. Paul, upon the centrality of faith, and so on were circulating widely among intellectuals and artisans in urban areas during the last decades of the fifteenth century and the early decades of the sixteenth century (see Olivieri 1992, 101–76; also Firpo 1993: 3–5).

What all this means is that we should not conceptualize the Reformation in Italy as mainly involving new and alien ideas that were thrust upon Italy from northern Europe. On the contrary, we come closer to the truth if we see Protestantism as a northern European tradition that was to a large extent pulled into Italy by the adherents of a preexisting and very similar tradition—evangelism.

Given the affinities between Protestantism and evangelism, neither can be explained in isolation from the other. This means that we must explain not only why both Protestantism and evangelism failed to win over local majorities in Italy but also why both, to the extent they were successful at all, were successful mainly in northern and central Italy[8]—and it is at this point that the Protestantism-as-liberation hypothesis proves unsatisfactory. As mentioned, it was a willingness to break with the organizational structure of the Roman Church that most of all made Protestantism a liberating ideology. By contrast, this willingness to break with the Roman Church was generally lacking in Italian evangelism. As Jung (1953, 523) notes: "It [evangelism] may have been at times heretical, but it was never schismatical." A more positive way of saying this is that Italian evangelicals took their association with the organizational structure of the Church as a given. Firpo (1993, 94–95) reminds us, for instance, that the *Benificio di Cristo*, the work most associated with Italian evangelism, was devoid of antipapal rhetoric despite its reliance on Calvin's works. In other words, it would appear that Italian evangelicals did borrow from Protestantism, but they borrowed selectively, and they did not borrow the one thing that made Protestantism distinct: a willingness to break with Rome.

The fact that a willingness to break with Rome was never part of the evangelical tradition makes it difficult to explain the appeal of evangelism (such as it was) in terms of a desire for liberation. But if evangelism was appealing for reasons having little or nothing to do with liberation, then perhaps Protestantism, whose fate was so intertwined with evangelism in Italy, was also appealing (to selected minorities in Italy) for these same reasons.

---

8. That evangelism was most popular in the same areas that Protestantism was popular is evident from all relevant discussions of evangelism, but see especially Welti (1985, 24–90).

Rejection of Image Cults and Relic Cults

In his introduction to a work by Juan de Valdés, Benedetto Croce, in 1938, characterized the early decades of the sixteenth century in this way:

> It was a time when the winds of change spread a new attitude towards life through-
> out Europe, and this attitude came as well to Italy and in particular to Naples. Part
> of this new attitude was an impatience with the old exterior forms of religion.
> There was a need for a more intense and interior form of religiosity, and a desire
> for . . . a spontaneous accord that would be felt among kindred souls in the most
> distant of communities. (cited in Jung 1953, 514)

Croce is talking about what subsequent commentators like Jung call evangelism, and like these subsequent commentators he is suggesting that an emphasis upon interior experience was central to the religion favored by the evangelicals. But Croce is also calling attention to the evangelical rejection of "exterior forms of religion" that is the logical consequence of this emphasis on interior experience. What makes the evangelical rejection of exterior forms important is that it led inevitably to the deemphasis or outright rejection of two things that have always been central to popular Catholicism in Italy: image cults and relic cults.

The tendency for Italian evangelicals to reject image and relic cults is evident in the warm reception accorded to the critiques leveled against such cults by Erasmus (1466–1536). Erasmus in fact singles out the veneration of images and relics for special criticism in his commentaries on popular Catholic practice (for a summary of Erasmus's views, see Eire 1986, 36–53; Gilmore 1975). In the case of image cults, Erasmus is willing to grant that images might have a didactic function (as Gregory's "images are books for the illiterate" suggested) but argues that more often than not images hinder piety because they draw attention more to themselves than to what they depict. In a letter written in 1531 to Jacopo Sadoleto (cited in Gilmore 1975, 86), Erasmus singles out for special condemnation the practice of praying to statues, as in the case of "a soldier about to go into mercenary service who genuflects before an image of St. Barbara and recites a few prayers very like magic in her honor and promises himself that he will return unharmed." Erasmus's criticism of relic cults is even more severe, since relics lack the potential didactic value of images.

In her study of Erasmian influence in Italy, Seidel Menchi (1987, 107–10) describes a number of incidents that illustrate the ways in which Italian evangelicals translated their dissatisfaction with image cults and relic cults into practice. It was common, for instance, for evangelicals to stop and talk with pilgrims in the streets of cities like Venice and Modena, asking these pilgrims why they were seeking Mary at some distant shrine like Loreto rather than seeking Christ in their own home. Likewise, in a discussion between two artisans at Modena in

1579, one advised the other to make a vow to the Annunziata at Florence in order to help his sick daughter. The girl's father, however, responded that "a person should appeal to the [madonna] in Heaven, not to the [madonna] at Florence." Martin (1987; 1988) uncovers a number of similar incidents in his study of evangelism among the artisan classes in Venice. Venetian evangelicals not only advocated praying directly to Christ but also spoke out against the cult of the saints, the saying of rosaries, and the miracles associated with the sanctuary at Loreto. One contemporary playwright satirizes the evangelicals in Venice and Padua by talking of those "who no longer keep vigils, who never go to church, and who give heed to no other images but those on their [playing and tarot] cards" (cited in Martin 1993, 27).

It was, I suggest, this evangelical rejection of image and relic cults that ensured that evangelism would never win over local majorities in Italy.

One More Time: What Causes What?

I argue in earlier chapters that ordinary Italian Catholics have long been psychologically predisposed to invest madonnine images and saintly relics with supernatural power and that this predisposition has constituted an unalterable constraint to which official Catholicism has had to adapt. Not to have adapted to this constraint would have meant losing the allegiance of the great mass of Italian Catholics. I also suggest that in northern Europe, Protestant leaders also adapted to the constraints of popular belief, arguing for instance that it was the popularity of iconoclasm in certain areas of Europe that led Calvin to make iconoclasm central to his doctrine. Such a formulation reverses the causality that usually guides the thinking of scholars investigating popular religion. I am arguing, that is, that it was not the doctrines passed down from on high that shaped popular practice but rather the logic of popular practice that shaped the doctrines passed down from on high.

Given this conceptual framework, the failure of both evangelism and Protestantism to win over local majorities in Italy is not particularly problematic: these ideologies failed because their underlying logic entailed a deemphasis (if not an outright elimination) of the image and relic cults to which Italian Catholics were unshakably attached. In short, the failure of both evangelism and Protestantism in Italy had little to do with the machinations and intrigues among religious elites (documented in such loving detail by generations of historians) and everything to do with the fact that these ideologies were not adapted (and did not adapt) to givens established by the logic of popular Catholicism.

The argument being advanced here also has consequences for the way we conceptualize one of the most important patterns associated with the Italian Reformation, namely, that the South was immune to Protestantism in a way the North was not.

The failure of Protestantism in southern Italy cannot be attributed to the fact that Protestant ideas never diffused there. In northern Europe, merchants and mobile artisans were among the first to embrace Protestantism, Calvinism in particular. One consequence of this was that Protestant ideas and literature tended to diffuse along established corridors of commercial activity throughout all of Europe. As Caponetto (1992, 377f) points out, this meant that during the sixteenth century Protestant ideas easily penetrated coastal areas, which were most involved in trade. Many of these areas were in the Italian North—Caponetto cites Venice, Savona, and Genoa in particular—but many were in the South. In particular, trade brought Protestant works to Cagliari (Sardinia), to Sicilian cities like Palermo, Messina, and Siracusa, to Naples, and to the Waldensian communities in Calabria and Apulia. In principle, these centers could have served as nodes for the distribution of Protestant ideas throughout the mainland South.

And yet, despite the availability of Protestant materials in the many areas of the South, Protestantism was not successful in southern Italy. The simplest explanation for this is that there was no "demand" for Protestantism in the Italian South the way there was in the Italian North. What we need to explain, of course, is why Protestantism held less appeal to southern Catholics.

Evangelism and Protestantism failed in Italy mainly because their emphasis on interior experience prevented them from adapting to one of the most important constraints established by the logic of popular Catholicism, the belief that images and relics can become infused with supernatural power. Given this general hypothesis, the fact that these ideologies failed most of all in southern Italy would make sense if the psychological predisposition to invest relics and images with supernatural power was much stronger in the South than in the North—and that conditions of life in the South created this predisposition. That is just the argument I want to make; to do that, however, I must leave Italy for a moment and consider the Reformation in Europe as a whole.

The Social Foundations of Reformation Success and Failure

In Europe generally, as in Italy in particular, there was a geographical patterning to the Reformation. In the end, the Reformation was most successful in northern Europe, especially in those areas where local populations spoke a proto-Germanic language. By contrast, the Reformation was far less successful in southern Europe, where local populations were more likely to speak a Romance language. The correlation is not perfect. German-speaking regions like Austria and Bavaria remained largely Catholic, and Calvinism enjoyed considerable success in French-

speaking regions. Still, a rough correlation does exist, and it would be easy to conclude that language serves as a marker indicating the presence of social institu-
tions or cultural traditions that predisposed local populations toward either Protestantism or Catholicism. Surprisingly, this is a possibility that has generally been
ignored in Reformation studies. The one exception is Swanson (1967).

For Swanson, the Catholic belief in immanence most distinguishes Catholicism from Protestantism. Immanence (in Swanson's discussion) refers to the belief that the essence of something sacred can infuse and merge with the essence
of persons or objects in the natural world. Among Catholics, he argues, a belief
in immanence is evident in the doctrine of the real presence, which holds that
after the act of consecration by a priest the Body and Blood of Christ is physically
present in the Eucharistic Host. A belief in immanence is also evident, Swanson
maintains, in the Catholic belief that the essence of Christ has infused and
merged with the organizational structure of the Church itself, so that the sacer-
dotal actions of the Church are in effect the actions of Christ.

Protestants, in Swanson's characterization, reject immanence. In the Protestant view, God can and does enter into relationships with persons and things of
this world and so can affect what happens here. Nevertheless, for the Protestant
there is always a strict separation between the human and the divine. Interactions
can occur across this great divide, but the divide itself is never blurred.

Citing Durkheim, Swanson argues that a society's experience with particular social structures predisposes the members of that society toward particular
religious beliefs. The social structure of greatest interest to Swanson was political
regime. Although Swanson originally delineated five types of regime, he later collapsed these into two basic types. One is found in those societies where the members see the society as being composed of separate social factions, each having a
legitimate right to use the central government to articulate its interests. In these
societies, people gain important positions in the operations of the central state
"as a consequence of their constituting or representing some autonomous special
interests" (Swanson 1968, 108). The other type includes those societies that are
not conceptualized as being composed of separate social factions. In these cases,
people gain important positions in the central government "only in their capacity as members of the commonalty" (ibid.). This contrast between factional and
communal regimes is then used to predict Reformation outcomes.[9]

For Swanson, factional regimes were more likely to embrace Protestantism,
since the emphasis upon social separation in such regimes predisposed their
members toward a religion (like Protestantism) emphasizing a rigid conceptual

9. The terms *factional* and *communal* do not come from Swanson but are introduced by Paige
(1974) in his discussion of Swanson's theory.

separation between divine power and the things of this world. Communal regimes, which had no such emphasis upon social separation, should have been
more predisposed toward Catholicism, since the Catholic belief in immanence
entails a belief in the merging (not the separation) of divine power and the material world.

Swanson tests his argument by identifying forty-one European societies and
coding each for type of central government and predominant religion (either the
official state religion or, if the society lacked an official state religion, the religion
of the majority of the population). He then correlates these two variables and
finds that in the vast majority of cases the data support the argument: factional
regimes tended to embrace Protestantism, communal regimes tended to remain
Catholic.

The Reaction to Swanson

Fellow sociologists have always been relatively uncritical of Swanson's argument, and they regularly cite it as a masterful application of a Durkheimian perspective to the study of European religion (see for instance Robertson and Lechner 1984). Even so, Swanson's work has not generated a large secondary literature,
which tries to assess and refine his argument in the manner, say, of Weber's con-
tentious thesis on the links between Protestantism and rational capitalism. Nor
has it generated among sociologists much interest in the Reformation generally.

Historians were at first very critical of Swanson's work. Several of them (see
for instance Davis 1969) were quick to see a methodological flaw in *Religion and
Regime* that was probably not obvious to most sociologists: in his sample of forty-
one societies, Swanson systematically excludes whole areas of Europe. All of the
imperial and ecclesiastical cities of the Holy Roman Empire, for instance, are
excluded, as are Finland and Norway. Swanson justifies such exclusions on the
grounds that he wanted to study only "autonomous states" so as to maximize the
independence of his cases. Quite apart from the fact that nearly a third of the societies in his sample are Swiss cantons (that in itself would seem to work against
the independence of the cases in his sample), the exclusion of so much of Europe
seriously undermines his claim to have studied the *European* Reformation.

The only Italian states in Swanson's sample are the city-states of Florence
and Venice, and he codes both of these as having a communal regime. Consistent
with his theoretical argument (which suggests that communal regimes should
have an affinity with Catholicism), he also finds that in both of these states "the
Reformation made no serious inroads in society." If the comparison is with Protestant states to the north, then Swanson's analysis here is mildly convincing. On
the other hand, the Veneto and Tuscany were among those areas of Italy in which
the Reformation scored its greatest successes in the sixteenth century, despite the

supposed communal nature of their regimes. This would seem to undermine the sort of Durkheimian argument that Swanson is making.

Historians also point to a theoretical flaw in Swanson's argument. Despite its claims to be Durkheimian, there are grounds for suggesting that his argument is not Durkheimian at all. What Durkheim suggests is that an individual's experience with a particular social structure predisposes that individual toward certain religious beliefs. Swanson's argument can be considered Durkheimian only if we grant that most members of the societies in his sample "experienced" the central governments that constitute his independent variable. Yet that seems unlikely. On the contrary, as Bouwsma (1968, 489) suggests, "for the vast majority of Europeans, social experience was almost exclusively local, and quite unconnected with the larger structures on which Swanson focuses attention." Davis (1971, 389–90) makes much the same point. It is generally felt that Swanson was led astray by his earlier studies (notably Swanson 1960), which focus on relatively small societies, in which it does make sense (at least more sense) to assume direct experience with the social structures.

After this first barrage of criticism, historians came increasingly to ignore Swanson. Not a single one of the sixteen review essays in Ozment's *Reformation Europe: A Guide to Research* (1982) makes any reference to Swanson or his work. A particularly significant failure to mention Swanson is Brady's (1982) survey of studies dealing with the social history of the Reformation, which does however mention "sociological" studies by Max Weber, Ernst Troeltsch, Reinhard Bendix, and Nicholas Luhmann.

Starting Again

Swanson begins his original analysis (1960) by suggesting that a belief in immanence was central to Catholicism, just as a rejection of that belief was central to Protestantism. At the level of formal doctrine and intellectual elites, he is likely correct. Protestant leaders like Zwingli and Calvin (though not Luther) did reject the doctrine of real presence, and all Protestant leaders (including Luther) rejected transubstantiation, which was (and is) the rationale offered by Catholic theologians to explain how Christ could be physically present in the Eucharistic Host. It is also the case that the intellectual leaders of the Counter-Reformation Church did consider belief in the real presence and in transubstantiation as what most distinguished loyal Catholics from Protestant heretics.[10]

On the other hand, neither Swanson nor anyone else can point to evidence that in most areas of Europe during the sixteenth century the laity understood,

---

10. For a study that documents the importance of transubstantiation to the leaders of the Catholic Counter-Reformation, notably the Jesuits, see Redondi's (1987) reanalysis of the Galileo case.

let alone were much concerned with, abstract issues like the real presence or transubstantiation. The same holds true for the other manifestation of a belief in immanence mentioned by Swanson, namely, that Christ was immanent in the structure of the Church. The real presence, transubstantiation, and Christ-immanent-in-the-Church—these were just not issues of any great concern to most Catholics. To suggest otherwise is to confuse official dogma with popular practice.

This is not to deny that popular Catholicism on the eve of the Reformation was permeated with a belief in immanence. As we have seen, ordinary Catholics in Italy saw divine power as immanent in images and relics. Cults organized around images and relics were among the first things eliminated in those areas of Europe where Protestantism triumphed. Like Swanson, then, though for somewhat different reasons, I take the issue of immanence to be central to any discussion of Reformation success or failure. Also, following both Durkheim and Swanson, I think it likely that social structure does shape religious worldview. But in pursuing this hypothesis we must avoid Swanson's wrong turn and focus specifically on those social structures that would have been experienced at the local level.

From a Durkheimian perspective, the fact that neither evangelism nor Protestantism was successful in southern Italy would make sense if southern Italians experienced a social organization that predisposed them toward religious traditions (like popular Catholicism) that embrace immanence. For the argument to work, however, this form of social organization would have to be either absent or less common in northern Italy, where immanence-rejecting traditions like evangelism and Protestantism had more success. In fact, there was a form of social organization experienced at the local level in southern Italy that seems relevant to the issue of immanence and was entirely absent in the north.

Barriers to Trent, Bulwarks of Catholicism

Today, Italian government bureaucrats define the Mezzogiorno, or southern Italy, as including Campania, Abruzzi and Molise, Apulia, Basilicata, Calabria, Sicily and Sardinia. But the characterization offered by De Martino (1968, 13) is probably more informative (and certainly more colorful): "Southern Italy includes the lands once encompassed by the old Kingdom of Naples, a kingdom held fast between the Papal States and the Mediterranean . . . [that is], between the Holy See and the saltwater sea." De Rosa consistently argues that the religious history of the Mezzogiorno is, for the most part, about how the reforms promulgated at the Council of Trent never came to be applied there in their entirety (see for instance De Rosa 1979, 172). At best, he argues, the tridentine reforms made themselves felt only in the large cities; their impact upon religious practice in the countryside was virtually nil, at least up until the nineteenth century. Concretely, this means that in the Mezzogiorno the tridentine emphasis on the Mass and the Eucharist was always subordinated to cultic activities organized around saints and madonnas. It also means that the antimagical emphasis at Trent, which worked to eliminate magical elements from Catholic practice in other areas of Catholic Europe, was absent. Indeed, I make a case elsewhere (see Carroll 1992, 112–28) that in southern Italy the inclusion of magical elements into Catholic ritual actually increased during the Counter-Reformation.

What makes De Rosa's argument relevant to our concerns here lies in what he sees as the primary cause of southern Italy's immunity to Trent: the peculiar nature and structure of the local churches in southern Italian communities, the *chiese ricettizie*. This term that does not translate well into English, although "churches of received priests" comes close.[11] Despite the fact that the Italian-language literature on this type of church is now extensive, the chiese ricettizie of southern Italy have not received much attention from English-speaking scholars.[12]

A chiesa ricettizia was, first and foremost, associated with a group of priests who were organized collegially and whose primary purpose was to manage and work the *massa commune*, the church property they held in common. The revenues from this common property were divided among the participating priests, with each priest receiving a share of those revenues. These churches could be either *numerate* or *innumerate*, depending upon whether the number of participating priests was fixed or open. They could also be either *curate* or *semplici*, depending on whether the priests involved were or were not responsible for the care of souls in the local community. If curate, then the clergy's religious duties were exercised collegially, with all participating priests being equally responsible for the administration of Extreme Unction, the saying of daily masses, preaching, and so on (on the collegial exercise of the care of souls, see Robertazzi delle Donne 1973, 1042).

In addition to the participating priests associated with a chiesa ricettizia, there were also a class of clergy who did not share in the revenues of the church.

11. On the likely origins of the term *ricettizie*, see De Rosa (1983, 163). The discussion of the ricettizie that follows is derived mainly from De Rosa (1973; 1979); Cestaro (1978); D'Andrea (1977); De Vitiis (1982); Ebner (1982).

12. In large part, this neglect of the chiese ricettizie derives from the fact that English-speaking scholars have always relied heavily upon anthropological investigations for information about popular Catholicism in southern Italy. The fieldwork that forms the basis of these anthropological reports was conducted during the twentieth century, by which time the ricettizie had ceased to exist.

These men started by performing menial tasks and were eventually admitted to the ranks of the participating priests after earning a certain seniority, with regard to either years of service or age or both. This period of nonparticipation could last a long time. In Potenza (Basilicata) during the late 1700s, men were admitted to a quarter share in the massa commune only after five years of service, to a half share after nine years, and to a full share after eleven years (De Rosa 1979, 64). Cestaro (1978, 151) reports that in some ricettizie in the diocese of Potenza it took fourteen years to be admitted to full membership.

Another distinctive feature, and in some ways the most distinctive feature, of the chiese ricettizie was the requirement that all members had to be of local origin, often a member of a particular local family. Even if a man met the local-origin requirement, his admission to the ricettizia was still contingent upon a secret vote of existing participants. In theory, those admitted to a ricettizia had to be certified as fit by the local bishop; in practice, bishops gave this approval fairly routinely, since the local-origin rule left them little room to maneuver. Moreover, bishops were explicitly excluded from interfering in any decisions relating to the massa commune. Indeed, prior to 1800 the autonomy of the ricettizie in these matters was enshrined in the civil law of the Kingdom of Naples, whose governing officials were only too happy to minimize the influence of a foreign power like Rome.

Each ricettizia had a rector or archpriest at its head, but these individuals (who were often elected and who held office only for limited periods) had nothing like the authority of the pastor in northern parishes, and any special title they possessed was for the most part honorary. In all matters relating to the administration of the massa commune, the rector could be overruled by the assembly of participating clergy (De Rosa 1979, 61).

The chiese ricettizie were first and foremost economic associations. In De Rosa's (1979, 58) words, "strictly speaking then, the ricettizia was not a parish at all, but a private association of local priests, or better, a closed corporation, to which no outsider could accede." In joining this private association, a man did not cut his ties to the secular world. On the contrary, members of a ricettizia often continued to live in their family home and often called upon family members for aid in managing or working the portion of the massa commune entrusted to their care. From a family's point of view, having a son admitted to a ricettizia was a valuable economic asset.

One important consequence of the structure of the ricettizie was that it insulated the ricettizie clergy from the zeal of reforming bishops, since the local-origin rule meant that bishops were relatively powerless to promote the careers of priests from outside who might have been committed to the tridentine reforms. This, together with the focus upon local economic concerns that flowed naturally from the organization of the ricettizie, explains for De Rosa why the tridentine reforms were implemented slowly if at all in the Mezzogiorno. But if we turn our attention from tridentine reform to the Reformation, De Rosa's analysis of the ricettizie raises an interesting puzzle that, as far as I know, neither he nor his followers confront.

De Rosa's analysis suggests that the structure of the chiese ricettizie insulated local communities in the Mezzogiorno from episcopal control. But if that is true, then why did Protestantism fail to flourish there? In other words, if southern bishops had so little control over religion in local communities, then why did local communities not become hotbeds of "heretical" activity, just like, say, the isolated alpine communities of Piemonte, where Waldensianism and (later) Calvinism flourished? Generally, the southern Italian case would seem to negate those arguments that blame the failure of the Reformation in Italy on the tight control exerted by the Church over local communities.

The solution to this puzzle lies in looking at the chiese ricettizie through a Durkheimian lens, since by doing that we detect a social arrangement as relevant to southern Italy's lack of enthusiasm for the Reformation as to the failure of the tridentine reforms. Everything about the ricettizie, but especially the local-origin requirement, predisposed the clergy of the ricettizie to share the values and sentiments of the local population (De Rosa 1979, 174). Just as important, the nature of a ricettizia worked to ensure that its priests were not seen as separate from the rest of the population. On the contrary, like other men in the community, the priests of the ricettizia rose each morning to work their land; they had sexual intercourse with women; they lived with the families into which they had been born; they dressed in the same clothes as everybody else (see De Rosa 1979, 30–32, 174–75). When local bishops complained (as they often did) about the corruption of the southern clergy, all they really meant was that the southern clergy were doing what the structure of the ricettizie predisposed them to do: behaving just like the other men in their communities.

Another way of saying this is that the nature of a chiesa ricettizia ensured that individuals intimately associated with religion in the eyes of the local community—namely, the ricettizia clergy—would not be seen as set apart from the rest of society. On the contrary, the ricettizia clergy was simply a segment of ordinary society that had been infused with certain religious rights and obligations. This lack of separation between the local clergy and the rest of the population is precisely what bothered reforming bishops committed to the tridentine model:

> The structure of the *chiesa ricettizia* . . . had led to the formation of a clergy that was more popular but also more disorderly and ignorant. During the eighteenth century Mezzogiorno bishops worked for a type of priest that differentiated himself from the surrounding population by his style of life and—most of all—by the dis-

charge of his priestly duties. But the risk that a priest would be socially segregated had never existed in the Mezzogiorno. A clerical career was a business . . . that one pursued like any other profession. (De Rosa 1983, 396)

From a Durkheimian point of view, this lack of separation between the local clergy and the rest of the population should have predisposed a local community toward a belief in immanence, that is, toward the belief that divine power could infuse material objects. In other words, the Durkheimian argument would suggest that the fusion of religion and society that characterizes communities organized around a ricettizia would give rise to the belief that divine power and the material world could be similarly fused. By the same reasoning, the experience of the ricettizie should have worked against the emergence of indigenous immanence-rejecting traditions in the Mezzogiorno, which otherwise might have encouraged Protestantism, in the way that evangelical traditions encouraged Protestantism in the North.

How Common Were the Ricettizie?

My argument requires that the local experience of the ricettizie be sufficiently widespread to influence the popular imagination throughout southern Italy, and here we encounter an issue that divides Italian scholars. Based on his analysis of the reports ad limina, De Rosa (1979, 58) argues that by the eighteenth century chiese ricettizie accounted for three-quarters of all the churches in the Mezzogiorno and that this figure did not begin to decline until the *decennio,* the period of French rule that lasted from 1806–15. But a number of critics challenge De Rosa in this regard, arguing that the ricettizie were never this common. These critics point out that the reports ad limina were usually more qualitative than statistical and that local bishops were naturally prone to emphasize that section of the local clergy who (from the bishop's point of view) were most problematic.

The earliest solid statistical data that we do have for the ricettizie appear in government reports and archival records that date from circa 1820. That data— reviewed in De Vitiis (1982)—suggest that at this time only 30 percent of the churches in the Mezzogiorno were ricettizie. This, however, is an average that masks substantial regional variation. In Naples and the immediately surrounding region the ricettizie constituted less than 4 percent of the total number of churches. This figure increases, but only to a moderate degree, in other areas on the Tyrrhenian (western) side of the Mezzogiorno. In Calabria (the "toe" of the Italian boot), for instance, roughly 23 percent of the churches were ricettizie, while the figure for the rest of Campania (outside Naples and the surrounding area) was 31 percent. The ricettizie become even more common when we move to the Adriatic side of the Mezzogiorno. In Apulia (the long strip that lies along the eastern edge of the Mezzogiorno and that includes the "heel" of the Italian boot), approximately 75 percent of the churches were ricettizie. But it was in the Basilicata (the region between Calabria and Apulia) where the ricettizie were most common, accounting for more that 93 percent of all churches.[13]

In De Vitiis's view, it is highly unlikely that the proportion of churches that were ricettizie could drop from 75 percent (the figure favored by De Rosa) to 30 percent with no trace of such a dramatic decline being left in the documentary record. He suggests instead that the proportion of churches that were ricettizie changed very little between 1750 and 1820; that is, that the percentage of churches that were ricettizie was roughly 30 percent, on average, throughout this entire period.

On the other hand, De Vitiis also argues that the ricettizie always had an economic importance that was greater than their relative numbers might suggest. His data indicate that, while the ricettizie may have accounted for only 30 percent of all churches in 1820, the income associated with the ricettizie accounted for 55 percent of the income associated with Mezzogiorno churches at this time. Since the documentary record does indicate that the decennio caused a dramatic reduction in the property (if not the numbers) of the ricettizie, it is quite possible that their economic importance was even greater in the eighteenth century. De Vitiis himself concludes that it is not unreasonable to suggest that circa 1750 the ricettizie might have accounted for three-quarters of church income in the Mezzogiorno.

In summary then, it is likely that by the middle of the eighteenth century the chiese ricettizie would have been perceived by local populations in most areas of the Mezzogiorno to have been important on account of either their relative numbers or their economic importance or both. This increases the plausibility of the Durkheimian hypothesis, namely, that the local experience of the ricettizie was sufficiently widespread and sufficiently intense to shape popular thinking throughout the Mezzogiorno.

Still, the eighteenth century is a long way from the sixteenth century and the key events of the Reformation in Italy. What do we know about the early history of the ricettizie? De Rosa (1983, 163) argues that the ricettizie began spreading throughout the Mezzogiorno during the twelfth century. Supporting this view are

---

13. The broad regional data reported here are derived from the tables presented in De Vitiis (1982, 468–73). De Vitiis himself presents his data on a diocese-by-diocese basis, and that data indicate that even within regions there was often substantial variation with regard to the proportion of churches that were ricettizie. Readers interested in the prevalence of ricettizie in any particular area of the Mezzogiorno should consult De Vitiis directly.

documents from the twelfth and thirteenth centuries that describe churches that seem to be ricettizie (see Rosa 1976, 152). By contrast, Robertazzi delle Donne (1973) argues that the ricettizie were transplanted to the Mezzogiorno from Spain during the period of Spanish domination in the early sixteenth century. The matter of exact origins aside, all commentators seem to agree that Spanish rule increased dramatically the number and dispersion of the ricettizie.

The first explicit reference to the ricettizie in any collection of ecclesiastical legislation occurs in a reform decree issued during the Council of Trent's twenty-fourth session, in which the council specified that when a "parochial church" falls vacant by death or resignation, the local bishop has the right to appoint a suitable vicar "who shall discharge the duties in that church til it has been provided with a rector [and this shall be the case] even if it be said that the charge of the church belongs to the bishop himself and is administered by one or more [and] also in churches called patrimonial or receptive" (Schroeder 1950, 106). The "churches called patrimonial or receptive" (ecclesiis patrimonialibus seu receptivis) are the chiese ricettizie, and what the council was trying to do here was to give bishops more control over their administration

We know in retrospect that both the ricettizie clergy and the royal government in the South prevented anything more than a purely symbolic implementation of this decree until after 1800 (see the discussion in De Vitiis 1982, 375). Nevertheless, this decree is evidence that by 1564 the ricettizie were in place and sufficiently important to be mentioned in ecclesiastical legislation. Phrased more dynamically, it appears that during the early sixteenth century, just as evangelism and Protestantism were achieving some limited success in northern Italy, an institution was spreading throughout southern Italy that would have predisposed local populations to reject religious traditions, like evangelism and Protestantism, that rejected immanence.

Back to the North

My argument also depends upon the chiese ricettizie being a peculiarly southern Italian phenomenon. On this there is no doubt: the ricettizie did not exist in northern Italy. During the Middle Ages the core element in the organization of northern Italian dioceses was the *pieve*.[14] There might be anywhere from ten to twenty pievi in a diocese, and the focus of each was a central church on which other churches in the pieve were dependent for the performance of certain liturgical functions. In particular, the central church was the only church in the pieve with a baptismal font and so was the church to which people came to have their chil-

14. For an account of pieve organization, see Hay (1977, 20–25); Moretti (1988).

dren baptized. On special occasions the clergy associated with the central church would travel to the satellite churches in the pieve to conduct religious rituals.

The number of dependent churches in a pieve could be large. In the twelfth century, for instance, twenty-one churches were dependent upon S. Maria dell'Impruneta in Tuscany (Paolucci, Pacciani, and Proto Pisani 1987, 5), and this was not an unusual number. Calvi (1676a; 1676b; 1677) routinely identifies central churches in his account of sacred events in the Bergamo region and commonly associates each of these with anywhere from fifteen to twenty-five satellite churches.

The pieve organization clearly worked against that merger of religion and society that was such a distinctive feature of the ricettizie in the South. Quite apart from the fact that it was never a requirement that the churches in a pieve be staffed by men of local origin (Tramontin 1977, 152), the hierarchial nature of the pieve system ensured that local priests were always tied to an organizational structure that transcended the local community. Moreover, on particularly important occasions the officiating clergy would not have been local at all but, rather, clergy associated with the central church, ensuring their separation from the local population in a way that was never true of the ricettizie clergy in the South.

The pieve organization began to break down when the satellite churches began to demand and be granted baptismal rights. But this breakdown, at least in the years after Trent, was accompanied by the emergence of a system in which the dioceses were divided into *vicariati foranei*, whose boundaries often corresponded to the boundaries of the old pievi. The priests who headed these new subunits were appointed by the bishop, and as Sebastiani (1982) points out, bishops were even freer than under the old pieve system to appoint administrators who thought the same way they did. In short, one hierarchial system was replaced by another. The local clergy in the North continued to be enmeshed in an organizational structure that transcended their local communities and so continued to be separate from those communities.

While the Durkheimian argument might explain the regional patterns associated with Protestant and evangelical success or failure, it cannot explain the more important pattern: that nowhere, neither in the North nor the South, did Protestantism win over a majority of the local population. Other factors, apart from the ricettizie, predisposed Italians toward a religiosity in which objects were invested with supernatural power—and those other factors were operative in both the North and the South.

I offer some preliminary speculations on some of these factors in the concluding chapter. Before that, however, I want to consider a type of relic cult that seems particularly relevant to the Reformation-era issues raised in this chapter.

Chapter Eight

"Preserved Whole and Entire"

The supernatural power immanent in saintly relics is usually implicit and invisible. This means that most relics do not bleed, cry, move, become surrounded by strange lights, and so on, in the manner of sacred images. There are two notable exceptions to this rule, however: dried blood relics that liquefy on a regular basis and saintly bodies preserved whole and entire.

A vial supposedly containing the dried blood of S. Gennaro, the principal patron of Naples, is exposed to the public in the Naples Duomo on eighteen occasions during the year. The records kept at the Duomo indicate that on most of these occasions the saint's dried blood did liquefy; indeed, it continues to liquefy annually. Other such relics still liquefying on a regular and predictable basis include a blood relic of S. Gennaro at Pozzuoli (just outside Naples), a blood relic of S. Patrizia at the Church of S. Gregorio Armeno in Naples, and a blood relic of S. Pantaleone at Ravello (along the Amalfi coast).[1] In earlier centuries, more than a dozen additional blood relics, found mainly in churches in and around Naples, have also liquefied on a regular basis.[2]

The second category of saintly relic whose appearance is affected by supernatural power has received less scholarly attention than the liquefying blood relics of Naples, but it is more important to the Catholic experience in Italy generally. The relics in this second category are saintly bodies preserved incorrupt.[3]

---

1. For an account of these relics as they appear during their period of liquefaction, see Carroll (1989, 189–96).

2. For an overview of the cults that have formed around liquefying blood relics at Naples and the surrounding area, see Carroll (1989, 57–78; 1992, 115–20).

3. Of the 103 cases from the hagiographical literature that Cruz (1977) located, 53 were found in Italy, 15 in France, and 13 in Spain.

An Example

Fra Marco Maffei da Marcianise (b. 1542) was one of the moving forces behind the reform of the Dominican order in the decades following the Council of Trent. During his lifetime he was widely known for his virtue and for his desire to extinguish vice and corruption.[4] When he died at Naples in 1616 there was little doubt in the mind of the public that he was a saint. As a result, Neapolitans came in large numbers to the Church of S. Maria della Sanità to view his body and to obtain relics. Some were content simply to touch their rosaries to his body in order to create a relic-by-contact. Others were more aggressive and pulled out hairs from da Marcianise's beard and scalp. Still others tore off bits and pieces of his clothing, and for this reason, D'Engenio (1623, 615) tells us, the corpse had to be reclothed twice. Eventually, da Marcianise was entombed in one of the side chapels at S. Maria della Sanità.

When his body was exhumed three months later, its appearance was not what would have been expected:

> His body was found to be entire and incorrupt [intiero & incorrotto], with his beard and hair looking as if he had only just died. But what most of all caused amazement and astonishment was that the skin on his head, on the front of his body, and under his beard seemed as it did when he was alive, and his hands, legs, and feet were as handsome as they had ever been. All this was true even though he had been buried in a very humid place. (ibid.)

In short, the natural processes that ordinarily lead to the decomposition of corpses were suspended in the case of this saintly Dominican. To the Neapolitans who saw de Marcianise's incorrupt body, the visual impact was probably as dramatic as the liquefaction of S. Gennaro's blood.

Incorruption in the Catholic Tradition

The incorruption of saintly bodies described in the hagiographical literature is understood to be of supernatural origin. The preservation of a corpse through embalming, for instance, is not considered incorruption. Also implicit in hagiographical accounts is that incorruption is a sign of saintliness. These understandings exist even though to the Church incorruption is neither a necessary nor a sufficient condition for sainthood, and saintliness must be based upon an evaluation of a person's life.

On the other hand, both Church officials and the general public recognize

---

4. Da Marcianise's career is discussed in D'Engenio (1623, 614–15); Miele (1963, 174–87).

that incorruption can happen to bodies that do not belong to saints. Burckhardt (1955, 95–96) reports that in 1485 the perfectly preserved body of a young girl, thought to be a Roman of the classical period, was discovered in a tomb along the Appian Way. Although her body was exhibited in Rome and attracted great crowds, no one suggested that she was a saint or a martyr. Norcini (1988, 50–52) tells us that during the early seventeenth century the body of a Cristofano Landino (d. 1504), a scholar who had written a commentary on Dante, was found "mummified but without any trace of corruption" in the parish church of Borgo alla Collina (Tuscany). Landino's body was kept in a simple wooden case, which was kept open for the benefit of the occasional curious visitor, but he was not venerated as a saint.

Even when an incorrupt body is judged to be that of a saint and to be the result of supernatural power, there is no expectation that that body is forever after impervious to harm or decay. Incorrupt bodies have been dismembered both by Catholics acquiring relics and by "heretics" bent on destruction, and yet this has not been seen to change the original incorruption. Also, to be considered incorrupt a body simply needs to have been preserved for a longer time than normal, even if it subsequently does decay. Stories are common of a saintly body found to be incorrupt at its first exhumation only to have decayed by a later exhumation.

Yet these caveats and conditions notwithstanding, the Church has enshrined incorrupt bodies of saints in crystal cases beneath altars in any number of churches (where many of these bodies can still be seen) and has approved hagiographical works that explicitly point to incorruption as a physical sign of saintliness. Even in the aftermath of the Second Vatican Council, a period that saw a general devaluation of the cult of saints, Church authorities have been unwilling to altogether abandon the traditional view of saintly incorruption. For instance, one of the very few references to incorruption in the *New Catholic Encyclopedia* (published in 1967) occurs at the end of the article, "Mystical Phenomena," in a paragraph that deals with liquefying blood relics and bodily incorruptibility:

> These phenomena [liquefying blood relics and incorruption] are well attested in the lives of the saints. Many cases could possibly have a natural explanation or be caused by diabolical power. Some are accepted as true mystical phenomena and testimonies from God concerning the holiness of an individual; others seem to be purely morbid and serve no spiritual purpose. (Aumann 1967, 174)

It would be difficult to write a paragraph that more neatly both affirms and denies that incorruption has a supernatural origin and is a sign of saintliness.

Previous Scholarship

The scholarly literature on saintly incorruption is not large. Cruz's (1977) book is mainly descriptive and tends to take the devotional literature at face value. Saintyves (1987, 708–40) treats incorruption as a folk belief, but his concern is more with the natural processes that might produce incorruption than with incorrupt bodies as the objects of cultic attention. Vauchez (1981), in his massive study of holiness in the late Middle Ages, mentions incorruption only in passing. The most authoritative analysis of incorruption in the Catholic tradition remains the one developed by Herbert Thurston, S.J. (1856–1939), whose work must be the starting point of any new analysis.

Thurston was a English Jesuit who wrote dozens of articles on popular Catholicism. His erudition and natural skepticism led him to challenge beliefs and traditions that were (and in many cases, still are) dear to his fellow Catholics. He systematically examines devotional accounts that associated saints and mystics with a variety of unusual behaviors (like levitation, the multiplication of food, living without eating, bodily elongation, tokens of mystic espousal, the stigmata) and almost always finds good reason for not taking these reports at face value. Thurston is also willing to debunk pious traditions surrounding popular Catholic devotions like the Rosary, the Brown Scapular of Our Lady of Mount Carmel, the Stations of the Cross, and the Angelus. His essays are exemplars of meticulous research and are valuable to anyone interested in popular Catholicism.[5]

Thurston's analysis of incorruption was developed in a series of articles that later became chapters in *The Physical Phenomena of Mysticism* (1952). His analysis of incorruption differs from his other analyses in that he does not reject supernatural claims. The otherwise skeptical Father Thurston, in other words, like the later editors of *The New Catholic Encyclopedia*, feels that incorruption (unlike levitation, living without food, etc.) just might occur and just might indicate saintliness. Two observations, in particular, lead him to entertain this possibility.

The first has to do with corpses of people not known to have led saintly lives. Thurston acknowledges that purely natural processes can sometimes produce results that look like incorruption. He describes in detail what he calls "saponification," a process that causes a fatty substance to collect and that works to preserve facial features and other distinguishing characteristics. He admits that the result might be mistaken for incorruption. Nevertheless, the important point for Thurston is that the overwhelming majority of corpses do decompose. He de-

---

5. Crehan (1952) presents an account of Thurston's life and career as well as an exhaustive listing of Thurston's publications.

scribes cases in which authorities had occasion to exhume and examine several hundred bodies at once. In 1840, for instance, Parisian authorities exhumed 574 bodies that had been buried hurriedly during the last days of the 1830 revolution. Some had been placed in coffins or wrapped in canvas, but most "had been buried as they had fallen, without wrapping or covering" (Thurston 1952, 256). Not one of these bodies exhibited any appearance of incorruption.

Thurston's second observation is that incorruption seems relatively common among saints and involves far more than simple saponification. He concedes that he cannot establish the incidence of incorruption among saints: the total runs into the thousands, and tracking down the relevant hagiographical literature would be, he says, too enormous a task. So Thurston settles for a more accessible sample: the forty-two saints who died since 1400 and who are included in Roman Martyrology, a listing of all the saints recognized as legitimate by the papacy. The list includes the day on which the feast in honor of each saint is to be celebrated in churches following the Roman rite. Evidence attests to incorruption in twenty-nine (70%) of these forty-two cases. This is true (as Thurston emphasizes over and over again) even though incorruption was never the reason that a saint was included in the list.

That incorruption was so rare among "ordinary" corpses yet so common among saintly corpses is what led Thurston to entertain the possibility that incorruption occurs, that it is of supernatural origin, and that it reflects saintliness. Thurston's argument depends upon the assumption that the saints in Roman Martyrology are a representative sample of saints in general. As we shall see later in this chapter, they are not. On the other hand, incorrupt saints do seem to be overrepresented in Roman Martyrology, and this in itself (as we shall see) is probably the most important pattern that emerges from Thurston's analysis.

Incorruption in Italy: Other Patterns

For the moment, I am not concerned with the precise physical attributes of saintly incorruption (though more on this later). I take a saintly body to be (or have been) incorrupt if that body is described as incorrupt in the devotional literature. Using this loose definition, I have located seventy-five cases of saintly incorruption in Italy (the fifty-three Italian cases described by Cruz 1977 plus twenty-two from other sources).[6] Although these seventy-five cases almost certainly do not exhaust all cases of saintly incorruption in Italy, I suspect that they

6. These twenty-two additional instances are described in: Alfano and Amitrano (1951, 262, 321); Arrigoni and Bertarelli (1936, 68, 141); Beltrano (1671, 149); Calvi (1676b, 341; 1677, 256, 345);

Table 8.1. Saintly Bodies Preserved Incorrupt in Italy, by Century of Death and Century of
First Declaration of Incorruption

Century	Number of (Incorrupt) Saints Dying in Century	Number of Saints First Declared Incorrupt in Century
Eleventh or earlier	4	0
Twelfth	2	1
Thirteenth	7	4
Fourteenth	14	5
Fifteenth	16	10
Sixteenth	13	11
Seventeenth	9	12
Eighteenth	5	3
Nineteenth	4	3
Twentieth	1	6
Information not available	0	20
Total	75	75

Sources: See text and n. 6.
Note: A saint, in this context, refers to someone who became the focus of an approved cult, regardless of official canonization.

constitute as complete and representative a sample as is likely to be developed in the foreseeable future.

With regard to gender, thirty-eight (51%) of the incorrupt saints in my sample are male, and thirty-seven (49%) are female. The split, in other words, is almost exactly fifty-fifty. Such a pattern suggests that male and female corpses are equally likely to be "struck" by incorruption.

And what about historic period? Table 8.1 shows the distribution of these seventy-five cases of saintly incorruption by century of death. As is evident, incorruption is very much a modern rather than, say, a medieval, phenomena, with a majority (64%) of incorrupt saints having died in the fifteenth century or later. But century of death, though easily determined, is not the best measure to situate the phenomenon. To understand why, consider the case of S. Cecilia, who in some sense is the oldest of all incorrupt saints.

According to traditions that emerged in the fifth century, Cecilia was a Roman aristocrat who converted to Christianity and was martyred for her faith sometime around the beginning of the third century A.D. Those same traditions suggest that Cecilia was laid to rest in the Catacomb of Calistus at Rome. In the early ninth century, Pope Paschal I sought to locate her body so that it could be

D'Engenio (1623, 71, 584, 615); Kempf (1916, 282); Musolino, Niero, and Tramontin (1963, 137, 147, 165, 241, 243); Piò (1615, 214, 461); Thurston (1952, 250); Vauchez (1981, 282). Information on S. Antonio Pierozzi was gathered during a visit to the church of S. Marco at Florence.

translated to the newly restored church of S. Cecilia at Rome. Unable to find her body in the Catacomb of Calistus, Paschal had a dream in which Cecilia directed him to look in the Catacomb of Pretextatus. Looking there, he did find the saint's body and did have it translated.

Nothing more is heard about Cecilia's body until 1599. At that time Cardinal Sfondrato set out to renovate and restore the Church of S. Cecilia, of which he was the titular head. When workmen came upon a sarcophagus of white marble near the main altar, the Cardinal insisted on being the one to open it. What he found inside was the incorrupt body of a woman whom he immediately declared to be S. Cecilia. This body was subsequently reburied and became the focus of a popular cult.[7]

Given the concerns of this book, it does not matter at all if the incorrupt body discovered in 1599 (or the one discovered in the early ninth century) belonged to S. Cecilia or not. It certainly does not matter if the historic S. Cecilia really died circa 300 or at some other point in time. If our concern is with the Catholic belief in incorruption (which it is), the key date is clearly 1599, since this is the point in time at which a belief in the incorruption of S. Cecilia's body first appears in the historical record.

Admittedly, the case of S. Cecilia is extreme, since in no other instance of incorruption is the delay between death and the discovery of incorruption so lengthy. Still, the basic point remains the same: the time a saint is first declared incorrupt conveys more information about the emergence of a belief in incorruption than time of death. Information on the time of this declaration is available for fifty-five of the seventy-five cases in my sample; distribution of these cases by century is given in the right-hand column of table 8.1. Forty-five (82%) of these fifty-five saints were declared incorrupt in the fifteenth century or later. These data, in other words, provide even stronger support for the conclusion that saintly incorruption is a modern phenomena.

An Illusion?

What causes Catholics to believe that certain corpses are preserved from the natural processes of decay? One obvious hypothesis is that the incorruption might be an illusion, that is, these corpses may be little different from ordinary corpses, and pious Catholics project the appearance of incorruption onto the corpse of someone with a reputation for saintliness.

---

7. Kirsch (1913) provides a critical account of the traditions surrounding S. Cecilia; the events surrounding the discovery of her incorrupt body in 1599 are described by Pastor (1933, 520–27).

Such a possibility must be considered if only because illusion is often the basis for other miraculous phenomena in the Catholic tradition. Reading through accounts of Marian apparitions, for example, it is common to find that there were people present at the scene who did not see Mary but who did report seeing something else (mysterious lights, etc.) in the region where other people saw the Virgin Mary. This suggests that the people who reported seeing Mary were projecting their image of Mary onto some ambiguous physical stimulus. As I argue elsewhere (Carroll 1986, 195–218), there are good reasons for believing that a misperception of naturally occurring phenomena was likely the cause of the well-known Marian apparitions at Pontmain (France) in 1871, at Knock (Ireland) in 1879, and at Zeitoun (Egypt) in 1968.

Even so, I doubt very much that misperception is an important factor in claims of incorruption. Remember that incorrupt saints are equally likely to be male or female. This is not what we would expect if Catholic expectations about saintliness were structuring the perception of incorruption. The vast majority of saints, after all, are male. In his statistical study of 2,610 Catholic saints, Delooz (1969) finds that male saints outnumber female saints by a ratio of roughly 4:1. This ratio holds even within particular national traditions and regardless of whether the saints were formally canonized or became "saints" as the result of local tradition (see ibid., 255–76). If perceptions about sainthood structure perceptions of incorruption, we would expect the vast majority of incorrupt saints (like the vast majority of saints in general) to be male, and this is not the case. We would also expect a correlation between perceived saintliness and incorruption, and this is not the case, either. Some of the best known and most popular saints in the Catholic tradition—like S. Francis, S. Dominic, S. Ignatius Loyola, S. Alphonso Liguori—were never found incorrupt. This lack of correlation between degree of saintliness and incorruption has been a recurring source of puzzlement for observers, who see incorruption to be the result of supernatural causation (see for instance the comments by Thurston 1952, 240–42).

Random Processes

A parsimonious way to account for at least two of the patterns associated with incorruption is to suggest that it is the result of natural processes (as yet unidentified) that occur randomly among bodies buried in sanctified ground. On the assumption that males and females are equally likely to be buried in sanctified ground, such a randomly occurring phenomenon would ensure that males and females would be equally represented with regard to incorruption (as they are). Seeing incorruption as something that strikes at random would also explain the general absence of a correlation between incorruption and degree of saintliness.

And what is the precise nature of these supposed random natural processes that produce the appearance of incorruption? Although some of my remarks later in this chapter bear on this issue, I really have no answer to this question nor any interest in finding an answer. My concern is with the *psychological appeal* of cults organized around saintly bodies that appear incorrupt, not with the physical processes that produce the appearance of incorruption. Readers who are curious about the purely natural processes that might lie behind the appearance of incorruption should consult Saintyves (1987), who explores a range of possibilities.

At first sight, the suggestion that incorruption results from random natural processes would seem to be at variance with the historic pattern, that is, with the fact that the incorrupt saints proliferated during the modern age. After all, if purely natural processes were at work, should the proportion of incorrupt corpses not have been relatively constant over time? In fact, the likelihood of a corpse being preserved incorrupt has been constant over time; what has changed is the likelihood of discovering such a corpse and, more importantly, the Church's attitude to saintly incorruption.

Beliefs about Incorruption

During the Middle Ages popular beliefs about bodily incorruption were not entirely consistent. On the one hand, incorruption was often seen as a sign of saintliness. But it could also be taken as a sign that the individual had been a sorcerer or a criminal (ibid.). Yet a third popular tradition suggested that someone who died while excommunicated would not decompose in the normal way. Writing in the fifteenth century, Florentine author Franco Sacchetti (1330 to circa 1400) took note of these contradictory folk attitudes in a passage where he criticizes the proliferation of saintly cults in Italy: "We [already] have [a large number of] canonized saints, and yet we seek those that as far as we know might not have existed . . . On the one hand we say that if someone died while excommunicated their body remains entire and does not decompose; on the other hand we say that if a dead body does not decompose it was the body of a saint." (Sacchetti 1970, 441). Of these various popular traditions, the only one endorsed by Church officials was that incorruption was a sign of saintliness. Nevertheless, the fact that incorruption was surrounded with contradictory associations in the popular mind probably explains why the medieval Church never chose to emphasize saintly incorruption.

The Church's attitude began to change in the decades following the Council of Trent, when we encounter for the first time a systematic and concerted effort by the Church to single out incorrupt saints in a special way. The tool used to do this has already been mentioned: the Roman Martyrology. In the early 1580s, Pope Gregory XIII appointed a commission to produce an authoritative work listing all the saints recognized as legitimate by the papacy as well as the days on which these saints were to be commemorated in churches that followed the Roman rite. Although the commission included several prominent cardinals, its driving force was Cesare Baronio (1538–1607). Baronio's first version of this new martyrology was published in 1586; a second was published in 1589. Additions and revisions to Baronio's martyrology would be made by Urban VIII in 1630 and by Benedict XIV in 1748. The only changes since then have been those occasioned by new canonizations.[8]

Among the saints in the Roman Martyrology, Thurston finds a high proportion of incorrupt bodies. Although he emphasizes that incorruption was not a criterion for inclusion in this martyrology, the proportion of incorrupt saints is far higher than would be expected if this were a random sample of saints. Of the 2,610 saints identified in Delooz (1969), more than 1,500 became the object of cultic devotion sometime after 1400 (the cutoff date used by Thurston). Yet Cruz (1977) was able to locate only 103 cases of saintly incorruption in the history of the Western Church.[9] Even allowing for considerable error on Cruz's part, it seems obvious that incorrupt saints are strongly overrepresented among the post-1400 saints listed in Roman Martyrology. Since one purpose of Roman Martyrology was to indicate which saints were to be honored on particular days of the year, this overrepresentation is evidence of a desire on the part of the Counter-Reformation Church to promote devotion to this particular sort of saint.

The Roman Martyrology aside, the Church's increased emphasis on saintly incorruption after Trent can also be seen in the new criteria for sainthood that emerged during the Counter-Reformation. During the Middle Ages the ideal saint was someone who had lived a virtuous life, which could serve as a model for other Catholics. But as De Maio (1973, 257–78) points out, this view began to change circa 1600. Specifically, in 1602 a group of Spanish theologians petitioning Clement VIII for the canonization of Teresa of Avila introduced the notion of heroic virtue as a way of measuring saintliness. *Heroic virtue* refers to an individual's ability and willingness to act virtuously in a manner far beyond what is expected of ordinary people. The idea proved popular with the Roman authorities and as the century progressed heroic virtue was increasingly mentioned in the deliberations surrounding proposed canonizations.

8. For a discussion of the Roman Martyrology and how it came to be, see Delehaye (1913).
9. Cruz, like Delooz, includes individuals who were either canonized or beatified as saints.

De Maio demonstrates that certain activities came to be seen as especially emblematic of heroic virtue (and so saintliness). Most people have an instinctive fear of pain, and so heroic virtue was seen in those individuals who willingly embraced extreme forms of penitential suffering. Heroic virtue was also seen in individuals willing to risk suffering and death in God's service, either as a missionary bringing the Catholic religion to pagans or as someone ministering to plague victims. Finally heroic virtue was seen in those who had been assaulted or tempted by the Devil and had emerged triumphant.

Church officials also argued that certain objective signs indicate the presence of heroic virtue. Two such signs, De Maio suggests, were particularly important. One was a "glorious tomb," that is, a tomb covered with ex-voto testifying to miracles obtained through that person's intercession. The second sign was a "precious death," by which was meant a death as much "beyond ordinary experience" as heroic virtue itself. Most often cited as evidence of a "precious death" in canonization proceedings were (1) that the person had prophesied the exact moment of his or her own death and (2) that the person's corpse remained incorrupt for a long period of time.

In the end, then, the Counter-Reformation Church took the association between incorruption and saintliness, which had existed since the Middle Ages, and made it more central to the official determination of saintliness. What still needs to be explained, of course, is why this happened.

Metaphor and Religious Belief

In a well-known and widely reprinted article, Burke (1984) suggests that the likelihood of someone being canonized in the period 1588–1767 was determined as much by whether that individual was associated with activities considered important by the Counter-Reformation Church as by any personal qualities the individual might have possessed. This is why, he argues, so many of the saints canonized during this period were missionaries, bishops who conformed to the tridentine model of the "good pastor," or the founders of religious orders (like the Jesuits and Theatines) concerned with promoting an awareness of tridentine Catholicism among the clergy and the laity.

Still, saints could be valuable to the Church not only for what they did (as Burke demonstates) but also for how they interpreted what they did. As mentioned, one measure of heroic virtue was being able to confront the assaults and temptations of the Devil and to emerge victorious. In deciding how well some particular individual had done in his or her battle with the Devil, it was usually necessary for Church authorities to rely on accounts of these struggles written by the individuals involved or at least communicated by these individuals to others. De Maio (1973, 266–67) points out that, although many of the "struggles with the Devil" described in these accounts might seem to the modern eye to have a strongly sexual flavor, the people involved invariably saw them differently. The Devil was seen less as an embodiment of evil or sin than as an "enemy of the Church" who had to be defeated so that the Church could carry out its apostolic mission. In other words, a saint's battle with the Devil was seen (by both the saint involved and the saint's promoters) as a metaphor for the Church's battle with its enemies. The fact that the saint emerged victorious implied that the Church would also emerge victorious.

But if the living saint could serve as a metaphor for the Church (as De Maio suggests), there is no particular reason why the body of the dead saint could not serve the same purpose. This suggests that the key to understanding the popularity of cults organized around incorrupt saints lies in determining the metaphorical connotations that saintly incorruption would have evoked in the minds of Counter-Reformation prelates—and this leads us to a question that I have until now avoided: What physical characteristics did a corpse have to possess to be defined as incorrupt?

The Physical Correlates of Incorruption

Cases of incorruption fall naturally into two general categories. First, there are those in which a saintly body is declared incorrupt before burial. An attribution of incorruption here seems to derive from what Thurston calls an "absence of cadaveric rigidity," along with the absence of discoloration and unpleasant odor. But this sort of incorruption is relatively infrequent; in the sample being used here, such cases account for only about 12 percent of the total.[10] Far more common are those cases that fall into the second category, which includes bodies that were buried and found incorrupt at a later exhumation. These are the cases, I suggest, that for most Catholics define the phenomenon of incorruption. What leads to attributions of incorruption here?

Devotional accounts often create the impression that incorrupt corpses have the appearance of bodies only just deceased. In fact, visual inspection of incorrupt corpses suggests otherwise. Visitors to the Church of S. Marco in Florence, for instance, can even now view the body of Antonio Pierozzi lying in a crystal case in a side chapel to the left of the main altar. The inscription below that case

10. Information relating to the circumstances surrounding the discovery of incorruption is available for fifty-nine of the seventy-five cases in the sample. Of these fifty-nine, seven (12%) were declared incorrupt before burial.

reads: "The incorrupt body of S. Antonio Pierozzi 1389–1459, Founder of the priory of S. Marco, Reformer of the Dominican Order, Archbishop and Patron of Florence." Only Pierozzi's face and hands are visible, but the skin is clearly desiccated and grey. The same is true of the skin covering the face and hands of S. Maria Maddalena de'Pazzi, whose corpse lies beneath the main altar in the convent church of the Carmelite nuns at Careggi (just outside Florence). On the other hand, despite their dry and desiccated skin, the facial features of both Pierozzi and de'Pazzi are sharp and clear, so it is likely that these centuries-old corpses do give viewers a sense of what these individuals looked like in life.

In other cases, however, the appearance of incorrupt corpses borders more on the hideous than on the lifelike. The incorrupt body of S. Rosa di Viterbo, for example, lies in the church dedicated to her at Viterbo (Lazio). In this case, the saint's face is severely flattened (her nose is all but gone), and her skin is dark and shiny. Also, the skin around her mouth has receded to expose her teeth. The overall effect is akin to what would be produced by placing a ghoulish leather mask over a skeleton.

The examples just considered of course have been incorrupt for centuries. But even in the case of fresh incorrupt corpses, the appearance of just having died is not central. A careful reading of devotional accounts of incorruption, for example, will almost always uncover evidence suggesting discoloration. Thus in 1599 a wealthy follower of Filippo Neri (1515–95) offered to build a silver shrine to house the body of this saintly man. Before proceeding, the priests of the oratory that Neri had founded thought it prudent to have the body inspected. A life of Neri published originally in 1622 by Father Bacci tells us what they found:

> On the 7th of May, 1599, after it had remained four years in the [tomb], they took down the wall and opened the coffin. They found the body covered with cobwebs and dust, which had got in through a crack in the lid of the coffin, caused by the moisture in the wall which had been built over it; his vestments were like so much dirt; the chasuble had become so rotten that it all fell to pieces . . . so that they expected to find his body reduced to dust. On the following evening however, having removed all the rubbish, they found not only his arms and legs and the whole body entire, but the breast and stomach so fresh and beautiful, and the skull and flesh so natural that every one was astonished; the breast moreover retained its whiteness. (Bacci 1902, 125–26).

The body was subsequently examined, Bacci (126) says, by three prominent medical doctors, and "they all three wrote upon the subject, showing that neither by nature nor by any artificial means could it have been preserved as it had been without the special aid of Divine Omnipotence." This story conforms to a formula typical of incorruption stories, namely: the body of a holy person is exhumed; conditions favor decomposition, and in fact observers expect to find the corpse decomposed; despite this, the body is discovered incorrupt to the amazement of all present; supernatural causation is considered to be the only possible explanation. But notice that Bacci very clearly says that Neri's "breast had retained its whiteness." This seems a implicit admission that the rest of his body had not retained its whiteness.

If it is not the appearance of just having died that leads to attribution of incorruption, what does? The answer, I think, can be glimpsed in that section of Bacci's account of Fillipo Neri's incorrupt body where he tells us that Neri was found with "his whole body entire." This line is important, because the terms *entire* or *whole and entire* are in fact the terms that appear most often in accounts of incorrupt corpses. Quite often a body's having been found entire or whole and entire are the only attributes mentioned in describing incorruption. The following passages are typical of the ways in which incorrupt corpses have been described in devotional accounts over the centuries:

The body [of Fra Ambrosio da Siena] was at first buried within the Sacristy of the monastery of S. Dominico. But a few years later it was transferred to fine marble sepulchre . . . and placed within a beautiful chapel in the middle of the church. During the translation the body was found entire [intero], fresh and beautiful, as if he had died that very day. (Piò 1615, 214)

Here lies the holy body [of Beata Sibillina Biscossi] that, except for the very tip of her nose, is still seen to be completely entire [tutto intiero], with the very clothes in which she was buried, despite the fact that it has been two hundred and forty-six years since her death. (Ibid., 394)

It was resolved to transfer the holy body of this great martyr [S. Pietro da Verona] to a more honorable place of burial. . . . When the holy body was raised from the place of its original burial it was found completely entire [tutto intiero] and without any sign of corruption or foul odor, just as if he had just died that day. (Ibid., 461)

Sister Maria Maddalena Carrafa was also a nun here [at the convent of S. Maria della Sapienza in Naples]. She flew to heaven on the 28th of December in the year 1613 . . . and her body can be seen today entire and incorrupt [intiero & incorrotto]. (D'Engenio, 1623, 71)

Preaching a lenten sermon in this church [Fra Giovanni Battista da Pesaro] predicted the date of his own death, and so it came to be. The entire city gathered around his corpse to venerate him because they considered him a saint. Several years after his death his body was found entire and incorrupt [intiero & incorroto]. (Ibid., 584)

After having lived for many years in Salerno, this holy pope [San Gregorio VII] passed over to enjoy another life in the year 1085 and was buried in a grand sepulchre in his church. After being worn down over time, the church was restored in the year 1578 by Archbishop Marsilio Colonna himself, who reported having found [the body] entire [intiero] and without damage, with its pontifical vestments incorrupt. (Beltrano 1671, 149)

F. Gottardo Ceni da Colognola, a Capuchin lay brother, dead in the odor of sanctity since the 18th of March 1624, was this year [1627] uncovered and found entire [trovato intiero]. (Calvi 1676b, 341)

A true portrait of . . . Margherita Columba . . . [who] chose to be buried among the penitents of S. Pelagia in the city of Milan, where even now her body lies entire and incorrupt [intiero, et incorrotto]. (Inscription on popular print, circa 1680; cited in Arrigoni and Bertarelli 1936, 68)

The Corpo di Cristo convent is among the noblest and richest of the convents [in Bologna]. This is where S. Caterina, called "of Bologna," is buried. Her body is as entire [intiera] as it was on the day of her death. (Jenkins 1775, 176–77)

Such passages suggest that being found "entire" or "whole and entire" is what leads to an attribution of incorruption. What *entire* seems to mean is that the limbs had not separated from the torso and the skin had not split apart to reveal tissue or bone. It was, I think, this sense of incorruption—as lack of separation—that made cults organized around incorrupt bodies so appealing to the leaders of the Counter-Reformation Church.

Incorruption and the Counter-Reformation View of Protestantism

As indicated in the last chapter, Lutheran ideas diffused quickly into Italy and were already circulating widely in some areas of northern Italy by the 1520s. How did the leaders of the Italian Church respond to these ideas? A few theologians did address the substance of Luther's arguments, but this was not the usual response. Niccoli's (1983) analysis of the references to Luther and Lutheranism in works by Catholic commentators in the 1520s and 1530s suggests that they made few if any references to Lutheran doctrine. On the contrary, if they discussed Lutheranism at all, it was mainly to mount ad hominem attacks against Luther as an individual (he was variously a drunkard, a sexual libertine, a blasphemer, a man consumed by pride, etc.) or to attack Lutheranism on account of the horrible social consequences to which it had given rise.

In this latter regard, they always saw the breakup of the Church as the most serious of the consequences that flowed from Lutheranism. In other words, Lutheranism's threat to the organizational integrity of the Church was the one attribute that most defined what Lutheranism meant to the leaders of the Italian Church during the first half of the sixteenth century. Niccoli (1983, 21) argues that this general neglect of doctrine and this focus on the threat to Catholic unity posed by Luther's heresy gave rise to the Italian practice of using the term *luterani* to describe all Protestants. After all, while Protestant groups might differ among themselves with regard to a variety of doctrinal matters, they were all similar to Luther in seeking to detach themselves from the Roman Church.

Most Italian prelates continued to avoid direct contact with Lutheran texts well into the middle of the sixteenth century. Even at the Council of Trent, the attending bishops usually left the business of preparing their doctrinal responses to Protestantism to professional theologians, with the result that these prelates themselves were often happily ignorant of the matters they were discussing. This explains how the archbishop of Palermo could deliver a report in 1562 that "confused the Elector of Saxony with the King of England and Luther with Tetzel, and argued that the religious protest in Germany has been caused by things like the denial of a matrimonial dispensation to Frederick of Saxony and the revocation of Luther's permission to preach indulgences" (Prosperi, 1983, 101).

The proceedings of the Council of Trent do contain a great many citations to Luther's work, but as Prosperi (113) notes, the overwhelming majority of these are to passages ripped from their original context and reproduced in texts written by Catholic commentators anxious to make some critical point. For some of the Italian prelates at Trent, this reliance on Catholic-supplied snippets of Lutheran thought was a point of pride. During the council's debate on matrimony in 1562, Giambattista Castagna, the archbishop of Rossano, cited passages from a variety of Protestant thinkers, including both Luther and Calvin, and concluded by saying "I have never read these [passages] in their books, nor do I have any wish to do so, [having relied instead] on the book by Ruard Tapper, the learned dean of Louvain, which reproduces them" (cited in ibid., 114).

This early response to Luther and Lutheranism established a formula that would structure the thinking of Italian prelates for centuries: Luther was a moral degenerate, his doctrines were attempts to satisfy the demands of this degeneracy, and the most important thing to understand about the Reformation was that it split apart the Church and set in motion a number of social ills. Occasionally, new details would be assimilated to the formula, but the formula itself was not changed. Thus the list of moral flaws attributed to Luther was often expanded (though never shortened) to reflect the specific concerns of the day. During the twentieth century, for instance, Luther became a disturbed personality, describable using the terminology of modern psychiatry (on this view of Luther, see Marcocchi 1983, 192–93).

Similarly, as new social evils emerged, Italian prelates were quick to tack these onto the list of horrible things that Luther's heresy had set in motion. During the eighteenth century, Luther's actions were seen to have been the ultimate cause of the French Revolution (Menozzi 1983, 163–64), just as in the nineteenth century Lutheranism was blamed for the revolutions that swept across Europe at midcentury and for the rise of socialism and communism (Miccoli 1983). Nevertheless, even though the list of social ills attributed to Luther grew, his most unpardonable sin was that his actions had split apart the organizational integrity of the Church. Though Catholic commentators in Italy no longer use the term *luterani* to denote all Protestants, they continued until quite recently to see the disruption of the Church's organizational unity as the most important feature of all Protestant sects (Bellini 1983, 232)

Given their preoccupation with organizational unity, Italian prelates would have been predisposed to promote devotions that provided (among both prelates and Catholics in general) a concrete metaphor for thinking about the organizational unity of the Church that had been lost during the Reformation. In promoting cults organized around saintly bodies that had been preserved incorrupt—which by definition meant bodies that had been preserved whole and entire—they were doing just that. Moreover, this metaphorical equivalence meant that the veneration of a saintly body miraculously preserved whole and entire was a way of rejecting the organizational disunity that Protestantism had engendered. This, I argue, is what made saintly incorruption so valuable to the Counter-Reformation Church.

Consistent with this interpretation is that fact that cults organized around incorrupt bodies have always been initiated at the top. Ordinary Catholics in Italy, for instance, have often been the ones to decide that some obscure madonnine image has suddenly begun to dispense favors, bleed, etcetera. The Church may have subsequently co-opted the resulting cult, but the fact remains that in the first instance these cults sprang from a purely popular predisposition. But a body buried on sanctified ground cannot casually be discovered incorrupt. On the contrary, in almost all cases bodies found incorrupt were exhumed upon the authorization of Church authorities, and every stage of these exhumations was carefully supervised by these same authorities. This means that the discovery of incorruption was under the direct control of Church authorities. If cults organized around incorrupt bodies proliferated after Trent, it was because these authorities wanted such cults to proliferate. Understanding the metaphorical value of these cults to prelates concerned with organizational unity helps us to understand why.

Summary

Since at least the Middle Ages, the belief that saintly bodies were sometimes preserved incorrupt has been part of both popular and official traditions surrounding the cult of the saints. I argue that natural processes can produce an appearance of incorruption and ensure that a certain proportion of the bodies buried in sanctified ground, when exhumed, will seem incorrupt. Partly, this means that the number of bodies found incorrupt will be a function of how many bodies are exhumed. I suspect, for instance, that the upsurge in saintly bodies found incorrupt in the fifteenth century (see table 8.1) has as much to do with the surge in renovations made to Italian churches during the Renaissance as with anything else.

Nevertheless, it was only during the Counter-Reformation that the Church chose to single out incorrupt saints for special cultic attention and to make incorruption more central to the definition of sanctity. This was done because Church leaders saw the incorrupt body of a saint—a body that had remained whole and entire after burial—as a metaphor for the organizational integrity of the Church, an integrity that had been the greatest casualty of the Reformation.

Conclusion

Back to Beginnings

I n October 1980 Alan Dundes presented his presidential address to the Annual Meeting of the American Folklore Society. His subject was German
folklore, and at first his audience laughed good-naturedly at the jokes that
were part of the presentation. But the laughter faded quickly as the speech
progressed. By the time Dundes finished, many listeners were obviously embar-
rassed. Several were visibly angry. One listener called the speech an "abuse of the
presidential podium"; another worried aloud that the speech might actually be
published in the Society's *Journal of American Folklore*. The editor of the mono-
graph series of the American Folklore Society would later decide against pub-
lishing Dundes's analysis, without even sending it out for review.

What had Dundes said to provoke such a strongly negative reaction? Three
things. First, he argued that folklore was a projective system that could be used to
assess national character, a concept that most social scientists in North America
regard as discredited. Second, he was concerned specifically with the German national character, and so to many listeners his analysis likely seemed vaguely remi-
niscent of the racial purity theories promulgated by the Nazis. Finally, Dundes
combined Freud's work on anal eroticism with the emphasis upon anal themes
that seems evident (he felt) in German folklore and concluded that German national character was, well, predominantly anal. Outside the psychoanalytic tradition, anality is not a subject that comes up often in scholarly circles. Eventually,
Dundes's analysis would be published in the *Journal of Psychoanalytic Anthropology* (an out-of-the-mainstream journal, which has since folded), and an expanded
version would appear as a book in 1984. Most North American reviewers were cool
to the book. Perhaps surprisingly, it was more favorably received in Germany itself.[1]

1. These events are described in Dundes (1981; 1989).

What has any of this to do with popular Catholicism in Italy? Not much, except that, like Dundes, I think that the time has come to take another look at the idea of national character. In particular, I argue that much of what is distinctive about popular Catholicism in Italy is the result of something that can reasonably be called the Italian national character.

The Rise and Decline of National Character Studies

In the decades following the First World War it became common for anthropologists studying non-Western societies to associate these societies with distinct personalities. For example, in her influential *Patterns of Culture* (1934), Benedict characterizes cultures as being either Dionysian or Apollonian. People in Dionysian cultures, she argues, sought emotional excess and emphasized individual experience; people in Apollonian cultures people sought moderation in all things and clung to tradition. Similarly, in *Sex and Temperament in Three Primitive Societies* (1935), Mead characterizes the Arapesh, both males and females, as being gentle, passive, and cooperative and the Mundugumor—again, both males and females—as being violent and aggressive. In a third society (the Tchambuli), Mead found a pattern that she feels is the reverse of the one in our own society, with men being emotionally dependent and women being impersonal and domineering.

As the world plunged into World War II, policy makers in America and Britain felt a need to develop a better understanding of the populations living in modern nation states, especially in those nation-states that were or would soon be most directly involved in the war. Several anthropologists (including Ruth Benedict, Margaret Mead, Gregory Bateson, and Geoffrey Gorer) responded to this need by arguing that modern nation states could be studied using the same conceptual tools developed to study small-scale societies. This meant that national societies, too, could be associated with distinct personalities.

Since wartime conditions made it impossible to do fieldwork in the societies being investigated, a new methodology was invented, what Mead (1953) calls "the study of culture at a distance." Partly this meant studying documentary sources (novels, newspapers, folklore collections, etc.), but mostly it meant interviewing exiles from the society in question. The method produced conclusions not much different from those derived from field investigations. For example, as a member of the Office of War Information, Benedict prepared a report on the "Dutch national character" in 1944, just before the American invasion of the Netherlands. Ginkel (1992) demonstrates that there is a strong congruence between Benedict's conclusions and those reached by Dutch scholars of the period (mainly historians, folklorists, and sociologists, not anthropologists) in reports that were not accessible to Benedict.

During the 1950s, however, a strong reaction against national character studies set in. Partly, this was the result of new evidence that cast doubt on some of the specific claims that had been made in these studies. In one particularly well-known study (indeed, for many critics it was *the* national character study), Gorer and Rickman (1949) relate the Russian practice of swaddling infants to personality traits supposedly characteristic of adult Russians. Specifically, these scholars argue that swaddling and the rage it generated in the infant gives rise to an adult personality characterized by a diffuse sense of guilt, rapid shifts between kindness and cruelty, and a preference for either strict equality or strict subordination. They then link these personality traits to several events that occurred in Russia since the 1917 Revolution. Unfortunately (for their argument), subsequent research failed to find evidence of extensive swaddling among groups comparable to the groups they studied; moreover, many of the traits they associate with the Russian personality seemed to evaporate with Stalin's death, suggesting that these traits were tied more to the nature of the Stalinist regime than to child-rearing practices (see Harris 1968, 444–48).

But the most serious objections to the national character tradition were and are methodological and theoretical, not empirical. Three objections are especially common and must be considered by anyone who argues for a reconsideration of the national character idea.[2] The first is that the concept of national character predisposes investigators to oversimplify, that is, to ignore variation within a national population. The second is that national character studies are reductionistic, that is, they tend to derive national character from some single factor, usually some specific child-rearing practice, and so ignore the obvious complexity of the processes that give rise to social behavior. Finally, these studies are accused of ignoring history, that is, of talking about the cluster of personality traits that define some particular national character as if it has existed for centuries, without doing the historical research that might establish (or discredit) such a premise.

Taken at face value, the oversimplification charge does a disservice to the scholars investigating national character. Without exception, they are well aware that modern populations are heterogeneous and that there is no one single personality type to which all members of national society conform, and they routinely allow for heterogeneity in one of two ways. Many studies, for example,

2. See Ginkel 1992, 63–67. Between 1945 and 1970, the debate over the validity of national character generated an enormous literature, partly because it was fueled by bitter controversies long since forgotten. For an introduction to this literature, see Mead (1951); DeVos (1968); Inkeles and Levinson (1969). For attempts to assess the national character of particular societies, see the collection of essays in Martindale (1967).

equate national character with modal personality, that is, with a cluster of personality traits that characterize the largest number of people in a society. By its nature, the modal personality concept acknowledges that other personality configurations exist in a society. Other studies conceptualize national character as akin to an ideal type in the Weberian sense, that is, as a idealized cluster of traits that exists in the subjective consciousness of individuals and that shapes, but does not precisely determine, their preferences and behaviors.

The second objection, that national character studies are reductionistic, is more legitimate but is misdirected. The matter of what cluster of attributes defines national character in some particular society is analytically and logically separate from the question of how that national character has come into existence. The fact that attempts to answer this second question might be simplistic or otherwise flawed does not discredit answers to the first question, nor does it undermine the concept of national character itself.

The third objection, that national character studies are ahistorical, is the most serious. Although the authors of these studies often talk about historic patterns, their statements in this regard are generally superficial and unsupported by any detailed discussion of the historical record. But here again the objection is less a reason for rejecting the concept of national character than a call for methodological rigor. It suggests that investigators establish that the cluster of traits they see as defining national character has persisted for a long of time.

In the end, then, I believe (with Dundes) that the idea of national character can be useful as long as we are careful not to make the reductionistic claims characteristic of earlier investigators and as long as we are careful to establish that the patterns that define national character have persisted for centuries. Given the strong emotions so often evoked by the national character label, I should also make clear that I take national character to be nothing more than a set of psychological predispositions and that the origins of these predispositions are to be found in cultural values and social arrangements, not in biology.

Like Dundes, I also believe that the psychological predispositions that define national character are best uncovered by examining the folk traditions of a society. The folk traditions examined by Dundes in his investigation of German national character include jokes, proverbs, and folk tales. In the investigation of the Italian national character that follows, my folk tradition of choice is popular Catholicism, and I make use of patterns established in earlier chapters of this book.

Predisposition to Merge Natural and Supernatural

One pattern made clear in earlier chapters is that Italian Catholics seem predisposed to merge the natural and the supernatural. This merging predilection is especially evident in the infusion of concrete objects, mainly madonnine images (chap. 1) and saintly relics (chap. 6), with supernatural power. I argue that this predisposition constitutes a given to which the Italian Church has had to adapt to maintain the allegiance of its constituency (chaps. 2 and 3). This predisposition also ensured that ideologies like Protestantism and evangelism, which reject a merging of supernatural power with concrete objects, would never be widely popular in Italy (chap. 7).

Because a predisposition to merge the natural and the supernatural is so central to the experience of popular Catholicism in Italy, it is reasonable (I suggest) to consider it a part of the Italian national character. What needs to be explained, of course, is where this popular predisposition comes from. Chapter 7 provides a partial answer, suggesting that in southern Italy the social experience of living in a community organized around a chiesa ricettizia facilitated such an emphasis on merging. I now want to explore a second possibility.

Psychoanalytic Considerations

Freud approaches religion in two ways. In *Totem and Taboo* (1913) and *Moses and Monotheism* (1939) he uses psychoanalytic insights to reconstruct the historical development of particular religious traditions. His arguments rest ultimately on a psycho-Lamarckian premise (namely, that unconscious memories can be transmitted from generation to generation) that has always been rejected even by scholars generally sympathetic to psychoanalysis. Freud's second approach to religion seeks to identify the psychological origins of religious belief. In *The Future of an Illusion* (1927) he argues that, when adults confront a world permeated by hostile forces beyond their control, they are reminded of the helplessness they felt as children. This leads them to believe in supernatural beings who have the power to protect them from the hostile forces of the adult world, just as their parents, the father in particular, had the power to protect them from the hostile forces of the child's world. The end result, he argues, is that infantile memories buried in the adult unconscious shape the adult's image of the supernatural world.

For a variety of reasons, Freud did not pursue this second hypothesis with the same zeal with which he pursues his investigations of the historic origins of religion.[3] One result is that he did not link his hypothesis on the psychological origins of religion to his work on infantile development. The two arguments, however, are obviously related. After all, one of Freud's central conclusions in regard to infantile development is that children pass through a series of stages, each

---

3. For some speculation on why Freud was more interested in the historic development of religion, see Carroll (1987).

characterized by a different set of erotic concerns, fears, parental images, etcetera. If this conclusion is combined with his hypothesis on the psychological origins of religion, then it leads to a clear prediction: the supernatural order that we create as adults will vary depending upon *which* infantile memories we use in constructing our image of the supernatural.

Although Freud does not link the different stages of infantile development to different religious beliefs in adults, he does something similar by linking the different stages of infantile development to different adult personalities. Most of his efforts here are concerned specifically with establishing a link between the infantile experience of anal eroticism and the development of the anal personality (a personality characterized by an emphasis upon cleanliness, order, and repetition) in the adult (see Freud 1908; 1917). Freud's work in this area was continued by Karl Abraham, who developed the classic psychoanalytic formulation relating infantile oral eroticism to adult personality. Abraham's discussion of the oral personality has a clear affinity with the merging emphasis of Italian Catholicism.

Abraham (1927) starts with the observation that the mouth's association with physical pleasure is only partly attributable to its association with the pleasures of eating. More important, he argues, is the fact that mouth is an erotogenic zone, that is, the physiology of the human mouth ensures that bringing things into contact with the lips and the surfaces inside the mouth produces a diffuse sense of physical pleasure. It is this that leads infants—all infants—to seek physical pleasure by sucking on objects. The most important of these objects is the mother's breast, but infants also derive pleasure from sucking on their own thumbs or whatever else is available.

In some cases, experiences at the oral stage lead to oral erotic desires that are especially strong and that continue to exert an influence on personality development even when the child moves into later developmental stages. Abraham emphasizes that strong oral erotic desires can emerge in individuals because their early oral erotic experiences were either especially pleasurable or especially frustrating. In the first case, the individual is seeking to repeat their pleasurable experiences, while in the second the individual is seeking to gain what was strongly desired but denied.

Ours is not a culture that strongly represses orality, which means that strong oral erotic desires can be gratified in relatively straightforward and undisguised ways. This is why (for Abraham) an emphasis upon food, eating, and talking, are characteristics of the oral personality.[4] But strong oral erotic desires can be grati-

---

4. As Abraham points out, this is dramatically different from what must happen in the case of strong anal erotic desires. Since all forms of anality are subject to strong repression in our culture, the gratification of such desires is subject to a great deal of disguise.

fied in less obvious ways as well. In particular, Abraham argues that such desires give rise to traits like sociability, an unwillingness to be alone, and an openness to new ideas.[5] His reasoning here is not entirely clear, but the basic idea seems to be that these traits (sociability, an unwillingness to be alone, an openness to new ideas) involve a desire for closeness with external objects (people or ideas) and that this is similar to the closeness achieved when infants engulf an object with their mouths.

Cognitive Consequences of Oral Eroticism

Abraham was concerned mainly with the emotional and behavioral sequelae of oral eroticism, as have been most subsequent researchers who have investigated the oral personality.[6] Less attention has been paid to how infantile oral eroticism might affect cognitive functioning, that is, how it might affect the schemas that adults use in thinking about the world. Freud (1905, 198) does say in passing that the physical act central to oral eroticism, putting an object into the mouth, becomes the prototype for identification, a cognitive process that plays an important role in later development.

Meissner (1971; 1981, 5–71) amplifies Freud's discussion by suggesting that we need to distinguish "identification" from "incorporation." Both are cognitive processes that involve internalizing an external object, and both are routinely encountered in clinical experience. The difference between the two is that incorporation aims to blur and eliminate the distinction between the external object and the self, while identification does not. In Meissner's words: "In incorporation the totality and globalness of the internalization of the object is such that the object loses its function and character as object. The external object is completely taken into the inner world of the subject. As a result, boundaries between the inner world and the outer world are decathected and dedifferentiated" (Meissner 1981, 18). For Meissner, incorporation is the more primitive process, since it derives directly from the oral stage and is modeled on the physical act of "incorporating" an object into the mouth.

Despite Meissner's penchant for diffuse language ("the totality and globalness of the internalization") and his reliance on jargon ("dedifferentiated"), it seems clear from his discussion that the cognitive process he calls "incorporation" strongly resembles the merging emphasis discussed earlier. In the case of Italian

5. Abraham links other personality traits to oral eroticism, but these traits depend on whether experiences at the oral stage are pleasurable or frustrating.
6. See Kline (1972, 6–94) and Masling (1986) for an overview of some of the relevant research here.

popular Catholicism, of course, the boundary that is blurred and eliminated is the boundary between the natural and the supernatural rather than the boundary between self and external object. Even so, the structural similarity seems apparent.

The hypothesis that emerges, and that I propose here, is that *the emphasis on merging that is so central to Italian popular Catholicism derives from strong unconscious oral erotic desires that predispose Italians toward modes of thinking that emphasize incorporation.*

Encountering and Countering Resistance

Taken collectively, previous chapters demonstrate that popular Catholicism in Italy is a complex and multilayered phenomenon. Do I really suggest that something so complex and multilayered has been shaped, even partially, by oral erotic experiences that date from the first year of life? Yes, I do. I make this suggestion even though I am fully aware that psychoanalytic arguments linking infantile experiences, infantile sexual experiences in particular, to the adult personality have always elicited a strongly negative reaction from audiences not already committed to the psychoanalytic tradition.

Freud (1916–17, 330–31) tells the story of an early psychoanalyst who was a medical officer during World War I. Stationed in Poland, the man had some unexpected successes with patients and so was asked by his colleagues to give a series of talks on psychoanalysis. At first his talks were well received. But when he began to discuss the Oedipus complex, his commanding officer rose and declared that he did not believe in such things and that it was "vile" to discuss such a topic with soldiers who were fighting for their country and who were in many cases fathers themselves. With that, he ordered the lectures stopped. A similar story, I suspect, could be told by every investigator who has tried to present psychoanalytic arguments to a wide audience. This is likely one reason why so many psychoanalytic investigators cloak their arguments in jargon and write only for other psychoanalytic investigators. After all, people are not likely to be upset over unintelligible arguments they never hear about.

What is the root cause of this negative response to psychoanalytic arguments? Many social scientists certainly are fond of justifying their negative judgments by importing grand rationales from the philosophy of science. A favorite here is the common claim that psychoanalytic explanations are no more than "just-so" stories tailor-made to fit whatever data happen to be at hand and so are not falsifiable in the manner of good, sound scientific arguments. There is no denying an element of truth in such a criticism. Psychoanalytic accounts, especially when they try to explain cultural phenomena, are often impossible to discredit, and psychoanalytic investigators who ignore this fact will never reach the larger audience that Freud tried to reach. But the "nonfalsifiability" charge can just as easily be leveled at explanations of cultural phenomena developed by functionalists, structuralists, sociobiologists, etcetera. Furthermore, though I have great sympathy for the feminist theorizing that has emerged since the mid-1980s, the analyses developed by these theorists are not more falsifiable than those developed by psychoanalysts. Yet these other traditions rarely attract the sort of hostility elicited by psychoanalytic explanations.

So we are left with the original question: Why the hostility to psychoanalytic accounts? I can think of at least two answers. The first was given some time ago by Freud (1916–17, 284–85) when he made his famous if immodest claim that Western science has delivered three great blows to human pride. The first occurred when Copernicus's heliocentric theory displaced us from the center of the universe. The second was delivered by Darwin and Wallace, who erased the sharp line dividing us from other species by demonstrating that we were animals descended from other animals. The third blow was delivered by psychoanalysis, which says that we are not even masters of our own minds.

Psychoanalysis demonstrates, Freud argues, that most of what we think or do is the result of desires and impulses of which we have no conscious awareness. Even worse, in identifying the origin of those desires and impulses psychoanalysis does not transcend the individual and talk about those grand and noble events of human history that involve groups, societies, nations, etcetera. On the contrary, psychoanalysis goes backward, into our earliest years, and says that we have been shaped mainly by banal and uninspiring desires that date from that period of our development. In the end, then, the hurt elicited by psychoanalytic explanations of culture is literally the hurt we felt as ten-year-olds when someone told us we were acting like babies or the hurt we feel as adults when someone tells us to stop being infantile.

But there is, I think, a second reason why psychoanalytic explanations elicit such strong opposition. Western social scientists traditionally draw a sharp distinction between what happens in public and what happens in private and have privileged the study of what happens in public in their analyses. Starting in the 1980s, however, any number of feminist theorists (see for example Harding 1986, 82–110; Lamphere 1987, 22–25; di Leonardo 1991) argue that this traditional orientation has been determined less by observation and evidence and more by a Eurocentric and androcentric bias. First (such theorists argue), the sharp distinction between public and private that seems so obvious to Western commentators is not found in all cultures. Second, even within the Western intellectual tradition, this private-public dichotomy became central to social theorizing only in the late nineteenth century. Finally, and most important, implicit in most formulations that assume a separation between the public and the private is the sense that what is public is more important than what is private. Given that males dominate the public sphere, such an implicit understanding has the effect of reinforcing patriarchy, and this is why modern social scientists find the public-private dichotomy so appealing.

So what does all this have to do with Freud? Feminism, after all, is usually seen as being antithetical to psychoanalysis, mainly because Freud's account of the Oedipal process (with its emphasis on the "anatomical difference between the sexes") seems pervaded by patriarchal bias. But at least in regard to challenging the public-private distinction, psychoanalysis and modern feminist theory are on common ground.

Unlike most theories in social science, psychoanalysis sees what happens between the child and its immediate environment—a process traditionally associated with the private sphere—as being of primary importance in explaining human behavior. More important, the psychoanalytic claim that culture is a projective system shaped by the human unconscious not only undermines that privileging of the public that is so central to Western social science but in fact breaks down any clear distinction between what happens in private and what happens in public. It is, I suggest, this implicit assault on the public-private dichotomy, a dichotomy still central to theorizing in the social sciences, that also accounts for much of the hostility to psychoanalytic explanations.

Generally, I see no particular reason for believing that psychoanalytic explanations are inherently more implausible than other theoretical explanations commonly offered in social science. Counterintuitive and often unappealing, perhaps, but not inherently implausible. In any event, the issue is not inherent plausibility but empirical plausibility, which depends on the fit between argument and evidence.

Following Cheshire (1975), I argue that the empirical adequacy of psychoanalytic arguments is best evaluated using a comprehensibility criterion. This means assessing the degree to which any given argument is able to order apparently disparate empirical patterns into a coherent whole. The greater the number of elements, and the more disparate they seem at first, the better the explanation. So far, the hypothesis being offered here—that Italian popular Catholicism has been shaped by strong unconscious oral erotic desires—has been used to account for the merging emphasis that appears in so many forms in this variant of Catholicism. Does this hypothesis help us to understand any other patterns?

Mothers and Infants, Tremors and Falls

As pointed out in chapter 1, the most popular madonnine images in Italy have always been of a Madonna con Bambino, which is not true of the madonnine images most popular with modern Catholics outside Italy. How old, precisely, is the child usually paired with an Italian madonna? In everyday discourse, the word *bambino* (the word Italians use to denote the child in these images) is applied to children ranging in age from newborns to seven or eight years old. The child paired with Italian madonnas, however, is in most cases an infant—that is, a child no more than two years old. This conclusion is reinforced by the fact that this bambino is usually being held or is sitting in the madonna's lap, rather than standing or walking (activities that would be associated with older children), and is often depicted as nursing or about to nurse at the madonna's breast. Why this emphasis upon a mother and her infant, rather than upon, say, a mother and an older child?

Given the logic of Freud's general argument, the experience of especially strong oral erotic desires at the oral stage produces a fixation at this stage. This in turn would mean (given his general argument) that images associated with the oral stage should become especially important in shaping the religious world-view of the adult. One of the most important of those images is that of the mother (where *mother* simply means female caretaker) being "with" her child—and the child in this case is a young child, an infant. Thus, I argue, Madonna con Bambino images are especially appealing to Italian Catholics because they are linked to the oral stage, which has been especially influential in shaping the religious worldview of adult Catholics in Italy.

In chapter 1, I call attention to the behaviors of some Italian Catholics when they approach an especially powerful miraculous image: they yell and scream, fall to the ground, and thrash about. The proximate cause of these behaviors has been traced to the cultural expectation that such behaviors make it more likely that the image will dispense favors. But what gives rise to this cultural expectation? That is, why are these particular behaviors seen as making it more likely that a madonnine image will dispense favors?

Although the behaviors in question are unusual in adults, they are not unfamiliar. On the contrary, they are behaviors routinely encountered in infants. Infants typically cannot stand up, and they often yell and thrash around, especially when they want to attract the attention of their caretakers. I am suggesting, in other words, that these behaviors be seen as a regression in the psychoanalytic sense. In Freud's (1916–17, 339–77) account, a regression occurs when an individual exhibits behaviors strongly similar to those associated with an earlier developmental stage. Most of all, an especially strong libidinous experience at a particular infantile stage makes it likely that the individual will regress to that stage later in life. Under this reasoning, especially strong oral erotic experiences early in life should predispose adults to behaviors typical of young children during the oral stage. Such behaviors include falling down and yelling and thrashing about in order to attract the attention of parental surrogates, which are, remember, the behaviors that Italian Catholics do routinely exhibit in front of powerful madonnine images.

Emphasis on the Visual

Jean Piaget and his associates established some time ago that for the first few months of life human infants equate existence with seeing, so that when objects pass out of sight they are assumed to no longer exist. But even after infants acquire a sense of object constancy, they rely heavily on visual cues in making sense of the world, and this reliance on the visual lasts a long time. Piaget's research established that it is this reliance on the visual that so often leads young children to make decisions that would seem inappropriate to older children and adults. Easily observable differences in, say, the height of two containers of water or the length of two rolled-out pieces of clay will be used to make inferences about amounts; differences in the appearance (or imagined appearance) of an adult, whether they appear angry or not, will be used to make decisions about what is right and wrong; and so on.

Given that this emphasis on the visual is a part of the predominant worldview of children at the oral stage, a religious worldview shaped by memories and desires from the oral stage should show evidence of this same emphasis. In fact, as we have seen in earlier chapters, popular Catholicism in Italy is permeated by a strong emphasis upon seeing and being seen.

Qualifications

The material covered in the last few sections is not meant to constitute proof of anything. My goal is to develop an argument that provides comprehensibility, an argument that orders disparate and seemingly unrelated observations into a coherent whole. What emerges is that elements central to popular Catholicism in Italy—namely, a predisposition to merge the natural and the supernatural; a preference for Madonna con Bambino images; an expectation that falling down, yelling, and thrashing about will elicit approval from powerful madonnas; and a strong emphasis upon the visual—can be ordered into a coherent pattern. The obvious next step is to determine the social arrangements that might have systematically induced such desires in Italian infants over the centuries.

As mentioned earlier, past national character studies were criticized for being reductionist, that is, for deriving national character from some one child-rearing practice (like swaddling). While this criticism has merit, it does not in itself invalidate the premise central to psychoanalytic thinking, which is that infantile desires shape the adult personality. On the contrary, such a criticism simply enjoins us to recognize that childhood experience is affected by many processes and so to recognize that identifying some of those processes does not preclude the existence of others.

In the sections that follow my concern is with a particular institutional arrangement that might be called the social organization of breast-feeding in Italy. Partly, my attention was drawn to this institutional arrangement for the entirely pragmatic reason that it has been well described by historians and partly because it is an arrangement that seems obviously relevant to infantile experience. But in reading through the literature on the social organization of breast-feeding in Italy, I was also struck by the fact that no one seems to have asked a question that flows inexorably from the psychoanalytic perspective: How would this institutional arrangement, which by everyone's account was widespread throughout the peninsula for centuries, have systematically shaped the personality of Italian adults? The answer to that question allows us to identify one, if only one, of the processes that have shaped the logic of popular Catholicism in Italy.

In Search of the Historical Bad Breast

During the fourteenth and fifteenth centuries, it was common practice in Florence and other Tuscan cities for upper- and middle-class fathers to keep a domestic journal that recorded familial events on a day-by-day basis. These journals provide a rare glimpse into the domestic life of these men. As both Klapisch-Zuber (1985, 132–64) and Ross (1974) point out, one clear finding that emerges from these accounts is that by the middle of the fifteenth century the vast majority of middle- and upper-class children in Florence were being handed over to *balie*, or wet nurses, within a few days of birth. These documents tell us much about the experiences of the infants placed with these balie.

First, there was usually an immediate and dramatic shift in the material environment in which an infant found itself. Although a balia did sometimes live in her employer's household, the more usual pattern was for a balia to take her young charge into her own household, and in most cases this meant taking the infant to the rural community where the balia lived. An infant's stay in this community was lengthy. On average, female infants were weaned from their balia's breast at age seventeen months; for male infants weaning took place a bit later, usually around the twentieth month (see the figures in Klapisch-Zuber 1985, 154–56). Infants were returned to their parental home within a month or two of weaning.[7] Most infants therefore remained with their balia for their first two years of life.

Middle- and upper-class children were not the only ones handed over to balie. Foundling homes in Tuscan cities also used rural balie, and Trexler (1973a; 1973b) shows that this practice became increasingly common as the number of children who were taken into these homes increased during the late fifteenth and early sixteenth centuries.

How would being sent to a rural balie for the first two years of life affect the oral erotic experiences of the infant? One factor to consider is the attitude of these balie toward their young charges. Although this cannot be assessed directly (the balie themselves, after all, left few written records), some reasonable inferences can be derived from what we do know about these women.

Klapisch-Zuber's (1985, 162) data indicate that about 40 percent of the balie in Tuscany had living husbands and another 40 percent were associated with men who might have been either husbands or fathers. Only about 20 percent were not explicitly linked, in the documentary record, with a male. The reason the records show balie linked with males is that the business of contracting for the service of balie was dominated entirely by men: the fathers of the infants, and the men who ran the foundling homes, on the one hand, and the husbands or fathers of the balie, on the other. The women who acted as balie were commodities, contracted out by men to serve the interests of other men.

In Klapisch-Zuber's (1985, 142) words, "behind her rustic husband the [wet] nurse remains a vague silhouette, and it is to her husband that the father gives the infant to be raised—and breast-fed." In keeping with her status as a commodity, a balia would be examined by a potential employer in a manner little different from the way an animal is examined before purchase. One fifteenth-century text (cited in Barbagli 1984, 373) instructs fathers to look for balie with breasts that are elevated and rounded, but not too large or soft, and with nipples that are large

7. Klapisch-Zuber (1985) suggests that the widespread use of balie by the middle and upper classes in Florence derived from the high valuation placed on fertility and from the belief that pregnancy caused a mother's milk to spoil and become unhealthy. This latter belief meant that mothers who nursed their own children would have to abstain from sexual intercourse, which would have limited the number of children she could bear in her lifetime. Sending a newborn to a balia was thus a way of permitting a husband and wife to have intercourse—and more children—without having to worry about giving "spoilt" milk to an infant. The use of balie does seem to have ensured that the spacing between births for middle- and upper-class wives was relatively brief. In the Klapisch-Zuber sample (158), the average interval between successive births was approximately twenty months.

and stand out. Obviously, this meant inspecting her breasts. A prospective balia was also required to express some of her milk so that a father might subject it to a number of tests to determine its quality. In short, the infants who came to suck at a balia's breast were there as the result of purely economic processes, over which the balia herself had little control and which reduced her to the status of a commodity. This is hardly a situation likely to induce warm feelings in the balia toward her charge.

A balia had usually recently given birth and was lactating. Prospective clients preferred balie whose own infants had died, since this meant that these balie would not be nursing their own children. Individuals responsible for finding balie often expressed regret when a balia's infant recovered from a serious illness (see Trexler 1973a, 100). It was also common for balie to seek pregnancy and then to abandon the resulting child so they could sell their milk. Certainly, many children came to the foundling home at Florence with notes saying that they were being abandoned so their mothers could hire themselves out as wet nurses (see Trexler 1973b, 274–75, for examples). Another possibility, equally plausible if more disturbing, is that balie were often made pregnant and then made to abandon their child by the same fathers and husbands who negotiated the contracts and who stood to gain the most financially from the exploitation of a balia's breast milk.

Common sense might dictate that balie had a financial incentive to keep their charges alive and in good health, but this is probably not true. The need for balie was sufficiently great that finding a replacement charge was usually not difficult (see Trexler 1973a, 113). Furthermore, especially in the case of the balie employed by foundling homes, their pay often came late or not at all, and in that event balie were perfectly willing to simply stop the flow of breast milk. Luigi Tansillo, an early-fifteenth-century Florentine poet, notes that if anything were refused a balia, "expect to see her breasts dry up" (cited in ibid.).

The emotional attitude of the balie toward her charge aside, other conditions would have produced relatively unpleasant oral erotic experiences for the infants being nursed by a balia. First, the amount of milk available to a lactating woman is partly a function of her diet, and the conditions of life in rural villages meant that the diet of these balie was often deficient. The flow of breast milk is also a function of a woman's general health, and the fact that many balie nursed more or less continuously over a period of several years, combined with the energy requirements of breast-feeding, would have ensured that many of them were in poor health. Lactation is also stimulated by rest and by frequent nursing during the course of a day. In her discussion of wet nursing in France, Fildes (1988, 227) points out that peasant wet nurses often worked alongside their husbands in the fields, especially during the summer months, and left their charges at home under the supervision of older children. The resulting lack of rest and reduced number of feeds, she concludes, would almost certainly have made it impossible for many of these women to maintain adequate levels of lactation. Fildes's remarks seem equally applicable to rural Italy, at least to those rural areas in (mainly) northern Italy, where the prevailing patterns of settlement ensured that families lived near the land they worked and so facilitated wives working alongside their husbands in the fields.

All of these conditions would have predisposed balie (and the men who brokered them) to use alternative foods, like animal milk or bread soaked in animal milk. One consequence of the use of such foods would have been increased mortality. Both Klapisch-Zuber's (1985, 153) data for middle- and upper-class infants and Trexler's (1973b, 276) data for urban foundlings show that mortality rates for infants placed with balie, especially when the infant was under the age of five months, did increase during the harvest months. Mortality aside, I assume that the meager supplies of breast milk and the use of alternative foods would have resulted in relatively frustrating oral erotic experiences and the consequent emergence of relatively strong oral erotic desires.

Balie were not supposed to be nursing any other infants, as a condition of their contract. If they had children under the age of two, it was expected that they would hire their own balie. But all commentators agree that supervision by Florentine fathers and foundling home officials was lax. It is likely that many balie were also nursing their own child, and this too would reduce the amount of milk available to their urban charge.

The very same conditions—the balia's poor diet, nursing over very long periods of time, working in the fields, nursing more than one infant at a time—that affected the urban infants placed in the balia's care would also have affected her own children. Certainly, the physical health of her own infants would have been affected. In fact, as the practice of using rural balie became more common, mortality rates among urban infants and rural infants increased (Trexler 1973b, 278). Physical death aside, it seems likely that these conditions would also have had a negative effect on the oral erotic experiences of these rural infants.

Although the social organization of breast-feeding in Italy has been most intensively studied in the case of Tuscany during the fourteenth and fifteenth centuries, the upper and middle classes in most others areas also used rural balie, a pattern that continued well into the eighteenth century. Cappelletto's (1983) study of the rural balie used by foundling homes in Verona during the eighteenth century, for instance, reaches more or less the same conclusions reached by Klapisch-Zuber, Ross, and Trexler. During the nineteenth century the practice of using balie did decline among the upper and middle classes, but this was accompanied by an increased use of balie among the urban working classes (Barbagli 1984, 366–92). The social organization of wet nursing in the Italian South has been less well studied. The literature that is available, however, suggests that balie were widely used there as well, though perhaps not as widely as in the North (see Livi Bacci 1977, 256–57).

In summary, then, we know that the practice of sending urban infants to rural wet nurses was widespread for most of the modern period and involved infants from all levels of urban society. In addition, there are several reasons for believing that this practice gave rise to frustrating oral erotic experiences, both for the infants turned over to balie and for the infants born to balie. This means that the widespread use of balie could have contributed significantly to a fixation at the oral stage, which under the hypothesis being offered here gave rise to a cognitive predisposition toward incorporation and merging that seems to underlie popular Catholicism in Italy.

Why Bother?

The widespread use of rural balie is only one of several processes that have shaped the logic of popular Catholicism in Italy and, moreover, possibly not even the most important one. Then why have I singled out this one factor, especially given the hostility typically engendered by psychoanalytic accounts? A good question, and my answer takes us back to the beginning of this book.

In the introduction, I criticize the top down approach to popular religion for denying to ordinary people the capacity to be creative, that is, to generate new forms of religiosity that go beyond simply mixing traditional folk beliefs with elements from the official Catholic tradition. One concern of earlier chapters is to show the wrongheadedness of such an approach by documenting the ways new Catholic devotions have emerged from below and have involved far more than simple mixing. We have also seen that this process of popular creativity has always been guided by an implicit logic. But if you grant the existence of this underlying popular logic, then you must ask where it comes from. I can see no basis for deriving it from the machinations of social elites documented so methodically by traditional historians nor from the processes of nation building, urbanization, and so on favored by more recent historians.

It strikes me as obvious that a logic that guides the creative responses of ordinary people must have its origins in the local experiences of those same people. This means that a full understanding of popular creativity must identify the nature of those local experiences, and this is what I have tried to do, by relating the logic of popular Catholicism in Italy to a community's experiences with a chiesa ricettizia and to the infantile experiences occasioned by the extensive use of balie. Subsequent investigators may identify other local experiences that can reasonably be linked to this logic and that prove more important than the ones identified here. So much the better. In the end, particular explanations are less important than the realization that, to study popular Catholicism, we must look to the people who have lived it and not to the experiences and concerns of the educated elites, who have not.

Past and Future Projects

I have long been concerned with those Catholic cults and devotions whose popularity seem to transcend national boundaries. Carroll (1986) deals with the historic development of the Mary cult in the Western Church and with those Marian apparitions that have become the focus of important cults; Carroll (1989) seeks to identify the psychological processes that make certain devotions (like those centered on the Rosary, the Scapular, the Angelus Bell) appealing. During the research for these two books, I came to appreciate that much of what is considered Catholic reflects the values and orientation of Italian prelates, who have for so long dominated the hierarchy of the Roman Catholic Church. This realization, plus a personal tie to Italy and things Italian, led to the investigation of popular Catholicism in Italy that was begun in Carroll (1992) and is continued here. There is a logical next step: to establish in some systematic way the relationship between Italian Catholicism and the variants of Catholicism associated with other national traditions.

In some regards, for example, it would appear that Italian Catholicism is considerably different from other national variants. In his statistical study of Catholic sainthood Delooz (1969), for example, finds that more saints have been created in Italy than in any other national tradition. Further, this cannot be attributed to the control exerted by an Italian-dominated hierarchy over the canonization process, since Italian saints predominate even when considering saints who are the objects of cults only as the result of local tradition. Delooz (179) himself concludes that Italians are more predisposed than other nationalities to create saints.[8] Similarly, studies of madonnine apparitions indicate that such apparitions have always been far more common, and by a wide margin, in Italy than in any other country (see Carroll 1986, 131).

In other regards, it appears that Italian Catholicism has affinities with Med-

8. For my explanation as to why Italian Catholics are more predisposed than other national groups to create saints, see Carroll (1992, 138–61).

iterranean Catholicism in general. In their survey of more than three thousand Catholic sanctuaries in Western Europe, the Nolans (1989, 115–59) find that in Italy, France, and Spain the majority of sanctuaries (about three out of four, in each case) were dedicated to Mary, with most of the rest being dedicated to a saint. By contrast, in northern European societies like the United Kingdom, Ireland, and the Netherlands, this pattern is reversed, with a clear majority of sanctuaries being dedicated to a saint. German-speaking regions fall in between these two extremes, with a slight majority of sanctuaries being dedicated to Mary and a substantial minority being dedicated to a saint. As I indicate elsewhere (Carroll 1986, 11–13), this difference in sanctuary dedications, at least between the British Isles and Mediterranean countries, exists even among sanctuaries erected before the Reformation.

Unfortunately, although statistical surveys of the sort conducted by Delooz and the Nolans are useful in detecting some general differences and similarities among national traditions, they provide little or no information bearing on issues that the analysis in this book suggests are important. Part of the problem is that statistical surveys make use of conceptual frameworks that originate within the official Catholic tradition.

The Nolans (1989), for example, divide sanctuaries into three basic categories, depending upon whether they are dedicated to Mary, to a saint, or to Christ. The Mary in this scheme is clearly the Mary of the official Church, and the Nolans have implicitly accepted the Church's view that it is this Mary who is being venerated at the sanctuaries involved. But in Italy, madonnas are independent beings with distinct personalities and differing amount of power and are only loosely associated with the Mary of the official Church. There are four to five hundred separate and distinct madonnas in Italy (see Carroll 1992a, 61–64). How does this compare to other national traditions? Are Italians more predisposed to create madonnas, as they are more predisposed to create saints and to experience apparitions? Such questions as yet have no answers, because studies that see every madonna as nothing more than a representation of Mary do not ask such questions.

And what about the Madonna con Bambino? Mary holding the Christ child is a theme favored by elite artists in all areas of Catholic Europe. But has this iconographic pattern been as popular with ordinary Catholics in Spain, Ireland, England, and so on as it has been with ordinary Catholics in Italy? Here again, this is a question that is never asked in studies that see madonnine images—with or without a child—as nothing more than images of Mary.

Popular Catholicism in Italy is often assumed to be similar to popular Catholicism in Spain. But how similar are they? Mitchell's (1990) analysis suggests that Spanish Catholicism is strongly Christocentric and marked by a Passional emphasis, in which the suffering of Christ is central. I suggest (chap. 3) that this Passional emphasis is less marked in Italy. But Christian's (1981, 181–208) overview of local religion in Spain suggests that the popularity of the Passion-related devotions increased steadily in moving from the sixteenth to the eighteenth centuries. In other words, the Passional emphasis discovered by Mitchell is the result of a centuries-long process. This in turn suggests that the Counter-Reformation campaign by the preaching orders to promote Passion devotions (a campaign waged in both countries; see chap. 3; Christian 1981, 189) proved more successful in Spain than in Italy. Why? That is, why did Spanish Catholics prove more receptive to these particular devotions than Italian Catholics?

Another promising area of study lies in investigating how the same cults came to acquire different meanings in different societies. The analysis of the Addolorata cult in Italy and Spain (chap. 3) is a brief example of what might be done. In Italy, the Addolorata was associated most with the female mourners at the traditional Mediterranean funeral, and the Addolorata cult was linked to the campaign by the Italian Church to eliminate that type of funeral. In Spain, however, the Addolorata was associated most with the view that lifelong suffering brings redemption from sin. But what about the Addolorata cult in France? In Germany and Austria? Poland? Did the Addolorata come to acquire distinct meanings in these societies as well? Generally, what other figures in the pantheon of the official Church have come to evoke sharply different connotations in different national traditions? Can these differences be correlated with differences in local experience? In ecclesiastical organization?

We need to look more carefully at the daily experience of popular Catholicism in national contexts. For instance, wayside shrines existed in England prior to the Reformation. Yet in the accounts of popular Catholicism in pre-Reformation England (Duffy 1992; Swanson 1989, 275–99) there is nothing to suggest that such shrines were as commonplace or as important to the everyday experience of Catholicism as edicole in Italy. Similarly, while English Catholics sometimes invested sacred images with supernatural power, and these images did sometimes bleed when struck (see Aston 1988, 62), cults organized around wonder-working images were never as common in England as in Italy. Why?

Finally, the differences among variants of popular Catholicism must never blind us to the elements common to all varieties of Catholicism, official and popular, and to the ways in which Catholicism differs from Protestantism. In this regard, I suggest that traditional notions of what causes what are too restricted. While most commentators take it as obvious that the spread of Calvinism promoted iconoclasm, I argue (chap. 7) that the reverse is just as plausible, namely, that the popularity of iconoclasm influenced Calvin to make it a central element in his doctrine. Similarly, I also argue that the official Church has always taken as a given the popularity of cults organized around images infused with supernatural power and has responded by developing doctrinal rationalizations that leave the behaviors associated with these cults intact. In both cases, the suggestion is that the popular imagination has shaped official doctrine more than has generally been recognized.

The possibilities opened up by this reversal of traditional notions of causality need to be explored further. For example, the use of wet nurses was far more common in Catholic areas of Europe than in Protestant areas. Most commentators assume that this correlation was produced by a causal process in which religious ideology was the independent variable. Fildes (1986, 105; 1988, 207), for example, suggests that Catholic theologians recommended the use of wet nurses because they accepted the taboo on sexual intercourse during lactation and so saw the use of wet nurses as a means by which married couples could resume intercourse soon after the birth of a child. By contrast, Fildes argues, Protestant theologians discouraged the use of wet nurses because it facilitated illegitimacy and child abandonment. But why could the causality not have worked in reverse, with the use of wet nurses promoting Catholicism? In fact, the argument sketched earlier—relating infantile oral eroticism to modes of thought emphasizing incorporation and merging—provides us with a basis for understanding just how this might have worked, given that all variants of Catholicism, both official and popular, give more emphasis to a merging of the natural and the supernatural than all variants of Protestantism.

For some readers, of course, the imagery here is all wrong. The argument just sketched suggests that it is the wet nurse—a poor, illiterate peasant woman whose breasts were exposed by her own husband so they could be inspected by some other woman's husband—whose image is to be found at the deepest levels of Reformation research. But appealing or not, the time has come to consider the possibility that the poor, exploited balie of Italy may have exerted as much of an influence on the outcome of the Reformation in Italy, and the shape of popular Catholicism in Italy, as Luther, Calvin, the Italian evangelicals, and De Rosa's reforming bishops together.

Epilogue

Ibegan this book by recounting the events that forced my maternal grandmother, Aurelia Demartini, to leave Italy. I want to end it by finishing her
story.

My grandmother was fifteen when she arrived in San Francisco. She had
relatives in the city, but none rich enough or concerned enough to provide her
with shelter. Instead, she lived with the family of a local Italian American doctor
who had been a friend of her mother, Antonietta. There is a vague and diffuse
family tradition suggesting that this man, Davide, had been in love with Antonietta and had persisted in his love even after her marriage to my great-grandfather
Felice. Whatever the truth of this story, Davide provided my grandmother with a
warm and secure home. She always spoke warmly of her time there. In particular
she liked to recount that Davide's family had given her a doll, her very first. It
seems that only with Davide's family was my teen-aged grandmother finally allowed to be the child she had never been in her own father's home.

Eventually, Aurelia got a job in a local cookie factory, and it was there she
met Pietro Ciarlanti, my grandfather. Pietro's family was from the Lunigiana, a
strip of land that lies astride the Magra River just at the border between Liguria
and Tuscany. Pietro had been born just outside Genoa and had emigrated to San
Francisco in 1912. Pietro and Aurelia were married in 1917. My mother was born
the following year, delivered at home by Doctor Davide. Aurelia and Pietro named
her Olga (Russian names being in vogue in San Francisco at the time), and that
is what they always called her. During World War II, however, when my mother
was in her twenties and working at the phone company, she had to pass a secu-
rity check. This meant looking up her birth certificate, and it was only then that
anyone realized Dr. Davide had recorded her name as Antonietta, the woman he
possibly loved.

My grandfather worked as a janitor for a number of companies in San Francisco, then signed on to a fishing boat that worked Alaskan waters, and finally became a cook in a local Italian restaurant. In the late 1920s, he opened his own

restaurant on Grant Avenue in North Beach. I remember that the neon sign outside said PETE'S CAFE—ITALIAN AND FRENCH CUISINE. To this day, I don't know what was French about his cooking, but it was solid, and it was Italian. My grandfather would preside over his restaurant for the next forty years, alternating between cooking, bartending, and supervising three or four waiters dressed in dark suits.

Aurelia and Pietro seem to have had a pleasant marriage. Still, some of the stories that have slipped through the generations make me wonder. My mother remembers an incident from the 1920s, when Aurelia had had her hair bobbed without telling Pietro beforehand. When he saw what she had done, he was furious and chased her around the kitchen table with a stick, just as her father had done back in Lòrsica.

My mother met and married a good-looking Irish American boy whose family had moved to San Francisco from the Midwest, and they also settled in North Beach. This is where I was born and where I spent the first five years of my life. Much of that time was spent with my grandmother. I have a surprising number of memories from that period, the most vivid being of the times she and I walked down to Fisherman's Wharf (which was still something of a real fisherman's wharf, and not the mix of elegant restaurants and cheap souvenir stands it is now). We shared a single shrimp cocktail and bought two comic books, to be read on the spot. Afterward, we walked to Aquatic Park and then to the Marina, where the rich people kept (and still keep) their yachts, to see if we could see the crabs that sometimes came out on the rocks on the bottom of the bay. Perhaps it wasn't as idyllic as I remember it, but then again perhaps it was.

My grandmother developed cancer in 1949. Hospitals were less tolerant of child visitors then, but some things are more important than rules, and my mother sneaked me down the hospital corridor to my grandmother's room. Aurelia had always been a tiny person, less than five feet tall, but she was tinier that night. The last thing I remember her saying to me was that the nurse had given her a popsicle and she had saved half for me. It was an orange popsicle, and my half was melting in a bowl on the table beside her bed. Aurelia died a few weeks later. She was fifty-three, an age that is a lot closer to my own than it used to be.

A few months after my grandmother's death, my family became part of that post–World War II exodus of second-generation Italian American families who left North Beach to settle in other, less distinctly Italian, San Francisco neighborhoods. My grandfather's restaurant, of course, ensured that we returned to North Beach every week. I recall playing outside on Grant Avenue, hearing the sounds of gambling behind the curtain in the Chinese shoe repair shop next door to the restaurant, and seeing beatniks (yes Virginia, there were beatniks) pass by engaged in intense conversations. I remember, too, the stores, mainly bakeries and butcher shops, where the signs were in Italian and the people inside spoke to each other mainly in Italian. Even so, we were no longer part of the North Beach community in the way we had been, and I was an outsider looking in.

In retrospect, the year of my grandmother's death was a watershed. It was the year I became an American of Italian descent rather than an Italian American. Writing this book has allowed me to move back to the other side of that watershed.

References

Abraham, Karl. 1927. "The influence of oral eroticism on character formation." In *The Selected Papers of Karl Abraham, M.D.* London: Hogarth.

Ahrweiler, Hélène. 1975. "The geography of the Iconoclast world." In *Iconoclasm: Papers Given at the Ninth Spring Symposium of Byzantine Studies, University of Birmingham, March 1975*, edited by Anthony Bryer and Judith Herrin. Birmingham: Centre for Byzantine Studies.

Alfano, G. B., and A. Amitrano. 1951. *Notizie storiche ed osservazioni sulle reliquie di sangue*. Naples: Arti Grafiche "Adriana."

Andrea, Alfred, and Paul Rachlin. 1992. "Holy war, holy relics, holy theft: The Anonymous of Soisson's *De terra Iherosolimitana*: An Analysis, Edition, and Translation." *Historical Reflections* 18 (1): 147–56.

Andreucci, Ottavio. 1857. *Il fiorentino istruito della Chiesa della Nunziata*. Florence: M. Cellini.

Anon. 1796. *Miraculous Events Established by Authentic Letters from Italy*. 3d ed. London: J. P. Coghlan.

Ariès, Philippe. 1981 (1977). *The Hour of Our Death*. New York: Oxford University Press.

Arrigoni, P., and A. Bertarelli. 1936. *Rappresentazioni popolari d'immagini venerate nelle chiese della Lombardia*. Milan: Impensis A. Bertarelli.

Aston, Margaret. 1988. "Iconoclasm in England: Official and clandestine." In *Iconoclasm versus Art and Drama*, edited by Clifford Davidson and Ann Eljenholm Nichols. Kalamazoo, Mich.: Medieval Institute Publications.

Aumann, J. 1967. "Mystical phenomena." In *New Catholic Encyclopedia* 10. New York: McGraw-Hill.

Bacci, Father. 1902 (1622). *The Life of Saint Philip Neri*. Vol. 2. London: Kegan Paul, Trench, Trubner.

Badone, Ellen. 1990. Introduction to *Religious Orthodoxy and Popular Faith in European Society*, edited by E. Badone. Princeton: Princeton University Press.

Barbagli, Marzio. 1984. *Sotto lo stesso tetto*. Bologna: Il Mulino.

Barbi, Silvana. 1980. "Le tavolette dipinte." In *Lo straordinario e il quotidiano*, edited by Angelo Turchini. Brescia: Grafo edizioni.

Barnard, L. W. 1974. *The Graeco-Roman and Oriental Background of the Iconoclastic Controversy*. Leiden, Netherlands: E. J. Brill.

Bellini, Alberto. 1983. "Lutero nella teologia cattolica moderna. Dalla confutazione polemica al confronto ecumenico." In *Lutero in Italia*, edited by Lorenzo Perrone. Casale Monferrato: Marietti.

Beltrano, Ottavio. 1671. *Descrittione del Regno di Napoli diviso in dodeci provincie*. Naples.

Benedict, Ruth. 1934. *Patterns of Culture*. New York: Houghton Mifflin.

Bernstein, Alan E. 1984. Review of *La naissance du purgatoire*, by Jacques Le Goff. *Speculum* 59 (Jan.): 179–83.

Boccaccio, Giovanni. 1982 (c. 1350). *Decameron*. Vol. 2, *Days VI–X*. Translated by John Payne. Revised and annotated by Charles S. Singleton. Berkeley: University of California Press.

Boesch Gajano, Sofia. 1990. "Riti, confini e scatole cinesi." In *Luoghi sacri e spazi della santità*, edited by S. Boesch Gajano and Lucetta Scaraffia. Turin: Rosenberg and Sellier.

Bontempi, Franco. 1983. "Conflitti politico-economici nella Valcamonica del '700." In *Immagini, arte, culture e potere nell'età di Beniamino Simoni (XVIII) e oltre*, edited by R. A. Lorenzi. Brescia: Luigi Micheletti editore.

Borrello, L. 1899. "I disciplinanti in Nocera Tirinese." *Archivio per lo studio della tradizione popolari* 18 (July–Sept.): 189.

Boswell, John. 1985. "Sympathy for the Devil." *New Republic* 192 (Mar. 18): 38–42.

Bouwsma, William J. 1971. "Swanson's Reformation." *Comparative Studies in Society and History* 10 (4): 486–91.

Braccesi, Simonetta Adorni. 1988. "Il dissenso religioso nel contesto urbano lucchese della Controriforma." In *Città italiane del '500 tra Riforma e Controriforma*, Atti del Convegno Internazionale di Studi, 13–15 ottobre 1983. Lucca: Maria Pacini Fazzi.

Brady, Thomas A. 1982. "Social history." In *Reformation Europe: A Guide to Research*, edited by Steven Ozment. St. Louis: Center for Reformation Research.

Bragaglia, Cesare. 1888. "I flagellanti in Ceccano." *Archivio per lo studio della tradizione popolari* 7 (July–Sept.): 563–66.

Breda, Giuliana. 1979. "La devozione mariana nei 'capitelli' di una valle veronese: la Valpolicella." In *I "capitelli" e la società religiosa veneta*, Atti del convegno tenutosi dal 17 al 19 marzo 1978. Vicenza: Istituto per le Ricerche di storia sociale e di storia religiosa.

Bruttini, Tiziana. 1983. "Legittimi e illegittimi: aspetti istituzionali dell'assistenza all'infanzia abbandonata a Siena nell'ottocento." *Bullettino senese di storia patria* 89: 221–42.

Bryer, Anthony, and Judith Herrin, eds. 1977. *Iconoclasm: Papers Given at the Ninth Spring Symposium of Byzantine Studies, University of Birmingham, March 1975*. Birmingham, U.K.: Centre for Byzantine Studies.

Burckhardt, Jacob. 1955. *The Civilization of the Renaissance in Italy*. London: Allen and Unwin.

Burigozzo, Gianmarco. 1842. "Cronica milanese di Gianmarco Burigozzo, merzaro dal 1500 al 1544." *Archivio storico italiano* 3:421–552.

Burke, Peter. 1984. "How to be a Counter-Reformation saint." In *Religion and Society in Early Modern Europe: 1500–1800*, edited by Kaspar von Greyerz. London: Allen and Unwin.

———. 1987. *The Historical Anthropology of Early Modern Italy*. Cambridge: Cambridge University Press.

Bynum, Caroline Walker. 1987. *Holy Feast and Holy Fast*. Berkeley: University of California Press.

Calvi, Donato. 1676a. *Effemeride sagro profana di quanto di memorabile sia successo in Bergamo, sua diocese, et territorio, da suoi principij fin' al corrente Anno*. Vol. 1. Milan: Francesco Vigone.

———. 1676b. *Effemeride sagro profana di quanto di memorabile sia successo in Bergamo, sua diocese, et territorio, da suoi principij fin' al corrente Anno*. Vol. 2. Milan: Francesco Vigone.

———. 1677. *Effemeride sagro profana di quanto di memorabile sia successo in Bergamo, sua diocese, et territorio, da suoi principij fin' al corrente Anno*. Vol. 3. Milan: Francesco Vigone.

Calvin, John. 1921 (1543). *Traité des reliques*. Introduction by Albert Austin. Paris: Editions Bossard.

———. 1960 (1559). *Institutes of the Christian Religion*. 2 vols. Philadelphia: Westminster.

———. 1986 (1536). *Institutes of the Christian Religion*. Translated and annotated by F. L. Battles. Grand Rapids, Mich.: Eerdmans.

Cameron, Euan. 1992. "Italy." In *The Early Reformation in Europe*, edited by Andrew Pettegree. Cambridge: Cambridge University Press.

Caponetto, Salvatore. 1987. *Studi sulla Riforma in Italia*. Florence: Università degli studi di Firenze.

———. 1992. *La Riforma protestante nell'Italia del cinquecento*. Turin: Claudiana.

———, ed. 1972. *Il beneficio di Cristo, con le versioni del secolo XVI, documenti e testimonianze*. Florence: Sansoni.

Cappelletto, Giovanna. 1983. "Infanzia abbandonata e ruoli di mediazione sociale nella Verona del settecento." *Quaderni storici* 53:421–43.

Cardini, Franco. 1983. *I giorni del sacro*. Milan: Editoriale Nuova.

Carmichael, Montgomery. 1901. *In Tuscany*. London: John Murray.

Carroll, Michael P. 1986. *The Cult of the Virgin Mary*. Princeton: Princeton University Press.

———. 1987. "Moses and Monotheism revisited: Freud's "Personal myth"? *American Imago* 44 (1): 15–35.

———. 1989. *Catholic Cults and Devotions*. Montreal: McGill-Queens University Press.

———. 1992. *Madonnas That Maim: Popular Catholicism in Italy since the Fifteenth Century*. Baltimore: Johns Hopkins University Press.

Casarini, Maria. 1982. "Maternità e infanticidio a Bologna: fonti e linee di ricerca." *Quaderni storici* 49:275–84.

Cattabiani, Alfredo. 1988. *Calendario: le feste, i miti, le leggende e i riti dell'anno*. Milan: Rusconi.

Cattaneo, Enrico. 1981. "Pietà liturgica e Pietà popolare a Milano fra l'ottocento e il novecento." In *Religion et culture dans la cité italienne de l'antiquité à nos jours*, Actes du Colloque du Centre Interdisciplinaire de Recherches sur l'Italie. Strasbourg: Université de Strasbourg.

Celano, Carlo. 1856 (1692). *Notizie del bello dell'antico e del curioso della città di Napoli*. Edited by Battista Chiarini. Vol. 2. Naples: Agostino de Pascale.

———. 1860 (1692). *Notizie del bello dell'antico e del curioso della città di Napoli*. Edited by Battista Chiarini. Vol. 5. Naples: Agostino de Pascale.

Cestaro, Antonio. 1978. *Strutture ecclesiastiche e società nel Mezzogiorno*. Naples: Editrice Ferraro.

————. 1980. *Studi di storia sociale e religiosa: scritti in onore di Gabriele De Rosa.* Naples: Editrice Ferraro.

Cheshire, Neil. 1975. *The Nature of Psychodynamic Interpretation.* London: John Wiley.

Chiara, Davide. 1988. *Alle porte del silenzio.* Ghedi: Primavera.

Chiovaro, F. 1967. "Relics." *New Catholic Encyclopedia* 12. New York: McGraw-Hill.

Christian, William A., Jr. 1981. *Local Religion in Sixteenth-Century Spain.* Princeton: Princeton University Press.

Ciocia, Aldo. 1985. "Il quartieri semicentrali a nord." In *Guida d'Italia: Milano.* Milan: Touring Club Italiano.

Cisotto, Gianni A. 1979. "Indagine sul sacro in una valle pedemontana Veneta: i 'capitelli' di Valdagno (Vicenza)." *Ricerche di storia sociale e religiosa* 15–16:237–59.

Cocchiara, Giuseppe. 1982 (1939). *Le immagini devote del popolo siciliano.* Palermo: Sellerio editore.

Cornaro, Flaminio. 1868. *Notizie storiche delle apparizioni e delle immagini più celebri di Maria santissima nella città e provincia di Bergamo.* New edition, with additions by Carlo Tacchi. Bergamo: Librajo editore.

Corrain, Cleto, and Pierluigi Zampini. 1970. *Documenti etnografici e folkloristici nei sinodi diocesani italiani.* Bologna: Forni.

Corsini, Carlo A. 1976. "Materiali per lo studio della famiglia in Toscana nei secoli XVII–XIX: gli esposti." *Quaderni storici* 33:998–1052.

————. 1988. "Per una storia della popolazione della Toscana fra XIV and XX secolo." In *Vita, morte e miracoli di gente comune.* Florence: La Case Usher.

Crehan, Joseph. 1952. *Father Thurston: A Memoir with a Bibliography of His Writings.* London: Sheed and Ward.

Cruz, Joan Carroll. 1977. *The Incorruptibles.* Rockford, Ill.: TAN Books.

Cusani, Francesco. 1865. *Storia di Milano.* Vol. 4. Milan: La Libreria Pirotta e C.

da Langasco, Cassiano. 1992. "Capitéi e Madonnelle." *La Madonna della Guardia: Bollettino mensile del santuario sul Monte Figogna* 97 (Aug.): 8–9.

d'Aloe, Stanislao. 1883 (circa 1660). "Catalogo di tutti gli edifizi sacri della città di Napoli e suoi sobborghi tratto da un ms. autografo della chiesa di S. Giorgio *ad forum.*" *Archivio storico per le province napoletane* 8:111–52, 287–315, 499–546, 670–737.

D'Andrea, Giampaolo. 1977. "La struttura sociale della parrocchia nelle diocesi lucane tra XVIII e XIX secolo." In *Società e religione in Basilicata nell'età moderna: comunicazioni,* Atti del Convegno di Potenza-Matera, 25–28 settembre. Salerno: D'Elia.

D'Antonio, Nino. 1979. *Gli ex voto dipinti e il rituale dei fujenti a Madonna dell'Arco.* Cava dei Tirreni: De Mauro editore.

Davis, Natalie Zemon. 1969. "Deforming the Reformation." *New York Review of Books* 7 (Apr. 10): 35–38.

————. 1971. "Missed connections: *Religion and regime.*" *Journal of Interdisciplinary History* 1:381–94.

————. 1985. Review of *The Birth of Purgatory,* by Jacques Le Goff. *New York Review of Books,* July 18, 31–33.

de Blasis, G. 1889. "Frammento d'un diario inedito napoletano." *Archivio storico per le province napoletane* 14:34–68, 265–352.

Degert, Antoine. 1913. "Veronica, Saint." *Catholic Encyclopedia* 15. New York: Encyclopedia Press.

Delehaye, Hippolyte. 1913. "Martyrology." *Catholic Encyclopedia* 9. New York: Encyclopedia Press.

———. 1934. *Cinq leçons sur la méthode hagiographique.* Brussels: Société des Bollandistes.

De Lellis, Carlo. 1654. *Parte seconda, o'vero supplimento a Napoli Sacra di D. Cesare D'Engenio Caracciolo.* Naples: Roberto Mollo.

———. 1977 (1666). *Aggiunta all Napoli Sacra del d'Engenio.* Edited by Francesco Aceto. Naples: Fiorentino editrice S.p.A.

del Grosso, Franco. 1983. "Origine del culto alla Madonna d'Impruneta e suoi rapporti con la città di Firenze." In *Impruneta; una pieve, un paese.* Atti del convegno Impruneta: una pieve, un paese. Cultura, parrocchia e società nella campagna toscana. Florence: Libreria Salimbeni.

Delooz, Pierre. 1969. *Sociologie et canonisations.* The Hague: Martinus Nijhoff.

Del Panta, Lorenzo. 1980. *Le epidemie nella storia demografica italiana (secoli XIV–XIX).* Turin: Loescher.

De Maio, Romeo. 1973. *Riforme e miti nella Chiesa del Cinquecento.* Naples: Guida editori.

———. 1983. *Pittura e Controriforma a Napoli.* Bari: Editori Laterza.

de Marco, Gerardo. 1975. *Dalle ceneri alla Settimana Santa.* Molfetta: Mezzina.

De Martino, Ernesto. 1968. *La Terra del rimorso.* Milan: il Saggiatore di Alberto Mondadori.

———. 1975 (1958). *Morte e pianto rituale.* Turin: Paolo Boringhieri.

D'Engenio, Cesare. 1623. *Napoli Sacra.* Naples: Ottavio Beltrano.

De Rosa, Gabriele. 1971. *Vescovi, popolo e magia nel Sud.* Naples: Guida editori.

———. 1973. "Organizzazione del territorio e vita religiosa nel Sud tra XVI e XIX secolo." In *La Società religiosa nell'età moderna,* Atti del Convegno studi di Storia sociale e religiosa, Capaccio-Paestrum, 18–21 maggio 1972. Naples: Guida editori.

———. 1979. *Chiesa e religione popolare nel Mezzogiorno.* Bari: Laterza.

———. 1983. *Vescovi, popolo e magia nel Sud.* 2d ed. Naples: Guida editori.

———. 1987. *Tempo religioso e tempo storico.* Rome: Edizioni di Storia e Letteratura.

de Stefano, Pietro. 1560. *Descrittione dei luoghi sacri della città di Napoli con li fondatori di essi, reliquie, sepolture et epitaphii, che in quelle si trovano.* Naples: Raimondo Amato.

De Vitiis, Vincenzo. 1982. "Chiese ricettizie e organizzazione ecclesiastica nel Regno delle Due Sicilie dal Concordato del 1818 all'Unità." In *Per la storia sociale e religiosa del Mezzogiorno d'Italia,* edited by Giuseppe Galasso and Carla Russo. Vol. 2. Naples: Guida editori.

DeVos, George. 1968. "National character." *International Encyclopedia of the Social Sciences* 11. New York: Macmillan.

Di Bella, Maria Pia. 1994. "Pietà e giustizia: la 'santificazione' dei criminali giustiziati." *La ricerca folklorica* 29 (Apr.): 69–72.

di Leonardo, Micaela. 1991. "Introduction: Gender, culture, and political economy." In *Gender at the Crossroads of Knowledge,* edited by M. di Leonardo. Berkeley: University of California Press.

Di Palo, Francesco. 1992. *Stabat Mater Dolorosa: La Settimana Santa in Puglia.* Brindisi: Schena editore

Dudden, F. Homes. 1905. *Gregory the Great: His Place in History and Thought.* Vol. 1. New York: Longmans Green.

Duffy, Eamon. 1992. *Stripping the Altars: Traditional Religion in England circa 1400 to circa 1580.* New Haven: Yale University Press.

Dundes, Alan. 1981. "Life is like a chicken coop ladder: A study of German national character through folklore." *Journal of Psychoanalytic Anthropology* 4 (3): 265–364.

———. 1989 (1987). *Life Is Like a Chicken Coop Ladder: A Study of German National Character through Folklore.* Detroit: Wayne State University Press.

Durkheim, Emile. 1915. *The Elementary Forms of the Religious Life.* London: Allen and Unwin.

Ebner, Pietro. 1982. *Chiesa, baroni e popolo nel Cilento.* Rome: Edizioni di storia e letteratura.

Edwards, Graham R. 1985. "Purgatory: 'Birth' or evolution?" *Journal of Ecclesiastical History* 36 (Oct.): 634–46.

Eire, Carlos. 1986. *The War against the Idols: The Reformation of Europe from Erasmus to Calvin.* Cambridge: Cambridge University Press.

Fappani, Antonio. 1980. "Santuari non mariani delle valli bresciane." In *Lo straordinario e il quotidiano,* edited by Angelo Turchini. Brescia: Grafo edizioni.

Fazzo, Vittorio. 1977. *La giustificazione delle immagini religiose dalla tarda antichità al Cristianesimo: I—La tarda antichità.* Naples: Edizione Scientifiche Italiane.

Febbraro, Antonio, and De Benedictus. 1988. *Soleto: Cittadella di Maria.* Soleto: Santuario Madonna delle Grazie.

Fenlon, Dermot. 1972. *Heresy and Obedience in Tridentine Italy: Cardinal Pole and the Counter-Reformation.* Cambridge: Cambridge University Press.

———. 1974. "*Encore une question*: Lucien Febvre, the Reformation and the school of *Annales*." *Historical Studies* 9:65–81.

Ferrari, Daniela, and Gioia Lanzi. 1985. "Pellegrinàggio bolognese." *Il santo* 25:135–72.

Fildes, Valerie. 1986. *Breasts, Bottles, and Babies.* Edinburgh: Edinburgh University Press.

———. 1988. *Wet Nursing: A History from Antiquity to the Present.* Oxford: Basil Blackwell.

Fineschi, Filippo. 1993. "La rappresentazione della morte sul patibolo nella liturgia fiorentina della congregazione dei Neri." *Archivio storico italiano* 553:805–46.

Firpo, Massimo. 1988. "Gli 'spirituali,' l'Accademia di Modena e il formulario di fede di 1542: controllo del dissenso religiosa e nicodemismo." In *Città italiane del '500 tra Riforma e Controriforma,* Atti del Convegno Internazionale di Studi, 13–15 ottobre 1983. Lucca: Maria Pacini Fazzi.

———. 1993. *Riforma protestante ed eresie nell'Italia del Cinquecento: Un profilo storico.* Bari: Editori Laterza.

Forget, J. 1913. "Jansenius and Jansenism." *Catholic Encyclopedia* 8. New York: Encyclopedia Press.

Fortescue, Adrian. 1913a. "Iconoclasm." In *Catholic Encyclopedia* 7. New York: Encyclopedia Press.

———. 1913b. "Images, veneration of." In *Catholic Encyclopedia* 7. New York: Encyclopedia Press.

Fragnito, Gigiola. 1989. "Evangelismo e intransigenti nei difficili equilibri del pontificato farnesiano." *Rivista di storia e letteratura religiosa* 25 (1): 20–47.

Franzonello, Lucia. 1946. *Il culto delle anime decollate in Sicilia.* Tesi di Laurea: Università di Palermo, Facoltà di Lettere e Filosofia.

Freud, Sigmud. 1905. "Three essays on the theory of sexuality." In *The Standard Edition of the Complete Psychological Works of Sigmund Freud.* Vol. 7. Edited and translated by James Strachey. 24 vols. London: Hogarth. The following works are also in these volumes.

———. 1908. "Character and anal eroticism." In *S.E.* 9.

———. 1913. *Totem and Taboo.* In *S.E.* 11.

———. 1916–17. *Introductory Lectures on Psychoanalysis.* In *S.E.* 15 and 16 (entire volumes).

———. 1917. "On transformations of instinct as exemplified in anal eroticism." In *S.E.* 17.

———. 1927. *The Future of an Illusion.* In *S.E.* 21.

———. 1939. *Moses and Monotheism.* In *S.E.* 23.

Fucini, Renato. 1977 (1877). *Napoli a occhio nudo.* Bologna: Massimiliano Boni editore.

Galante, Gennaro Aspreno. 1985 (1872). *Guida sacra della città di Napoli.* Edited and with an introduction by Nicola Spinosa. Naples: Società Editrice Napoletana.

Ganzer, Klaus. 1993. "Aspetti dei movimenti cattolici di riforma nel XVI secolo." *Cristianesimo nella storia* 14 (Feb): 33–67.

Geary, Patrick. 1978. *Furta sacra: Thefts of Relics in the Central Middle Ages.* Princeton: Princeton University Press.

———. 1984. "The saint and the shrine." In *Wallfahrt kennt keine Grenzen,* edited by L. Kriss-Rettenbeck and G. Möhler. Munich: Schnell and Steiner.

Gentilcore, David. 1994. "Adapt yourself to the people's capabilities: Missionary strategies, methods, and impact in the Kingdom of Naples, 1600–1800." *Journal of Ecclesiastical History* 45 (2): 260–96.

Giannone, Pietro. 1821. *Opere postume di Pietro Giannone.* Vol. 1. Naples: No publisher.

Gigli, Giuseppe. 1893. *Superstizioni, pregiudizi e tradizioni in Terra d'Otranto.* Florence: No publisher.

Gilmore, Myron. 1975. "Italian reactions to Erasmian humanism." In *The Profile of the Italian Renaissance in the Mirror of Its European Transformations,* edited by H. A. Oberman and T. Brady. Leiden, Netherlands: E. J. Brill.

Ginkel, Rob van. 1992. "Typically Dutch—Ruth Benedict on the national character of the Netherlanders." *Netherlands Journal of Social Sciences* 28 (Apr.): 50–71.

Ginzburg, Carlo. 1980 (1976). *The Cheese and the Worms.* Baltimore: Johns Hopkins University Press.

———. 1983 (1966). *The Night Battles.* Baltimore: Johns Hopkins University Press.

Gorer, Geoffrey, and John Rickman. 1949. *The People of Great Russia.* London: Cresset.

Gramsci, Antonio. 1966 (1948). *Il materialismo storico e la filosofia di Benedetto Croce.* Turin: Giulio Einaudi editore.

Granata, Francesco Monsignor. 1988 (1766). *Storia sacra della chiesa metropolitana di Capua.* Photographic reproduction. Bologna: Arnaldo Forni editore.

Greeley, Andrew. 1993. Review of *Madonnas That Maim. Contemporary Sociology* 22 (1): 121–22.

Grendi, Edoardo. 1976. "Le confraternite come fenomeno associativo e religioso." In *Società, Chiesa e vita religiosa nell'Ancien Régime,* edited by C. Russo. Naples: Guida.

Grigioni, Elisabetta Gulli. 1975. "L'empio giocatore nelle leggende dell'*Atlante mariano.*" *Il santo* 15 (1–2): 345–51.

Grisanti, Cristoforo. 1895. "Usi e costumi siciliani in Isnello." *Archivio per lo studio della tradizione popolari* 14 (Jan.–Mar.): 76–83.

Guastella, Serafino Amabile. 1968 (1884). *La parità morali.* Rocca San Casciano: Cappelli editore.

Hanna, Edward J. 1913. "Purgatory." *Catholic Encyclopedia* 12. New York: Encyclopedia Press.

Harding, Sandra. 1986. *The Science Question in Feminism.* Ithaca: Cornell University Press.

Harline, Craig. 1990. "Official religion–popular religion in recent historiography of the Catholic Reformation." *Archive for Reformation History* 81:239–62.

Harris, Marvin. 1968. *The Rise of Anthropological Theory.* New York: Thomas Y. Crowell.

Hartland, E. Sidney. 1910. "The cult of executed criminals at Palermo." *Folk-lore* 21 (June): 168–79.

Hay, Denys. 1977. *The Church in Italy in the Fifteenth Century.* Cambridge: Cambridge University Press.

Hertling, L., and E. Kirschbaum. 1949. *Le catacombe romane e i loro martiri.* Rome: Pontificia Università Gregoriana.

Hilgers, Joseph. 1913. "Sabbatine privilege." *Catholic Encyclopedia* 13. New York: Encyclopedia Press.

Holweck, F. G. 1913. "Sorrows of the Blessed Virgin Mary." *Catholic Encyclopedia* 14. New York: Encyclopedia Press.

Hunecke, Volker. 1989. *I trovatelli di Milano.* Bologna: Il Mulino.

Inkeles, Alex, and Daniel J. Levinson. 1969. "National character: The study of modal personality and sociocultural systems." In *The Handbook of Social Psychology*, edited by Gardiner Lindzey and Elliot Aronson. Vol. 4. Reading, Mass.: Addison-Wesley.

Jedin, Hubert. 1972 (1935). "Genesi e portata del decreto tridentino sulla venerazione delle immagine." In *Chiesa della fede, Chiesa della storia: saggi scelti.* Brescia: Morcelliana.

Jenkins, Thomas. 1775. *La vera guida per chi viaggia in Italia.* Rome: Paolo Giunchi.

Jung, Eva-Maria. 1953. "On the nature of Evangelism in sixteenth-century Italy." *Journal of the History of Ideas* 14 (4): 511–27.

Kempf, Constantine. 1916. *The Holiness of the Church in the Nineteenth Century.* New York: Benziger Brothers.

Kertzer, David I. 1993. *Sacrificed for Honor: Italian Infant Abandonment and the Politics of Reproductive Control.* Boston: Beacon.

Kertzer, David I., and Caroline Bretell. 1987. "Advances in Italian and Iberian family history." *Journal of Family History* 12 (1–3): 87–120.

Kirk, James. 1992. "Iconoclasm and reform." *Scottish Church History Society—Records* 24 (3): 366–83.

Kirsch, J. P. 1913. "Cecilia, Saint." *Catholic Encyclopedia* 3. New York: Encyclopedia Press.

Klapisch-Zuber, Christianne. 1985. *Women, Family, and Ritual in Renaissance Italy.* Chicago: University of Chicago Press.

Kline, Paul. 1972. *Fact and Fantasy in Freudian Theory.* London: Methuen.

Lamphere, Louise. 1987. "Anthropology and feminism: The struggle to reshape our thinking about gender." In *The Impact of Feminist Research in the Academy*, edited by C. Farnham. Bloomington: Indiana University Press.

Lanari, Sergio. 1986. "Le edicole sacre nelle strade dell'Anconetano." *Antiqua* 8:22–24.

Lancellotti, Arturo. 1951. *Feste tradizionali.* 2 vols. Milan: Società Editrice Libraria.

La Sorsa, Saverio. 1925. *Usi, costumi e feste del popolo pugliese.* Bari: F. Casini and Figlio.

Lazzaretto, Alba. 1978. "I capitelli e la società religiosa veneta." *Ricerche di storia sociale e religiosa* 13:305–10.

Le Goff, Jacques. 1983. *The Birth of Purgatory.* Chicago: University of Chicago Press.

Lerner, Robert E. 1982. Review of Jacques Le Goff, *La naissance du Purgatoire. American Historical Review* 87 (5): 1374–75.

Livi Bacci, Massimo. 1977. *A History of Italian Fertility during the Last Two Centuries.* Princeton: Princeton University Press.

Lombardi Satriani, Luigi M. 1979. *Il silenzio, la memoria e lo sguardo.* Palermo: Sellerio editore.

———. 1981. "La teatralizzazione del sangue." In *Rappresentazioni arcaiche della tradizione popolare,* Atti del Vi Convegno di Studio, 27–31 Maggio 1981. Viterbo: Union Printing.

Lombardi Satriani, Luigi M., and Mariano Meligrana. 1982. *Il ponte di San Giacomo.* Milan: Rizzoli editore.

Longo, Bartolo. 1981. *Storia del santuario di Pompei.* Pompei: Pontificio santuario di Pompei.

Luther, Martin. 1958. *Luther's Works.* Vol. 40, *Church and Ministry II.* Philadelphia: Fortress Press.

———. 1959. *Luther's Works.* Vol. 51, *Sermons I.* Philadelphia: Fortress Press.

Maarbjerg, John P. 1993. "Iconoclasm in the Thurgau: Two related incidents in the summer of 1524." *Sixteenth Century Journal* 24 (3): 577–93.

Marchesi, Giambattista. 1898. "In Valtellina: costumi, leggende, tradizioni." *Archivio per lo studio delle tradizioni popolari* 17:411–26.

Marchetti, Giovanni. 1797. *De' prodigj avvenuti in molte sacre immagini, specialmente di Maria Santissima secondo gli autentici Processi compilati in Roma.* Rome: Zempel.

Marcocchi, Massimo. 1983. "L'immagine di Lutero in alcuni manuali di storia ecclesiastica tra '800 e '900." In *Lutero in Italia,* edited by Lorenzo Perrone. Casale Monferrato: Marietti.

Mariella, Michele. 1979. *Il santuario di Capurso nella storia e nella tradizione.* Bari: Favia.

Martin, Edward J. 1930. *A History of the Iconoclastic Controversy.* London: Society for Promoting Christian Knowledge.

Martin, John. 1987. "Popular culture and the shaping of popular heresy in Renaissance Venice." In *Inquisition and Society in Early Modern Europe,* edited by Stephen Haliczer. London: Croom Helm.

———. 1988. "Salvation and society in sixteenth-century Venice: Popular evangelism in a Renaissance city." *Journal of Modern History* 60 (2): 205–83.

———. 1993. *Venice's Hidden Enemies.* Berkeley: University of California Press.

Martindale, Don. 1967. *National Character in the Perspective of the Social Sciences: The Annals of the American Academy of Political and Social Science* 370 (Mar.): 1–163.

Maselli, Domenico. 1980 (1865). Introduction to *Memorie,* by Scipione de'Ricci. Pistoia: Libreria Editrice Tellini.

Masling, Joseph. 1986. "Orality, pathology, and interpersonal behavior." In *Empirical Studies of Psychoanalytic Theories,* edited by Joseph Masling. Hillsdale, N.J.: Analytic Press.

McGrath, Alister. 1990. "Justification and the Reformation." *Archive for Reformation History* 81:5–19.

McGuire, Brian Patrick. 1989. "Purgatory: The Communion of Saints and medieval change." *Viator* 20:61–84.

McNair, Philip. 1967. *Peter Martyr in Italy.* Oxford: Clarendon.

———. 1981. "The Reformation of the sixteenth century in Renaissance Italy." In *Religion and Humanism,* edited by Keith Robins. Oxford: Basil Blackwell.

Mead, Margaret. 1935. *Sex and Temperament in Three Primitive Societies.* New York: Morrow.

———. 1951. "The study of national character." In *The Policy Sciences,* edited by Daniel Lerner and Harold Lasswell. Stanford: Stanford University Press.

———. 1953. "The study of culture at a distance." In *The Study of Culture at a Distance,* edited by M. Mead and R. Métraux. Chicago: University of Chicago Press.

Mead, Margaret, and Rhoda Métraux, eds. 1966. *The Study of Culture at a Distance.* Chicago: University of Chicago Press.

Medica, Giacomo M. 1965. *I santuari mariani d'Italia.* Turin: Leumann.

Meissner, W. W. 1971. "Notes on identification—II. Clarification of related concepts." *Psychoanalytic Quarterly* 40 (2): 277–302.

———. 1981. *Internalization in Psychoanalysis.* New York: International Universities Press.

Mellano, Maria Franca. 1986. *Popolo religiosità e costume in Piemonte sul finire del '500.* Turin: Centro studi piemontesi.

Menozzi, Daniele. 1983 "La figura di Lutero nella cultura italiana del Settecento." In *Lutero in Italia,* edited by Lorenzo Perrone. Casale Monferrato: Marietti.

Mercati, Angelo. 1961. *Sommario del processo di Giordano Bruno.* Città del Vaticano: Biblioteca Apostolica Vaticana.

Meyer, Judith. 1993. "The success of the French Reformation: The case of La Rochelle." *Archive for Reformation History* 84:242–75.

Miccoli, Giovanni. 1983. "'L'avarizia e l'orgoglio di un frate laido' . . . problemi e aspetti dell'interpretazione cattolica di Lutero." In *Lutero in Italia,* edited by Lorenzo Perrone. Casale Monferrato: Marietti.

Miele, Michele. 1963. *La riforma Domenicana a Napoli nel periodo post-tridentino (1583–1725).* Rome: S. Sabina.

Miller, S.J. 1994. "The limits of political Jansenism in Tuscany: Scipione de' Ricci to Peter Leopold, 1780–1791." *Catholic Historical Review* 80 (4): 762–67.

Mioni, Ugo. 1908. *Il culto delle reliquie nella Chiesa Cattolica.* Turin: Tipografia pontificia.

Mitchell, Timothy. 1990. *Passional Culture: Emotion, Religion, and Society in Southern Spain.* Philadelphia: University of Pennsylvania Press.

Molinari, Franco, and Antonio Fappani. 1982. "Religiosità popolare e giansenismo in Valcamonica: la Via Crucis di Cerveno." In *Economia, istituzioni, cultura in Lombardia nell'età di Maria Teresa,* edited by A. De Maddalena, E. Rotelli, and G. Barbarisi. Vol. 2. Milan: Società editrice il Mulino.

Mondello, Fortunato. 1874. *San Francesco d'Assisi: discorsi sacri, con l'aggiunta di vari panegirici e sermoni.* Palermo: Stabilimento tipografico Lao.

———. 1882. *Spettacoli e feste popolari in Trapani.* Trapani: Stamperia Economica Trapanese.

Moretti, Italo. 1988. "La demografia medievale attraverso le testimonianze architettoniche e urbanistiche." In *Vita, morte e miracoli di gente comune*, edited by Carlo A. Corsini. Florence: GEF.

Moroni, Marco. 1986. "Le edicole sacre del territori recanatese." *Studia Picena* 51:31–59.

Muir, Edward. 1991. "Introduction: Observing trifles." In *Microhistory and the Lost Peoples of Europe*, edited by Edward Muir and Guido Ruggiero. Baltimore: Johns Hopkins University Press.

Muir, Edward, and Guido Ruggiero. 1991. *Microhistory and the Lost Peoples of Europe*. Baltimore: Johns Hopkins University Press.

Musolino, G. A. Niero, and S. Tramontin. 1963. *Santi e beati veneziani: quaranta profili*. Venetia: Edizioni Studium Cattolico Veneziano.

Naselli, Carmellina. 1960. "Notizie sui disciplinati in Sicilia." In *Il movimento dei Disciplinati nel settimo centenario dal suo inizio*, Convegno Internazionale, Perugia, 25–28 settembre 1960. Spoleto: Arti Grafiche Panetto and Petrelli.

Nelli, Athanasio. 1571. *Origine della Madonna della Quercia di Viterbo*. Revised and translated by Aurelio Cosini Senese. No publisher.

Niccoli, Ottavia. 1983. "Il mostro di Sassonia. Conoscenza e non conoscenza di Lutero in Italia nel Cinquecento (1520–1530 ca.)." In *Lutero in Italia*, edited by Lorenzo Perrone. Casale Monferrato: Marietti.

Niero, Antonio. 1986. "Per una storia della società religiosa lombarda: la pietà popolare." In *Chiesa e società*, edited by A. Caprioli, A. Rimoldi, and L. Vaccaro. Brescia: Editrice La Scuola.

Nieto, Jose C. 1970. *Juan de Valdés and the Origins of the Spanish and Italian Reformation*. Geneva: Librairie Droz.

Nolan, Mary Lee, and Sidney Nolan. 1989. *Christian Pilgrimage in Modern Western Europe*. Chapel Hill: University of North Carolina Press.

Norcini, Franca Loretta. 1988. *Casentino santo: storie e tradizioni religiose di una vallata toscana*. Cortona: Calosci.

Novi Chavarria, Elisa. 1982. "L'attività missionaria dei Gesuiti nel Mezzogiorno d'Italia tra XVI e XVIII secolo." In *Per la storia sociale e religiosa del Mezzogiorno d'Italia*, edited by Giuseppe Galasso and Carla Russo. Vol. 2. Naples: Guida editori.

Olivieri, Achille. 1979. *La Riforma in Italia*. Milan: Mursia.

———. 1992. *Riforma ed eresia a Vicenza nel Cinquecento*. Rome: Herder editrice e libreria.

Oltranto, Giorgio. 1982. "Una mostra per la città." In *Vicoli e santi: S. Nicola nella edicole religiose della città vecchia di Bari*, edited by G. Cioffari et al. Bari: Edizioni Levante.

Ott, Michael. 1913. "Jacopo de Voragine." *Catholic Encyclopedia* 8. New York: Encyclopedia Press.

Ozment, Steven. 1975. *The Reformation in the Cities: The Appeal of Protestantism to Sixteenth-Century Germany and Switzerland*. New Haven: Yale University Press.

———. 1982. *Reformation Europe: A Guide to Research*. St. Louis, Mo.: Center for Reformation Research.

Paglia, Vincenzo. 1982. *La morte confortata: riti della paura e mentalità religiosa a Roma nell'età moderna*. Rome: Edizioni di Storia e Letteratura.

Paige, Jeffery. 1974. "Kinship and polity in stateless societies." *American Journal of Sociology* 80 (2): 301–20.

Paleotti, Gabriele. 1961 (1594). "Discorso intorno alle imagini sacre e profane." In *Trattati d'arte del cinquecento fra manierismo e controriforma*, edited by Paolo Barocchi. Vol. 2. Bari: Laterza.

Paolucci, Antonio, Bruno Pacciani, and Rosanna Proto Pisani. 1987. *Il tesoro di Santa Maria all'Impruneta*. Florence: Becocci editore.

Pardo, Italo. 1981. "Il tempo controllato." *M & m: media & messaggi* 1 (Dec.): 104–9.

———. 1982. "L'elaborazione' del lutto in un quartiere tradizionale di Napoli." *Rassegna italiana di sociologia* 23 (4): 535–69.

Pastor, Ludwig von. 1933. *The History of the Popes from the Close of the Middle Ages*. Vol. 24, *Clement VIII (1592–1605)*. London: Kegan Paul, Trench, and Trubner.

Payton, James R. 1993. "Calvin and the legitimation of icons: His treatment of the Seventh Ecumenical Council." *Archive for Reformation History* 84:222–41.

Pellizari, Pietro. 1889a. "I flagellanti in Terra d'Oltranto." *Archivio per lo studio della tradizione popolari* 8 (July–Sept.): 345–53

———. 1889b. "I flagellanti in Modica." *Archivio per lo studio della tradizione popolari* 8 (July–Sept.): 551–52.

Peter, Carl J. 1987. Review of *The Birth of Purgatory*, by Jacques Le Goff. *Catholic Historical Review* 73 (1): 108.

Petersen, Joan M. 1984. *The "Dialogues" of Gregory the Great in Their Late Antique Cultural Background*. Toronto: Pontifical Institute of Mediaeval Studies.

Piccaluga, Gabriella Ferri. 1983. "Le radici iconografiche della Via Crucis settecentesca in territorio bresciano: immagini, antropologia, storia." In *Immagini, arte e poteri nell'età di Beniamino Simoni (XVIII secolo) e oltre*, edited by Roberto Andrea Lorenzi. Brescia: Luigi Micheletti editore.

Piccaluga, Gabriella Ferri, and Gianvittorio Signorotto. 1983. "L'imagine del suffragio." *Storia dell'arte* 49:235–48.

Piò, Giovanni Michele. 1615. *Della nobile et generosa progenie del P.S. Domenico in Italia*. Bologna: B. Cochi.

Pitrè, Giuseppe. 1969 (1881). *Spettacoli e feste popolari siciliane*. Photographic reproduction. Bologna: Forni editore.

———. 1978a (1888). *Usi e costumi, credenze e pregiudizi del popolo siciliano*. Vol. 2. Photographic reproduction. Palermo: Edizioni Il Vespro.

———. 1978b (1889). *Usi e costumi, credenze e pregiudizi del popolo siciliano*. Vol. 3. Photographic reproduction. Palermo: Edizioni Il Vespro.

———. 1978c (1889). *Usi e costumi, credenze e pregiudizi del popolo siciliano*. Vol. 4. Photographic reproduction. Palermo: Edizioni Il Vespro.

———. 1978d (1913). *Cartelli, pasquinate, canti, leggende, usi del popolo siciliano*. Photographic reproduction. Palermo: Edizioni Il Vespro.

Prandi, Carlo. 1983. *La religione popolare fra potere e tradizione: per un sociologia della tradizione religiosa*. Milan: Franco Angeli editore.

Prodi, Paolo. 1968. *Lo sviluppo dell'assolutismo nello stato pontificio (secoli XV–XVI)*. Bologna: Casa Editrice Prof. Riccardo Pàtron.

———. 1987. *The Papal Prince, One Body and Two Souls: The Papal Monarchy in Early Modern Europe*. New York: Cambridge University Press.

Prosperi, Adriano. 1965. "Note in margine a un opuscolo di Gian Matteo Giberti." *Critica storica* 4:367–402.

———. 1980. "*Oltras Indias*: missionari della controriforma tra contadini e selvaggi." In *Scienze, credenze occulte, livelli di cultura*, Convegno internazionale di Studi, Firenze, 26–30 giugno 1980. Florence: Leo S. Olschki editore.

———. 1982. "Il sangue e l'anima, ricerche sulle compagnie di giustizia in Italia." *Quaderni storici* 51:959–99.

———. 1983. "Lutero al Concilio di Trento." In *Lutero in Italia*, edited by Lorenzo Perrone. Casale Monferrato: Marietti.

Redon, Odile. 1983. "A proposito delle reliquie logica dei corpi spezzettati nella *Legenda aurea*?" In *Il linguaggio, il corpo, la festa: per un ripensamento della tematica di Michail Bachtin*, edited by P. Clemente et al. Milan: Franco Angeli editore.

Redondi, Pietro. 1987. *Galileo Heretic*. Princeton: Princeton University Press.

Ricci, Scipione de'. 1980 (1865). *Memorie*. 2 vols. Introduction by Domenico Maselli. Pistoia: Libreria Editrice Tellini.

Rienzo, Maria Gabriella. 1980. "Il processo di cristianizzazione e le missioni popolari nel Mezzogiorno. Aspetti istituzioni e socio-religiosi." In *Per la storia sociale e religiosa del Mezzogiorno d'Italia*, edited by Giuseppe Galasso and Carla Russo. Vol. 1. Naples: Guida editori.

Riflessioni in difesa di M.r. Scipione de'Ricci e del suo sinodo di Pistoja sopra la costituzione Auctorem fidei pubblicata in Roma il di 28. Agosto 1794. 1796. Rome.

Riolfi, Walter. 1980. "La protesta dei 'morti della fossetta' ovvero San Rocco di Ghedi." In *Lo straordinario e il quotidiano*, edited by Angelo Turchini. Brescia: Grafo edizioni.

Rivera, Annamaria. 1988. *Il mago, il santo, la morte, la festa*. Bari: Edizioni Dedalo.

Robertazzi delle Donne, Enrica. 1973. "Le Chiese ricettizie nella legislazione borbonica." In *La Società religiosa nell'età moderna: parte seconda*, Atti del Convegno studi di Storia sociale e religiosa, Capaccio-Paestrum, 18–21 maggio 1972. Naples: Guida editori.

Robertson, Roland, and Frank Lechner. 1984. "On Swanson: An appreciation and an appraisal." *Sociological Analysis* 45 (3): 185–204.

Robertson Smith, W. 1972 (1889). *The Religion of the Semites*. New York: Schocken.

Rosa, Mario. 1976. *Religione e società nel mezzogiorno tra cinque e seicento*. Bari: De Donato editore.

Ross, James B. 1974. "The middle-class child in urban Italy." In *The History of Childhood*, edited by Lloyd deMause. New York: Psychohistory Press.

Rossi, Annabella. 1969. *Le feste dei poveri*. Bari: Editori Laterza.

Russo, Carla. 1984. *Chiesa e comunità nella diocesi di Napoli tra cinque e settecento*. Naples: Guida editori.

Sacchetti, Franco. 1970 (c. 1392). *Il trecentonovelle*. Turin: Giulio Einaudi.

Saintyves, Pierre. 1987 (1931). *En marge de la Légende Dorée: songes, miracles et survivances*. Paris: Robert Laffont.

Sassu, Pietro. 1981. "La Settimana Santo a Castelsardo." In *Rappresentazioni arcaiche della tradizione popolare*. Viterbo: Atti del VI Convegno di Studio.

Saunders, George R. 1993. "Critical ethnocentrism and the ethnology of Ernesto De Martino." *American Anthropologist* 95 (4): 875–93.

Scavizzi, Giuseppe. 1992. *The Controversy on Images from Calvin to Baronius*. New York: Peter Lang.

Schroeder, H. J. 1950. *Canons and Decrees of the Council of Trent*. St. Louis, Mo.: B. Herder.

Schutte, Anne J. 1989. "Periodization of sixteenth-century Italian religious history: The post-Cantimori paradigm shift." *Journal of Modern History* 61 (2): 269–84.

Sebastiani, Lucia. 1982. "Parrocchie e comunità in età teresiana." In *Economia, istituzioni, cultura in Lombardia nell'età di Maria Teresa,* edited by A. De Maddalena, E. Rotelli, and G. Barbarisi. Milan: Il Mulino.

Seidel Menchi, Silvana. 1987. *Erasmo in Italia: 1520–1580.* Turin: Bollati Boringhieri.

Serraino, Mario. 1968. *Trapani nella vita civile e religiosa.* Trapani: Cartograf.

Servetti Donati, Fedora. 1970. *Nascita e vita di un santuario di campagna: La Madonna dell'Olmo in Budrio.* Bologna: Centro Studi O.S.M.

Shaffern, Robert. 1993. "Learned discussions of indulgences for the dead in the Middle Ages." *Church History* 61 (4): 367–81.

Signorotto, Gianvittorio. 1983a. "Guadagnini e la fortuna del 'pio esercizio.'" In *Immagini, arte, culture e potere nell'età di Beniamino Simoni (XVIII) e oltre,* edited by R. A. Lorenzi. Brescia: Luigi Micheletti editore.

———. 1983b. "Gli esordi della *via crucis* nel Milanese." In *Il Francescanesimo in Lombardia.* Milan: Silvana editoriale.

———. 1983c. "Un eccesso di devozione. Preghiere pubbliche ai morti nella Milano del XVIII secolo." *Società e storia* 6:305–36.

———. 1985. "Cercatori di reliquie." *Rivista di storia e letteratura religiosa* 21 (3): 383–418.

Sordi, Italo. 1983. "La Santa Croce: ideologia e forme di un rituale folklorico." In *Immagini, arte, culture e potere nell'età di Beniamino Simoni (XVIII secolo) e oltre,* edited by R. A. Lorenzi. Brescia: Luigi Micheletti editore.

Staurenghi, Cesare. 1916. *L'Ospedale Maggiore di Milano e i suoi antichi sepolcri, particolarmente il foppone ora detto la Rotonda.* Milan: Ulric.

Stella, Pietro, ed. 1986. *Atti e decreti del concilio diocesano id Pistoia dell'anno 1786.* Vol. 1, *Ristampa dell'edizione Bracali.* Florence: Leo S. Olschki editore.

Strocchia, Sharon. 1992. *Death and Ritual in Renaissance Florence.* Baltimore: Johns Hopkins University Press.

Strong, John S. 1987. "Relics." In *Encyclopedia of Religion,* edited by M. Eliade. Vol. 12. New York: Macmillan.

Swanson, Guy E. 1960. *The Birth of the Gods.* Ann Arbor: University of Michigan Press.

———. 1967. *Religion and Regime.* Ann Arbor: University of Michigan Press.

———. 1968. "To live in concord with society: Two empirical studies of primary relations." In *Cooley and Sociological Analysis,* edited by A. Reiss. Ann Arbor: University of Michigan Press.

Swanson, R. N. 1989. *Church and Society in Late Medieval England.* Oxford: Basil Blackwell.

Tamburro, Nunzio. 1987. *Pompei fondata da Bartolo Longo.* Pompei: Tipografia Francesco Sicignano.

Tentori, Tullio. 1982. "An Italian religious feast: The *fujenti* rites of the Madonna dell'Arco, Naples." In *Mother Worship,* edited by James J. Preston. Chapel Hill: University of North Carolina Press.

Thurston, Herbert. 1913. "Relics." *Catholic Encyclopedia* 12. New York: Encyclopedia Press.

———. 1952. *The Physical Phenomena of Mysticism.* London: Burns Oates.

Tocchini, Anna Petroni. 1972. "La sagra degli ossessi." In *La sagra degli ossessi: il patrimo-*

nio delle tradizioni popolari italiane nella società settentrionale, edited by Carlo Tullio Altan. Florence: Sansoni.

Toschi, Paolo. 1955. *Le origini del teatro italiano.* Turin: Boringhieri.

Tramontin, Silvio. 1977. "Dibattito sulle relazioni De Rosa, De Maio, Guarnieri, Aymard." In *Società e religione in Basilicata nell'età moderna—Relazioni e dibattito*, Atti del Convegno di Potenza-Matera, 25–28 settembre 1975. Salerno: D'Elia.

Trexler, Richard. 1973a. "Infanticide in Florence: New sources and first results." *History of Childhood Quarterly* 1 (1): 98–116.

———. 1973b. "The foundlings of Florence, 1395–1455." *History of Childhood Quarterly* 1 (2): 259–84.

Triputti, Anna Maria. 1978. "Le tavolette votive del santuario della Madonna del Pozzo a Capurso." *Lares* 44:183–214.

Tubach, Frederic. 1969. *Index exemplorum: A Handbook of Medieval Religious Tales.* Helsinki: Suomalainem Tiedeakatemia Akademia Scientiarum Fennica.

Turchini, Angelo. 1990. "Storie ordinarie e storia sacra." In *La Madre Bella*, edited by Pietro Caggiano, Michele Rak, and Angelo Turchini. Pompei: Pontifico santuario di Pompei.

Vannugli, Antonio. 1991. "La 'Pietà' di Jacopino del Conte per S. Maria del Populo: dall'identificazione del quadro al riesame dell'autore." *Storia dell'arte* 71:59–93.

Varese, Ranieri. 1969. *Francesco Cavazonni: critico e pittore.* Florence: Marchi and Bertolli.

Vauchez, André. 1981. *La sainteté en Occident aux derniers siècles du Moyen Age.* Rome: Ecole française de Rome.

Venturi, Silvio. 1901. "La Settimana Santa in Calabria." *Archivio per lo studio della tradizione popolari* 20:358–64.

Verzella, Emanuela. 1993. "Il giansenismo piemontese tra polemica e storiografia." *Rivista di storia e letteratura religiosa* 29 (3): 589–622.

Viscardi, Giuseppe Maria. 1993. "La religiosità popolare nel Cilento fra XVI e XIX secolo." *Ricerche di storia sociale e religiosa* 22 (July/n/Dec.): 7–46.

Vismara Chiappa, Paola. 1982. "Forme della pietà barocca nelle campagne lombarde tra sei e settecento." In *Economia, istituzioni, cultura in Lombardia nell'età di Maria Teresa*, edited by A. De Maddelena, E. Rotelli, and G. Barbarisi. Vol. 2. Milan: Società editrice Il Mulino.

———. 1988. *Miracoli settecenteschi in Lombardia tra istituzione ecclesiastica e religione popolare.* Milan: Istituto Propaganda Libraria.

Warner, Marina. 1976. *Alone of All Her Sex.* New York: Knopf.

Welti, Manfred E. 1985. *Breve storia della Riforma italiana.* Casale Monferrato: Marietti.

Wroth, William. 1982. *Christian Images in Hispanic New Mexico.* Colorado Springs: Taylor Museum.

———. 1991. *Images of Penance, Images of Mercy: Southwestern Santos in the Late Nineteenth Century.* Oklahoma City: University of Oklahoma Press.

Wuthnow, Robert. 1987. *Meaning and Moral Order: Explorations in Cultural Analysis.* Berkeley: University of California Press.

———. 1989. *Communities of Discourse.* Cambridge: Harvard University Press.

Zanchi, Goffredo. 1988. "La religiosità popolare a Bergamo nell'età moderna: caratteristiche e linee evolutive." In *Storia religiosa della Lombardia: Diocesi di Bergamo*, edited by A. Caprioli, A. Rimoldi, and L. Vaccaro. Bergamo: Editrice La Scuola.

Zarri, Gabriella. 1982. "Purgatorio 'particolare' e ritorno dei morti tra riforma e controri-
  forma: l'area italiana." *Quaderni storici* 50:466–97.
Zimmerman, Benedict. 1904. "The origin of the scapular—III (from original sources):
  The Sabbatine indulgence." *Irish Ecclesiastical Record* 15 (Apr.): 331–51.

Index

abandoned souls, 134–35
abandonment, child, 26–27
Abraham, Karl, 231–32
Addolorata, 29; carried in procession, 85; contrasted with Pietà, 93–94; cult in Italy, 92–100; Spanish cult contrasted with Italian cult, 100–102, 244–45
ad limina reports, 9, 204
Ahrweiler, Hélène, 51
Alamanni, Giuseppe, 40–42
Alcantarines, 62–63
Alfano, G. B., 212n
anal eroticism, 226, 231n
Andalusia, 100
Andrea, Alfred, 168, 171n
Andreuci, Ottavio, 33
Angelus, 211, 243
Anzani, Angelo, 9–10
Apollonian cultures, 227
apparitions, 48n, 215
Aquinas, Thomas, 131, 132
Arapesh, 227
Arcene, 16–17
Ariès, Phillipe, 122–23
aristocracy, landed, 12
Arrigoni, P., 25, 26, 29, 156, 212n, 222
Aston, Margaret, 245
Auctorem Fidei, 23
Augustinians, 141
Aumann, J., 210
Avola, 89

Bacci, Father, 220
Badone, Ellen, 5
Baldinucci, Antonio, 87
balie. See wet nurses
Barbagli, Marzio, 239
Barbi, Silvana, 139

Bari, 34–35, 61
Barnard, L. W, 50
Baronio, Cesare, 217
Battles, F. L., 56
beheaded souls, cult of, 142–46, 151
Bellarmino, Roberto, 132
Bellini, Alberto, 224
benandanti (agrarian cult), 13-14
Benedict, Ruth, 227
Benificio di Cristo, 192
Bennardini, Gierolamo, 181–84
Bergamo, 127, 169; skeletal dead cults at, 140–41
Bernstein, Alan, 121
Bitonto, 86
blood: and breast milk, 158; and flagellation, 83–85
blood relics, 208
Boccaccio, 167
Boesch Gajano, Sofia, 170
Bologna, 24–25, 35
Bonito, 136
Bontempi, Franco, 18n
Boronio, Cesare, 60
Borrani, Giambattista, 152–54
Borrello, L., 91, 92
Borromeo, Carlo, 60, 86; and relic cults, 171–72
Borromeo, Federico, 172, 181, 185
Boscoreale, 74
Bosio, Antonio, 175
Boswell, John, 129–30
Bouwsma, William, 199
Bracessi, Simonetta, 188–89
Brady, Thomas, 199
Bragaglia, Cesare, 90
brandea, 164
breast-feeding, 238–42

Breda, Giuliana, 32, 35
Brescia, 26, 33, 118
bridge to otherworld, 146–50
Bruttini, Tiziana, 27
Bryer, Anthony, 50n
Budrio, 30–31, 32
Burckhardt, Jacob, 210
Burigozzo, Gianmarco, 132
Burke, Peter, 179–80, 218
Bynum, Caroline, 157–59

Cagliari, 97
Calvi, Donato, 31, 46, 127, 140–41, 179, 207, 222
Calvin, John: on images, 53–54, 56, 245–46; and immanence, 199; on Purgatory, 127; on relics, 176–77. See also Calvinism
Calvinism, in Italy, 187, 192. See also Calvin, John
Cameron, Euan, 186, 189
Campagna, 9
Campbell, Lori, 73
Caponetto, Salvatore, 3n, 186, 192n, 196
Cappelletto, Giovanna, 26, 241
Cappi, Silvio, 182
Capuchins, 63, 79, 154
Capurso, 61–64
Cardini, Franco, 91
Carmelites, 79; and Sabbatine Privilege, 126, 128–29
Carmichael, Montgomery, 22
carnival, 86
Carroll, Michael P., 10–11, 41, 48, 64, 80, 83, 123, 201, 215, 230n, 243
cartapesta, 88
Casarini, Maria, 27
Castelsardo, 89–90
Castoldi, Giovanni, 181–85
catacombs, 115, 175–78, 181
Cattabiani, Alfredo, 93
Cattaneo, Enrico, 169
Cavazzoni, Franceso, 24, 25
Celano, Carlo, 39, 172, 161–62
Cestaro, Antonio, 8n, 201n
character, national. See national character
Cheshire, Neil, 235
Chiara, Davide, 116n, 117
chiesa ricettizia, 9, 200–206, 230, 243
Chiovaro, F., 171

Christian, William, 5, 245
Christocentrism, 17, 79–81, 90, 159, 245
Ciocia, Aldo, 157
Cisotto, Gianni, 35
Clement VIII, 94
Cocchiara, Giuseppe, 25, 29
Cologne, 182, 183
Colonna, Vittoria, 188n
confraternities, 70, 94, 154–55, 161; and condemned criminals, 149–50, 156; and Purgatory, 123–24
Congregation of Apostolic Missions, 82, 85
conspicuous consumption, and relic cults, 178–85
Constantine V, 51
Constantine VI, 51
Constantinople, 168
Contarini, Gasparo, 188
Copernicus, 234
Cornaro, Flaminio, 16n
Corrain, Cleto, 97, 147
Corsini, Carlo, 26
Cosenza, 26
Cosimo I, 20
Council of Constance, 125
Council of Constantinople, 51
Council of Elvira, 53
Council of Hieria, 51
Council of Nicea (787 A.D.): cited by Calvin, 53–54; and Council of Trent, 55; on image cults, 51–52
Council of Trent, 3, 8, 188n; on images, 54–56; Jansenist views on, 18; on justification, 188; and Lutheranism, 223; on Purgatory, 127–28
Counter-Reformation: and Addolorata cult, 96–100; and criteria for sainthood, 217–18; and flagellation, 78–79, 83–84, 90; and missionary activity, 3–15, 81–86; and relic cults, 171–85; response to Luther, 222–25; and saintly incorruption, 222–25; and souls in Purgatory, 129
Crehan, Joseph, 211
Croce, Benedetto, 194
crusaders, 168
Cruz, Joan Carroll, 208n, 211
Cusani, Francesco, 156

da Langasco, Cassiano, 37
d'Aloe, Stanislao, 161

da Marcianise, Marco Maffei, 209
D'Andrea, Giampaolo, 201
D'Antonio, Nino, 43, 47
Darwin, Charles, 234
da Vinci, Leonardo, 102
Davis, Natalie Zemon, 7, 121, 198, 199
dead, cult of: and executed criminals, 141–50,
    156; and plague victims, 66, 116–17, 139–
    41, 148, 151–55, 161–62; skeletal imagery,
    139–40; and soul's journey to otherworld,
    146–50; and souls in Purgatory, 116–138;
    two distinct cults, 118–19, 150–51; and
    young children, 160
death, acceptance of, 148–50
de Blasis, G., 36
Decameron, 167
de Fusco, Countess, 68, 71
Degert, Antoine, 80
Delehaye, Hippolyte, 167n, 170–71
De Lellis, Carlo, 161, 172, 178
del Grosso, Franco, 21
del latte madonnas, 157–60
Delooz, Pierre, 215, 217, 243
Del Panta, Lorenzo, 27–28, 116, 161n
Delumeau, Jean, 7
De Maio, Romeo, 33, 129, 172, 217–18, 219
de Marco, Gerardo, 89
De Martino, Ernesto, 96–98, 149, 200
D'Engenio, Cesare, 38–39, 45, 47, 124, 161,
    172–74, 209, 213, 221
De Rosa, Gabriele, 6–7, 26, 27, 74n, 81, 82, 246;
    on chiese ricettizie, 200–204, 205–6
de Stefano, Pietro, 172–74
De Vitiis, Vincenzo, 201n, 204–6
DeVos, George, 228n
dialectical models of religion, 7
Di Bella, Maria, 149
di Leonardo, Micaela, 234
Dini, Taddeo, 167–68
Dionysian cultures, 227
Di Palo, Francesco, 3n, 4, 81, 82, 84, 86, 87, 89,
    94, 95, 96, 99, 100
dismemberment, saintly, 164–65
Dominicans, 57, 59, 79; and papal authority,
    125; and Purgatory, 122
Dudden, F., 163, 164
Duffy, Eamon, 5, 12, 245
dulia, 53
Dundes, Alan, 226–27, 229

Durkheim, Emile, 21, 197, 199, 203, 207

Ebner, Pietro, 201
Ecce Homo, 91–92
edicole, 31–37, 106–7, 245; for beheaded souls,
    145; with skulls, 139, 141
Edwards, Graham, 121
Eire, Carlos, 56, 194
England, 12, 244, 245
epidemics, 27–28, 139. *See also* plague
Erasmus, 191, 194
eroticism. *See* anal eroticism; oral eroticism
Eusebius, 53
evangelism, Italian, 191–96, 230, 246
evil eye, 68
executed criminals, cult of, 142–46, 148–51
exempla, 131
ex-voto, 58, 61, 218; for beheaded souls, 144; at
    Budrio, 31; at Capurso, 61, 63; at Ghedi,
    118, 139; at Pompei, 67; removed during
    episcopal investigation, 64; for Vincenzo
    Camuso, 137
eyes, madonnine images move, 23–24

Fappani, Antonio, 139
Fara d'Adda, 16
Fatima, Our Lady of, 25
Fazzo, Vittorio, 50n, 51
Febbraro, Antonio, 47
feminism, 234–35
Fenlon, Dermot, 188, 191
Ferrari, Daniela, 33, 35, 36
Fildes, Valerie, 240, 246
Fineschi, Fillipo, 149–50
Firmian, Count, 155
Firpo, Massimo, 186n, 192n, 193
flagellant movement, 7
flagellation, 83–84, 90; at Nocera Terinese, 78,
    91–92
Florence, 20, 26, 33, 167, 238
fopponi, 152–53
Forget, J., 18
Fortescue, Adrian, 49
France, 12, 122–23, 240–41, 244
Franciscans, 79, 81; and papal authority, 125;
    and Purgatory, 122; and Stations of the
    Cross, 129
Franzonello, Lucia, 142–43, 145, 151
Freud, Sigmund, 226, 230–31, 232, 233

Fucini, Renato, 42–43
funerals, 96–98. *See also* souls, folk beliefs
    about

Gaeta, Muzio, 62–63
Galante, Gennaro, 162
Galileo, 199n
Ganzer, Klaus, 186
Garibaldi, 144n
Geary, Patrick, 165
Genoa, 123–24
Gentilcore, David, 81
Germany, 226, 244
Ghedi, 112–13, 116–19, 139, 154
Giannone, Pietro, 130
Giberti, Gian Matteo, 146–47
Gilmore, Myron, 194
Ginkel, Rob van, 227
Ginzberg, Carlo, 13–14
Golden Legend, 166
Good Friday rituals, 77
Gorer, Geoffrey, 228
Gramsci, Antonio, 7–8, 11
Great Schism, 14, 125
Greeley, Andrew, 7
Gregory the Great, 76; on images, 49–50, 53,
    194; on purgatory, 120; and relics, 163–65
Gregory II, 51
Gregory III, 51
Grendi, Edoardo, 123–24
Grigioni, Elisabetta, 46
Grisanti, Cristoforo, 90
Guadalupe, Our Lady of, 25
Guastella, Serafino Amabile, 133

Hanna, Edward, 132
Harding, Sandra, 234
Harline, Craig, 5, 11
Harris, Marvin, 228
Hartland, Sidney, 142n, 144–45
Hay, Denys, 206
heroic virtue, 217–18
Hertling, L., 175
Hilgers, Joseph, 128
Holweck, F. G., 93
Holy Name of Jesus, 80
Holy Saturday, 77
Holy Week celebrations, 86–100
Hunecke, Volker, 26

iconoclasm, 30; in Eastern Church, 50–52; in
    France, 54–55; and Gregory the Great,
    49–50; Protestantism and, 52–57, 245–46
Iconoclast controversy, 30, 50–52. *See also*
    iconoclasm
identification, 232
illusion, and incorruption, 214–15
image cults: and catacombs, 176; Council of
    Trent on, 54–56; and evangelism, 194–95;
    Jansenist views on, 18–24; official views on,
    after Trent, 57–60. *See also* images, miracu-
    lous
images, miraculous: at Arcene, 16–17; behav-
    iors in front of, 40–44, 236–37; Episcopal
    investigations of, 61–67; expectations about,
    29–31; and Iconoclast controversy, 50–52;
    and Jansenism, 19–24; and merging of nat-
    ural and supernatural, 229–30; Protestant
    views on, 52–54, 56–57; static vs. dynamic,
    28–29, 80; and supernatural signs, 37–40,
    62; two dimensional vs. three dimensional,
    24–25; and veiling, 19–22, 65. *See also* image
    cults; *and specific madonnine titles*
immanence, 197–98, 208
Impious gamesplayer (folktale), 46–48
incontro (ritual), 98–100
incorporation, 232
incorruption, saintly: associated patterns, 212–
    13; as illusion, 214–15; as metaphor, 218,
    222–25; official views on, 208–10, 216–18;
    popular traditions about, 216; physical cor-
    relates of, 219–22; previous scholarship on,
    211–12; as result of random processes, 215–
    16
indulgences, 33, 35, 125–26, 134–36
infanticide, 27
Inkeles, Alex, 228
Inquisition, 13–14, 186, 187, 192n
Ireland, 244
Irene (regent), 51
Italian Indies (metaphor), 3

Jansenism: and image cults, 18–24, 66; and
    Purgatory, 117, 134; and skeletal dead cults,
    155
Jedin, H., 52n, 54
Jenkins, Thomas, 222
Jesuits, 79, 81; missionary activity, 3–4, 95; and
    Sacred Heart, 80; and souls in Purgatory,
    129

John XXII, 126
Jung, Eva-Marie, 191

Kaunitz, Prince, 155–56
Kempf, Constantine, 213n
Kertzer, David, 26, 27
Kingdom of Naples, 3–4
Kirk, James, 56
Kirsch, J. P., 214n
Klapisch-Zuber, Christianne, 238–39, 241
Kline, Paul, 232n
Knock, 215

lactation, 240
lamentation (at funerals), 10, 94, 97–98. See
    also Addolorata
Lamphere, Louise, 234
Lanari, Sergio, 32
Lancelloti, Arturo, 87, 88, 90, 99
Landino, Cristofano, 210
La Sorsa, Saverio, 83, 88
Last Supper (painting), 102
latria, 53
lazarreto, 152–53, 156–57
Lazzareto, Alba, 36
Lecce, 34–35, 97
Legenda aurea. See Golden Legend
Le Goff, Jacques, 7, 119–23, 127, 130
Leo XIII, 76
Leopold, Peter, 18, 19, 21, 22
Lerner, Robert, 121
Liguori, Alphonso, 132
Livi Bacci, Massimo, 242
Lombardi Satriani, Luigi, 84, 91, 99, 147, 160
Longo, Bartolo, 68–76
Loreto, 58, 67, 108
Lourdes, Our Lady of, 25
Lucarelli, Clarinda, 71
Lucca, 41
Lucera, 34–35
luterani, 223
Luther, Martin: Counter-Reformation view of,
    222–25; on images, 52; and immanence,
    199; on Purgatory, 127

Maarbjerg, John, 56
Madonna con Bambino, as preferred pattern,
    25–28, 80, 236
Madonna dei Miracoli, 95
Madonna della Quercia, 57–58

Madonna dell'Archetto, 23
Madonna dell'Arco, 36, 43–44, 47n
Madonna del Latte, 157–60
Madonna delle Grazie, 17, 30–31, 95, 102
Madonna dell'Impruneta, 20–21, 104–5
Madonna del Pozzo, 61–64
Madonna del Rosario. See Madonna di Pompei
Madonna di Caravaggio, 41n
Madonna di Pompei: history of her cult, 67–
    76, 108; compared with Vincenzo Camuso,
    137
Madonna di San Luca, 24n
Madonna di Trapani, 21
madonnas: contrasted with Mary, 48; and
    madonnine images, 45–46. See also images,
    miraculous; and specific madonnine titles
madonnine (term), compared to "marian," 17n
madonnine images. See images, miraculous;
    and specific madonnine titles
Marchesi, Giambattista, 140
Marchetti, Giovanni, 23, 45
Marocchi, Massimo, 224
Martin, Edward, 50n
Martin, John, 191, 195
Martindale, Don, 228
Martire, Pietro, 33
Marxist approach to religion, 7
Maselli, Domenico, 23n
Masling, Joseph, 232n
McGrath, Alister, 190
McGuire, Brian, 121
McNair, Philip, 186n, 191n, 192n
Mead, Margaret, 227, 228n
Medica, Giacomo, 95
Medjugorje, 26
Meissner, W., 232
Mellano, Maria, 40
mendicant orders, 79
Menocchio (miller), 13
Menozzi, Daniele, 224
merging, predisposition towards, 229–30
Messina, 146
metaphor, and religious belief, 218–19
Meyer, Judith, 190–91
Mezzogiorno: defined, 200; and Protestantism,
    187, 195–96
Miccoli, Giovanni, 224
Michelangelo, 188n
microhistory (scholarly tradition), 13–14

Middle Ages, beliefs about incorruption during, 216
Miele, Michele, 39, 209n
Milan (Archdiocese), 64–66; and skeletal dead cults, 151–57
Milan (city), 102, 132; and Sacred Treasure, 181–84
milk, breast: and blood, 158; and del latte madonnas, 157–60
Miller, S. J., 18n
Mioni, Ugo, 164, 165, 177
miraculous images. *See* images, miraculous
Miraculous Medal, 25
missions, 3–4, 69–70, 81–86
misteri, 87–89
Mitchell, Timothy, 100–101, 244–45
Molfeta, 89
Molinari, Franco, 18n
Mondello, Fortunato, 88, 149
Mondovì, 40–42
Monreale, 33
Montevergine, 42–43, 67, 108, 137
Moretti, Italo, 206
Morone, Giovanni, 188
Moroni, Marco, 32
Muir, Edward, 13n, 14n
Mundugumor, 227
Musolino, G. A., 213n
mystery plays, 87n
mystics, female, 158–59

Naples, 36, 38–39, 67–68, 85, 86, 100, 209; and abandoned souls, 135–36; churches dedicated to the dead at, 161–62
Naselli, Carmellina, 90
national character: Dundes on, 226–27; German, 226; Italian, 227, 229, 236–42; rise and decline of concept, 227–226
Nelli, Athanasio, on images, 57–58, 75
Neri, Filippo, 175, 220
Netherlands, 244
Niccoli, Octavia, 222
Nicea. *See* Council of Nicea
Niero, Antonio, 33
Nieto, Jose, 192n
Nocera Terinese, 77–79, 91–92, 110–11
Nolan, Mary Lee, 24, 165, 244
Novi Chavarria, Elisa, 81n, 82, 84, 85, 86
Nuestra Señora de la Soledad, 101
Nunziata (image), 20, 58, 195

Ochino, Bernardino, 187
Oedipus complex, 233
Oliveri, Achille, 193
Oltranto, Giorgio, 33, 35
oral eroticism, 231–33
Ornago, 66
otherworld, journey to, 146–50
Ott, Michael, 166n
Ozment, Steven, 190, 199

pagan-survivals hypothesis, 6–7
Paglia, Vincenzo, 123, 129, 149
Paige, Jeffrey, 197n
Paleotti, Gabriele, 59–60
Palermo, 90, 100, 142–46
Paolucci, Antonio, 207
Paolucci, Scipione, 3–4, 82, 84, 95
papacy, 125
Papal states, 23, 31
parables, Sicilian, 133
Pardo, Italo, 135–36, 147n, 148
Passion, 81n, 83, 85, 86–96, 245
Passionists, 82
Passion symbols, 89–90
Pastor, Ludvig von, 214n
pastoral visits, 9
Paul III, 187
Paul IV, 188
Payton, James, 56
Pellizari, Pietro, 90
penitential mission, 81–86
penitential procession, 85
Perugia, 78
Petersen, Joan, 164
Philip III, 184
Piaget, Jean, 237
Piccaluga, Gabriella, 117, 159–60
Pietà, 77; contrasted with Addolorata, 93–94
pieve, 206–7
Piò, Giovanni, 213n, 221
Pious Workmen, 82
Pisa, 22
Pistoia, Synod of. *See* Synod of Pistoia
Pitrè, Giuseppe, 86, 99; on beheaded souls cult, 142–46
Pius VI, 23
plague, 116, 161n, 167. *See also* dead, cult of; plague victims, devotion to
plague victims, devotion to: at Bergamo, 140–41; at Ghedi, 116–19, 139; at Naples, 161–62

Pole, Reginald, 188

Pompei. *See* Madonna di Pompei

Ponte di San Giacomo, 146–50; and Via Lattea, 159–60

Pontmain, 215

popular Catholicism: De Rosa on, 8–10; model used in this book, 10–11. *See also* popular religion

popular religion: approaches to, 12–14; definitions of, 5–6; in Italy, 6–11. *See also* popular Catholicism

power, of saints and madonnas compared, 170

Prandi, Carlo, 96

preaching orders: and Catholic reform, 79–86; and Purgatory, 122, 125, 131

precious death, 218

Prodi, Paolo, 125

Prosperi, Adriano, 3n, 81n, 149, 223

Protestantism: Counter-Reformation view of, 222–25; and image cults, 52–54, 56–57; and Italian evangelism, 191–93; Purgatory, 127; rejects merging of natural and supernatural, 230; and saintly relics, 175–77

psychoanalysis: hostility toward, 233–35, 242; view of religion, 230–31. *See also* anal eroticism; oral eroticism

Purgatory (place): and confraternity titles, 123–24; emergence and development of doctrine on, 119–23; and preaching orders, 122, 125; and rejection of Protestantism, 127–29. *See also* Purgatory, souls in

Purgatory, souls in: abandoned, 134–36; and beheaded souls, 142; cult of, in Italy, 123–25; power to help the living, 129–34; sea of flames motif, 112, 139, 145; and skeletal dead, 150–51; two categories of, 134–36; and Vincenzo Camuso cult, 136–37. *See also* Purgatory (place)

quarantina, 33n

real presence, 199–200

Redemptorists, 82

Redon, Odile, 166

Redondi, Pietro, 199n

Reformation: debates on image cults, 52–57; and Italian evangelism, 191–95; in Italy, 186–89; Swanson's hypothesis on, 196–200; and urbanism, 189–91

refrisco, 136

regression, 236–37

relic cults: and conspicuous consumption, 178–85; and Counter-Reformation, 171–85; distorted histories of, 170–71; in early Church, 163–65; and evangelism, 194–95; during Middle Ages, 168; at Naples, 172–75; and rejection of Protestantism. *See also* relics, saintly

relics, saintly: blood relics, 208; and catacombs, 175–78; increased emphasis on, during Counter-Reformation, 171–75; meaning of, to ordinary Catholics, 168–170; and merging of natural and supernatural, 230; at Milan, 181–85; not clearly distinguished from saint, 169; and power, 170; theft of, 165–66. *See also* relic cults

Renaissance, 14, 55

Resurrection, 99, 101

Ricci, Scipione de', 18–19, 80. *See also* Jansenism

ricettizia. *See* chiesa ricettizia

Rienzo, Maria, 81n, 83

Riolfi, Walter, 116n, 117, 118, 139

Rivera, Annamaria, 170

Robertazzi delle Donne, Enrica, 201, 206

Robertson Smith, W., 21

Roman Martyrology, 212, 217

Rome, 45, 51

Rosa, Mario, 81n, 85

Rosary, 143, 211, 243; and Madonna di Pompei, 67–69

Ross, James, 238, 241

Rossi, Annabella, 136

ruota, 27

Russia, 228

Russo, Carla, 24n, 25, 94, 96, 124

Sabbatine Privilege, 126, 128–29

Sacchetti, Franco, 167–68, 216

Sacred Heart, 80

Sacred Treasure (relics), 181–85

S. Anastasia (community), 43, 47

S. Antonio di Padua, 67

S. Antonio Pierozzi, 213, 219–20

S. Augustine, 50, 53

S. Bernardino of Siena, 80

S. Caterina da Siena, 67, 72

S. Cecilia, 213–14

S. Dimas (Dismas), 182

S. Dominic, 67

S. Filippo Neri, 221–21
S. Gennaro, 208, 209
S. Giovanni Battista Decollato, 143
S. Ignatius of Loyola, 79
S. Lawrence, 163, 167
S. Nicolà, 166
S. Paul, 163, 165
S. Reparata, 167
S. Rocco, cult of, 116–17, 139
S. Rosa, 70, 72
S. Rosa di Viterbo, 220
S. Teresa of Avila, 217
saints: dismemberment of, 163–65; and heroic
    virtue, 217–18; and incorruption, 208–25;
    ratio of male to female, 215; relationship
    with relics, 168–70. See also specific names
Saintyves, Pierre, 211, 216
San Bernardino alle Osse (church), 152
sanctuary, dedications, 95
Santa Maria della Sanità (church), 38–39
saponification, 211
Sassu, Pietro, 90
Saunders, George, 96n
Savonarola, 191
Scapular, 211, 243
Scavizzi, Giuseppe, 56
Schutte, Anne, 187, 191n, 192
sea of flames (motif), 112, 139, 145
Sebastiani, Lucia, 207
Seidel Menchi, Silvana, 192, 194
Seregno, 65
Serenus, 49–50, 76
sermons, dramatic, 82–83
Servetti Donati, Fedora, 17n
Servites, 79, 93
Shaffern, Robert, 125
Sicily, 86–87, 142–46, 151
Signorotto, Gianvittorio, 18n, 129, 132n, 152–
    56, 172, 177, 181–84
Sixtus V, 9
skeletal dead, 139–62; and del latte madonnas,
    157–60; devotion to, at Milan, 151–57; and
    Ghedi cult, 112–13, 116–19, 139; and souls
    in Purgatory, 150–51, 153. See also dead,
    cult of
skeletal imagery, 139–40
smallpox, 27–28. See also epidemics
Soleto, 47
Sordi, Italo, 139
Sorrows of Mary, 93

soul, folk beliefs about, 146–50. See also dead,
    cult of
souls in Purgatory. See Purgatory, souls in
southern Italy. See Mezzogiorno
Spain, 244. See also Spanish Catholicism
Spanish Catholicism, contrasted with Italian
    Catholicism, 100–102
Stations of the Cross, 81, 99, 129, 211
Staurenghi, Cesare, 153
Stella, Pietro, 19
Strocchia, Sharon, 140
Strong, John, 171
swaddling, 228
Swanson, Guy, 196–200
Swanson, R. N., 245
syncretism, pagan/Catholic, 6–7
Synod of Pistoia (1786): on image cults, 18–
    24; on Purgatory, 134; on relics, 169. See also
    Jansenism

Tamburro, Nunzio, 72n, 73
Tansillo, Luigi, 240
Tanzella, Domenico, 61–63
Tchambuli, 227
teeth, human, as relics, 183
"theater of blood," 84
Theatines, 129
Theodora (regent), 52
Thurston, Herbert, 164, 211–12, 213n, 215
Tocchini, Anna, 41n
tongue dragging, 83, 146
Toschi, Paolo, 86, 87, 98
Tramontin, Silvio, 207
transubstantiation, 199–200
Trapani, 88, 146
Trevi fountain, 23n, 100
Trexler, Richard, 239, 240, 241
trigram, 80
Triputti, Anna Maria, 61
Triumph of Death (motif), 140
Turchini, Angelo, 72, 73
Turin, Shroud of, 59
Tuscany, 238

United Kingdom, 244
urbanism, and Reformation, 189–91

Valdés, Juan de, 191, 194
Vannugli, Antonio, 94
Varese, Ranieri, 24, 26, 29

Varese (community), 65
vattente. *See* Nocera Terinese
Vauchez, André, 211, 213
veiling of images, 19–22, 65
Venice, 186
Venturi, Silvio, 90
Vermigli, Pietro Martire, 187
Verona, 241
Veronica story, 80
Verzella, Emanuela, 18n
Via Lattea, 159–60
vicar-general, 141
Vismara Chiappa, Paola, 64–66, 129
visual, emphasis on, 237
Viterbo, 57, 58, 188n
Voragine, Iacopo da, 166

Waldensians, 166, 186–87, 203
Warner, Marina, 157–58
Weber, Max, 198, 229
Welti, Manfred, 186, 189, 191, 193n
wet nurses, 238–42
witches, 13–14, 68
Wroth, William, 101
Wuthnow, Robert, 12, 191

Zanchi, Goffredo, 169
Zarri, Gabriella, 131–32
Zeitoun, 215
Zimmerman, Benedict, 126, 128
Zwingli, Ulrich: on images, 52–54; and imma-
    nence, 199

Library of Congress Cataloging-in-Publication Data

Carroll, Michael P., 1944–
    Veiled threats : the logic of popular Catholicism in Italy / Michael P. Carroll.
        p.   cm.
Companion vol. to the author's Madonnas that maim, c1992.
Includes bibliographical references and index.
ISBN 0-8018-5290-0 (alk. paper)
    1. Catholics—Italy—Religious life. 2. Italy—Religious life and customs.
I. Carroll, Michael P., 1944–   Madonnas that maim.   II. Title.
BX1543.C353   1996
282'.45'0903—dc20   95-50982